PASS TRAK 6

Principles & Practices

Investment Company/ Variable Contracts Limited Representative

16th Edition

Dearborn Financial Publishing, Inc.

At press time, this 16th edition of PassTrak Series 6 contains the most complete and accurate information currently available for the NASD Series 6 license examination. Owing to the nature of securities license examinations, however, information may have been added recently to the actual test that does not appear in this edition.

While a great deal of care has been taken to provide accurate and current information, the ideas, suggestions, general principles and conclusions presented in this text are subject to local, state and federal laws and regulations, court cases and any revisions of same. The reader is thus urged to consult legal counsel regarding any points of law—this publication should not be used as a substitute for competent legal advice.

Executive Editor: Kimberly K. Walker-Daniels
Managing Editor: Nicola Bell
Associate Product Editor: Brian K. Fauth

©1981, 1982, 1983, 1984, 1985, 1986, 1987, 1988, 1989, 1990, 1991, 1993, 1994
by Dearborn Financial Publishing, Inc.
Published by Dearborn Financial Publishing, Inc.®

All rights reserved. The text of this publication, or any part thereof, may not be reproduced in any manner whatsoever without written permission from the publisher.

Printed in the United States of America.

95 96 10 9 8 7 6 5 4 3 2

Library of Congress Cataloging-in-Publication Data

PassTrak series 6, Investment company/variable contracts limited
  representative. Principles & practices. — 16th ed.
    p.   cm.
  Includes index.
  ISBN 0-7931-0602-8
  1. Mutual funds—Examinations, questions, etc. 2. Stockbrokers—
Examinations, questions, etc. I. Dearborn Financial Publishing.
II. Title: PassTrak series 6, Investment company/variable contracts
limited representative. III. Title: Pass Trak six, Investment
company/variable contracts limited representative. IV. Title:
Investment company/variable contracts limited representative.
HG4530.P35 1993
332.63'27—dc20   92-36822
                                                                  CIP

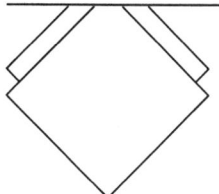

Contents

	Introduction to PassTrak Series 6	ix
1.	**Equity Securities**	**1**
	Corporate Ownership and Common Stock	2
	What Is Stock?	2
	The Rights of Corporate Ownership	4
	Benefits and Risks of Owning Common Stock	7
	Preferred Stock	8
	Return on Investment	11
	Tracking Equity Securities	13
	Review Questions	15
2.	**Debt Securities**	**19**
	Characteristics of Bonds	20
	Rating and Analyzing Bonds	21
	Bond Yields	24
	Characteristics of Corporate Bonds	27
	Types of Bonds	27
	Zero-coupon Bonds	28
	Liquidation	29
	Tracking Corporate Bonds	30
	Review Questions	31
3.	**Corporate Special Securities**	**35**
	Convertible Securities	36
	Calculating Conversion Parity	37
	Rights and Warrants	39
	Issuance	39

	Characteristics of Rights	39
	Warrants	40
	American Depositary Receipts	41
	Introduction to Options	42
	Review Questions	44
4.	**U.S. Government, Agency and Municipal Securities**	**47**
	Marketable Government Securities	48
	Nonmarketable Government Securities	51
	Agency Issues	52
	Introduction to Municipal Bonds	54
	General Obligation Bonds	55
	Revenue Bonds	56
	Review Questions	57
5.	**Money-market Securities and Interest Rates**	**61**
	The Money Market	62
	Money-market Instruments	63
	Review of Interest Rates	65
	Review Questions	66
6.	**Issuing Securities**	**69**
	The Regulation of New Issues	70
	Registration of Securities	71
	Civil Liabilities under the Act of 1933	74
	The Underwriting Process	75
	Underwriting Corporate Securities	75
	Participants in a Corporate New Issue	75
	Types of Offerings	76
	Types of Underwritings	77
	Review Questions	79
7.	**Trading Securities**	**81**
	The Regulation of Trading	82
	The Securities Exchange Act of 1934	82
	Securities Markets and Broker-Dealers	84
	Securities Markets	84
	Role of the Broker-Dealer	86
	Review Questions	88

8.	**Client Accounts**	**91**
	New Accounts	93
	Classification of Accounts	93
	Opening New Accounts	94
	Documenting New Accounts	94
	Cash Accounts and Margin Accounts	95
	Opening Accounts for Employees of Other Brokers	97
	Types of Accounts	98
	Discretionary Accounts	99
	Uniform Gifts to Minors Act Accounts	101
	Review Questions	104
9.	**Brokerage Office Procedures**	**107**
	Brokerage Support Services	108
	Transactions and Trade Settlement	108
	Dividend Department	109
	Rules of Good Delivery	112
	Ethics in the Securities Industry	113
	Ethical Business Practices	113
	Prohibited Practices	115
	Criminal Penalties	122
10.	**Economics and Analysis**	**123**
	Economics	124
	Government Economic Policy	127
	Fiscal Policy	129
11.	**Investment Recommendations and Taxation**	**133**
	Know Your Customer	134
	Financial Profile	134
	Nonfinancial Investment Considerations	135
	Analyzing Financial Risks and Rewards	138
	Suitability	138
	Investment Risks	138
	Analyzing Investment Returns	141
	Portfolio Analysis	142
	Portfolio Management Strategies	142
	Modern Portfolio Theory	143
	Federal and State Taxation	145
	Taxation and Investment Portfolios	146
	Review Questions	150

12.	Investment Company Products	153
	Investment Company Offerings	154
	The Investment Company Act of 1940	154
	Investment Company Purpose	154
	Types of Investment Companies	155
	Characteristics of Mutual Funds	160
	The Mutual Fund Concept	160
	Advantages to Investors	160
	Investment Objectives	161
	Comparing Mutual Funds	165
	Investment Company Registration	168
	Registration of Investment Companies	168
	Registration of Investment Company Securities	169
	Restrictions on Operations	171
	Management of Investment Companies	173
	Board of Directors	173
	Investment Adviser	173
	Affiliated and Interested Persons	174
	Custodian Bank	176
	Transfer Agent (Customer Services Agent)	177
	Underwriter	177
	Bonding of Directors and Employees	178
	Information Distributed to Investors	178
	Mutual Fund Marketing, Pricing and Valuation	180
	Methods of Marketing Mutual Fund Shares	180
	Determining the Value of Mutual Fund Shares	181
	Sales Charges	182
	Mutual Fund Pricing	184
	Sales Charges and Quantity Discounts	186
	Breakpoint Sales	188
	Exchanges Within a Family of Funds	189
	Redemption of Fund Shares	189
	Mutual Fund Purchase and Withdrawal Plans	191
	Types of Mutual Fund Accounts	191
	Dollar Cost Averaging	196
	Withdrawal Plans	197
	Mutual Fund Distributions and Taxation	198
	Distributions from Mutual Funds	198
	Taxation of Mutual Funds	201
	Tracking Investment Company Securities	204
	Review Questions	207

13.	**Retirement Planning**	**209**
	The Employee Retirement Income Security Act	210
	Individual Retirement Accounts	212
	Participation in an IRA	212
	IRA Contributions	212
	IRA Custodians and Investments	214
	IRA Rollovers	214
	IRA Transfers	215
	IRA Withdrawals	215
	Taxation on IRA Distributions	215
	Keogh (HR-10) Plans	217
	Comparison of Qualified Retirement Plans	219
	Corporate Retirement Plans	220
	Nonqualified Corporate Retirement Plans	223
	Taxation	223
	Types of Plans	223
	Annuity Plans	225
	Types of Annuity Contracts	225
	Purchasing Annuities	228
	Variable Annuity Sales and Redemption Practices	229
	Annuity Payout Options	229
	Annuity Accounting	230
	Taxation of Annuities	232
	Qualified Annuity Plans	234
	Tax Advantages	234
	Eligibility Requirements	234
	Variable Life Insurance	238
	Conventional Life Insurance	238
	Variable Life Insurance	239
	Variable Universal Life	244
	Review Questions	245
14.	**U.S. Government and State Rules and Regulations**	**249**
	The Investment Advisers Act of 1940 and SEC Release IA-1092	250
	Insider Trading and Securities Fraud Enforcement Act of 1988	252
	Securities Investor Protection Corporation	253

15.	**Other SEC and SRO Rules and Regulations**	255
	Registration and Regulation of Broker-Dealers	256
	Securities Exchange Act of 1934	256
	NASD Bylaws	257
	Administration of the NASD	257
	NASD Membership and Registration	259
	Qualifications Examinations	262
	Ineligibility and Disqualifications	263
	NASD Definitions	264
	Codes of Procedure and of Arbitration Procedure	265
	Code of Procedure	265
	Code of Arbitration Procedure	267
	Communications with the Public	270
	Advertising and Sales Literature	270
	NASD Rules Concerning Public Communications	272
	Review of NASD Regulations	276
	Review Questions	278
	Glossary	281
	Index	337

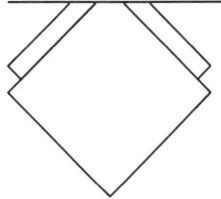

Introduction to PassTrak Series 6

Welcome to PassTrak Series 6. Because you probably have a lot of questions about the course and the exam, we have tried to anticipate some of them and provide you with answers to help you on your way.

The Course

How is the course structured?

PassTrak Series 6 is divided into two volumes: a textbook and an exam book. The textbook, titled *Principles & Practices*, consists of fifteen chapters, each devoted to a particular area of investment company/variable contract products (IC/VC) trading and regulation that you will need to know in order to pass the IC/VC Limited Representative Qualification Exam (the Series 6). Each chapter is divided into study sections devoted to more specific areas with which you need to become familiar.

The exam book, titled *Questions & Answers*, contains review exams that test the topics covered in *Principles & Practices;* it concludes with three comprehensive and three final exams composed of questions similar to those you will encounter on the Series 6 exam.

What topics are covered in this course?

The information needed to pass the Series 6 exam is covered in PassTrak Series 6 through the following chapters:

Chapter 1:	Equity Securities
Chapter 2:	Debt Securities
Chapter 3:	Corporate Special Securities
Chapter 4:	U.S. Government, Agency and Municipal Securities
Chapter 5:	Money-market Securities and Interest Rates
Chapter 6:	Issuing Securities
Chapter 7:	Trading Securities
Chapter 8:	Client Accounts
Chapter 9:	Brokerage Office Procedures
Chapter 10:	Economics and Analysis

Chapter 11: Investment Recommendations and Taxation
Chapter 12: Investment Company Products
Chapter 13: Retirement Planning
Chapter 14: U.S. Government and State Rules and Regulations
Chapter 15: Other SEC and SRO Rules and Regulations

How much time should I spend studying?

You should plan to spend approximately 30 to 40 hours reading the material and working through the questions. Your actual time, of course, may vary from this figure depending on your reading rate, comprehension, professional background and study environment.

Spread your study time over the two to three weeks prior to the date on which you are scheduled to take the Series 6 exam. Select a time and place for studying that will allow you to concentrate your full attention on the material at hand. You have a lot of information to learn and a lot of ground to cover. Be sure to give yourself enough time to learn the material.

What is the best way to approach the exams?

Approach each exam as if you were preparing to take the actual Series 6 test. Read each question carefully and write down your answer. Then check your answers against the key and read the accompanying rationale. Making yourself go through all of these steps (rather than simply reading each question and skipping directly to the rationale) will greatly increase your comprehension and retention of the information in the book.

Do I need to take the final exams?

The final exams test the same knowledge you will need in order to answer the questions on the Series 6 exam. By completing these exams and checking your answers against the rationale, you should be able to pinpoint any areas with which you are still having difficulty. Review any questions you miss, paying particular attention to the rationale for those questions. If any subjects still seem troublesome, go back and review those topics in *Principles & Practices*. At the end of each rationale, you will find a page reference that directs you to the page in *Principles & Practices* where the information is covered.

The Exam

Why do I need to pass the Series 6 exam?

Your employer is a member of the National Association of Securities Dealers (NASD) or another self-regulatory organization that requires its members and employees of its members to pass a qualification exam in order to become registered. To be registered as a representative qualified to sell investment company and variable contract products, you must pass the Series 6 exam.

What is the Series 6 exam like?

The Series 6 is a 2-hour-and-15-minute, 100-question exam administered by the NASD. It is offered as a computer-based test at various testing sites around the country. A paper-and-pencil exam is available to those candidates who apply to and obtain permission from the NASD to take a written exam.

What topics will I see covered on the exam?

This course covers the wide range of topics that the NASD has outlined as being essential to the IC/VC representative. The NASD exam is divided into four broad topic areas:

	% of Exam
Securities, Securities Markets and Investment Risk	20%
Investment Companies	35%
Variable Contracts and Retirement Plans	20%
Securities Regulation	25%

What score must I achieve in order to pass?

You must answer correctly at least 70% of the questions on the Series 6 exam in order to pass and become eligible for NASD registration as an IC/VC representative.

How long does the exam take?

You will be allowed 2 hours and 15 minutes in which to finish the exam. If you are taking the computerized version of the exam, you will be given additional time before the test to become familiar with the PROCTOR® terminal.

Are there any prerequisites I have to meet before taking the exam?

There are no prerequisite exams you must pass before sitting for the Series 6.

How do I enroll for the exam?

To obtain an admission ticket to the Series 6 exam, your firm must file the proper application form with the NASD, along with the appropriate processing fees. The NASD will then send you a directory of Certification Testing Centers and a PROCTOR® enrollment valid for a stated number of days. To take the exam during this period, you must make an appointment with a Certification Testing Center as far in advance as possible of the date on which you would like to sit for the test.

What should I take to the exam?

Take one form of personal identification that bears your signature and your photograph as issued by a government agency. You are not allowed to take reference materials or anything else into the testing area. Calculators will be available upon request; you will not be allowed to use your personal calculator.

Scratch paper and pencils will be provided by the testing center, although you will not be permitted to take them with you when you leave.

What is the PROCTOR® System?

The Series 6 exam, like many professional licensing examinations, is administered on the PROCTOR® computerized testing system. PROCTOR® is a nationwide, interactive computer system designed for the administration and delivery of qualifications examinations. Included with your PROCTOR® enrollment, you will receive a brochure describing how the exam is formatted and how to use the computer terminal to answer the questions.

When you have completed the exam, the PROCTOR® System promptly scores your answers and within minutes displays a grade for the exam on the terminal screen.

How well can I expect to do on the exam?

The examinations administered by the NASD are not easy. You will be required to display considerable understanding and knowledge of the topics presented in this course in order to pass the Series 6 exam and qualify for registration. If you study and complete all of the sections of the course, and consistently score at least 80% on the review and final exams, you should be well prepared to pass the Series 6 exam.

1 Equity Securities

Key Terms

authorized stock
callable preferred stock
cash dividend
combination preferred stock
convertible preferred stock
cumulative preferred stock
dividend
issued stock
market value
no-par stock
outstanding stock

par value
participating preferred stock
preemptive right
preferred stock
prior preferred stock
property dividend
residual claim
statutory voting
stock dividend
treasury stock
voting right

Overview

Of all the different types of investments available to today's consumer, people are most familiar with stock and the various markets on which it is traded. The Dow Jones Industrial Average (an indicator of the general direction in which the stock market is moving) is frequently a topic of discussion on the news, in the business section of the newspaper, in the office and on the street.

Many people own stock in one form or another. Some receive stock as a gift, others buy stock regularly through payroll savings plans, some acquire stock indirectly through pension or profit-sharing programs and many purchase stock for its growth and income potential. The buying and selling of stock in its various forms constitutes a major portion of the business of many Wall Street investment firms.

Chapter 1 lays the groundwork for the study of stock and the stock market. In this chapter, you will be exposed to the important characteristics of common and preferred stock, the rights of stockholders, the different ways of valuing and classifying stock, the stock certificate and how to track traded equity securities.

Corporate Ownership and Common Stock

What Is Stock?

Ownership

Shares of stock represent individual pieces of ownership (or equity) in a corporation. Companies issue stock as their primary means of raising business capital, and investors who buy those shares (either during the initial public stock offering or later, in the secondary market) are the owners of those companies. Whatever property a business owns (that is, its assets) less the claims of its creditors (its liabilities) belongs to the owners of the business, its stockholders.

A company can also issue bonds as a means of raising capital, but the bondholders have no equity interest in the corporation; they are considered lenders, not owners.

Diversified Ownership, Centralized Management

If a company issues 100 shares of common stock (a **round lot**), each of those shares represents a 1% ownership of that company and gives its holder one vote in the company's management. A person who owns ten shares of stock would own 10% of the company (and be entitled to ten votes) and so on. In today's business world, it is not unusual to see companies that have issued 10,000, 100,000, 1 million or more shares of common stock. Because each of these shares carries with it the same rights and privileges as every other share, it is easy to see how conflicts could arise regarding the management of these companies by their many rightful owners, the stockholders.

For this reason, most corporations are organized in such a way that the holders of their common stock regularly vote for and elect a limited number of people to a board of directors to manage the company's business for them. By electing a board of directors, stockholders still have a say in the management of the company, but do not have to bother with the day-to-day details of its operations.

Different Types, Different Rights

In addition to its common stock, corporations will often have reasons to issue a second type of stock called preferred stock. Although preferred stockholders also acquire equity in the corporation, they usually do not have the same voting rights as the holders of common stock. As the name "preferred" indicates, however, they do enjoy some privileges not granted common stockholders, some of which will be covered later in this chapter.

Classifying Stock by Its Holder

Authorized stock. As part of its original charter, a corporation receives authorization from the state to issue (that is, sell or distribute) a specific number of shares of stock. It must amend its charter if its board of directors ever decides that there is a need to issue more shares than are currently authorized.

Issued stock. A corporation may distribute (issue) fewer than the total number of shares authorized by the state (and many do) and reserve the excess (the unissued stock) for future needs such as:

- raising new capital for expansion;
- paying stock dividends;
- providing stock purchase plans for employees or stock options for corporate officers;
- exchanging common stock for outstanding convertible bonds or preferred stock; and
- redeeming outstanding stock purchase warrants.

Treasury stock. Treasury stock is stock a corporation has issued and subsequently repurchased from the public in the secondary market. The corporation has the privilege of holding this stock indefinitely, reissuing it or retiring it. A corporation could reissue its treasury stock to fund stock option plans or other employee bonus arrangements, or could distribute it to holders of record in the form of a stock dividend.

Treasury stock does *not* carry the rights of other common shares, including such basic ones as voting rights and the right to receive dividends. A corporation will buy back its stock for a number of reasons, such as to:

- increase earnings per share;
- have an inventory of stock available to distribute as stock options, employee pension plans, and so on; or
- use for future acquisitions.

A corporation with extra cash available may buy back its own shares as a means of increasing earnings per share. By purchasing its own shares in the open market, the corporation reduces the number of shares outstanding. If there are fewer shares outstanding, and operating income remains the same, earnings per share will increase.

Outstanding stock. Outstanding stock includes any shares that have been issued by the corporation and that have not subsequently been repurchased by the company (that is, they are still in the hands of investors).

Summary of Stock Classifications

Authorized stock is the number of shares that the state has permitted the corporation to issue; issued stock is the number of shares that have actually been sold (or otherwise distributed) to stockholders. Any authorized stock that has not been sold or distributed is referred to as unissued stock. Stock that has been repurchased and is being held by the company is known as treasury stock. Outstanding stock represents all shares still in the possession of investors.

Putting a Value on Common Stock

Like they do with many other retail goods, the laws of supply and demand determine a stock's price in the marketplace. A stock's market price is not the only measure of its value, however. Other measures include **par value** (an arbitrary value assigned to a stock by its board of directors) and **book value** (a figure calculated from the corporation's assets and liabilities).

Par Value

A stock's par value is the arbitrary dollar value given to the stock by the company in its articles of incorporation. If a stock has been assigned a par value, this value is usually printed on the face of the stock certificate. A stock's par value normally bears little or no relationship to its market price and tends to be a small dollar amount: $1 par, $5 par, and so on. The par value of a share of stock may change at some future date in the event that the company's board of directors decides to arrange a stock split.

Most states also authorize the issuance of **no-par stock**. Unless state statutes or the corporate charter state a minimum price for no-par stock, it can be sold for any amount. Some states require that no-par stock be given a stated value and that any sale proceeds exceeding that value be recorded as paid-in surplus. There is no discernible difference to the investor between a stock with a par value and one with a stated value.

When stock is sold, the amount of money received in excess of the par value is recorded on the corporate balance sheet as capital in excess of par (also called *paid-in surplus, capital surplus* or *paid-in capital)*. In practical terms, this means that stockholders cannot be assessed at some point in the future for deficiencies in the company's operating capital.

Book Value

While a stock's par value is a stable figure, its book value is not. Book value per share is a measure of how much a holder of common stock could expect to receive for each share if the corporation were to be liquidated. The figure is based on the difference between the value of a corporation's assets (including inventory, investments, cash on hand and facilities) and its liabilities (money owed lenders, suppliers, payroll, etc.) divided by the number of shares outstanding.

Market Value

For many people, the most familiar measure of a stock's worth is its price in the marketplace, its market value. Market value is directly influenced by supply (the number of shares available to investors) and demand (the number of shares investors would like to buy). Information about stocks and their prices (including the day's high, low and closing prices) can be found daily in many newspapers. In general, there is no direct relationship between the market value and the book value of a stock.

The Rights of Corporate Ownership

Voting Rights

Holders of common stock exercise control of a corporation by electing a board of directors and by voting on corporate policy at annual meetings. In addition to voting for members of the board of directors, stockholders are entitled to vote on matters involving:

- issuance of senior securities or additional common stock
- stock splits
- substantial changes in the corporation's business

Stockholders have the right to vote on the issuance of senior securities because, in the event of a bankruptcy or dissolution of the company, senior securities would have a prior claim on the company's assets. Stockholders are entitled to vote on stock splits because a split would change the stated (par) value of the stock. Stockholders do not have the right to vote on either the timing or the amount of cash or stock dividends. Those matters are left to the discretion of the board of directors.

Calculating the Number of Votes

A stockholder is entitled to cast one vote for each share of stock she owns. Depending on the bylaws of the company and on applicable state laws, a stockholder may cast her votes in one of two ways. These two ways are known as *statutory voting* and *cumulative voting*.

Statutory voting. Under the statutory voting system, a stockholder who votes in an election of members to the board of directors may cast one vote per share owned for each position.

To illustrate, if three directors are to be elected, the stockholder with 100 shares may cast from 0 to 100 votes for each of the three positions. In the event that the stockholder casts fewer than 100 votes for a candidate for one of the available seats, the remainder of those 100 votes may not be cast for another candidate for the same seat.

A candidate needs only to receive a simple majority (more than 50% of the votes cast) to be elected to the board. Statutory voting tends to put majority stockholders (those who own large blocks of stock) at an advantage over investors who own smaller amounts of stock in the company.

Cumulative voting. Cumulative voting entitles the stockholder to the same total number of votes as the statutory system, but places no restriction upon allocation of those votes.

In the example above, the stockholder has a total of 300 votes (one vote per share times the number of candidates). Under a cumulative voting system, those 300 votes could be cast in any manner the stockholder chooses. The stockholder could cast all 300 votes for a single candidate or split them in any fashion between two or more candidates.

In companies with cumulative voting rights, minority stockholders have a better chance of electing directors, thereby gaining representation on (although not necessarily control of) the board. Election under cumulative voting requires a plurality of the votes cast (the most votes, rather than just a simple majority).

Preemptive Rights

When a corporation raises capital through the sale of common stock (or securities convertible into common stock), it may be required by law or by its corporate charter to offer the securities to its common stockholders before it offers them directly to the public. Stockholders then have what is known as a preemptive right to purchase enough newly issued shares to protect their proportionate ownership in the corporation.

To illustrate, a person who already owns 1% of the stock of MicroScam Corporation (MCS) will have a preemptive right to purchase 1% of any new stock issue. Preemptive rights help ensure that stockholders' rights (such as voting rights) are not diluted at the issuance of new stock.

The subscription price for such an issue of additional stock (that is, the price at which existing stockholders will be able to acquire new shares) is usually lower than market value at the time the rights are offered.

Other Stockholder Rights

Limited Liability

Stockholders cannot lose more than they have invested in the stock of a particular corporation (in other words, they cannot be forced to pay off the debts of a corporation going through bankruptcy proceedings).

Inspection of Corporate Books

Stockholders have the right to obtain lists of stockholders, receive annual reports, and so on. Inspection rights do not include the right to examine the detailed books of accounts, the minutes of directors' meetings or financial records.

Protection of the Corporation

Stockholders may take the company's management (including members of the board of directors) to court if they believe that it has committed wrongful acts that could harm the corporation.

Restraint of Illegal Acts

Stockholders may take action against the board of directors of a corporation to restrain it from acting in a manner inconsistent with the corporate charter.

Residual Claims to Assets

When a corporation ceases to exist (liquidates), the stockholder, as owner, has a right to corporate assets. The right is residual in that a common stockholder may make a claim only after all debts and other security holders have been satisfied (that is, the common stockholder is at the bottom of the liquidation priority list).

Benefits and Risks of Owning Common Stock

Benefits of Owning Stock

Among the various securities issued by corporations, common stock tends to offer investors the greatest potential return. Two of the rewards people expect to receive when they invest in common stock are growth and income.

Growth. The almost unlimited potential for increase in the market price of shares owned is known as capital appreciation. Historically, owning common stock has provided investors with greater real returns than any other investment.

Income. Many corporations distribute a portion of their profits on a regular basis in the form of dividends. These regular distributions can be a significant source of income and are a major reason many people invest in corporate stock.

Risks of Owning Stock

Decreased or no income. Common stockholders must assume certain risks in exchange for the high profit potential of stock ownership. One of these risks is the possibility of dividend income decreasing or ceasing entirely during periods of corporate unprofitability (a corporation will usually distribute dividends to common stockholders only after satisfying the claims of other securities such as bonds and preferred stock).

Low priority at dissolution. A second risk that holders of common stock face is that, in the event of a company's bankruptcy, owners of common stock have the lowest priority in claims against corporate earnings and assets. In the event of the company's dissolution, the holders of corporate bonds and preferred stock may enter claims against corporate earnings and assets before common stockholders. Because of this advantage, some refer to those investments as senior securities. Common stockholders have only what are known as residual rights to corporate assets upon dissolution.

Fall in price. A third risk of owning stock is that there always exists the possibility that other investors in the marketplace will not value as highly as the investor does the shares she holds. This is reflected every day in the financial section of the newspaper as supply and demand drive the price of every stock up and down.

Preferred Stock

To many people, preferred stock appears to be a cross between an equity and a debt security. Although it is an equity security and represents ownership in the issuing corporation, it does not provide all of the privileges of ownership that are normally associated with common stock. Like a debt instrument, preferred stock is often (though not always) issued as a fixed income security with a stated dividend. Its price fluctuations tend to be affected more by changes in interest rates than by supply and demand. Unlike common stock, most preferred stock is issued as nonvoting stock.

Although preferred stock does not typically have the same growth potential as common stock (because its price is more likely to be affected by changes in interest rates than by changes in company profits), the owners of preferred stock generally have an advantage over common stockholders in two ways:

- when dividends are declared by the board of directors, owners of preferred stock receive their dividends (plus any dividends in arrears) first; and
- if a corporation goes bankrupt after paying off creditors, preferred stockholders have a prior claim on the remaining assets. Common stockholders' claims are typically the last ones paid.

Dividend Preference over Common Stock

Dividends (once they have been declared by the board of directors) must be paid to preferred stockholders before they can be paid to common stockholders. This gives holders of preferred stock a higher probability of receiving regular income than the holders of common stock.

Stated (Fixed) Rate of Return

To most owners of preferred stock, the stock's most attractive feature is its fixed dividend (although preferred stocks with variable dividends exist, they are not common). If the stock has been assigned a par value (a value normally much higher than that assigned to the corporation's common stock), it will state the annual dividend payments in terms of percentage of par value. A preferred stock with a par value of $100 that pays $6 in annual dividends would be known as a 6% preferred. No-par value preferred stock has a dividend stated in a dollar amount. A $6 no-par preferred would pay a $6 annual dividend.

Adjustable-rate Preferred

Some preferred stocks are issued with an *adjustable* (or *variable*) rate of interest. The dividend on an adjustable-rate preferred is tied to the rate of some other interest rate (such as the Treasury bill rate or money-market rates) and can be adjusted as often as quarterly.

Prior Claim over Assets at Dissolution

Holders of preferred stock can make a claim against the assets of the corporation (in the event of its liquidation) before common stockholders can.

Limited Ownership Privileges

Preferred stocks usually do not carry either voting rights or preemptive rights. There are exceptions, however, including those times when a company is in financial difficulty and the occasional issue of preferred stock with full or limited voting rights.

No Maturity Date or Set Maturity Value

Unlike corporate bonds (or other debt securities), preferred stock has no preset date at which it matures or is scheduled for redemption by the corporation.

Classes of Preferred Stock

Just as they can issue more than one class of common stock, corporations can issue more than one class of preferred. Separate classes of preferred may differ in terms of rate of dividend, in profit participation privileges or in any number of other ways. All, however, maintain a degree of preference over common stock. The classes are frequently referred to as *Preferred A* (prior preferred) and *Preferred B* (second preferred).

Prior Preferred

Prior preferred stock has a prior claim over other preferred stock in receiving dividends, as well as in the distribution of assets in the event of liquidation.

Cumulative Preferred

One of the primary reasons investors buy preferred stock in a corporation is the preferred stock's predictable dividend flow. Holders of preferred stock can expect payment of a predetermined amount at regular intervals. Common stockholders, on the other hand, do not have this advantage; their dividends (if they receive any at all) are paid only after all of the corporation's other debt obligations and preferred stock dividends are paid and only when (and if) the board of directors votes to pay them.

If a corporation is experiencing financial difficulties, however, its board of directors may vote to reduce or suspend payment of dividends to both common and preferred stockholders. Common stockholders do not have any recourse if this occurs; any dividends they miss may (or may not) be made up by the corporation at a later date. An investor who has purchased cumulative preferred stock, though, has a definite advantage. Any and all dividends due will accumulate on the company's books until such time as the corporation is able to pay them. When the company is able to resume full payment of dividends, holders of cumulative preferred stock will receive the current preferred dividend plus the total accumulated dividends (dividends in arrears) before any dividends are distributed to common stockholders.

Participating Preferred

In addition to the fixed dividend characteristic of other classes of preferred stock, participating preferred stock offers its owners another benefit. These stockholders receive a share of any corporate profits that remain after all dividends due other securities are paid. The percentage to which participating preferred stock actually participates is usually printed right on the stock certificate. If a preferred stock is described as "XYZ 6% Preferred Participating to 9%," the company will pay its holders up to 3% in additional dividends in profitable years.

Owners of participating preferred stock do not participate in a corporation's profits until the company has paid:

- interest to bondholders
- dividends to other preferred stockholders
- the basic dividend rate
- dividends to common stockholders

Convertible Preferred

A preferred stock is convertible if the holder has the right to convert its shares into shares of common stock at some future point in time. To illustrate, a convertible preferred stock with a $100 par value might be convertible into common stock at $25 per share. For each share of $100 par value preferred an investor owns, she can exchange it for four shares of common stock. As long as the price of the common stock in this example remains below $25 per share, the preferred stockholder would have little incentive to take advantage of the conversion feature.

If the market price of this corporation's common stock were to move above $25 per share, however, the preferred stockholder could profit by converting her shares into common stock at the preset below-market conversion price. Because the value of convertible preferred is linked to the value of common stock in this way, it tends to fluctuate more in price than do other fixed income securities.

Convertible preferred is usually issued with a lower stated dividend rate than nonconvertible preferred due to the special advantages it offers stockholders. In addition, the conversion of preferred stock into shares of common increases the total number of common shares outstanding, thereby decreasing (or diluting) total earnings per common share.

Callable Preferred

Occasionally, a corporation may decide to issue a special class of stock known as callable (or redeemable) preferred. With this type of stock, a company retains the right to call (or buy back) the stock from investors. The company does this by notifying the investors that it will buy back the shares from them at a specified price on a particular date. Companies often issue preferred stock with a call feature during periods of high interest rates. The right to call back the stock allows them to eliminate a relatively high fixed dividend obligation sometime in the future and sell in its stead an issue of preferred stock with a lower dividend.

Stockholders do not have to surrender their stock when it is called by the corporation, but most will because dividend payments and conversion rights generally cease on the call date. The stock will retain its par value even if it is not surrendered. In return for the call privilege, the corporation usually pays the stockholder a premium over the stock's par value at the call (such as $103 for a $100 par value stock).

Combinations

A corporation may decide to issue a preferred stock with more than one of the features described above. A single preferred issue can include participating, cumulative, convertible and/or callable features.

Return on Investment

Dividends

Dividends represent the sharing of a company's profits with its owners (the stockholders). Although many investors buy stock primarily for its income (or dividend) potential, stockholders are entitled to dividend distributions only if the company board of directors votes to make such a distribution.

Stockholders are automatically sent any dividends to which their shares entitle them.

Cash Dividends

Cash dividends are normally distributed by corporations to stockholders in the form of checks representing the stockholders' share of the companies' profits (most corporations do this quarterly). Some companies take great pride in their long, uninterrupted history of regular or increasing cash dividend payments, and investors tend to view companies with consistent dividend payment histories favorably.

Stock Dividends

A company may not want to pay out cash dividends from its profits, however. Often, young companies developing new products or services (or even long-established companies engaging in expansion or acquisitions) may want to use some or all of their available cash for these purposes.

To satisfy investors (and at the same time to conserve cash), a company's board of directors may declare a stock dividend instead of a cash dividend. Under these circumstances, the company issues shares of its common stock as a dividend to its current stockholders. When a stock dividend is declared, all common stockholders receive the same percentage of stock as a dividend; this way, the dividend does not increase any single investor's proportionate share of ownership in the company. The market price of the stock tends to decrease after a stock dividend, but the total market value of the position remains the same.

Property Dividends

Sometimes a corporation that owns securities in other companies as an investment will distribute some of those securities as a property dividend. For example, with a holding company that owns stock in one or more subsidiaries, the parent corporation may divest itself of a subsidiary by distributing the stock it owns in the subsidiary to the stockholders as a dividend (i.e., a property dividend).

Property dividends, in some circumstances, may actually be a company product. Proctor and Gamble, as an example, could distribute shampoo as a property dividend. Property dividends are declared and identified as such and should not be confused with gifts of the sort given to stockholders who attend annual meetings (a common practice among corporations).

Calculating Return on Investment

One way to evaluate the return on an investment in common stock is to calculate the dividend (or current) yield, the annual rate of return for an investor. To determine the **current yield**, divide the yearly dividend (which is normally four times the quarterly dividend) by the current market price of the stock.

If, for example, the yearly dividend paid by This Can't Be Sushi (TCBS) on its common stock is $1 (a quarterly dividend of $.25) and the market price of the stock is $20, the current yield for TCBS would be 5%. If TCBS paid $.25 for the first two quarters of the year and then raised its dividend to $.35 for each of the last two quarters, at a current market value of $20, TCBS's current yield would be 6% ($1.20 ÷ $20 = 6%).

Tracking Equity Securities

Common and preferred stocks are listed in newspapers and other financial publications such as *Barron's* and *The Wall Street Journal*. Consolidated stock tables, which represent the most complete information, are printed in most major newspapers. Figure 1.1 is an example of an NYSE Composite Transactions listing as it might be printed in the *The Wall Street Journal*. It reports activity for the previous day.

The market price of a stock is quoted in whole dollars plus fractions of a dollar, also known as points (for example, 1/2 a point equals 1/2 of a dollar, or $.50). If a stock is quoted at 25, this means that the market price for that stock is $25 per share. A stock quoted at 25 1/2 is selling for $25.50 per share.

The securities industry divides amounts less than one dollar (referred to as a point) into 1/8ths of a dollar, each with a value of 12 1/2 cents ($.125). Very low-priced stocks may be quoted in fractions of a dollar as small as 1/16ths ($.0625, or 6 1/4 cents), 1/32nds ($.03125, or 3 1/8 cents) and 1/64ths ($.015625, or 1 9/16 cents).

Figure 1.1   NYSE Composite Transactions Listing

New York Stock Exchange Composite Transactions

Tuesday, September 13, 1998
Quotations include trades on the Chicago, Pacific, Philadelphia, Boston and Cincinnati Stock Exchanges and reported by the National Association of Securities Dealers and INSTINET.

	52 Weeks High	Low	Stock	Div	Yld %	PE Ratio	Sales 100s	High	Low	Close	Net Chg.
	80	40	ABCorp	.75	.1	12	3329	78	71	73	- 1 1/2
n	8 3/8	6 1/2	ACM IncFd	1.01	12.4	...	178	8 1/4	8 1/8	8 1/8	- 1/8
	42 5/8	26 7/8	ALFA	2.40	5.6	12	x 1265	42 5/8	41 1/4	42 5/8	+1 1/4
	35	24 5/8	Anchor	1.48	4.9	36	1960	30	29 3/4	30	+ 1/4
	27 1/4	25	ANR pf	2.67	10.3	...	6	26	26	26	...
	6	1 7/8	ATT Cap wt	...	...	...	20	5 7/8	5 3/4	5 3/4	- 1/4
s	22 3/4	14	AVEMCO	.40	1.9	17	6	21 1/2	21 3/8	21 1/2	...
	84 1/4	40	BrlNth	2.20	3.7	13	2701	59 3/8	58 1/4	58 3/4	+ 1/2
	4 3/4	1/2	Brooke rt	...	...	...	26	4 5/8	4 5/8	4 5/8	...
	7	2 1/2	CV REIT	.25	4.0	...	10	6 3/8	6 1/4	6 1/4	...
	3 1/8	2 1/4	CalifREIT	.40	13.9	...	3	2 7/8	2 7/8	2 7/8	...
	39 3/8	17 7/8	Circus wi	...	...	...	14	39 1/4	38 7/8	39 1/4	+ 5/8
	82 1/2	39 5/8	Dsny	.32	.6	17	6211	53 3/4	52	53 1/4	+1 1/4
	38 3/8	19 1/2	Fubar	.24	.9	13	z 1454	28	26 7/8	27 3/8	+ 1/4
	8 3/4	3 5/8	Navistr	...	...	...	6484	4 1/2	4 1/8	4 1/4	...

EXPLANATORY NOTES
The following explanations apply to New York and American Exchange listed issues and the National Association of Securities Dealers Automated Quotations system's over-the-counter securities.
The 52-week high and low columns show the highest and lowest price of the issue during the preceding 52 weeks. Dividend rates, unless noted, are annual disbursements. Yield is the dividends paid by a company on its securities, expressed as a percentage of price. The PE ratio is determined by dividing the price of a share of stock by its company's earnings. Sales figures are quoted in 100s (00 omitted).
a-Extra dividend. b-Annual rate of the cash dividend and a stock dividend was paid. n-Newly issued in the past 52 weeks. pf-Preferred. rt-Rights. s-Stock split or dividend greater than 25% in the past 52 weeks. vi-In bankruptcy or receivership. wd-When distributed. wi-When issued. wt-Warrants. ww-With warrants. x-Ex-dividend or ex-rights. xw-Without warrants. z-Sales in full, not in hundreds.

Normally, stock prices are quoted in minimum increments of 1/8ths of a dollar. The yearly range of prices is shown in the first two columns. This range is for the previous 52 weeks plus the current week, but not the latest trading day. ALFA, for example, has hit a high of 42 5/8 ($42.625) and a low of 26 7/8 ($26.875) per share.

The name of the stock and the annual dividend follow the 52-week price range. The dividend is quoted as an annual dollar amount based on the most recent quarter. ALFA is paying an annual dividend of $2.40 per share. The "Yld" column reports the current yield of the security. For ALFA, the yield is 5.6% ($2.40 ÷ 42 5/8 = 5.6%).

The "PE Ratio" (price-earnings ratio) column follows the "Yld" column. It gives the ratio of the current price of the stock to its earnings during the past twelve months. ALFA's PE ratio is 12.

The "Sales" column reports the number of shares sold during the day. Trading is reported in round lots of 100 shares each. The entry for ALFA is 1265, which means that 126,500 shares of stock were traded the previous day. The "*x*" before the sales volume indicates that the stock is selling ex-dividend, or ex-rights, meaning that a buyer will not receive the next dividend check.

The two columns after "Sales" list the daily range of prices, the security's high and low prices for the day. ALFA sold for a high of 42 5/8 and a low of 41 1/4. The column labeled "Close" shows the final price for the day. ALFA closed at 42 5/8 at the top of its 52-week range.

The net change in price is reported in the final column. The net change is the difference between the closing price on the trading day reported and the previous day's closing price. ALFA closed up 1 1/4 points from the previous day's (Monday's) close, which would have been 41 3/8 on that day (42 5/8 − 1 1/4 = 41 3/8).

◆ Review Questions

1. Which of the following represent(s) ownership (equity) in a company?

    I. Corporate bonds
    II. Common stock
    III. Preferred stock
    IV. Mortgage bonds

    A. I and IV only
    B. II only
    C. II and III only
    D. I, II, III and IV

2. Which of the following statements describe treasury stock?

    I. It has voting rights and is entitled to a dividend when declared.
    II. It has no voting rights and no dividend entitlement.
    III. It has been issued and repurchased by the company.
    IV. It is authorized but unissued stock.

    A. I and III
    B. I and IV
    C. II and III
    D. II and IV

3. In which of the following ways may a company declare dividends?

    I. Cash
    II. Stock
    III. Stock of another company

    A. I only
    B. I and II only
    C. II and III only
    D. I, II and III

4. ABC Company currently has earnings of $4 and pays a $.50 quarterly dividend. The market price of ABC is $40. What is the current yield?

    A. 1.25%
    B. 5%
    C. 10%
    D. 15%

5. A corporation must have stockholder approval to

    A. split its stock 3 for 1
    B. repurchase 100,000 shares of stock for the treasury
    C. declare a 15% stock dividend
    D. declare a cash dividend

6. Limited liability regarding ownership in a large, publicly held U.S. corporation means all of the following EXCEPT

    A. investors might lose the amount of their investment
    B. investors might lose their investment plus the difference between their investment and par value
    C. investors' shares are nonassessable
    D. investors are not liable to the full extent of their personal property

7. Stockholders' preemptive rights include which of the following rights?

    A. Right to serve as an officer on the board of directors
    B. Right to maintain proportionate ownership interest in the corporation
    C. Right to purchase treasury stock
    D. Right to a subscription price on stock

8. Common stockholders' rights include a

   I. residual claim to assets at dissolution
   II. vote for the amount of stock dividend to be paid
   III. vote in matters of recapitalization
   IV. claim against dividends that are in default

   A. I
   B. I and III
   C. II and III
   D. III and IV

9. When a corporation holds treasury stock, it has the option of

   A. reissuing it as debt securities
   B. not disclosing it to the registrar
   C. retiring it
   D. registering it under any name it chooses

Table 1.1

NEW YORK STOCK EXCHANGE COMPOSITE TRANSACTIONS
Tuesday, September 13, 1998

52 Weeks High	52 Weeks Low	Stock	Div.	Yld %	P-E Ratio	Sale 100s	High	Low	Close	Net Chg.
91 3/8	57 1/2	Time	1.00	1.4	11	5106	70 5/8	69	69 7/8	-3/8

10. According to Table 1.1, the closing price for Time on the preceding trading day was

    A. 69 3/8
    B. 69 7/8
    C. 70 1/4
    D. 71

◆ Answers & Rationale

1. **C.** Owning either common or preferred stocks represents ownership (or equity) in a corporation. The other two choices represent debt instruments. Clients purchasing corporate or mortgage bonds would be considered lenders, not owners.

2. **C.** Treasury stock is stock a corporation has issued but subsequently repurchased from investors in the secondary market. The corporation can either reissue the stock at a later date or retire it. Stock that has been repurchased by the corporation has no voting rights and is not entitled to any declared dividends.

3. **D.** Cash dividends are normally declared by corporations, but corporations can also declare stock dividends (where stockholders receive additional shares) or declare dividends that are securities in another company the corporation owns. This type of dividend is known as a *property dividend.*

4. **B.** The current yield on a stock is calculated by dividing the yearly dividend by the current market price of the stock.

5. **A.** One of the corporate matters that stockholders are entitled to vote on is stock splits. The other choices are decisions that are made by the board of directors and don't require a stockholder vote.

6. **B.** An advantage of owning stock is that an investor's liability is limited to the amount of money he invested when the stock was purchased.

7. **B.** Preemptive rights deal with stockholders maintaining their proportionate ownership when the corporation wants to issue more stock. If a stockholder owns 5% of the outstanding stock and the corporation wants to issue more stock, the stockholder has the right to purchase enough of the new shares to maintain a 5% ownership position in the company.

8. **B.** Choices I and III are common stockholder rights. Dividend declarations are decided by the board of directors, not by the stockholders. Claims against dividends in default can be made only by preferred stockholders.

9. **C.** The corporation always has the option of retiring treasury stock. Stock cannot be reissued as debt. The registrar has to know how many shares are outstanding at any given time in order to keep accurate records.

10. **C.** The close shown is 69 7/8, down 3/8, which means that the previous day's close was 3/8 higher, or 70 1/4.

Equity Securities

2 Debt Securities

Key Terms

collateral trust bond
current yield
debt service
discount
equipment trust certificate
mortgage bond

nominal yield
par
premium
senior security
yield to maturity (YTM)
zero-coupon bond

Overview

Bonds of various types (including those issued by municipalities, corporations, the U.S. government and governmental agencies) are commonly referred to as *debt securities*; that is, they represent a loan by an investor to the issuer. In return for this loan, the issuer promises both to repay the debt at a specified date in the future and to pay the investor interest on the amount borrowed. Because the interest rate an investor receives is normally set by the issuer at the time the bond is issued, bonds are also referred to as *fixed income securities*.

A bond represents an issuer's promise to repay money it has borrowed (the principal of the loan) at some point in the future. The individual bonds that make up the entire bond issue usually have a face (or par) value of $1,000.

Characteristics of Bonds

Unlike stockholders, bondholders do not have ownership interest in the issuing corporation (or government) or a voice in management. In return for their lending the issuer money, bondholders receive the corporation's promise to repay principal and pay interest on the debt. As creditors of the corporation, bondholders receive preferential treatment over common and preferred stockholders in certain instances. When a corporation files for bankruptcy, the claims of creditors (including bondholders) are settled before the claims of stockholders. For this reason, bonds are sometimes called *senior securities*.

Issuers

Municipalities. Municipal securities are the debt obligations of state and local governments and their agencies. Most are issued to raise capital to finance public works and construction projects that benefit the general public (as opposed to financing the municipality's current expenses).

Corporations. Corporate bonds are debt securities, issued by corporations that need to raise money for working capital or for capital expenditures such as plant construction, equipment purchases, expansion and so forth. Corporate bonds are commonly referred to as *funded debt*.

U.S. government and government agencies. The federal government is not only the nation's largest borrower, it is its most secure credit risk. The bills, notes and bonds it issues to finance operations are backed by the full faith and credit of the government and by the government's almost unlimited powers of taxation.

Interest

In return for the money loaned to it by investors, the bond issuer promises to pay investors interest for that loan at a fixed rate and on particular dates. Those interest payment dates are set when the bonds are issued. The interest rate (or coupon) is calculated from the par value of the bond. Interest on the outstanding loan balance of a bond accrues daily and (in most cases) is paid in semiannual installments over the life of the bond. For example, an investor who owns a $1,000 bond that pays 7% interest will receive $70 ($1,000 × 7% = $70) in income each year in the form of two $35 semiannual installments. An investor who owns $10,000 of the same 7% bond will receive $700 each year in two $350 payments. In bond quotes, "M" is sometimes used as shorthand for "$1,000" and interest rates are expressed in the form "7s." A $10,000 TCBS bond paying 7% is referred to as "10M TCBS 7s."

The final interest payment will be made on the date the bond is scheduled to mature, and is normally combined with repayment of the principal amount. As an example, if a bondholder has been receiving semiannual payments of $300 on a $10,000 bond (a 6% interest rate), she will receive a check for $10,300 when the bond matures. Bond principal and interest are paid in the legal tender of the country in which they are issued.

Pricing

Par, Premium and Discount

All debt securities are issued with a face (or par) value, typically $1,000. **Par** represents the dollar amount of the contract between the issuer and the investor and is the amount repaid to investors per bond when the bond is due. The maturity date is the point at which the issuer redeems the debt obligation at par value and interest no longer accrues. Issues of less than $1,000 are referred to as *baby bonds* and are not popular with investors because they tend to be less marketable.

Either before or after bonds begin to trade in the secondary market, they may sell at any price. Investors can expect to see bonds issued or trading at par, below par (that is, at a **discount**) or above par (at a **premium**). If someone refers to a bond's premium, they are referring to the difference between par and its higher market value. If someone refers to a bond's discount, they are referring to the difference between par and its lower market value. The two primary factors affecting a bond's market value are the market's perception of the investment quality of the bond and overall interest rates.

Quotes on bonds are stated as percentages of the principal amount of the bond (although there are slight differences between the way corporate, municipal, U.S. government and government agency bonds are quoted). For example, a bid of 100 means 100% of par, or $1,000. Changes in bond prices are quoted in newspapers and other business-oriented periodicals in points, and a bond point is equal to $10 (1% of $1,000). A bond quote of 98 1/8 means 98 and 1/8th percent (98.125%) of $1,000. The minimum variation for most corporate and municipal bond quotes is 1/8th (.125%). The price moves from 98 to 98 1/8 to 98 1/4 and so on.

Rating and Analyzing Bonds

Various rating services, such as Standard & Poor's, Moody's and Fitch's, evaluate and publish their ratings of bond issues. Standard & Poor's and Moody's rate both corporate and municipal bonds; Fitch's rates corporate bonds, municipal bonds and commercial paper. Standard & Poor's, Moody's and Fitch's base their bond ratings primarily on the issuer's creditworthiness—that is, the ability of the issuer to make interest and principal payments as they come due. The less likely the issuer is to make payments as promised, the lower the rating given the bond. If the prospects are good that the issuer will be able to make the required payments and make them on time, the bond will be granted a high rating. Also taken into consideration is a company's **debt-to-equity ratio**—that is, how much of its capital is in the form of debt (bonds) and how much is in the form of equity (stock). Debt financing is a form of **leverage**.

The rating organizations rate only those issues that either pay to be rated or have enough outstanding securities to generate constant investor interest. The fact that a bond is not rated is not an indication of its quality; many unrated bonds can be safe and worthwhile additions to an investor's portfolio.

For an example of various bond ratings, see Figure 2.1.

Figure 2.1 Bond Ratings

Standard & Poor's	Moody's	Interpretation
Bank grade (investment grade) bonds		
AAA	Aaa	Highest rating. Capacity to repay principal and interest judged high.
AA	Aa	Very strong. Only slightly less secure than the highest rating.
A	A	Judged to be slightly more susceptible to adverse economic conditions.
BBB	Baa	Adequate capacity to repay principal and interest. Slightly speculative.
Speculative (non-investment grade) bonds		
BB	Ba	Speculative. Significant chance that issuer could miss an interest payment.
B	B	Issuer has missed one or more interest or principal payments.
C	Caa	No interest is being paid on bond at this time.
D	D	Issuer is in default. Payment of interest or principal is in arrears.

Relationship of Rating to Yield

Generally, the higher the bond rating, the lower the yield. Investors are willing to accept a lower return on their investment if they know that their principal is safe and interest payments are predictable. On the other hand, some bonds will sell at deep discounts, producing high yields. These bonds may have low ratings, and a degree of uncertainty may surround the safety of the investment and the ability of the issuer to continue interest payments. Other bonds, however, may be selling at deep discounts because they have low coupons.

When interest rates are expected to rise, prudent investors buy very short-term instruments such as municipal notes. When interest rates are expected to decline, prudent investors buy long-term bonds. The reasons for this are twofold. First, if interest rates do decline, the bonds that will appreciate most in price are long-term bonds. Second, investors may want to lock in high yields for a long time because they believe they may not have another chance to receive these returns.

Qualitative assessments. Analyzing bonds involves more than just numbers. Other more qualitative factors evaluated are the stability of an industry, strength of the company in that industry, quality of management and regulatory climate.

Comparative Safety of Securities

U.S. government securities. When comparing the safety of different types of securities, a person should know that the *highest safety* is found in securities backed by the U.S. government. These securities include:

- U.S. Treasury bills, notes and bonds (Series EE and HH bonds)
- Government National Mortgage Association bonds (Ginnie Maes or GNMAs)
- Public Housing Authority bonds (PHAs)

The *second highest degree of safety* is found in securities that, although not backed by the U.S. government, are issued by government agencies and government-sponsored corporations. These include:

- Federal Farm Credit Banks
- Federal Home Loan Bank (FHLB)
- Federal National Mortgage Association (FNMA)
- Inter-American Development Bank (IADB)
- International Bank for Reconstruction and Development (IB)

Municipal issues. Generally, the next highest degree of safety is found in securities issued by municipalities. General obligation bonds (GOs) are usually safer than revenue bonds.

Corporate issues. The next highest category of safety is found in corporate debt securities. Usually, these securities are ranked as follows:

1. equipment trust certificates
2. first mortgage bonds
3. debentures
4. income bonds

These rankings simply provide rough guidelines. For example, some AAA rated corporate bonds are safer than many municipal bonds.

Marketability and Liquidity

Many factors work together to determine a bond's marketability and liquidity. Chief among these factors are:

- quality
- rating
- maturity
- call features
- coupon rate and current market value
- issuer
- existence of a sinking fund
- type of registration

Bond Yields

Comparing Yields

One way investors evaluate debt securities is by comparing their yields. Affecting the buyer's yield are interest rate, time to maturity, price at purchase and sale, and call features. Investors must make sure they are comparing yields calculated by the same method. Bonds frequently are quoted and traded by their yields rather than by dollar amounts.

Nominal Yield

A bond's nominal yield (or coupon rate) is a fixed percentage of the bond's par value (normally $1,000). It is set at issuance and printed on the face of the bond. A coupon of 6%, for instance, means the issuer will pay $60 interest every year until the bond matures.

Current Yield

The interest an investor receives (the nominal yield) does not tell the whole story of potential return, however. Although the interest rate is calculated on the bond's face value of $1,000, the investor may not have paid that amount for the bond. Current yield is a measure of the return an investor receives compared to the current price of the security, as shown in the following equation:

$$\frac{\text{Annual interest}}{\text{Current market price}} = \text{Current yield}$$

Relationship of yield to price. A bond traded at par ($1,000) will have identical nominal and current yields. An investor who pays $1,000 for a 6% bond actually will receive a 6% return on investment, or $60 per year. A bond purchased at a discount will have a current yield that is higher than its nominal yield. For example, a 4 1/2% coupon bond trading at a discounted price of $750 has an annual interest payment of $45 and a current yield of 6% ($45 ÷ $750 = 6%). Conversely, a bond purchased at a premium will have a current yield that is lower than its nominal yield. Therefore, an investor who buys a 10% coupon bond trading at a premium of $1,200 receives an annual interest payment of $100 and a current yield of 8.33% ($100 ÷ $1,200 = 8.33%).

While current yield accounts for the dollars actually invested in the bond, it does not take into account a gain or loss on the sale of the bond or whether the bond is held to maturity.

Figure 2.2 illustrates how bond prices affect bond yields.

Figure 2.2 Relationship Between Bond Prices and Yields

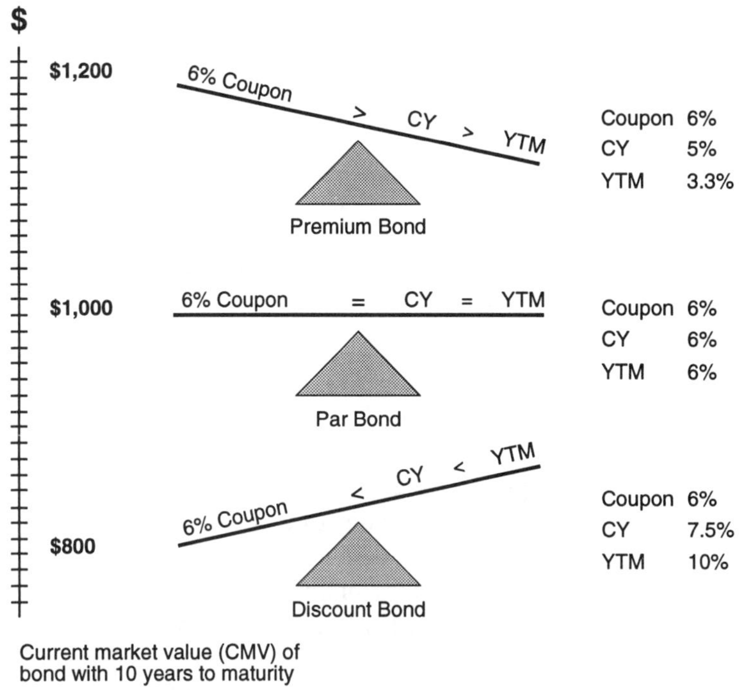

```
$
 $1,200   6% Coupon
                  > CY > YTM           Coupon  6%
                                        CY      5%
              Premium Bond              YTM     3.3%

 $1,000   6% Coupon = CY = YTM         Coupon  6%
                                        CY      6%
              Par Bond                  YTM     6%

                              YTM
                     < CY <            Coupon  6%
          6% Coupon                     CY      7.5%
  $800                                  YTM     10%
              Discount Bond
```

Current market value (CMV) of
bond with 10 years to maturity

Yield to Maturity

A bond's yield to maturity (YTM) is a measure of the annual return on investment (ROI) from purchase until maturity. This measure of yield accounts for the difference between the amount an investor pays for the bond and the amount the investor receives at the time the bond matures. For example, an investor who purchases a 10% coupon bond at 105 (or $1,050 per bond) can expect $100 in interest per year. If he holds that bond to maturity, he will have realized a loss of $50 on his investment (the purchase price of $1,050 less the maturity value of $1,000). This capital loss should be taken into account when calculating the actual yearly earnings of a bond bought at a premium.

Yield and Price

Bond prices and yields have an inverse relationship. As bond prices go up, yields go down (and vice versa). If a bond is trading at a discount, the current yield increases; if a bond is trading at a premium, the current yield decreases.

As a rule of thumb, when comparing two premium or two discount bonds, the bond with the interest rate that is farther away from the current market rates will be more volatile in price.

Yield and price have an inverse relationship—

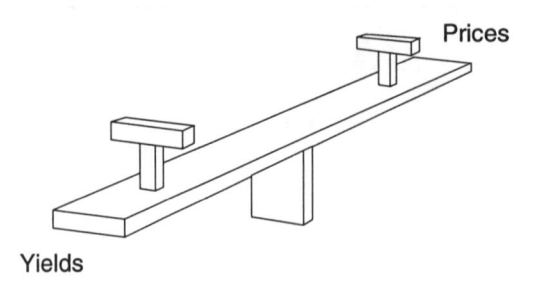

as one goes up, the other goes down.

Short-term and Long-term Yields

A positive yield curve (as depicted in Figure 2.3) is referred to as a *normal curve* due to the fact that most investors are willing to pay a higher price for the benefits of liquidity (the ease with which an investment can be converted to cash without an excessive loss of principal). Short-term investments tend to be more easily bought and sold (more liquid) than long-term investments of the same type and quality, so investors are generally willing to accept lower yields for shorter maturities. Conversely, investors who assume more risks by purchasing longer term maturities (risks that include lower marketability, the effects of changing interest rates on principal, and the time value of money) demand a higher yield in return.

A yield curve typically is plotted on a graph that depicts the yields of bonds of the same quality, with maturities ranging from near to far away. The resulting curve allows an investor to analyze whether short-term interest rates are higher or lower than long-term rates in today's market.

Changing interest rates have a greater effect on bonds with long maturities than on those with short maturities. As interest rates rise, the price of long-term bonds drops more quickly than the price of short-term bonds. Investors who put money into longer term investments will find that long-term yields and prices tend to be more volatile (changeable) than short-term yields and prices.

Figure 2.3   Positive Yield Curve

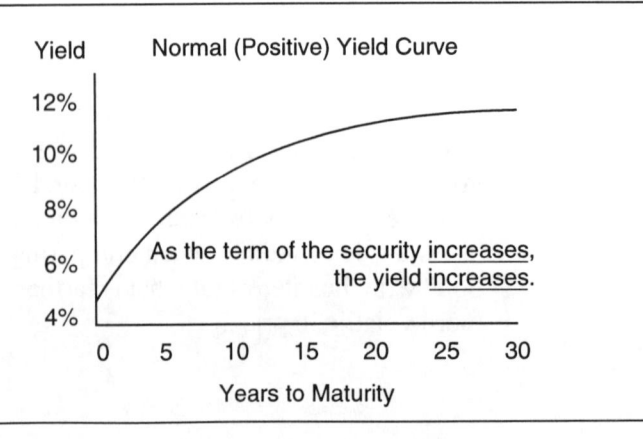

Normal (Positive) Yield Curve

As the term of the security increases, the yield increases.

Characteristics of Corporate Bonds

Types of Bonds

There are two primary types of corporate bonds: secured and unsecured.

Secured Bonds

The term "secured" is used when the issuer has set aside certain identifiable assets as collateral for the prompt payment of interest and the repayment of principal. In a default (that is, when the issuer has failed to meet its obligations to pay principal, interest or both), bondholders can lay claim to the assets.

Mortgage bonds. Mortgage bonds are considered relatively safe investments. In reorganization or liquidation, mortgage bonds have absolute priority among claims on the assets pledged to secure them. For this reason, they are sometimes called *senior debt securities* (also known as *senior lien securities*). While mortgage bonds as a whole are considered relatively safe, individual bonds are ranked against other bonds and given high or low ratings by the various bond-rating organizations.

Not all mortgage bonds, however, are equal. First claim on the pledged property goes to first-mortgage bonds, second claim to second-mortgage bonds and so on.

Collateral trust bonds. Collateral trust bonds are usually issued by corporations that own securities of other companies as investments (these other companies may be subsidiaries of the parent company issuing the collateral trust bonds or nonaffiliated independent corporations). The corporation issues bonds secured by a pledge of these investment securities as collateral. The trust indenture (the written agreement between a corporation and its creditors that details the terms of the debt issue) will usually contain a covenant requiring that the pledged securities be held by a trustee.

Collateral trust bonds may be backed by one or more of the following securities:

- stocks and bonds of partially or wholly owned subsidiaries;
- prior lien long-term bonds of the pledging company that have been held in trust to secure short-term bonds;
- another company's stocks and bonds; or
- installment payments or other obligations of the corporation's clients.

Equipment trust certificates. Railroads, airlines, trucking companies and oil companies use equipment trust certificates (or equipment notes and bonds) to finance the purchase of transportation equipment.

Title to the newly acquired equipment is held in trust (usually by a bank) until all certificates have been paid in full. Because certificates usually mature before the equipment wears out, principal is generally less than the value of the property securing the certificates.

Few other corporate securities are backed as strongly as equipment trust certificates. Though mortgage bonds are technically safe, real estate is not as easily sold as transportation equipment. Equipment trust certificates, therefore, are generally considered to offer greater safety of principal. Consequently, yields on these certificates may be quite low.

Unsecured Bonds

Unsecured bonds have no specific collateral backing and are classified into two primary types: debentures and subordinated debentures.

Debentures. Debentures are backed by the general credit of the issuing corporation. In other words, investors simply believe that the corporation will pay its debts. The owner of a debenture is considered a general creditor of the corporation. Debentures are considered less safe than secured bonds, but safer than subordinated debentures or preferred stock. The issuing corporation promises to pay back principal and interest, just as it does with secured bonds.

Subordinated debentures. Subordinated debentures are so called because the claims of their owners are subordinated to the claims of other general creditors, including owners of ordinary debentures. Subordinated debentures appeal to investors because the debentures generally offer higher income than either straight debentures or secured bonds and often have conversion features.

Zero-coupon Bonds

Issuing zero-coupon bonds. As we have already discussed, most debt securities are issued as fixed income securities—they are issued and can be redeemed by investors at face (par) value, and the issuer pays the owner of the bond a fixed rate of interest (coupon) in semiannual payments. In 1981 a new type of debt security was created by the financial community—the **zero-coupon bond**. Zero-coupon bonds, like all bonds, are debt obligations of the issuer. The difference between ordinary bonds and zero-coupon bonds is that the issuers of zero-coupon bonds do not make interest payments to the owners of zeros. Instead, the issuers sell these debt obligations to investors at a deep discount from the face value (often as low as $100 or $200 for a $1,000 bond) with a promise to redeem the bonds at face value when they mature. The difference between the deeply discounted purchase price and the full face value at maturity is the return (interest) the investor receives.

When pricing a zero-coupon bond at issuance, the issuer and the underwriter take into account several factors. They consider the interest rates being paid by regular debt obligations of similar safety and maturities, the premium investors might want in return for giving up a regular income stream, and the time value of money. Once these and other important considerations are factored in, the price of the zero-coupon bond is set and the bond is offered to the public.

Zero-coupon bonds are issued by corporations, municipalities and the U.S. Treasury (e.g., Separate Trading of Registered Interest and Principal of Securities—STRIPS), and they may be created by broker-dealers from other types of securities, including those issued by the federal government.

Advantages and Disadvantages of Zero-coupon Bonds

Investors in zero-coupon bonds do not purchase them as income investments, but rather, see them as a means of locking in an acceptable rate of interest for the life of the bond. One advantage of an investment in zero-coupon bonds is that there is no **reinvestment risk** (also known as **interest rate risk**) for the purchaser. What this means is that the purchaser does not have to be concerned about reinvesting the interest payments as they are received at current interest rates (an important consideration when you take into account the power of compounding interest). A disadvantage of an investment in zeros is that they are more subject to **market risk** (also known as **price risk**) than are interest-paying debt obligations. Market risk is the risk that the price of the investment will fluctuate during its life (due to changes in market conditions, interest rates, investor sentiment and so on). Zero-coupon bond prices tend to be extremely volatile because of their deep discount and low (zero) interest rate. If interest rates change dramatically, investors in zeros could experience significant losses or gains if they sell their zeros before maturity, more so than investors in ordinary interest-paying debt securities.

Taxation of Zero-coupon Bonds

Even though interest is not paid until the bond matures, the investor who owns corporate or government zeros owes income tax each year on a portion of that amount, just as though it had been received in cash (interest from municipal obligations, including municipal zeros, is generally federally tax-exempt). Because the annual interest is not prorated on a straight-line basis and the investor is apportioned a different amount each year, the issuer of the bond is required to send the investor an Internal Revenue Service (IRS) Form 1099OID annually showing the amount of interest subject to taxation. Final determination of the amount of taxable interest may be made by the IRS.

Liquidation

Liquidation priority. The backing of a bond is of greatest concern when a corporation goes into liquidation. In such a case, strict rules are followed for paying off the corporation's employees (who are paid first), creditors and stockholders. In order of priority, liquidation occurs as follows:

1. unpaid wages
2. IRS (taxes)
3. secured claims (mortgages)
4. secured liabilities (bonds)
5. unsecured liabilities (debentures) and general creditors
6. subordinated debt
7. preferred stockholders
8. common stockholders

Tracking Corporate Bonds

Bonds are listed in newspapers and other financial publications such as *Barron's* and *The Wall Street Journal*. Figure 2.4 is an example of a New York Stock Exchange bond table as it might appear in a financial publication. Take, for example, Alabama Power 9s 2000. The symbol for the bond (AlaP) and the description of the bond (9s 2000) indicate that the bond pays 9% interest and matures in the year 2000. The current yield is given as 8.9%, which indicates that the bond is selling at a premium. The "Vol" (volume, or sales) column states how many bonds traded the previous day (the day being reported). In this case, 18 bonds, or $18,000 par value, were traded in Alabama Power 9s of 2000.

The next three columns explain the high, low and closing prices for the day. For AlaP, the high was 100 3/4, the low was 100 5/8 and the bonds closed at (last trade) 100 3/4. Net change (the last column) refers to how much the bond's closing price was up or down from the previous day's close. Alabama Power 9s of 2000 closed up 1/4 of a point, or $2.50. AlaP closed yesterday at 100 1/2 (100 3/4 – 1/4).

Note that the Allied Chemical (AlldC) zr bonds have "..." in the current yield column. This indicates that these are zero-coupon bonds that do not pay interest.

Figure 2.4   Corporate Bond Quotations

New York Exchange Bonds
Quotations as of 4 pm Eastern Time
Friday, July 16, 1995
Corporation Bonds
Volume $45,198,000

Bonds	Cur Yld	Vol	High	Low	Close	Net Chg
AForP 5s 30r	9.6	50	52 1/4	51 7/8	52	+3/4
AbbtL 7 5/8s 96	7.6	21	99 3/4	99 3/4	99 3/4	...
Advst 9s 08	cv	72	103 1/2	103	103	...
AetnLf 8 1/8s 07	8.5	15	95 3/4	95 3/4	95 3/4	– 1
AirbF 7 1/2s 11	cv	32	114	112	114	+1
AlaP 9s 2000	8.9	18	100 3/4	100 5/8	100 3/4	+1/4
AlaP 8 1/2s 01	8.6	13	98 3/8	98 3/8	98 3/8	– 3/8
AlaP 8 7/8s 03	8.5	65	102 7/8	102 1/2	102 1/2	– 3/8
AlldC zr 12	...	10	91 1/2	91 1/8	91 1/2	– 1/8
viAmes 7 1/2s 14f	cv	79	15 1/2	14 3/4	15	+1
Ancp 13 7/8s 02f	cv	10	91	89 3/8	91	+2

EXPLANATORY NOTES

Yield is current yield. cld–Called. cv–Convertible bond. dc–Deep discount. f–Dealt in flat. m–Matured bonds, negotiability impaired by maturity. na–No accrual. r–Registered. zr–Zero coupon. vi–In bankruptcy or receivership or being reorganized.

◆ Review Questions

1. Which of the following are characteristics of bonds?

   I. They represent a loan to the issuer.
   II. They give the bondholder ownership in the entity.
   III. They are issued to finance capital expenditures or to raise working capital.
   IV. They are junior securities.

   A. I, II and IV only
   B. I and III only
   C. II and III only
   D. I, II, III and IV

2. Interest payments on bonds are based upon the security's

   A. par value
   B. discount value
   C. market value
   D. book value

3. A 5% bond is issued at par. It is now selling at 90 and is redeemable at par. What is the owner's annual income from this investment?

   A. $20
   B. $50
   C. $500
   D. $5,000

4. Which of the following is commonly referred to as *funded debt*?

   A. Corporate bonds
   B. Municipal bonds
   C. Preferred stock
   D. Government bonds

5. Equipment trust certificates would MOST commonly be issued by

   I. airline companies
   II. railroad companies
   III. farm equipment companies
   IV. automobile manufacturers

   A. I and II
   B. II
   C. III
   D. III and IV

6. Bonds that are secured by other securities placed with a trustee are called

   A. mortgage bonds
   B. collateral trust bonds
   C. debenture bonds
   D. guaranteed bonds

Use the following information to answer questions 7 through 9.

Company	Sales	High	Low	Close	Change
Best 7 3/4's '95	5	92 1/2	91 1/4	92	– 1/2
Bre 7's '96	10	84 1/4	83 3/8	83 7/8	– 3/8
Bzdt 7 1/2's '99	30	95 3/8	95	95 7/8	+ 5/8

7. How many Bzdt bonds were sold on this day?

   A. 3
   B. 30
   C. 300
   D. 30,000

8. Best's bonds closed the day before at

   A. 91 1/2
   B. 92
   C. 92 1/2
   D. This cannot be determined from information given.

9. The current yield for Bre's 7% bonds is

   A. 8.25%
   B. 8.31%
   C. 8.35%
   D. 8.54%

10. The newspaper reports a Burlington Northern bond is priced at $1,012.50. This price is written as

   A. 100 1/8
   B. 101 1/4
   C. 101 1/2
   D. 101.25

◆ Answers & Rationale

1. **B.** Bonds give the bondholder the status of lender, not of owner. Because they represent a debt the corporation owes, they are senior securities.

2. **A.** $1,000 is considered a bond's par value or principal amount. If a bond is issued with a 6% coupon, this means the corporation will pay 6% of $1,000, or $60, each year in interest.

3. **B.** A 5% bond will continue to pay $50 a year, regardless of its market price in the secondary market.

4. **A.** Corporate bonds are referred to as *funded debt* because corporations issue the bonds to raise money for working capital or for capital expenditures such as plant construction, equipment purchases, expansion and so forth.

5. **A.** Equipment trust certificates are debt obligations backed by equipment. Consequently, they are most commonly issued by the users of the equipment, such as airlines and railroads, not by the manufacturers.

6. **B.** Debt issued by a corporation that is backed by stocks or bonds of another issuer and held by a trustee for safekeeping is called a *collateral trust bond.*

7. **B.** Sales on bonds are quoted in $1,000 par value unit. 30 = 30 $1,000 bonds = $30,000 face amount.

8. **C.** Today, Best closed at 92, down 1/2. Therefore, Best closed the day before at 92.50, or 92 1/2.

9. **C.**

$$\frac{\text{Annual interest}}{\text{Bond price}} = \frac{\$70}{\$838.75}$$

$$= .0835 = 8.35\%$$

10. **B.** Corporate bond prices are expressed as percentages of the principal amount of a bond, or $1,000. Each bond point is equal to $10, with the minimum variation for bond quotes at 1/8 of a point. Therefore, a quote of 101 1/4 is equal to $1,012.50 (101.25 × $10). A quote expressed as 101.25 is used for government securities quotations and is equal to 101 25/32.

3 Corporate Special Securities

Key Terms

American depositary receipt (ADR)
call
conversion price
conversion ratio
convertible security
option
parity

preemptive right
put
right
subscription right certificate
warrant
when issued (WI)

Overview

Some corporate securities may be converted by their owner into other securities of the same corporation (such as stocks into bonds). These are called *convertibles* and are usually debentures, subordinated debentures or preferred stock.

Technically, convertible bonds are classified as debt securities. Their holders are creditors of the corporation. But debentures, in reality, are like both debt and equity securities. Though they have a fixed interest rate and a maturity date established at the time of issuance, they can also be converted into common stock of the issuing corporation.

Convertible Securities

Why Corporations Issue Convertible Securities

A corporation will add a conversion feature to its bonds and preferred stock issues to make them more marketable. During strong bull markets, when investors are interested in stocks and the market for new fixed income securities is poor, the conversion privilege makes a bond more attractive. In exchange for the investor benefits offered by a conversion feature, many corporations will pay a lower rate of interest on convertible securities.

When the bond market is strong, convertible debentures are frequently issued as a means of raising equity capital on a postponed basis. When (and if) the debentures are converted, the corporation's capitalization changes from debt to equity.

The Market for Convertible Securities

Theoretically, the convertible bondholder has the best of two markets: the investment safety of the fixed income market and the potential appreciation of the equity market. This leads to several advantages:

- As a debt security, a convertible debenture pays interest at a fixed rate and will be redeemable for its face value at maturity, provided the debenture is not converted. As a rule, interest income is usually higher and surer than dividend income on the underlying common stock. Similarly, convertible preferred stock usually pays a higher dividend than does common stock.
- If the corporation should experience financial difficulties, the convertible bondholder has priority over common stockholders in the event of a corporate liquidation.
- In theory, the market price of a convertible debenture will tend to be more stable during market declines than the price of common stock. Its value in the marketplace will be supported by current yields of other competitive debt securities.
- Because convertibles can be exchanged for common stock, their market price tends to move upward if the stock price moves up. For this reason, convertible securities are more volatile in price during times of steady interest rates than are other fixed income securities.

Critics of convertible securities contend that convertibles do not necessarily offer the best of the equity and debt markets. The critics say that convertibles do not offer interest rates commensurate with lack of principal safety (nonconvertible debentures offer higher interest yields) and have a tendency to depress common stock prices because of the possible dilution effect.

Conversion Price and Conversion Ratio

Conversion price. Conversion price is the amount of par value of the convertible bond that can be converted into one share of common stock. For example, Hammermill Paper has a convertible debenture with a conversion price of $40. This means each $40 worth of par value will be converted into one share of common stock. In other words, for every bond a holder converts, the bondholder will receive 25 shares of stock (a 25-to-1 conversion ratio). The conversion ratio is simply a factor of the conversion price. The conversion ratio times the conversion price will equal the bond's par value.

Conversion ratio. Conversion ratio (also called *conversion rate*) expresses the number of shares of common stock obtainable by converting $1,000 par value of the bonds. A debenture with a conversion price of $40, for example, has a conversion ratio of 25 to 1 ($1,000 ÷ $40 = 25). Conversion terms are stated in the indenture agreement, either as a conversion ratio or as a conversion price. A preferred stock normally has a par value of $100, so a conversion price of $50 would mean a conversion ratio of 2 to 1.

Calculating Conversion Parity

Investors holding convertible securities naturally are curious about which is worth more, the security they own or the security they could own by converting. Answering that question involves finding the prices that will put the two securities at **parity** (or equality). If the securities are not at parity, then one is worth more to the investor than the other.

Parity means that two securities (in this case, a convertible preferred stock or bond and the common stock into which it can be converted) are of equal dollar value. If a corporation issues a convertible preferred stock that has a par value of $100 and is convertible at $50, the conversion ratio is 2 to 1. The investor can receive two shares of common stock for one share of the preferred. Then the question about relative value becomes simpler: Which is worth more on the market, one share of the preferred or two of the common?

Suppose, for example, that a convertible preferred is selling in the market at 104 and is convertible into two shares of common stock. The market price of the common would have to be 52 to have the same dollar value as (to be at parity with) the convertible preferred. Why? Because two shares of common stock at 52 per share are equal in value to one share of the preferred at $104 per share. If the common stock is selling below 52 (below parity), the investor can make more by selling the preferred than by converting and selling the common. If the common is selling above 52, the investor can make more money by converting to common and selling that.

Parity can also be calculated the other way around, beginning with the market price of the common stock and calculating the parity price of the preferred. Knowing that the common is trading at 52 and that the convertible preferred has a conversion ratio of 2 to 1, you can multiply 52 by 2 to calculate that the preferred's parity price is 104. An investor would find a conversion profitable only if the common has a price of more than $52 (greater than one-half the preferred's price of $104).

The following formulas allow calculation of the parity prices of convertible securities and their underlying common shares:

$$\frac{\text{Market price of convertible}}{\text{Conversion ratio}} = \text{Parity price of common}$$

$$\text{Market price of common} \times \text{Conversion ratio} = \text{Parity price of convertible}$$

In a rising market, the market value of the convertible rises with the common stock. In a declining market, the market price of the convertible tends to level off when the yield becomes competitive with bonds that are not convertible and may not decline in price as far as the common stock.

Rights and Warrants

Issuance

A corporation, when issuing new shares of common stock, may choose to sell its shares to existing stockholders before going to public investors. This may be because the company believes its stockholders would be the best prospects to buy additional shares of the company, or it may be because the corporation's stockholders have preemptive rights.

Preemptive right refers to the right of an existing stockholder to purchase shares of a new issue of stock in proportion to the number of shares the investor already owns. A concern is that if new shares are issued by a corporation, the present stockholders' ownership of the company will be diluted if they are not able to purchase a proportionate share of the new issue. Their voting percentage, earnings per share and net worth per share will be reduced. In addition, the additional supply of stock available to the market may cause the market price of the stock to decrease.

The rights entitle the stockholder to purchase common stock below the current market price. This means that the rights are valued separately and trade in the secondary market during the subscription period. A stockholder who receives rights may take one of the following actions:

- exercise the right to buy stock (by sending the rights certificates and a check for the required amount to the rights agent), thereby maintaining proportionate interest in the corporation;
- sell the right: because the rights certificate is a negotiable security, the investor can sell the right and profit from its market value (although by selling the right, the investor forgoes any potential profit from exercising the right and owning the stock); or
- let the right expire, thus reducing proportionate ownership and losing the value of the right or of the stock it could have been used to acquire.

Approval by Vote of Stockholders

Decisions to issue additional stock must first be approved by the board of directors. If the additional stock to be issued through the rights offering increases the total stock issued beyond the amount authorized in the charter, the stockholders must vote to amend the charter.

Characteristics of Rights

Subscription Right Certificate

A rights offering is a short-term (typically 30 to 45 days) privilege a stockholder receives from a corporation, and a subscription right is the actual certificate representing that privilege. One right is issued for each share of common stock the investor owns. Therefore, an investor with 100 shares of common stock receives a certificate representing 100 rights.

Warrants

A **warrant** is a certificate giving the holder the right to purchase securities at a stipulated price from the issuer. Unlike a right, a warrant is usually a long-term instrument, affording the investor the option of buying shares at a later date at the subscription price, subject to the warrant's expiration date.

Warrants may be detachable from the underlying security, or they may be nondetachable. If detachable, they trade in the market purely as speculation on the price of the underlying stock (because the warrants do not receive dividends or represent any other right of a corporate owner). While the exercise price is set above the market price of the stock when the warrant is first issued, the investor hopes the stock's price will increase in the market. The investor can (1) exercise the warrant and buy the stock below the price he would have to pay in the market or (2) sell the warrant in the market at a price based on the benefit the purchaser can get by exercising the warrant and buying the stock below market price.

Origination of Warrants

Warrants are usually offered to the public as a sweetener in connection with other securities (usually debentures) to make these securities more attractive. Investors enjoy the security of owning a bond, note or preferred stock, but might also benefit from the opportunity to participate in the appreciation of the common stock. The market price of the common stock is normally lower than the exercise price stated in the warrants when they are first issued.

Warrants are occasionally bundled with other securities and offered as part of *units*. For example, Datawaq may make an offering of 1,000,000 shares of new preferred stock, bundling it into units of 2 shares of preferred and 1 warrant for 1/2 a share of common stock exercisable at a specific price. An investor who purchases 100 units will receive 200 shares of preferred stock plus warrants redeemable for 50 shares of common (100 units times 1 warrant for 1/2 a share of common per unit).

American Depositary Receipts

Facilitate Trading in Foreign Securities

A U.S. investor interested in buying stock of foreign corporations need not always arrange to receive the foreign certificates. Instead, the investor can, in many cases, buy **American depositary receipts** (**ADRs**), also known as *American depositary shares (ADSs)*.

ADRs facilitate the ownership of foreign securities by U.S. citizens. An ADR is a negotiable security and represents a receipt for a given number of shares of stock (typically one to ten) in a non-U.S. corporation. The ADR itself is an instrument that can, like a stock, be bought and sold in the U.S. securities markets on an exchange or over the counter.

Rights of ADR Owners

Most rights normally held by common stockholders are also rights of holders of ADRs. These rights include voting rights and the right to receive dividends when declared, but do not include preemptive rights. Because ADRs are registered on the books of the U.S. bank responsible for them, dividends are sent to the custodian bank as registered owner. The custodian bank collects any dividends paid (or processes any stock splits declared) by the foreign issuer, converts the payments into U.S. funds for U.S. owners and withholds any required payments of foreign taxes.

The custodian bank also acts as subscription agent in the event of the distribution of stock rights or warrants. When the bank receives the rights or warrants from the issuer, it does not distribute them directly to the ADR owners (which would require registering the securities with the SEC). Instead, the bank sells the rights and warrants in a market of the issuer's own country and distributes the sale proceeds in cash to the ADR owners.

Introduction to Options

Calls and Puts

An option is a **contract** between two people. The purchaser (also known as the **holder**, **buyer** or **owner**) of the contract has paid money for the *right* to buy or the *right* to sell securities. The **seller** (or **writer**) of the option contract, on the other hand, has accepted money for taking on an *obligation*. The option seller *must* buy or *must* sell the specified security if asked to do so by the option's buyer. A stock option contract represents an agreement between two people (a buyer and a seller) to buy or sell 100 shares (a round lot) of stock.

There are two types of options: **calls** and **puts**.

- A call option is the *right to call* (buy) a security away from someone. You can buy that right for yourself, or you can sell that right to someone else.
- A put option is the *right to put* (sell) a security to someone. You can buy that right for yourself, or you can sell that right to someone else.

A *call* is the right to *buy* a set amount of a specific investment instrument at a set price for a set period of time. A *put* is the right to *sell* a set amount of a specific investment instrument at a set price for a set period of time. The money the buyer of an option contract pays the seller to take on the obligations in the contract is called the option's **premium**. The following illustrates the rights and obligations of buyers and sellers.

The buyer of an option has acquired a *right*.

The seller of an option has taken on an *obligation*.

In general, bullish investors (those who believe that the market or the stock underlying the corporation is going to move up in price) buy calls and sell puts. Bearish investors (those who believe that the market or the stock underlying the corporation is going to move down in price) buy puts and sell calls. Figure 3.1 illustrates this relationship.

Disposing of an option. The holder of an option contract (a put or call buyer) has three choices. The holder can:

- **exercise** the option (that is, use it to purchase or sell the security specified in the contract);
- let the option **expire**; or
- **sell** the option contract to another investor before the expiration date.

Underlying Instruments

In theory, options can be created on any item with a fluctuating market value, such as securities, houses, cars, gold coins, baseball cards and comic books, including:

- corporate stock;
- broad- and narrow-based indexes (Major Market Index, Technology Index, Gold/Silver Index, etc.);
- Treasury bonds, Treasury notes and Treasury bills; and
- major foreign currencies.

The most familiar options are those issued on common stocks; they are called **equity options**.

Figure 3.1 Determining Market Side for Position Limits

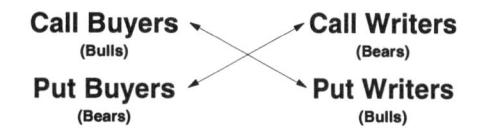

Call Buyers (Bulls) ⤫ **Call Writers** (Bears)
Put Buyers (Bears) ⤫ **Put Writers** (Bulls)

Call buyers and put writers are on one side of the market as bulls, and put buyers and call writers are on the other side of the market as bears.

Review Questions

1. Which of the following statement(s) concerning convertible bonds is(are) true?

   I. Coupon rates for convertible bonds are usually lower than for nonconvertible bonds of the same issuer.
   II. Convertible bondholders are creditors of the corporation.
   III. If the underlying common stock should decline to the point where there is no advantage to converting the bonds into common stock, the bonds will sell at a price based on their inherent value as bonds, disregarding the convertible feature.

   A. I only
   B. I and III only
   C. III only
   D. I, II and III

2. ABC bonds are convertible at $50. If the bonds are selling in the market for 60 ($600) and the common stock is selling for $30, which two of the following statements are true?

   I. The bonds are trading below parity to the common.
   II. The stock is selling at conversion parity.
   III. There would be a profitable arbitrage situation.
   IV. The bonds can be converted into 20 shares of common.

   A. I and II
   B. I and III
   C. II and IV
   D. III and IV

3. Which of the following instruments does NOT receive dividends?

   A. warrants
   B. common stock
   C. preferred stock
   D. convertible preferred stock

◆ Answers & Rationale

1. **D.** Coupons on convertible bonds are lower because, in exchange for the conversion option, investors are willing to settle for lower interest income. Bondholders are creditors of the corporation. If the price of the underlying declines sharply, then the conversion feature is unimportant and the bond will sell in the secondary market as if it was a nonconvertible bond.

2. **C.** With a conversion price of $50 the investor would receive 20 shares ($1,000 par value ÷ $50 = 20). To calculate the parity of the common stock, divide the current market price by the number of shares at conversion: $600 ÷ 20 = $30. The stock is selling at parity.

3. **A.** A warrant is not evidence of ownership in a corporation qualifying for dividends. It is a certificate giving the holder the right to purchase securities from the issuer at a stipulated price. Eventually the warrant expires.

4 U.S. Government, Agency and Municipal Securities

Key Terms

agency issue
Federal National Mortgage
　Association (FNMA)
General obligation bond (GO)
Government National Mortgage
　Association (GNMA)
pass-through security
revenue bond
savings bond

Separate Trading of Registered Interest
　and Principal of Securities (STRIPS)
Series EE bond
Series HH bond
Treasury bill
Treasury bond
Treasury note
Treasury receipt
zero-coupon bond

Overview

The federal government is not only the nation's largest borrower, it is its best credit risk. Securities issued by the U.S. government (or by governmental agencies) to finance its operations are backed by its full faith and credit. The full faith and credit backing the U.S. government gives the securities it issues is largely based on its power to raise money through taxation.

The Public Debt Act of 1942 gave the U.S. Treasury department the authority to determine the number and types of government securities to be sold to meet the needs of the federal budget. The Treasury, however, does not set the rate on its new issues; the marketplace does. The marketplace also dictates, to a degree, the form and features of those securities. In general, government securities are exempt from state and municipal taxation, but subject to federal taxation.

Some government securities (in particular, registered or bearer bonds) are issued in definitive form, which means that the investor receives a certificate. Others are issued in book-entry form; that is, the investor's name is stored in a computer, and the investor receives no certificate.

Marketable Government Securities

Treasury Bills

Issuance and trading. T bills are issued by the Treasury Department at a discount from par in a **competitive bid** auction. Large U.S. government securities dealers, pension plans and money managers submit bids (also known as **tenders**) for large blocks of T bills at the weekly auctions. Competitive tenders are submitted with the price that the bidder is willing to accept (such as 99.247), a price that reflects the interest rate the bidder wishes to receive. The Treasury then awards the bills to the highest bidders (who are actually bidding the lowest interest rates), starting at the top of the list and working down. A firm that submits a competitive bid may not have its bid filled if it bids too low. Competitive bids are usually submitted for amounts of $500,000 and up and settle in federal funds (as do all U.S. government securities).

T bills may also be purchased by submitting a **noncompetitive bid**. The investor who submits a noncompetitive bid agrees to pay the average of the competitive bids accepted at that auction and is guaranteed to have his order filled. Noncompetitive bids are limited to a maximum amount of $500,000.

T bills are highly liquid securities actively quoted and traded in the secondary market. They trade at a discount and do not pay interest (that is, they are traded **flat**); an investor's return on T bills is the difference between the price the investor paid and the price at which the investor sells or redeems them.

Book entry. Treasury bills are issued in book-entry form. An owner receives no certificate, but a record of the purchase is kept on computer. Because a record of the bill's ownership is kept on computer, T bills are considered *registered* securities. When the T bill matures, the principal amount is sent to the owner of record. The investor, meanwhile, has the confirmation as proof of purchase.

Maturities and denominations. Treasury bills are short-term issues with maturities of one year or less. Issued in denominations of $10,000 to $1 million (in $5,000 increments), they mature in 13 weeks, 26 weeks or 52 weeks. T bills with 13-week and 26-week maturities are auctioned weekly, while those with 52-week maturities are auctioned every four weeks. At the bill's maturity, the investor can either request cash or request that the investment be rolled over into another T bill.

Pricing. Treasury bills are quoted at a discount from par. A quote of 5.50%, for example, means a T bill is selling at 5 1/2% less than its face value. For a $10,000 52-week Treasury bill, that would be a price of $9,450. A T bill quote might read as follows: Maturity April 6, bid 5.50%, asked 5.35%. The bid appears higher than the asked because the bidder wants to pay less for the bill to achieve a higher yield and thus bids at a deeper discount from par.

Treasury Notes

Issuance and trading. T notes pay interest every six months. They are issued in book-entry form only.

Maturities and denominations. Issued in denominations of $1,000 to $1 million, T notes are intermediate-term bonds maturing in one to ten years (notes typically have maturities of at least two years).

Pricing. T notes are issued, quoted and traded at a percentage of par. T notes and bonds are quoted in 1/32nds of a percent of par. A quote of 98:24 (which can also be expressed as 98-24 or 98.24) on a $1,000 note means that the note is selling for 98 and 24/32% of its par value of $1,000. In this instance, :24 is not a decimal; instead, it designates 24/32nds of 1%. A quote of 98:24 is equal to 98.75% of $1,000, or $987.50.

Other examples are as follows:

A bid of:	Means:	In dollars:
98:1	98 + 1/32% of $1,000	$980.3125
98:2	98 + 2/32% of $1,000	$980.6250
98:3	98 + 3/32% of $1,000	$980.9375
......	......	......
98:10	98 + 10/32% of $1,000	$983.1250
98:11	98 + 11/32% of $1,000	$983.4375
98:12	98 + 12/32% of $1,000	$983.7500

Redeemable at face value. At maturity, T notes can be redeemed for cash at par or they can be refunded. If a T note is refunded, the government offers the investor a new security with a new maturity date as an alternative to a cash payment for the existing securities. Bondholders may always request the principal amount in cash if they do not wish to reinvest.

Treasury Bonds

Issuance and trading. Treasury bonds constitute the smallest portion of the government's marketable debt. Interest is payable every six months. Before June 30, 1983, they were issued in bearer and registered forms. Now T bonds are sold in book-entry form only.

Callable. Some Treasury bonds have optional call dates, ranging from three to five years before maturity. For example, a quote of "5s 11/16" indicates that they could be called at any time from 2011 until they mature in 2016. Before calling the bonds, however, the Treasury department must give bondholders four months' notice. U.S. government securities are always called at par and never at a premium.

Maturities and denominations. Treasury bonds are issued in denominations of $1,000 to $1 million, and with maturities of ten years or more.

Pricing. T bonds, like T notes, are issued, quoted and traded in 1/32nds of a percent of par. A quote of 98:04 (98-04 or 98.04) on a $1,000 bond means that the bond is selling for 98 and 4/32% of its par value of $1,000. A quote of 98:04 is equal to 98.125% of $1,000, or $981.25.

Table 4.1 compares Treasury bills, notes and bonds.

Table 4.1 Marketable Government Securities

Bond	Maturity	Denomination	Pricing	Form
Treasury bills	Ninety days to one year	$10,000 to $1,000,000	Interest rate basis	Book entry
Treasury notes	One to ten years	$1,000 to $1,000,000	Percentage of par	Book entry
Treasury bonds	Ten to thirty years	$1,000 to $1,000,000	Percentage of par	Book entry

Zero-coupon Securities

Brokerage firms have the permission of the Treasury department to create zero-coupon bonds (**Treasury receipts**) from U.S. Treasury notes and bonds. Broker-dealers buy Treasury securities, place them in trust at a bank, and then sell receipts against the principal and coupon payments separately to investors. Unlike Treasury securities, Treasury receipts are not backed by the full faith and credit of the U.S. government.

Treasury receipts are collateralized by Treasury securities held in escrow for the investor by a custodial bank. Because the underlying Treasury notes and bonds pay semiannual interest to the custodial bank, zero-coupons are issued with maturities at six-month intervals.

Treasury receipts are priced at a discount from face value. You can think of a $1,000 10-year Treasury note with a 6% coupon as a 21 separate obligations: the obligation to pay $30 in six months, in a year, in a year and a half and so on to maturity and the obligation to pay $1,000 at maturity. An investor interested in purchasing a Treasury receipt worth $1,000 when it matures in ten years may pay as little as $400 or $500 for that receipt, depending on current interest rates, the time value of money, alternative investments and so on.

One of the appeals of zero-coupon bonds is that investors are not subject to **reinvestment risk**. Because there are no interest payments during the life of the bond, the investor does not have to be concerned with reinvesting those payments at a comparable or better interest rate.

STRIPS. In 1984 the Treasury department itself entered the growing zero-coupon bond market by designating certain Treasury issues as suitable for stripping into interest and principal components. These special securities became known as STRIPS, which stands for "Separate Trading of Registered Interest and Principal of Securities." STRIPS were issued as book-entry securities—that is, evidence of ownership of each STRIP is maintained on computer at the Fed. Treasury STRIPS are not to be confused with zero-coupon bonds that broker-dealers create by buying Treasury securities and issuing receipts against them or by stripping the coupons from corporate or municipal bonds and selling them separately.

While the securities underlying Treasury STRIPS are the direct obligation of the U.S. government, the actual separation and trading is performed by major banks and dealers.

Brokerage zero-coupon bonds. The original zero-coupon bonds were created by brokerage firms and tend to be identified by such memorable acronyms as TIGRs (Treasury Investors Growth Receipts), CATS (Certificates of Accrual on Treasury Securities), LIONs (Lehman Investment Opportunity Notes), ETRs (Easy-growth Treasury Receipts) and TBRs (Treasury Bond Receipts).

Nonmarketable Government Securities

Savings Bonds

Savings bonds differ from other government securities in that they cannot be used as collateral and are not negotiable. They are **nonmarketable securities** because they are nontransferable. They are not bought and sold on an exchange or over the counter; rather, they are purchased from the Treasury department through various issuing agents, including commercial banks and post offices. They can be redeemed by only the purchaser or a beneficiary.

Series EE bonds. Series EE bonds are discount bonds: bondholders earn the discount over the 12-year life of the bond, and can continue to receive interest for up to thirty years. They can be redeemed for the face value at maturity (although they may be redeemed before they mature). Series EE bonds are issued at 50% of their face value in denominations from $50 to $10,000 (with a minimum purchase of $25, a $50 face bond). In the early years, only small amounts of interest accrue; the bulk of the interest accrues in later years. Series EE bonds can be redeemed before maturity, but will receive a lower rate of return (giving the bondholder an incentive to hold bonds until maturity). A minimum return is guaranteed on Series EE bonds, a return tied to 85% of the average return of five-year Treasury securities. The tax on accrued interest on EE bonds can be paid annually or deferred until the bond matures. Tax can be deferred further by trading EE bonds for HH bonds.

Series HH bonds. Series HH bonds differ from Series EE bonds in that they pay interest semiannually. They are designed for investors who want regular income. Series HH bonds can be purchased only by trading in Series EE bonds at maturity. Series HH bonds come in denominations of $500 to $10,000 and mature in ten years, although the investor can redeem them at face value at any time.

Table 4.2 compares Series EE and HH bonds.

Table 4.2 Comparison of Series EE and HH Bonds

Bond	Maturity	Denomination	Pricing	Form
Series EE	Twelve years	$50 to $10,000	Issued at a discount	Registered
Series HH	Ten years	$500 to $10,000	Issued at par	Registered

Agency Issues

Authorization. Congress authorizes certain agencies of the federal government to issue marketable debt securities. Some of these agencies (reported daily in many newspapers) are:

- Federal Farm Credit Banks
- Federal Home Loan Mortgage Corporation (FHLMC or Freddie Mac)
- Government National Mortgage Association (GNMA or Ginnie Mae)
- Inter-American Development Bank (IADB)

Other agency-like organizations that are operated by private corporations include:

- Federal Home Loan Banks (FHLBs)
- Federal National Mortgage Association (FNMA or Fannie Mae)

The term "agency" is sometimes used to refer to entities that are not technically government agencies, but that do have ties to the government. The Federal Home Loan Banks, for example, are owned by the private savings and loan associations that are members of the FHLB system. Yet the FHLB operates under federal charter and regulates its members. Whatever its technical status, therefore, it functions as a government agency. The Federal National Mortgage Association (Fannie Mae) is also privately owned, but government regulated.

Yields and maturities. Agency issues sell at higher yields than do direct obligations of the federal government (partially attributable to a slightly higher level of risk), but they frequently sell at lower yields than those available on corporate debt securities. The maturities of these issues vary from very short (money-market instruments) to relatively long term. Agency issues are quoted at a percentage of par and are traded on the secondary market prior to their maturity.

Backing. Agency issues have a very slight risk of failing to pay interest and principal because the issuing agency backs them with revenues from taxes, fees or income from lending activities. Agency issues are backed in several ways: by collateral, such as cash, U.S. Treasury securities and the debt obligations; by a U.S. Treasury guarantee; by the right of the agency to borrow from the Treasury; or, in a few cases, by the full faith and credit of the government.

Taxation. Interest on government agency issues is sometimes exempt from state and local income taxes, but is always subject to federal income tax. Fannie Mae and Ginnie Mae securities, for example, are taxed at federal, state and local levels.

Federal National Mortgage Association

The Federal National Mortgage Association is a publicly held corporation (not a government agency) that provides mortgage capital. FNMA purchases conventional and insured mortgages from agencies such as the Federal Housing Administration (FHA) and the Department of Veterans Affairs (VA). The securities are backed by FNMA's general credit.

Types of issues. FNMA issues debentures, short-term discount notes and mortgage-backed securities (like GNMA). The notes are issued in denominations of $5,000, $25,000, $100,000, $500,000 and $1 million. Debentures (3- to 25-year maturities) have denominations from $10,000 up in increments of $5,000. Interest is paid semi-annually. They are issued in book-entry form only.

Taxation. Interest from FNMA securities is taxed at federal, state and local levels.

Government National Mortgage Association

The Government National Mortgage Association, established in 1968, is a wholly U.S. government-owned corporation that supports the Department of Housing and Urban Development. Ginnie Maes are backed by the full faith and credit of the government.

Types of issues. GNMA buys FHA and VA mortgages and auctions them to private lenders, which pool these mortgages (along with GNMA mortgages acquired from other sources) and sell pass-through certificates based on them. These certificates represent proportionate interests in the mortgages. Each month, principal and interest payments from the pool of mortgages pass through to investors (after deduction of GNMA fees). The amount of principal represented by a GNMA certificate is therefore constantly decreasing. In this regard, a GNMA certificate is similar to a single mortgage.

GNMA pass-throughs are popular investments, primarily because they pay a higher rate of interest than comparable Treasury securities and they are guaranteed by the federal government. GNMA also guarantees timely payment of interest and principal. Because GNMAs are backed directly by the government, risk of default is nearly zero. Yields, however, may fluctuate as prices rise and fall in relation to current interest rates. If interest rates fall, homeowners may pay off their mortgages early, which affects the yield on certificates. If mortgage interest rates rise, certificates may mature more slowly.

GNMAs are issued in minimum denominations of $25,000. Quoted yields for GNMAs are based on early payment, because few mortgages last for the full term. Yields are based on a twelve-year prepayment assumption; that is, the balance of the mortgage should be prepaid in full after twelve years of normally scheduled payments.

Taxation. Interest earned on GNMA certificates is fully taxable at federal, state and local levels.

Introduction to Municipal Bonds

In the ranking of investments by safety of principal, municipal securities are considered second only to U.S. government and U.S. government agency securities. The degree of safety, of course, varies from issue to issue and from municipality to municipality. Much of the safety of any municipal issue is based on the viability of the issuing municipality and the community in general.

Each new municipal issue is accompanied by documentation that:

- sets forth the terms of the loan and the schedule of repayment;
- attests to the issuing municipality's authority to issue the debt obligation;
- lists the specific features of the issue;
- describes the intended use of the borrowed funds; and
- provides financial information about the economic health of the municipality and the community.

Tax Benefits

The interest paid by most municipal securities is exempt from federal income taxation. The federal government does not tax the interest from debt obligations of municipalities; municipalities reciprocate by not taxing the interest from federal debt securities. This **doctrine of reciprocal immunity** was established by the Supreme Court in a decision handed down in 1895. To qualify for the exemption from federal taxation, the municipal security must be issued to fund government (public rather than private) activities.

In many cases, interest from municipal bonds is also exempt from state taxation if the bond (1) is issued by a municipality in that state and (2) is sold to an investor who lives in that state. Some states also exempt from taxation bonds issued by a territory of the United States.

This tax-advantaged status of municipal bonds allows municipalities to raise money at a lower cost than can corporations: municipalities are able to offer tax-exempt bonds at lower interest rates than offered by similar taxable bonds. Because municipal rates are generally lower than corporate rates, municipal securities are more attractive to investors in high tax brackets than to those in lower brackets (avoiding a 39% tax liability on interest is more important than avoiding a 15% tax liability). Investors should always carefully calculate a bond's overall yield, including tax savings, before choosing it for their portfolios.

As an example, assume that two investors, one in a 15% tax bracket and one in a 30% tax bracket, are considering purchasing $10,000 worth of a new municipal issue with a coupon of 7%. Corporate bonds with similar maturities and ratings are currently being issued at 8.5%. What would the **tax-equivalent yield** of this municipal issue be for each investor?

The investor in the 15% tax bracket would receive a tax-equivalent yield of 8.2%. To calculate this, divide 7% by 100% minus his tax rate of 15%, or 7% divided by 85%, which equals 8.2%. The municipal bond would not be a good choice for this investor because he could get a higher rate of return by investing in corporates.

The investor in the 30% tax bracket would receive a tax-equivalent yield of 10% (7% divided by 100% minus his 30% tax rate, or 7% divided by 70%, which equals 10%) and, therefore, would receive a higher after-tax yield from the municipal.

Municipal bonds, like most other bonds, pay interest semiannually on a schedule set at issuance.

Issuers

The three primary entities legally entitled to issue municipal debt securities are territorial possessions of the United States (Puerto Rico, the Virgin Islands and Guam), state governments and legally constituted taxing authorities (county and city governments and the agencies they create). Public authorities that supervise ports and mass transit systems (such as the Milwaukee Port Authority and the Ohio Turnpike Authority) are also permitted to issue municipal debt securities.

Types of Issues

There are only two major categories of municipal security issues: **general obligation bonds** (GOs—bonds backed by the full faith, credit and taxing powers of the municipal borrower) and **revenue bonds** (bonds backed by revenues generated by the financed facility).

General Obligation Bonds

GO bondholders have a legal claim to the revenues received by a municipal government for payment of the principal and interest due them. GOs are used to raise funds for those municipal capital improvements that typically do not produce revenues (building a new city hall, for example). The financial support for city and county bonds is ad valorem taxes (which means *according to the value of* the property). Sales and income taxes are the support for state bonds. GOs are also known as *full faith and credit bonds*.

Sources of Funds

GOs are backed by taxes. State-issued debt securities are backed by income taxes, license fees and sales taxes. Cities, towns and counties issue debt securities backed by property taxes, license fees, fines and all other sources of revenue to the municipality. School, road and park districts may also issue municipal bonds that are backed by property taxes.

Revenue Bonds

Revenue bonds are a common type of municipal issue and can be used to finance any municipal function that generates income. The typical sources of revenue that finance the principal and interest payments to revenue bondholders include user charges for public utility facilities (such as a municipal water or sewer authority); tolls, concessions and fees from the operation of turnpikes, bridges, airports and other facilities; and rental payments under lease-rental arrangements between the issuing authority and a state or political subdivision.

Revenue bonds are payable only from the earnings of specific revenue-producing enterprises. An analysis of the quality of revenue bonds would include sources of revenue, feasibility studies, maturity structure, call provisions, application of revenues and protective covenants of the indenture. Also taken into account are the construction period costs (including capitalized interest). Unlike GOs, revenue bonds are subject to no statutory debt limits and require no voter approval. Revenue bonds may be issued by any municipally authorized political entity.

Sources of Revenue

In contrast to the interest and principal payments of GOs, the interest and principal payments of revenue bonds are payable to bondholders only from the specific earnings and net lease payments of revenue-producing facilities such as:

- utilities (water, sewer, electric)
- housing
- transportation (airports, toll roads)
- education (college dorms, student loans)
- health (hospitals, retirement centers)
- industrial (industrial development, pollution control)

They are not payable from general or real estate taxes and are not backed by the full faith and credit of the issuer.

Municipal Bond Insurance

Issuers of municipal bonds can insure the principal and interest payments on their securities by purchasing insurance from the investor-owned Municipal Bond Investors Assurance Corp. (MBIA) or AMBAC Indemnity Corporation (AMBAC). Insured bonds can be issued with lower coupon rates because investors are willing to pay a premium for the added safety insurance affords. Lower coupon rates for new issues equate to lower costs to the issuer. Standard & Poor's has agreed to rate all AMBAC- and MBIA-insured bonds AAA. Moody's does not take into consideration purchased insurance when it rates municipal bonds.

◆ Review Questions

1. Government bonds and notes are quoted
   A. in 1/8ths
   B. as a percentage of par
   C. on a yield to maturity
   D. as a percentage of par on a discounted annualized basis

2. The maximum maturity on a T note is
   A. 1 year
   B. 3 years
   C. 5 years
   D. 10 years

3. Which of the following statements are true regarding T bills?
   I. T bills trade at a discount to par.
   II. T bills have maturities of one year or less.
   III. Most T bill issues are callable.
   IV. A T bill is a direct obligation of the U.S. government.

   A. I and II
   B. I, II and III
   C. I, II and IV
   D. II and IV

4. Which of the following U.S. government securities state a rate of interest on their face?
   I. Treasury bonds
   II. Treasury notes
   III. Treasury bills

   A. I and II only
   B. I and III only
   C. II and III only
   D. I, II and III

5. All of the following are characteristics of Series EE and Series HH bonds EXCEPT
   I. EE bonds do not generate interest income; HH bonds have a fixed coupon
   II. HH bonds can be borrowed against
   III. EE bonds are registered; HH bonds are bearer bonds
   IV. EE bonds are sold at a discount; HH bonds are sold at par

   A. I and II
   B. I and IV
   C. II
   D. II and III

6. Which of the following is an original issue discount obligation?
   A. GNMA certificate
   B. T bill
   C. Corporate bond
   D. FNMA bond

7. If you invest $10,000 in T bills over a period of years, which of the following statements are true?
   I. The principal is stable.
   II. The interest is volatile.
   III The interest is stable.
   IV. The principal is volatile.

   A. I and II
   B. I and III
   C. II and IV
   D. III and IV

8. The function of the Federal National Mortgage Association is to
   A. purchase FHA-insured, VA-guaranteed and conventional mortgages
   B. issue conventional mortgages
   C. provide financing for government-assisted housing
   D. guarantee the timely payment of interest and principal on FHA and VA mortgages

9. GNMA pass-through certificates pay interest
   A. monthly
   B. quarterly
   C. semiannually
   D. annually

10. Which of the following are types of municipal bonds?
    I. Federal National Mortgage Association
    II. General obligation
    III. Revenue
    IV. Reciprocal immunity

    A. I and II
    B. I, III and IV
    C. II and III
    D. III and IV

◆ Answers & Rationale

1. **B.** U.S. government notes and bonds are issued, quoted and traded at a percentage of par.

2. **D.** Treasury notes are intermediate-term bonds maturing in one to a maximum of ten years.

3. **C.** Treasury bills are issued at a discount from par in a competitive bidding auction. They are short-term issues with maturities of one year or less and they are a direct obligation of the U.S. government. Because of their short maturity, they are not callable.

4. **A.** Treasury bonds and notes are issued and quoted at a percentage of par; they pay a stated rate of interest each year until maturity. Treasury bills are sold at a discount from par and pay no interest; they mature at par.

5. **D.** Series HH bonds cannot be borrowed against. Both EE and HH bonds are issued in registered form. EE bonds do generate taxable interest income. Although HH bonds are issued at par, they can only be purchased by exchanging Series EE bonds at maturity.

6. **B.** Treasury bills are issued at a discount from par. The other three choices are issued at or near par.

7. **A.** Because Treasury bills are short-term instruments, they are vulnerable to upward and downward changes in short-term interest rates. As they are direct obligations of the U.S. government, however, the principal is not at risk.

8. **A.** FNMA is a publicly held corporation that provides mortgage capital. FNMA purchases conventional and insured mortgages from agencies such as the Federal Housing Authority (FHA) and Veterans Administration (VA). The securities FNMA issues are backed by its general credit.

9. **A.** GNMA certificates represent proportionate interests in the underlying mortgages. Each month, principal and interest payments from the underlying pool of mortgages are passed through to investors.

10. **C.** Municipal bonds are issued as either general obligation or revenue bonds. FNMA is a government agency. The doctrine of reciprocal immunity concerns the taxation of U.S. government and municipal issues.

5 Money-Market Securities and Interest Rates

Key Terms

banker's acceptance (BA)
broker loan (call) rate
capital market
certificate of deposit (CD)
commercial paper

federal funds rate
money market
prime rate
repurchase agreement (repo)

Overview

In the financial marketplace, a distinction is made between the *capital market* and the *money market*. The capital market serves as a source of intermediate to long-term funding for corporations and municipal and federal governments. This funding usually takes the form of debt and equity securities with maturities of more than one year.

The money market, on the other hand, exists to provide very short-term funds to corporations, municipalities and the U.S. government. The money-market securities that generate these funds are primarily short-term debt issues and loans.

The Money Market

The economy cannot survive on long-term capital alone. Although an advantage of long-term capital is that it can be raised in large amounts at competitive rates, raising that capital is often a long, complex process. A company in need of cash today to meet a payroll may not be able to wait the weeks, months or even years it could take to raise that cash through a traditional stock or bond offering.

The U.S. economy requires a constant availability of short-term funds, both cash and credit. Banks must be able to meet demands for currency immediately, even if those demands are unusually large. Businesses must be able to finance current operations as bills come due. Municipalities must pay salaries, services and contractors while waiting for revenues or bond issues to generate money. Money-market instruments provide ways for businesses, financial institutions and governments to meet their short-term obligations and cash requirements yet avoid the time and expense of SEC registration of securities (required for maturities of 270 days and greater).

Moving money. The business of the money market is to shift funds from institutions with temporary excesses of money to institutions with temporary deficiencies. Among the borrowers in the money market are the U.S. Treasury, large commercial banks, corporations, dealers in money-market instruments and many states and municipalities. Large institutions such as banks, trust companies and insurance companies are often the lenders, the buyers of money-market instruments.

Liquidity and safety. Most of the debt and fixed income securities discussed so far offer a wide range of maturities, from a few months to more than 30 years. Money-market instruments, by contrast, are fixed income securities with short-term maturities—typically one year or less. Because they are short-term instruments, money-market securities offer investors a highly liquid investment. Money-market instruments also provide investors with a relatively high degree of safety; most issuers of money-market securities have high credit ratings.

Issuers. Money-market securities are issued by a number of different entities. Money-market instruments issued by the U.S. government and its agencies include:

- Treasury bills that have begun trading in the secondary market (as new issues they are not considered money-market instruments);
- tax anticipation notes (TANs);
- Federal Farm Credit Bank short-term notes and bonds maturing in one year;
- Federal Home Loan Bank (FHLB) short-term discount notes and interest-bearing notes;
- Federal National Mortgage Association (FNMA) short-term discount notes; and
- short-term discount notes issued by various smaller agencies.

Municipalities issue tax-exempt money-market instruments that include:

- bond anticipation notes (BANs)
- tax anticipation notes (TANs)
- revenue anticipation notes (RANs)

- construction loan notes (CLNs)
- tax and revenue anticipation notes (TRANs)

Corporations and banks have a number of methods for raising short-term funds in the money market, including:

- repurchase agreements (repos)
- reverse repurchase agreements
- bankers' acceptances (time drafts)
- commercial paper (prime paper)
- negotiable certificates of deposit
- federal funds
- brokers' and dealers' loans

Money-market Instruments

Repurchase Agreements

Although broker-dealers typically hold large amounts of capital on hand, the security positions they take are often many times the value of that capital. Because of this imbalance, dealers need a source of ready cash with which to finance their securities transactions.

One method a dealer can use to raise cash is to find a temporary buyer for some of the securities it holds and then to sign a contract with that party in which the dealer agrees to buy the securities back at a later date. A transaction of this sort is called a **repurchase agreement** (**repo**). A repo is simply that—an agreement between a buyer and a seller to conduct a transaction (the purchase) and then to reverse that transaction (the repurchase) at some point in the future. U.S. government and municipal securities dealers are big users of repos.

A repo will include a repurchase price and maturity date in the contract. If the agreement sets a specific date, the repo is considered a fixed agreement. If the maturity date is left to the discretion of the initial buyer, the repo is known as an *open repo* and becomes a demand obligation callable at any time.

Though technically a sale of securities, a repo is very similar to a fully collateralized loan. Instead of borrowing money and putting up securities as collateral for the loan, the dealer sells the securities and agrees to buy them back later at a higher price. The interest on the loan takes the form of the difference between the sale price and the repurchase price. The effective rate at which the loan is made is negotiated between the two parties involved and generally is lower than the rate on a loan with similar terms from a bank. In the event the dealer defaults on the agreement to buy back the securities, the lender (the investor making the initial purchase) can sell the securities in the open market.

Repos serve both as a way to raise short-term capital and as instruments of Federal Reserve monetary policy. Among the primary users of repos are:

- U.S. government and municipal securities dealers financing their inventories;
- commercial banks raising short-term funds; and

- the Federal Reserve effecting short-term changes in member bank reserves (fine tuning the monetary supply).

Bankers' Acceptances

A **banker's acceptance** (**BA**) is a short-term time draft with a specified payment date drawn on a bank—essentially a postdated check or line of credit. Bankers' acceptances are used extensively by American corporations as a means of financing international trade (imports and exports of goods and services). The payment date on a banker's acceptance is normally between 1 and 270 days after it is written.

In a typical transaction, a banker's acceptance can be used by a corporation to pay for goods and services in a foreign country. As an example, assume a U.S. company enters into an agreement with a firm in another country to purchase bolts of cloth. The U.S. company asks its bank to send a time draft to the foreign company as payment for the goods, but to postdate the draft six months in the future. The U.S. company wants the draft postdated so that it will have sufficient time to sell the cloth in the United States and raise the cash to cover the purchase. The foreign company accepting the time draft as payment for the cloth presents the draft to its local bank, and this bank gives the company somewhat less than the face value in cash. The foreign firm now has immediate cash, and the U.S. company has the goods it needs.

The foreign bank then sends the draft to the U.S. bank on which the draft is drawn for payment. The U.S. bank agrees to *accept* (guarantee) the draft and puts its own credit behind this guarantee of payment. When a time draft is accepted in this manner by a bank, it becomes a banker's acceptance, a security tradeable in the money market. If the acceptance is drawn on certain major banks that meet specific financial qualifications, it is known as a *prime acceptance* and becomes eligible for trading and purchase by the Fed and the Federal Open Market Committee (FOMC).

Once a time draft is returned and accepted by the bank, the bank sells the new banker's acceptance in the money market at a discount from face value (thereby raising the cash to cover the payment to the foreign bank). When the acceptance eventually matures, the U.S. firm makes good on the amount it borrowed and the current holder redeems the banker's acceptance for its face value at the accepting bank.

Bankers' acceptances are considered one of the few secured money-market instruments because the holder has a lien against the trade goods in the event the accepting bank fails. Bankers' acceptances frequently are used by banks as collateral against Federal Reserve Bank (FRB) loans.

Commercial Paper

Corporations issue short-term, unsecured **commercial paper** (promissory notes) as a means of raising the cash to finance both accounts receivable and seasonal or unusually large inventories. Many corporations view commercial paper as a less expensive alternative to borrowing from banks when they need short-term funds. Rates in the commercial paper market are usually lower than comparable bank loan rates, and securities with maturities of less than 270 days are exempt from registration under the 1933 act and are therefore less expensive to issue. Both the maturities and the rates of commercial paper are negotiable.

Commercial paper issues have fixed maturities that range from 1 to 270 days, although most are issued to mature in less than 90 days. Commercial paper normally is issued in bearer form and at a discount from face value. Dealers in commercial paper generally consider $250,000 in face value as a minimum round lot, but issues of $1 million and more are not uncommon.

Commercial paper is issued primarily by large, well-known companies with excellent credit ratings and is considered a very safe investment. Most corporations sell their paper directly to investors, although some use a dealer as an intermediary. The primary purchasers of commercial paper in the money market are money-market funds, commercial banks, pension funds, insurance companies, corporations and nongovernmental agencies.

Certificates of Deposit

Certificates with fixed interest rates and minimum face values of $100,000 (although minimums of $1 million and up are more common) are issued and guaranteed by banks and can be traded in the secondary market. The FDIC offers insurance on jumbo certificates of deposit.

Review of Interest Rates

The yields of money-market instruments and interest rates are as follows:

- **Prime rate**. The base rate on corporate loans at large U.S. money center commercial banks. The prime rate is relatively stable and moves only when the major money center banks react to changes in the money supply.
- **Federal funds rate**. The interest rate charged on reserves traded among member banks for overnight use in amounts of $1 million or more. The federal funds rate is the most volatile of the interest rates, changing daily in response to the needs of the borrowing banks, and represents a daily average of the rates charged by the lending banks.
- **Commercial paper**. The rate on commercial paper placed directly by GMAC or the rate on high-grade unsecured notes sold through dealers by major corporations.
- **Certificates of deposit**. Average top rates paid by major New York banks on new issues of negotiable CDs, usually on amounts of $1 million or more. The minimum unit is $100,000.
- **Treasury bills**. Results of the auction of short-term U.S. government bills sold at a discount from face value in units of $10,000 to $1 million.

◆ Review Questions

1. All of the following are money-market instruments EXCEPT

    A. Treasury bills
    B. municipal notes
    C. commercial paper
    D. newly issued Treasury bonds

2. Which of the following describes money-market instruments?

    A. Short-term debt
    B. Long-term debt
    C. Short-term equity
    D. Long-term equity

3. The maximum maturity of commercial paper is how many days?

    A. 90
    B. 180
    C. 270
    D. 360

4. Which of the following characteristics describes commercial paper?

    A. Secured note issued by a corporation
    B. Guaranteed note issued by a corporation
    C. Promissory note issued by a corporation
    D. Promissory note issued by a broker

5. Which of the following money-market instruments finances imports and exports?

    A. Eurodollars
    B. Bankers' acceptances
    C. ADRs
    D. Commercial paper

6. A banker's acceptance is a

    A. promissory note
    B. capital-market instrument
    C. time draft
    D. means of facilitating the trading of foreign securities

7. A U.S. government bond dealer sells bonds to another dealer with an agreement to buy back the securities in a specified period of time. This is a(n)

    A. repurchase agreement
    B. reverse repurchase agreement
    C. open market certificate
    D. open market note

◆ Answers & Rationale

1. **D.** Money-market instruments provide ways for businesses, financial institutions and governments to meet short-term financial requirements. By their nature they need to have short-term maturities. Because Treasury bonds don't mature for at least 10 years, they are not considered money-market instruments.

2. **A.** By definition, a money-market instrument is a debt security with a fixed interest rate and a short-term maturity, usually one year or less.

3. **C.** Commercial paper issues have fixed maturities that range from 1 to 270 days, although most are issued to mature in less than 90 days.

4. **C.** Commercial paper is an unsecured, short-term promissory note issued by corporations for short-term financial needs.

5. **B.** Bankers' acceptances are used extensively by U.S. corporations as a means of financing international trade (exports and imports).

6. **C.** A banker's acceptance is a short-term time draft with a specified payment date, drawn on a bank.

7. **A.** When a dealer lends securities to another dealer with an agreement to buy back the securities at a later date, this is a repurchase agreement.

6 Issuing Securities

Key Terms

all or none (AON)
best effort
cooling-off period
firm commitment
Glass-Steagall Act of 1933
indication of interest
investment banker
Maloney Act
mini-max offering

new issue market
preliminary prospectus
primary offering
red herring
registration statement
secondary offering
Securities Act of 1933
Securities Exchange Act of 1934

Overview   In general, securities come to market in one of two ways: as new issues (primary distributions) from a corporation, municipality or federal government or in secondary trades between investors. This chapter introduces you to the market for newly issued securities, beginning with a review of the stock market crash of 1929, the calamity that precipitated the legislation now governing securities trading. From there, the chapter discusses the process of registering a new securities offering and the role an investment banker plays in various types of offerings. And, because offerings may be brought to market by more than one firm, you will read about the formation and functioning of an underwriting syndicate.

The Regulation of New Issues

The Crash of 1929

During the early 1900s, America enjoyed a long-term bull market that promised to last forever. Attracted by the dream of easy money, Americans turned en masse to Wall Street, poring over stock price tables and learning the language of trading operations. For the first time, the general public became a significant factor in the market; but often they purchased securities knowing little or nothing about the issuing company or its plans for spending their money.

Investors borrowed heavily (that is, they bought securities *on margin*). Doing so was an act of faith in the perpetual bull market and an outcome of generous credit policies that allowed investors to borrow most of the purchase price of stock. By the summer of 1929, over a million Americans held stock on margin.

The rest is familiar history. Stock prices reached new heights in early September 1929. Then things fell apart. By the third week of September, tumbling prices brought the Dow Jones averages down 19 points. A month later, averages were 50 points below the September high mark. The downward spiral of prices gained momentum, breaking through crumbling layers of anticipated buying support.

Rapidly declining prices meant investors' stocks were no longer adequate security for the loans they had taken out to buy them. Securities purchased on very low margins, therefore, were sold to raise money, and this caused even deeper drops in market prices. Stock dumping destroyed grassroots investors and wealthy traders alike, including those supposedly safe investment trusts, which unloaded their holdings for whatever they could bring.

The Legislative Reaction

After the crash, the market continued to decline for several years. During that time, Congress examined the causes of the debacle and passed several laws meant to prevent its recurrence. This legislation included, among other acts, the Securities Act of 1933, the Glass-Steagall Act of 1933, and the Securities Exchange Act of 1934.

The Securities Act of 1933. The Securities Act of 1933 requires issuers of securities to provide sufficient information for investors to make fully informed buying decisions. This information must be registered with the federal government and published in a prospectus. The act outlaws fraud committed in connection with the underwriting and issuing of all securities (including exempt securities).

The Glass-Steagall Act (Banking Act) of 1933. Securities firms were not the only financial companies to go belly-up in the early 1930s. Banks, too, went broke in vast numbers. Congress concluded that one factor in the general financial collapse was the fact that commercial bankers engaged in investment banking. In their role as commercial bankers, they took deposits and financed commercial enterprises. As investment bankers, they underwrote stocks, using deposits to finance their securities ventures. Losses on the investment side of the bank, therefore, affected the health of the commercial operations.

With the Glass-Steagall Act (Banking Act) of 1933, Congress attempted to erect a wall between commercial banking and investment banking. The act forbids commercial banks to underwrite securities (except municipal general obligation bonds) and denies investment bankers the right to open deposit accounts or make commercial loans.

The Securities Exchange Act of 1934. The Securities Exchange Act of 1934 addresses secondary trading of securities, personnel involved in secondary trading and fraudulent trading practices. It also created the Securities and Exchange Commission (SEC, a government agency) to oversee the industry.

In 1938, the act was broadened when it was amended by the **Maloney Act**, which provides for the establishment of a self-regulatory body to help police the industry. Under the provisions of the Maloney Act, the National Association of Securities Dealers (NASD) regulates over-the-counter (OTC) trading in much the same way as the exchanges regulate their members.

The Trust Indenture Act of 1939. The Trust Indenture Act of 1939 was created, in part, to provide the same sort of protection to the purchasers of debt securities as is afforded to investors in equities. The term "debt securities" includes all notes, bonds, debentures and other similar evidences of indebtedness. The term "trust indenture" covers any mortgage, trust or other indenture, or any similar instrument or agreement.

As its major focus and means of protecting the public interest, the act prohibits the sale of any corporate debt security unless it has been issued under a **trust indenture**. In addition to full disclosure about the nature of the debt issue and the issuer, the trust indenture identifies the rights and powers of the trustee, as well as the trustee's responsibilities.

The trust indenture is the contract that gives the appointed trustee the powers necessary to enforce the issuer's obligations and the debt holders' rights. Among the trustee's responsibilities is the representation of the future investors in the preparation of the indenture.

Registration of Securities

The Legislation

The Securities Act of 1933 regulates new issues of corporate securities sold to the public. The act is also referred to as the *Full Disclosure Act*, the *New Issues Act*, the *Truth in Securities Act* and the *Prospectus Act*. The main purpose of the act is to ensure that the investing public is fully informed about a security and its issuing company when the security is first sold (in the **primary market**). The act requires the registration of new issues (both debt and equity) of nonexempt securities with the SEC if the mails or any other means of interstate commerce are used to offer or sell the security to the public. It also requires that a prospectus (which contains information derived from the registration statement) be given to buyers.

The 1933 act protects the investor who is considering purchase of new issues by:

- requiring registration of new issues that are to be distributed interstate;
- requiring the issuer to provide full and fair disclosure about itself and the offering;
- requiring the issuer to make available all material information necessary for the investor to judge the merit of the issue;
- regulating the underwriting and distribution of primary and secondary issues; and
- providing criminal penalties for fraud in the issuance of new securities.

When a corporation wants to issue its securities to the public, the SEC requires it to:

- supply detailed information about itself and its securities to the SEC; and
- supply the relevant portion of that information to the general investing public.

A **registration statement** disclosing material information must be filed with the SEC by the issuer. Part of the registration statement is a prospectus, which must be provided to all purchasers of the new issue. A prospectus contains much of the same information included in the registration statement, but without the supporting documentation. The registration statement must contain:

- a description of the issuer's business;
- the names and addresses of key people in the company, officers and directors, their salaries and a five-year business history of each;
- the amount of corporate securities owned by these key people and by owners of 10% or more of the company;
- the company's capitalization, including its equity and the amount of funded debt;
- a description of how the proceeds will be used; and
- whether the company is involved in any legal proceedings.

The Prospectus

The preliminary prospectus. After an issuer files a registration statement with the SEC, a **cooling-off** period begins. During the cooling-off period (a 20-day period during which the SEC reviews a security's registration statement), a registered rep may discuss the new issue with clients and provide them with a **preliminary prospectus** (also known as a **red herring**). A registered rep *may not* send any other material to potential customers with the preliminary prospectus, including research reports, *Value Line* sheets, marketing letters and so on.

A red herring need not include the final price of the securities, commissions, dealer discounts or net proceeds to the company (although pricing formulas and other information are often included). The document must carry a legend to the effect that a registration statement has been filed with the SEC, but is not yet effective. By law, this disclaimer message must be printed in red ink.

SEC rules prohibit the sale of public offering securities other than by prospectus, which means that no sales are allowed unless and until the buyer is furnished with a final prospectus.

However, the SEC does allow the use of preliminary prospectuses (essentially all the same information found in a final prospectus, but with only an offering price range or no price at all) as prospecting tools. The underwriters and selling group members thus have a document to use as they test for investor receptivity and gather **indications of interest**.

An indication of interest is just that—a broker-dealer's or investor's declaration that it might be interested in purchasing some of the security from the underwriter after the security comes out of registration. An indication of interest on the part of the broker-dealer or investor is *not* a commitment to buy because sales are prohibited until after the security clears registration.

The final prospectus. When the registration statement does become effective, the issuer amends the preliminary prospectus and adds information, including the final offering price and the underwriting spread. This revised report becomes the final prospectus. Registered representatives may then take orders from those customers who indicated an interest in buying during the cooling-off period.

A copy of the final prospectus must precede or accompany all sales confirmations. The prospectus should include all of the following information:

- description of the offering
- price of the offering
- selling discounts
- date of the offering
- use of the proceeds
- description of the underwriting, but not the actual contract
- statement of the possibility that the issue's price may be stabilized
- history of the business
- risks to the purchasers
- description of management
- material financial information
- legal opinion concerning the formation of the corporation
- SEC disclaimer

SEC review. The SEC reviews the prospectus to ensure that it contains whatever material facts the SEC deems necessary, but it does not guarantee the accuracy of the disclosures. Further, the SEC does not approve the issue, but simply clears it for distribution. Implying that the SEC has approved the issue is a violation of federal law. Finally, the SEC does not pass judgment on the investment merit of the issue. The front of every prospectus must contain a clearly printed SEC disclaimer clause specifying the limits of the SEC's review procedures. A typical SEC disclaimer clause reads as follows:

> These securities have not been approved or disapproved by the Securities and Exchange Commission nor has the Commission passed upon the accuracy or adequacy of this prospectus. Any representation to the contrary is a criminal offense.

The information supplied to the SEC becomes public information (accessible to anyone) once a registration statement is filed. (This is one of the reasons why issuers look for ways to sell securities to the public without having to file registration statements.)

Civil Liabilities under the Act of 1933

Untruths in Registration Statements

If a registration statement contains untrue statements of material fact or omits material facts, any person acquiring the security may sue any or all of the following:

- those who signed the registration statement;
- directors and partners of the issuer;
- anyone named in the registration statement as being or about to become a director or partner of the company;
- accountants, appraisers and other professionals who contributed to the registration statement; and
- the underwriters.

A civil lawsuit to recover damages incurred owing to untrue statements or omissions of material facts in a registration statement must be filed within three years after the sale of the security.

Untruths in Prospectuses and Communications

The seller of any security being sold by prospectus (which includes oral communications based on information contained in a security's prospectus) will be liable to the purchaser if the prospectus contains misstatements or omissions of material facts. To avoid civil liability, the seller must prove that he did not know of the misstatements or omissions and that reasonable care was exercised at the time of the sale to prevent communicating any untrue or misleading information of a material nature.

Unlawful Representations

It is unlawful for a seller to tell a purchaser of a security that the information contained in the registration statement (and, therefore, in the prospectus) must be 100% true and complete as evidenced by the fact that the SEC has not issued a stop order.

The Underwriting Process

Underwriting Corporate Securities

The first successful securities underwriting in the United States is attributed to Jay Cooke. During the Civil War, he and his force of bond salesmen placed over $2 billion in U.S. government bonds with private investors throughout the North. By fostering these financial ties between government and investors, Cooke's sales force reinforced the loyalty and patriotism of many investors.

After the war ended, securities underwriting continued to be critical to the economic development of the United States. Today, publicly owned and financed corporations dominate U.S. business. Each year, the underwriting activities of investment bankers provide billions of dollars in new equity and debt financing.

Investment Banking

A business or branch of government that plans to issue securities usually works with an **investment banker**, a securities broker-dealer that may also specialize in underwriting new issues by helping to bring securities to market and sell them to investors.

An investment banker's functions may include:

- advising corporations on the best ways to raise long-term capital
- raising capital for issuers by distributing new securities
- buying securities from an issuer and reselling them to the public
- distributing large blocks of stock to the public and to institutions

Participants in a Corporate New Issue

Securities and Exchange Commission. When a corporation issues new securities, the SEC is responsible for the following:

- reviewing the registration statement filed for the offering (accomplished during the cooling-off period between the filing date and the effective date);
- sending a deficiency letter to the issuer if the review uncovers problems, thus halting the review until deficiencies are corrected, at which point the cooling-off period continues; and
- declaring the registration statement effective—that is, releasing the securities for sale.

The issuer. The issuer is the party selling the securities to raise money. The issuer's duties include:

- filing the registration statement with the SEC;
- filing a registration statement with the states in which it intends to sell securities (also known as *blue-skying the issue);* and

- negotiating the price of the securities and the amount of the spread with the underwriter.

National Association of Securities Dealers. The NASD Committee on Corporate Financing reviews the underwriting spread to determine fairness and reasonableness of underwriting compensation.

The individual states. State security laws, also called **blue-sky laws**, require state registration of new issues, broker-dealers and registered reps. As mentioned above, registering securities with the state is called **blue-skying the issue**. The issuer or investment banker may blue-sky an issue by one of the following three methods:

- **Qualification.** The issue is registered with the state independent of federal registration, meeting all state requirements.
- **Coordination.** The issuer registers simultaneously with the state and the SEC. Both registrations become effective on the same date.
- **Notification.** Certain states allow some new issues to blue-sky by having the issuers notify the state of registration with the SEC. In this case, no registration statement is required by the state, although certain other information must be filed.

The underwriter. The underwriter not only assists with registration, but also may advise the corporate issuer on the best way to raise capital. The underwriter will consider at least the following matters:

- **Whether to offer stock or bonds.** If stocks are currently selling at depressed prices, bonds may seem the more attractive alternative. If bonds are currently selling at high interest rates, the company may choose to issue stock.
- **Tax consequences of the offering.** The interest a corporation must pay on its bonds is tax deductible. The stock dividends it pays investors are paid out of aftertax profits.
- **Whether to go to the money market for short-term funds or to the capital market for long-term funds.** If the corporation decides to go to the capital market, it will issue one of the following types of securities: secured bonds, debentures, preferred stock or common stock.

Under the provisions of the Securities Act of 1933, offering such securities normally requires registration with the SEC unless a specific exemption applies.

Types of Offerings

Securities Markets

The **new issue market** consists of companies "going public"—privately owned businesses raising capital by selling common stock to the public for the very first time. New issue securities are also known as **initial public offering (IPO)** securities.

The **additional issue market** is made up of new securities issues from companies that are already publicly owned (that is, they already have stock outstanding with the public). These companies are now increasing their equity capitalization by issuing more stock. This is accomplished when an underwriter either distributes the stock in a public offering or arranges for the shares to be sold in a private placement.

Table 6.1 Offerings and Markets

	New Issue (IPO) Market	Additional Issue Market
Primary Offering	Company is going public; underwriting proceeds go to the company.	Company is already public; underwriting proceeds go to the company.
Secondary Offering	Company is going public; underwriting proceeds go to the selling stockholders.	Company is public; underwriting proceeds go to the selling stockholders.

In addition to being classified by whether they represent initial or additional issues of new securities, offerings can be classified by the final distribution of their proceeds.

Primary Offering

A primary offering is one in which the proceeds of the underwriting go to the **issuing corporation**. The corporation increases its capitalization by selling stock (either a new issue or previously authorized but unissued stock). It may do this at any time and in any amount, provided the total stock outstanding never exceeds the amount authorized in the corporation's bylaws.

Secondary Offering

A secondary offering is one in which one or more major stockholders in the corporation are selling all or a major portion of their holdings. The underwriting proceeds are paid to the stockholders rather than to the corporation itself. Typically, secondary offerings occur in situations where the founder of a business, and perhaps some of the original financial backers, determine that there is more to be gained by going public than by staying private.

Table 6.1 shows a comparison of primary and secondary offerings.

Types of Underwritings

Firm Commitment

The **firm commitment** is the most widely used type of underwriting contract. Under its terms, the underwriter contracts with the issuing corporation (or selling stockholders, or both) to buy the securities described in the contract, within a defined price and quantity range, on or about a given date—all of which is spelled out in a **letter of intent** prepared for signatures of both the underwriter and the issuer (or the selling stockholders, or both) during the early stages of negotiation.

The underwriter is committing to buying securities from the issuer and paying the underwriting proceeds to the company (or individual sellers). The underwriter does this without full assurance that the securities can be resold to the public. If part of an issue that is being distributed under a firm commitment contract goes unsold, any losses incurred are prorated among the underwriting firms according to their participation.

Best Efforts

The **best efforts** arrangement calls for the underwriter to buy securities as agent from the issuing corporation (or from the selling stockholders), contingent on the underwriter's ability to either sell them in a public offering or place them with select investors in a private placement.

For example, if the corporation's plan is to issue 100,000 shares of common stock at $20 per share, but—after exerting *best efforts*—the underwriter is able to distribute only 80,000 shares, the extent of the underwriter's commitment is limited to 80,000 shares (for proceeds of $1.6 million), and not the full 100,000 shares (for $2 million).

All or None

An **all or none (AON)** underwriting puts more control over the outcome of the offering in the hands of the issuing corporation (or the selling stockholders). The issuer, in effect, is saying to the underwriter, "Distribute all one million shares at $20, and send us the full $20 million proceeds; if that is not possible, cancel the underwriting entirely." Because of the uncertainty over the actual issuance of securities in an AON offering, SEC rules demand that any purchase amounts collected from investors during the offering period be held **in escrow**, pending final disposition of the underwriting.

Mini-max

A **mini-max** offering is a best efforts underwriting with a floor and a ceiling on the amount of securities the issuer is willing to sell. The underwriter must locate enough interested buyers to support the minimum (floor) issuance requirement. Then, with the minimum requirement covered, the underwriter will be free to expand the offering up to the maximum (ceiling) amount of shares specified by the issuer. Mini-max underwriting terms are most frequently found in limited partnership program offerings.

Standby Underwritings

Standby underwritings come into play when a publicly held corporation proposes to issue additional common stock. In such cases, the corporation may be obliged to protect the *proportional ownership interest* of the current stockholders (subject to the securities laws of the issuer's state of incorporation and the corporation's articles of incorporation). If this is the case, the company must first offer any additional issue of the same class of stock to the existing stock owners before offering the securities to the general public. This is done through a **subscription rights offering**. Typically, any number of a company's current stockholders will not exercise their *preemptive rights* (right of first refusal); for whatever reason, they have no desire to buy more stock in the company. Thus, the issuing corporation needs an underwriter standing by to step in and buy up the unused rights.

◆ Review Questions

1. Which of the following are types of underwritings?

    I. Firm commitment
    II. All or none
    III. Standby
    IV. Best efforts

    A. I and II only
    B. I, III and IV only
    C. II and III only
    D. I, II, III and IV

2. In a best efforts offering, an underwriter

    A. makes no guarantee that an offering will be sold
    B. makes a best efforts attempt to reduce the underwriting spread
    C. guarantees a minimum price and makes a best efforts attempt to increase that price
    D. makes a best efforts attempt to bring the security to market within the cooling-off period

3. A standby underwriting is used

    A. by a company going public for the first time
    B. in a secondary offering
    C. in a best efforts underwriting
    D. in a rights offering

4. The principal functions of an investment banker are to

    I. distribute securities to the public
    II. provide a secondary market
    III. provide financing for an individual
    IV. advise the issuer about alternatives in raising capital

    A. I and II
    B. I and IV
    C. II and III
    D. III and IV

5. All of the following acts are prohibited during the cooling-off period EXCEPT

    A. promising a certain amount of the issue to a customer
    B. soliciting indications of interest
    C. taking an order
    D. accepting a check from a customer to purchase the issue

6. The red herring typically includes all of the following information EXCEPT

    A. a list of company officers
    B. the price of the issue
    C. a list of principal underwriters
    D. the number of shares

7. The Securities Act of 1933 does all the following EXCEPT

    A. require SEC registration of most new issues of securities
    B. require publication of material information about the issue
    C. provide for the establishment of self-regulatory organizations
    D. exempt certain types of securities from registration

8. Which of the following best describes the underwriting manager?

    A. Employee who supervises the underwriting activities of an investment banker
    B. Broker-dealer that supervises the activity of the issuer on authority of the SEC
    C. Broker-dealer that publishes the offering prospectus
    D. Broker-dealer that supervises the activity of the underwriting syndicate and selling group

◆ Answers & Rationale

1. **D.** All four choices are types of underwriting. They differ as to the level of commitment by the broker-dealer to sell all or part of the issue. In a firm commitment underwriting, the broker-dealer purchases all the securities and then resells them. In an all or none underwriting, the broker-dealer tries to sell the entire issue. If the entire issue is not sold, the offering is canceled.

2. **A.** In a best efforts underwriting, the firm sells as much as it can with no obligation to purchase any part of the unsold offering.

3. **D.** In a standby commitment, a firm agrees to purchase any part of an issue that has not been subscribed to through a rights offering.

4. **B.** The primary roles of a broker-dealer are to distribute securities to the public and advise issuers on the best ways to raise capital. Broker-dealers do not have to provide a secondary market for any security. Providing individual financing is the role of commercial banks and other lending institutions.

5. **B.** The only action that can be taken during the cooling-off period is to determine investor interest in the security.

6. **B.** The offering price of the issue is one of the last details to be determined. As a result, the issue's price will not be known until much closer to the time the issue actually comes to market.

7. **C.** The 1933 act was designed to protect investors considering the purchase of new issues. Beginning with the Securities Exchange Act of 1934, legislation was enacted to provide for industry self-regulatory organizations.

8. **D.** In addition to negotiating with the issuer, the underwriting manager directs the entire underwriting process from registration to directing the sales process with the other firms in the syndicate and selling group.

7 Trading Securities

Key Terms

American Stock Exchange (AMEX)
broker
Consolidated Tape
dealer
exchange market

New York Stock Exchange (NYSE)
over-the-counter (OTC) market
position trading
specialist
third market

Overview

Wall Street is a marketplace where merchants, agents and customers of the financial industry meet to buy and sell stocks, bonds and other securities. Much buying and selling of stocks and bonds takes place on exchanges where stocks are traded in a two-way auction process. The major exchanges include:

- the New York Stock Exchange (NYSE)
- the American Stock Exchange (AMEX)
- regional stock exchanges

Other trades take place in the nationwide network of broker-dealers known as the over-the-counter (OTC) market.

This chapter introduces the terminology and language of trading securities.

The Regulation of Trading

The Securities Exchange Act of 1934

After the Securities Act of 1933 was enacted regulating primary issues of securities, attention turned to the need for regulating secondary trading. The intent of the Securities Exchange Act of 1934 is to maintain a fair and orderly market for the investing public. It seeks to attain this goal by regulating the securities exchanges and the over-the-counter markets. Commonly called the **Exchange Act**, it formed the Securities Exchange Commission and gave the Commission authority to oversee the securities markets and to register and regulate the exchanges.

According to the Securities Exchange Act of 1934, several other entities must also register with the SEC, including exchange members and broker-dealers that trade securities OTC and on exchanges and individuals who effect securities trades with the public.

The Securities Exchange Act of 1934, which has much greater breadth than the act of 1933, addresses the:

- creation of the SEC
- regulation of exchanges
- regulation of credit by the Federal Reserve Board
- registration of broker-dealers
- regulation of insider transactions, short sales and proxies
- regulation of trading activities
- regulation of client accounts
- customer protection rule
- regulation of the OTC market
- net capital rule

The Securities and Exchange Commission

The SEC, created by the act of 1934, was given responsibility and authority to regulate the securities markets. The SEC is made up of five commissioners appointed by the president of the United States and approved by the Senate. One of the primary responsibilities of this group is to enforce the act of 1934.

The SEC has established rules regarding net capital requirements for broker-dealers, hypothecation of customers' securities, commingling of broker-dealer securities with those of customers, the use of manipulative and deceptive devices and broker-dealer recordkeeping. The SEC enforces the Securities Exchange Act of 1934 (and others) by providing rules and prescribing penalties for violations.

Registration of Exchanges and Firms

Under the 1934 act, the national securities exchanges must file a registration statement. When they register, the exchanges agree to comply with and help enforce the rules of this act. Each exchange gives the SEC copies of its bylaws, constitution and articles of incorporation. Any amendment to rules must be disclosed as soon as it is adopted. The exchange must also institute and enforce disciplinary procedures for members who do not use just and equitable practices.

In addition to the registration of exchanges, the act of 1934 requires companies that list securities on those exchanges to register with the SEC. Each listed company must file quarterly and annual statements (Form 10Q and 10K, respectively) informing the SEC of its financial status (as well as other information).

Many firms with securities that are traded OTC must also register. Those firms with 500 or more stockholders and assets of $1 million or more are required to do so. Exchange members who do business with the public must register as well as broker-dealers that do business OTC or that use the mail (or telephone, TV, radio, etc.) to conduct OTC business.

The Maloney Act, an amendment to the Securities Exchange Act of 1934, permitted the establishment of a national securities association of broker-dealers transacting business in the OTC market. According to the act, SROs such as the NASD could be established and registered with the SEC.

There are also some exemptions from registration, including small local exchanges and any broker-dealer that deals only on an intrastate basis. An *intra*state firm, however, cannot use the mail or other instruments of *inter*state commerce and still qualify for the exemption from registration.

Net Capital Rule

To ensure broker-dealer solvency, the act of 1934 states that broker-dealers must maintain a certain level of net capital. A firm must not let its debts exceed 15 times its net capital.

Financial Statements Sent to Customers

Every broker-dealer must furnish financial statements to customers. A customer is any person for whom the broker-dealer holds funds or securities or anyone who has made a securities transaction at any time up to one month before the date of the financial statement. Excluded from the definition of "customer" are other broker-dealers, partners or officers of the broker-dealer, and subordinated lenders. NASD rules require a broker-dealer to provide a copy of its current balance sheet to any active customer who makes a written request for one.

Regulation of Credit

The act of 1934 empowered the FRB to regulate margin accounts (that is, to regulate credit extended in the purchase of securities). Within FRB jurisdiction are:

- **Regulation T**—regulates the extension of credit by broker-dealers
- **Regulation U**—deals with the extension of credit by banks
- **Regulation G**—deals with the extension of credit by anyone else

Securities Markets and Broker-Dealers

Securities Markets

A market is the exchange (or system) in which trades of securities occur. The market in which securities are bought and sold is also known as the *secondary* market (as opposed to the *primary* market for new issues). All of the securities transactions in which people, corporations, governments and institutions engage take place in one of four trading markets.

Exchange Market

The NYSE and other exchanges on which *listed* securities are traded compose the **exchange market**. The term "listed security" refers to any security listed (quoted) for trading on an exchange.

Over-the-counter Market

The dealer market in which *unlisted* securities (securities not listed on any exchange, also known as *nonexchange securities*) are traded is called the **over-the-counter (OTC) market**.

The OTC market is a computer and telephone connected interdealer market represented by about 600 securities dealers across the country. More than 15,000 different securities are traded OTC (including all municipal and U.S. government securities), compared to the 4,500 or so securities registered for listed trading on the various exchanges.

The NASD governs and enforces rules and regulations covering all facets of OTC trading and market-making activities. To bring some order into OTC trading, the NASD's Automated Quotation System (Nasdaq) provides a computer link between broker-dealers that trade OTC. Nasdaq lists frequently traded OTC securities in much the same way as an exchange lists exchange-traded securities.

Third Market (OTC-listed)

The **third market** is a trading market for institutional investors in which *exchange-listed* securities are bought and sold (usually in large blocks) in the OTC market. These transactions are arranged and negotiated through the services of a broker-dealer registered as an OTC market maker in listed securities.

All securities listed on the NYSE and American Stock Exchange (AMEX) plus most exclusively traded securities listed on the regional exchanges are eligible for OTC trading, provided that trading information (volume and execution price) is reported for public display on the **Consolidated Tape** within 90 seconds after the execution of any transaction.

Fourth Market (INSTINET)

INSTINET is a market for institutional investors in which large blocks of stock (both listed and unlisted) change hands in privately negotiated transactions between banks, mutual funds, pension managers and other types of institutions, unassisted by a broker-dealer.

Registered with the SEC as a broker-dealer, INSTINET includes among its subscribers a large number of mutual funds and other institutional investors. All INSTINET members are linked by computer terminals. Subscribers can display bid and ask quotes, and their sizes, to others in the system.

Trading Hours

Exchange business hours. Both the NYSE and AMEX begin trading at 9:30 am EST each business day and close trading at 4:00 pm EST.

OTC business hours. Normal hours for retail OTC trading are the same as those of the NYSE: 9:30 am to 4:00 pm EST, Monday through Friday.

To accommodate institutional investors in the third market, NASD members functioning as registered market makers in listed securities may remain open for business beyond the normal 4:00 pm market close until 6:30 pm EST. However, if a registered market-maker broker-dealer stays open beyond 4:00 pm, but *not* until the 6:30 pm final close, the NASD requires orderly closing times on the hour or half hour, from 4:00 pm to 6:30 pm.

Comparison of Listed and OTC Markets

Listed Markets

Location. Listed markets (such as the NYSE or AMEX) have a central marketplace and trading floor facilities.

Pricing system. Listed markets operate as **double-auction markets**. Floor brokers compete among themselves to execute trades at prices most favorable to the public.

Price dynamics. When a floor broker representing a buyer executes a trade by taking stock at a current offer price higher than the last sale, a plus tick occurs (market up); when a selling broker accepts a current bid price below the last sale price, a minus tick occurs (market down).

Major force in the market. The **specialist** is charged with maintaining an orderly market and providing price continuity. The specialist fills limit and market orders for the public and trades for his own account to either stabilize or facilitate trading when serious supply and demand imbalances occur.

Transactions away from the main market. As a rule, dealers do not maintain inventories in listed stocks and do no principal business in them, except in connection with third market transactions. Customer orders are routed to an exchange trading floor for execution, and the originating firm charges a commission for services rendered.

OTC Markets

Location. There is no central marketplace for OTC trading. Trading takes place over the phone, over computer networks and in trading rooms across the country.

Pricing system. The OTC market works through an **interdealer network**. Registered market makers compete among themselves to post the best bid and ask prices. The OTC market is a *negotiated* market.

Price dynamics. When a market maker raises its bid price to attract sellers and outpace other market makers, the price of the stock rises; when a market maker lowers its ask price to attract buyers and outpace other market makers, the price of the stock declines.

Major force in the market. The **market makers** post the best current bid and ask prices. The best price at which the public can buy (best ask) and the best price at which the public can sell (best bid) are called the **inside market**.

Subject to certain minimum capital requirements, any NASD member can apply for registration as a market maker in any number of OTC securities.

Transactions away from the main market. Unlike the situation in listed stocks, many dealers maintain inventories in OTC stocks (or stand ready to buy or sell for their own accounts) without registering as market makers. Such firms have the choice of filling customer orders either as principal trades (from inventory) or as agency trades (executed with a registered market), similar to the way listed stocks are handled.

Role of the Broker-Dealer

Those engaged in buying and selling securities must register as broker-dealers. Most firms act both as brokers and dealers, but not in the same transaction.

Brokers. Brokers are agents that arrange trades for clients and charge them a commission. The broker does not buy shares, but simply arranges a trade between a buyer and seller.

Dealers. When firms act as dealers (principals), they buy and sell securities for their own accounts (inventory). A broker-dealer that is buying and selling for its own account is sometimes said to be **position trading**. Taking a position in a security also can be referred to as *in control* of that amount of the security. Members may not trade excessively for their own accounts because that would obstruct the maintenance of a fair and orderly market. Any trading practice that manipulates the market or deceives the investing public is a violation of SEC regulations.

When selling from their inventory, dealers charge their clients a markup rather than a commission. A markup is the difference between the current interdealer offering price and the actual price charged the client. When a price to a client includes a dealer's markup, it is called the *net price*. The dealer does not just arrange a trade, but actually sells the client shares from its inventory.

Filling an order. A broker-dealer may fill a customer's order to buy securities in any of the following ways:

- The broker may act as the client's agent by finding a seller of the securities and arranging a trade.

- The dealer may buy the securities from the market maker, mark up the price and resell them to the client on a dealer basis.
- If the dealer has the securities in its own inventory, it may sell the shares to the client from that inventory.

Broker-dealer role in transactions. A firm is prohibited from acting as both a broker and a dealer in the same transaction. For example, your firm cannot make a market in a stock, mark up that stock and add an agency commission. If the firm acts as a broker, it may charge a commission. If it acts as a dealer, it may charge a markup (or markdown).

The following chart compares brokers and dealers:

Broker	Dealer
Acts as an agent, transacting orders on behalf of the client.	Acts as a principal, dealing in securities for its own account and at its own risk.
Charges a commission.	Charges a markup or markdown.
Is not a market maker.	Makes markets and takes positions (long or short) in securities.
Must disclose to the client its role and the amount of its commission.	Must disclose to the client its role, but not necessarily the amount or source of the markup or markdown.

An easy way to remember these relationships is to memorize the letters "BAC/DPP." The letters stand for "**B**rokers act as **A**gents for **C**ommissions/**D**ealers act as **P**rincipals for **P**rofits."

◆ Review Questions

1. The New York Stock Exchange serves investors by

   A. offering securities for sale
   B. buying securities for members
   C. both of the above
   D. none of the above

2. Which of the following brokers would be allowed to trade on the NYSE?

   I. Registered representative
   II. Specialist
   III. Registered trader
   IV. Commission broker

   A. I and II only
   B. II and III only
   C. II, III and IV only
   D. I, II, III and IV

3. The over-the-counter market is a(n)

   A. negotiated market
   B. auction market
   C. transfer market
   D. double-auction market

4. Which of the following statements are true regarding the OTC market?

   I. It facilitates the trading of stock not listed on an exchange.
   II. It is a connection of broker-dealers via computers and phones.
   III. Stocks of banks and insurance companies typically trade in the over-the-counter market.

   A. I and II only
   B. I and III only
   C. II and III only
   D. I, II and III

5. An over-the-counter trader attempting to buy stock is given a quote of "16–17 work out." This indicates that the quote is

   A. $16 with a suggested broker-dealer markup of $1
   B. firm
   C. bona fide
   D. approximate

6. All of the following are usually traded over the counter EXCEPT

   A. mutual fund shares
   B. foreign securities and ADRs
   C. exchange-listed stocks
   D. closed-end investment company securities

◆ Answers & Rationale

1. **D.** The primary objective of the NYSE is to provide a central location for the transaction of its members' business—the trading of securities.

2. **C.** The NYSE permits only specialists, registered traders and commission brokers to trade on the Exchange floor. Registered representatives deal with the investing public and initiate orders that are transmitted for execution to the Exchange floor.

3. **A.** The OTC market is not an auction market like the NYSE. Prices are negotiated between broker-dealers.

4. **D.** All three statements are true of the OTC. Some stocks cannot meet the NYSE listing requirements so they trade over the counter. Bank and insurance company stocks typically trade in this market because many of them have only regional interest rather than national interest. The OTC market is a system of telephone and computer connections between broker-dealers.

5. **D.** A workout quote is usually given as a range of prices within which the dealer or broker thinks it can make the trade. A firm quote would be "The market is 16–17," or, "It is currently 16–17."

6. **A.** Because mutual fund shares are redeemed by the issuer, there is no secondary market trading.

8 Client Accounts

Key Terms

- cash account
- credit agreement
- custodial account
- custodial trading authorization
- custodian
- discretionary account
- discretionary trading authorization
- donor
- fiduciary trading authorization
- full power of attorney
- guardian
- hypothecation agreement
- indefeasible title
- irrevocable gift
- joint account
- joint tenants in common (JTIC)
- joint tenants with right of survivorship (JTWROS)
- limited power of attorney
- loan consent agreement
- margin account
- new account form
- Regulation T (Reg T)
- retirement account
- single account
- special cash account
- trading authorization
- trustee
- Uniform Gifts to Minors Act (UGMA)
- Uniform Transfers to Minors Act (UTMA)

Overview

The client account (and any statements generated by it) serves as a record of the client's investment activity. The account also functions as a file in which the firm can record any and all information it requires about the investing client.

There are a number of different types of accounts that a registered rep can open for a customer. Among the variables to be considered when opening a customer account are:

- the type of investing the customer intends to do
- the number of people who will have access to the account
- whether the customer intends to borrow money in the course of investing

Both the registered rep and the principal must become familiar with the various forms and paperwork necessary to open accounts and the handling of investment transactions.

Every account (and every transaction in an account) has its own records and recordkeeping requirements. Some account and order forms provide companies with the information they need in order to keep track of the daily business of their customers; others are required by the Securities and Exchange Commission (SEC) and the self-regulatory organizations (SROs), such as the National Association of Securities Dealers, Inc. (NASD) and various other government agencies, as a means of monitoring industry practices.

New Accounts

For every type of account (and for every variation of every type), there are specific forms and paperwork that must be filled out, filed, sent to the appropriate regulatory body and/or kept on file by the broker. Some forms, such as the new account form (or card), need to be filled out for every account opened. Other forms have their own specific applications, including:

- customer agreements
- loan consent agreements
- IRA contracts
- Keogh forms
- partnership agreements
- corporate charters
- simplified employee pension plan (SEP) applications
- annuity contracts
- trust documents
- mutual fund applications
- full or limited powers of attorney

Classification of Accounts

Account ownership. Procedures and relevant regulations vary according to the type of person, group or business that owns the account. The principal types of ownership are:

- individual
- joint (for example, a husband and wife or two business associates)
- corporate
- partnership

Trading authorization. The primary types of trading authorization are:

- **Discretionary.** After receiving written authority from the customer, the registered representative enters trades without having to consult the customer before each trade.
- **Fiduciary.** The individual given fiduciary responsibility enters the trades for the account.
- **Custodial.** The custodian for the beneficial owner enters all trades.

Payment method. Customers may pay for securities in one of two ways: cash or margin. In cash accounts, clients must pay the full purchase price of securities. In margin accounts, clients may borrow part of the purchase price of a security from the broker-dealer.

Securities traded. Clients must have special approval to make certain types of trades in their accounts, and additional special requirements exist for options accounts.

Opening New Accounts

Before opening any new account, the broker-dealer and registered representative should evaluate the prospective customer as to character and credit references, financial reliability and specific financial goals and objectives.

Required information. According to NYSE Rule 405 ("Know Your Customer"), exchange members must exercise due diligence to learn essential facts about every customer and account. General guidelines suggest the registered rep interview the client in order to obtain an inventory of the client's present holdings and discover the client's financial situation, needs and objectives.

Generally, any competent person may open an account. Any person declared legally incompetent may not open an account. Fiduciary or custodial accounts may be opened for minors or legally incompetent individuals.

Approval and Acceptance of an Account

Without exception, every new account must be approved by a partner or a principal of the firm, in writing on the account form, before any trading can take place. The principal may initial the new account form to indicate that the account is approved and the firm has accepted the account.

Documenting New Accounts

New account form. The registered rep must fill out a new account form for every new account she opens. On this form the rep should enter certain details regarding client identification and information concerning suitability. The firm must have a record of the following information about each client who will have access to the account:

- full name;
- address and telephone number (business and residence numbers);
- Social Security or tax identification number;
- occupation, employer and type of business;
- citizenship;
- whether the person is of legal age;
- bank and brokerage references;
- whether the client is an employee of a member broker-dealer;
- how the account was acquired;
- name and occupation of the person(s) with authority to make transactions in the account; and
- signatures of the representative opening the account and a principal of the firm (the client's signature is not required on a new account form).

If the customer refuses to disclose or provide all of the financial information requested by the firm, the firm may still open the account if it determines by other means that the customer has the financial resources to carry the account and that whatever trades the customer seeks to enter are suitable.

Client information should be updated periodically as situations change. Transactions placed by the customer and judged unsuitable by the registered rep may still be entered by the customer. For unsuitable trades (as well as for any trade requested by a customer without the rep's recommendation), the rep should note on the ticket that the transaction was unsolicited. If the ticket is not marked, the trade will be assumed to be solicited.

Signature Cards

Many firms ask their customers to fill out a signature card. Although the customer is not legally required to fill one out for a cash account, the card provides both protection and convenience; it enables a customer to send written orders to the registered rep or sponsor, who can then verify the accuracy of the order by comparing the signature on the letter to the one that the firm has on file.

Mailing Instructions

When a new account form is filled out, the client gives specific mailing instructions. Statements and confirms may be sent to someone other than the client (his agent or attorney, for example) if the client requests it in writing or if duplicate confirms are also sent to the client. A member firm may hold the client's mail for up to two months if the client is traveling in the United States, and for up to three months if the client is abroad.

Cash Accounts and Margin Accounts

When a customer has opened an investment account with a brokerage firm, the account will be designated as either a cash account or a margin account. Each type of account carries certain rights and responsibilities, depending on how the customer chooses to pay for any securities purchased.

Cash Accounts

The cash account (also known as the **special cash account**) is the securities industry's basic investment account. Anyone who is eligible to open an investment account can open it as a cash account. In a cash account, a customer is expected to pay in full for any securities purchased.

Certain accounts may be opened *only* as cash accounts; among these are personal retirement accounts (IRAs, Keoghs and TDAs), corporate retirement accounts and custodial accounts (UGMAs).

Margin Accounts

The margin account came into being as a way for clients to borrow money for the purpose of investing. The term "margin" refers to the minimum amount of cash or marginable securities that a customer is required to deposit on the purchase of securities.

The Federal Reserve Board's Regulation T

Because leveraging is a two-way street, several rules apply to margin accounts. The Securities Exchange Act of 1934 grants the Federal Reserve Board (FRB) authority to regulate credit extended in the purchase of securities. The FRB established Regulation T, which sets forth the equity or margin required in a purchase of securities in a margin account. Regulation T prevents the overextension of credit in securities transactions. It also stipulates which securities may be purchased on margin. The board establishes the rules and regulations governing margin accounts, and then delegates the enforcement of them to the SEC.

Opening a Margin Account

If a customer wishes to open a margin account, the firm holding the account first satisfies itself that the client can meet certain minimum financial requirements (the securities industry's equivalent of a credit check). After that, the client is allowed to place orders for investments and is asked to deposit only a percentage of their cost (and to pay interest on the unpaid balance). The securities purchased are held for the customer in the account in street name. The rate of interest on margin accounts is based on the broker call rate, a rate typically more favorable than the rates offered by banks and savings institutions for similar loans.

Documenting a margin account. When opening a margin account, the client signs a margin agreement disclosing the terms under which credit will be extended. The margin agreement contains a credit agreement, a hypothecation agreement and an optional loan consent.

- The **credit agreement** discloses the terms under which credit is extended. The SEC requires that the firm disclose the annual rate and method of computing interest and the conditions under which interest rates and charges will be changed. The firm is also required to send the customer an assurance that statements accounting for interest charges will be sent at least quarterly. If the firm fails to make these disclosures, changes in interest rates are permitted only with 30 days' notice to the customer.
- The **hypothecation agreement** gives the firm permission to pledge (or hypothecate) securities held on margin. The hypothecation agreement is a mandatory part of the margin agreement.
- The **loan consent agreement** gives the firm permission to lend the customer's securities held in a margin account to other brokers (usually for delivery on short sales). A customer signature to a loan consent is not mandatory under NASD rules. A typical loan consent would read as follows:

"Until you receive written notice of revocation from the undersigned, you are hereby authorized to lend to yourselves as brokers, or to others, any securities held by you on margin for the account of, or under the control of, the undersigned."

Retirement Account Agreements

Each separate type of personal and corporate retirement account has its own forms and applications. The most important ones are those that establish the firm's custodial relationship with the owner of the retirement account, necessary for Internal Revenue Service (IRS) approval.

Business Accounts

When a registered rep opens a business account of any type, it is necessary to establish three items:

1. the business's legal right to open an investment account;
2. any limitations that the owners, stockholders, a court or any other entity has placed on the investments in which the business will be allowed to invest; and
3. who will be allowed to represent the business in transactions involving the account.

A copy of the legal documents that established the business will usually contain this information and must be kept on file together with all other account forms.

Trading Authorization/Power of Attorney

Any time a power of attorney or a discretionary power to the broker has been established for an investment account, a signed copy of that document must be kept on file.

Opening Accounts for Employees of Other Brokers

The NASD, NYSE and MSRB all have rules that require broker-dealers to give special attention to accounts opened by certain individuals. This special attention typically involves permission from or written notification to some other broker-dealer regarding the establishment of the account. Accounts opened by the following individuals fall within these rules:

- employee of a broker-dealer
- spouse or minor child of an employee of a broker-dealer
- (in certain cases) employee of a non-NYSE member financial institution

NASD requirements. NASD rules do not require the employee of one NASD member firm to get the employer's permission to open an account with another NASD member. The rules do require the firm opening the account to notify the client's employer. The employee is responsible for disclosing that she is an NASD member when opening the account. Duplicate confirmations and statements must be sent to the employer broker-dealer only if the employer requests them.

Types of Accounts

When an account is opened, it is registered in the name(s) of one or more people. They are the owners of the account and are the only individuals who will be allowed access to and/or control of the investments in the account. When a representative opens an account, he asks the customer to specify the names in which the account is to be registered.

Single Accounts

In general, if the customer will be the only person who has access to the account, his name is the only one that appears on it, and it is known as a **single account**. In a single account, there is only one beneficial owner. The account holder is the only person who can:

- control the investments within the account
- request distributions of cash or securities from the account

"Single account" refers only to the number of owners and does not limit in any way the owner's ability to trade or margin the securities in the account.

Joint Accounts

If the names of two or more people appear on the account and each will be allowed some form of control over the account (that is, two or more individuals are cotenants or co-owners of the account), it is called a **joint account**.

In addition to the appropriate new account form, a joint account agreement must be signed, and the account must be designated as either joint tenants in common (JTIC), or joint tenants with right of survivorship (JTWROS).

The account forms must be signed by all owners. Both types of joint account agreements provide that any or all tenants may transact business in the account. Checks must be made payable to the name(s) in which the account is registered (and must be endorsed for deposit by all tenants), although mail need only be sent to a single address. To be in good delivery form, securities sold from a joint account must be signed by all tenants.

Joint tenants in common. JTIC ownership provides that a deceased tenant's fractional interest in the account is retained by that tenant's estate and is not passed to the surviving tenant(s), if any. As an example, if a JTIC agreement provides for 60% ownership interest by one owner and 40% ownership interest by the other, that is the fraction of the account that would pass into the deceased owner's estate if he died. The JTIC agreement may be used by more than two individuals.

Joint tenants with right of survivorship. JTWROS ownership stipulates that a deceased tenant's interest in the account passes to the surviving tenant(s).

Power of Attorney

An individual will occasionally want another person to have access to (or control of) her investment account. If that person is not named on the account as an owner, custodian, trustee or some other form of legal account manager, then the client must file written authorization with the broker-dealer giving that person access to the account. This trading authorization usually takes the form of a power of attorney. There are two basic types of trading authorization: full and limited powers of attorney.

Full Power of Attorney

The beneficial owner of an account can direct the broker-dealer to allow another person access to her account. The account owner does this by supplying the broker-dealer with what is known as a full power of attorney. A full power of attorney allows someone who is not the beneficial owner of an account to:

- deposit or withdraw cash and/or securities; and
- make investment decisions for the owner of the account (i.e., buy, sell, trade or in any other manner affect the account's holdings).

Custodians, trustees, guardians and other people filling similar legal duties typically have been given full power of attorney.

Limited Power of Attorney

If the beneficial owner of an account would like another individual to have some (but not total) control over the account, he will file a limited power of attorney with the broker-dealer that clearly states the rights and responsibilities he is giving this person. Limited powers of attorney must be filed by clients who want to give their brokers discretionary power over their accounts.

Discretionary Accounts

Customers occasionally want to give a registered rep the authority to make transactions on their behalf without having to ask for specific approval each time. An account set up with this type of preapproved authority is known as a *discretionary account*. "Discretion" is defined as the *authority to decide*:

- the security
- the number of shares (or units)
- whether to buy or sell

Discretion *does not* apply to decisions regarding only the *timing* of the investment or the *price* at which it is acquired. An order from a customer worded: "Buy 100 shares of Datawaq for my account whenever you think the price is right" is not a discretionary order.

Authorization for discretionary accounts. There are a number of rules and regulations regarding discretionary accounts of which the registered rep must be aware. A customer can give a registered rep discretionary power over his account(s) only by filing a trading authorization or a limited power of attorney with the registered rep's broker-dealer. No transactions of a discretionary nature can take place without this document on file. Once trading authorization has been given, the customer is legally bound to accept the registered rep's decisions although the customer may continue to enter orders on his own. If the customer has orally authorized the registered rep to exercise discretion in a transaction, the rep must follow up by obtaining written authorization *within ten business days*.

The customer may only give authority to make decisions for the account to specific individuals, and cannot give blanket authorization to the firm. If the registered rep (or other person named in the power of attorney) leaves the firm or in any other way stops working with the account, the discretionary authority does not pass on to the next account representative. It ends immediately and will not restart unless the account owner files a new power with the company.

The power of attorney remains in force for no more than three years (and must be kept on file for at least three years), at which point it can be renewed at the discretion of the customer.

In addition to other information required, on every discretionary account the registered rep needs to record whether the customer is of legal age and the occupation of the customer, as well as the signature of each person authorized to exercise discretion in the account. The account file must also include the signature of the registered rep who introduced the account and the signature of the member, partner or other company officer who accepted the account for the firm.

Uniform Gifts to Minors Act Accounts

Until the Tax Reform Act (TRA) of 1986 changed the favorable tax status of UGMA and its successor, the Uniform Transfers to Minors Act (UTMA) adopted by the National Conference of Commissioners of Uniform State Laws in 1983, many people used these accounts as a means of transferring highly taxable income and capital gains to a child in a lower tax bracket through gifts of money or securities (children are normally in a low tax bracket and subject to lower taxes on most types of income).

The regulations surrounding these gifts are very specific in their application. They were developed over time as a means of protecting the interests of the recipient (the minor or donee), the gift giver (the donor) and the custodian of the account.

UGMA and UTMA accounts require an adult (or bank trust department) to act as custodian for a minor (the beneficial owner). Any kind of security—cash, life insurance, annuity contracts and other forms of property—may be given, and there is no limitation on the dollar amount of the gift.

Donating Securities

When a person makes a gift of securities to a minor under the UGMA laws, that person is referred to as the **donor** of the securities. A gift under UGMA is a complete, irrevocable donation of the donor's interest to another person. Once the gift is donated, the donor gives up all rights to the property.

A gift to a minor through an UGMA gives the minor what is known as **indefeasible title**; that is, title that cannot be made null or void. The minor is considered the beneficial owner of the account and its contents. The gift is *irrevocable*: the donor may not take back the gift, nor may the minor return the gift until she has reached the age of majority or the age that the laws of her state have set as the age when the custodianship will terminate. When the minor reaches the specified age, the property in the accounts is transferred into her name.

Bearer securities are generally not permitted but, if they are, gifts of bearer securities must be accompanied by a *deed of gift*.

Custodian

Any securities given to a minor through an UGMA account are managed by a custodian until the minor attains the age of majority. The custodian may be either the donor or a person appointed by the donor, but not necessarily a family member. The custodian has full control over the minor's account and can:

- buy or sell securities
- exercise rights or warrants
- liquidate, trade or hold securities

The custodian may also use the property in the account in any way that person deems proper for the support, education, maintenance, general use or benefit of the minor. However, the account may not be used to discharge the liabilities normally associated with raising the child, such as for payment of food, shelter, and so on.

There are few restrictions as to who can act as a custodian for a minor's account:

- The donor of the securities can act as custodian or can appoint someone else to the responsibility (the laws do state, however, that there may be only one custodian and one minor or beneficial owner for each account).
- One person may not be the custodian for two minors in a joint account, nor can there be two people sharing custodial duties for one minor.
- A minor can be the beneficiary of more than one account and a person may serve as custodian for more than one UGMA as long as each account benefits only one minor.
- Parents, unless acting as custodians for a minor's account, have no legal control over, or recourse to, the account or any of the securities in it.

The registered rep is not responsible for determining whether the appointment is valid or whether the custodian's activities are actually within his authority. However, the rep should determine whether securities being given are already owned by the minor.

Opening an UGMA Account

When opening an UGMA account for a customer, the rep must ensure that the account application contains the custodian's name, the minor's name and Social Security number, and the state in which the UGMA is registered.

Registration of UGMA Securities

Any securities in an UGMA account are registered in the name of the custodian for the benefit of the minor; they cannot be registered *in street name*. Typically, the securities will be registered to "Joan R. Smith as custodian for Brenda Lee Smith," or a variation of this form. When the minor reaches the age of majority, all of the securities in the account will be registered in her name.

The gift of the securities is considered to have been made when this registration has been completed.

Fiduciary Responsibility

The UGMA custodian is charged with fiduciary responsibilities in the management of the minor's account. Certain restrictions have been placed on what is deemed to be proper handling of the investments in an UGMA. The most important limitations are:

- UGMAs may only be opened and managed as cash accounts.
- Securities in the account may not be purchased on margin or pledged by the custodian as collateral for a loan.
- All cash proceeds, dividends and interest must be reinvested by the custodian within a reasonable period of time. Cash proceeds from sales or dividends

may be held in a noninterest-bearing custodial account for a reasonable period, but should not remain idle for long.
- Investment decisions must take into account the age of the minor and the custodial relationship; commodities futures, naked options and other high-risk securities are examples of inappropriate investments. Options may not be placed or purchased in a custodial account because no evidence of ownership is issued to an option buyer.
- Stock subscription rights or warrants must be either exercised or sold.
- A custodian for an UGMA may not grant trading authority to a third party.
- A custodian may loan money to the account, but may never borrow from it.

The custodian may be reimbursed for any reasonable expenses incurred in the management of the account.

Taxation

The minor's Social Security number appears on the account, and the minor must file an annual income tax return and pay taxes on any income produced by the UGMA at *the parent's top marginal tax rate*, regardless of the source of the gift, until the minor reaches the age of 14 (there are exclusions available totalling $1,000, indexed for inflation).

The law specifies that when the minor reaches age 14, any taxes incurred by the account will be charged at the minor's rate, rather than at the parent's rate.

In most states, although the minor is the beneficiary of the account and is responsible for any and all taxes on the account, it is the custodian's responsibility to see that the taxes are paid.

Death of the Minor, Custodian or Donor

If the minor beneficiary of an UGMA dies, the securities in the account pass to the minor's estate, not to the parents' or custodian's estates. In the event of the death or resignation of the custodian, a new custodian must be appointed by either a court of law or the donor. If the donor dies, additional gifts to a minor's UGMA may not be made by will (although, in some states, a gift under UGMA may be made through a will, trust or estate).

◆ Review Questions

1. An employee of another NASD member broker-dealer would like to open an account with your firm. All of the following statements regarding the employee and the account are true EXCEPT the

   A. employer must receive duplicate copies of all transactions made in the account if requested
   B. employer must be notified of the opening of the account
   C. opening member must notify the employee in writing that the employer will be notified of the employee's intent to open the account
   D. broker-dealer holding the account must approve each transaction made by the person before entry of the order

2. All of the following client information is required on a new account form EXCEPT

   A. name
   B. date of birth
   C. Social Security number
   D. occupation

3. Which of the following client information should the registered rep normally attempt to obtain when opening a new account?

   I. Occupation
   II. Financial condition
   III. Investment objective

   A. I and II only
   B. I and III only
   C. II and III only
   D. I, II and III

4. A customer would like to open a custodial UGMA/UTMA account for his nephew, a minor. The uncle

   A. can open the account provided the proper trust arrangements are filed first
   B. can open the account and name himself custodian
   C. needs a legal document evidencing the nephew's parents' approval of the account
   D. can be custodian for the account only if he is also the minor's legal guardian

5. Which of the following characteristics describe a joint tenants with right of survivorship account?

   I. Orders may be given by either party.
   II. Checks must be made out in the name of the account.
   III. Mail may be sent to either party.
   IV. In the event of the death of one of the tenants, the surviving party assumes control of the entire account.

   A. I and IV only
   B. II and III only
   C. III and IV only
   D. I, II, III and IV

◆ Answers & Rationale

1. **D.** The broker-dealer has no obligation to approve every transaction prior to entry.

2. **B.** The registered rep must ascertain that the client is of legal age in that state, but is under no obligation to determine an exact birth date.

3. **D.** When opening a new account, the registered rep would normally obtain information on, among other things, the client's occupation, financial condition and investment objectives.

4. **B.** No documentation of custodial status is required to open an UGMA account.

5. **D.** In a JTWROS account, any party named on the account may enter orders for the account but distributions from the account must be sent in the names of all of the owners.

9 Brokerage Office Procedures

Key Terms

breakpoint sales
churning
confirmation
ex-date
frozen account
good delivery
regular way
Rules of Fair Practice
selling away
selling dividends
settlement date
uniform delivery ticket

Overview

The business of trading securities is not without its share of paperwork. Registered representatives and principals are responsible for providing accurate and thorough information for processing transactions. Some of the procedures they follow are particular to their firms. Other procedures are required of all firms by securities regulations such as the NASD's Uniform Practice Code.

Brokerage Support Services

Transactions and Trade Settlement

Receipt and Delivery of Securities

When a representative accepts a buy order from a customer, the representative must inquire of and be assured that the customer agrees to receive the securities and will pay for them at the agreed upon price. When a rep accepts a sell order from a customer, the rep must be assured that the customer has the security (in a long position) and can deliver it within five business days of the trade.

Trade Confirmations

A confirmation is a printed document that confirms the trade, settlement date and amount of money due from or owed to the client. For each transaction, a client must be sent or given a written confirmation of the trade *at or before the completion of the transaction* (known as the **settlement date**). An exception to this rule is made for wire order purchases of mutual funds for which confirmation may be sent by the selling agent as late as the day after the settlement date. The registered rep receives a copy of the customer's confirmation and checks its accuracy against the order ticket.

Transaction Settlement Dates and Terms

Settlement date is the date on which ownership changes between buyer and seller. It is the date on which a customer is expected to pay for securities bought and make delivery on securities sold. Settlement is made when the selling broker-dealer delivers the securities to the buying broker-dealer's office. The NASD's Uniform Practice Code standardizes the dates and times for each type of settlement.

Regular Way Settlement

Except for transactions in U.S. government securities and money-market instruments, regular way settlement is usually the *fifth business day* following the date of trade (which is different from the seven-business-day Reg T payment date). Unless there is an intervening holiday, settlement is always one calendar week later (for example, a trade entered on a Monday settles the next Monday). If the seller delivers prior to the settlement date, the buyer may either accept the security or refuse it without prejudice.

For U.S. government notes and bonds, regular way settlement is always the *next business day.* For money-market securities (commercial paper, bankers' acceptances, certificates of deposit and U.S. Treasury bills), settlement is the *same day* (except for small retail transactions, which are billed for next day settlement).

Extensions

If for good reason a buyer is unable to pay for a trade within seven business days (Reg T payment date) from the trade date, the broker-dealer may request an extension from an SRO (such as the NASD) on the seventh day. The broker-dealer has the option of ignoring amounts of less than $500 without violating Reg T requirements.

Frozen accounts. If a customer buys securities in a cash account and sells them before paying for the buy side in full by the seventh business day, the account is *frozen*—any additional transactions must be on a cash-and-carry basis (full payment or securities on deposit in advance of a sell transaction). Frozen account status continues for a period of *90 calendar days*. If a customer buys and sells as described previously but pays for the buy side not later than the seventh business day, frozen account status is lifted.

Dividend Department

Dividend Disbursing Process

Declaration date. A company's board of directors approves the payment of a dividend, announcing the amount, payment date and date on which it will be determined who is and who is not a registered stockholder (known as the *dividend record date*). The SEC requires any corporation that intends to pay cash dividends or make other distributions to notify the NASD (or the appropriate exchange, if the stock is listed) at least ten business days prior to the intended record date. This timely notification enables the NASD (or an exchange) to establish the ex-date.

Ex-dividend date. Based on the dividend record date announced previously, the NASD Uniform Practice Committee (or an exchange, if the stock is listed) will post an **ex-date** for trading and price continuity purposes. The ex-date is *four business days* before the announced record date. Because most trades settle regular way—five business days after the trade date—a customer would have to purchase the stock five business days before the record date in order to qualify for the dividend.

On the ex-date, the opening price of the stock drops to compensate for the fact that customers who buy the stock that day or later will not qualify for the dividend. Trades executed regular way on or after the ex-date will not settle until after the record date.

Neither purchaser (the one who buys before the ex-date or the one who buys after the ex-date) is at an advantage. The customer who buys the stock before the ex-date receives the dividend, but pays a higher price for the stock (and is said to have *bought the dividend*). The customer who buys the stock after the ex-date does not receive the dividend, but pays a lower price for the stock.

Cash trades. Cash trades settle the same day, so cash trades go ex-dividend on the day after the record date because there is no lag between the trade date and the transaction settlement.

Dividend record date. The record date is the date selected by a corporation that is used to determine who is and who is not stockholder of record for dividend payment or rights distribution purposes.

Payable date. Three or four weeks after the record date, the transfer agent (or another company-authorized entity) cuts dividend checks and mails them to all stockholders whose names appear on the books as of the record date.

Late receipt of information. If the Uniform Practice Committee does not receive the necessary declaration date information in time to schedule a normal ex-date, it will set as the ex-date the first practical date in view of all surrounding circumstances.

Ex-date and Record Date Relationship

The following example and the accompanying figure illustrate the relationship between the ex-date and the record date.

Assume that a company declares a cash dividend of $.75 payable to stockholders whose names appear on the company's books on June 21st. The NASD (or an exchange, if the stock is listed) sets an ex-date for trading purposes four business days in advance of the record date, which makes the ex-date June 15th in this case.

On June 14th, a transaction is executed for regular way settlement on June 21st, the record date. The stock's market price on June 14th includes the $.75 upcoming dividend payment. In effect, the buyer is buying the dividend and the seller is collecting the dividend early.

On the settlement date, the buyer's name replaces the seller's on the company's books. Later, on the payable date, the buyer will get the dividend.

On June 15th, the ex-date, another transaction is executed for regular way settlement, this time on June 22nd. This is past the record date, which means it is too late to get the buyer's name on the company's books in time for the dividend payment. Instead, the seller will get the dividend, even though she already has sold the stock. To compensate both parties, the stock's market price on the ex-date dropped by $.75.

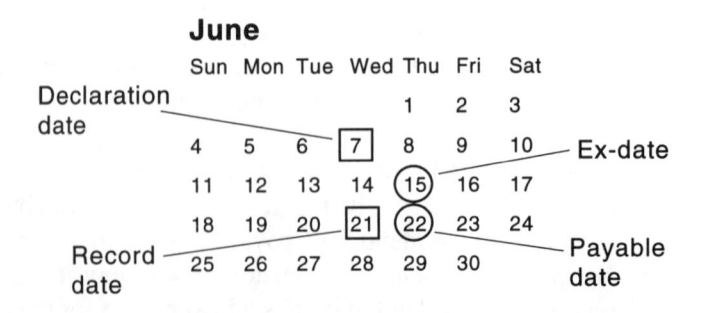

June

	Sun	Mon	Tue	Wed	Thu	Fri	Sat	
Declaration date				1	2	3		
	4	5	6	**7**	8	9	10	Ex-date
	11	12	13	14	(15)	16	17	
	18	19	20	**21**	(22)	23	24	Payable date
Record date	25	26	27	28	29	30		

Summary of Ex-dates

Whether the buyer or the seller of a security is entitled to its distribution (dividends, rights or warrants) is determined by the ex-date. Table 9.1 compares the different kinds of transaction dates.

Table 9.1　Summary of Ex-dates

Transaction/Ex-date	Definition	Duration/Expiration
Trade date	Date on which the transaction occurs.	Initiation date for all types of payment contracts. Due date for cash settlement.
Settlement date	Date on which payment must be received under NASD, NYSE or MSRB rules.	Varies according to type of delivery contract: same day for cash; five business days for regular way; 60 days for seller's or buyer's option.
Record date	Date that determines who is eligible to receive dividends or rights distributions. Fixed by the issuing corporation.	The investor must have settled the transaction to be considered the stockholder of record on the record date.
Ex-date (Ex-dividend date)	Date set by the Uniform Practice Committee after being informed of the distribution declaration by the issuer. Date on which stock is sold without (ex-) the right to receive the dividend.	One-day period dictated by the record date for distributions. Normally four business days before the record date. Stock trades without (ex-) rights or dividends.
Ex-rights date	Date on which the seller of the underlying security is entitled to receive the stock rights.	Fourth business day preceding the record date.
Ex-warrant date	Date on which the seller of the underlying security is entitled to receive the warrants.	Fourth business day preceding the expiration of the warrant.

Rules of Good Delivery

Before a security that has been sold can be delivered to the buyer, it must be in good delivery form. It is the registered rep's responsibility to inquire of a customer who calls with a sell order whether the security is negotiable, is in compliance with the contract of sale, can be delivered to the broker-dealer within five business days and is ready to be transferred from seller to purchaser.

"**Good delivery**" describes the physical condition, signatures, attachments and denomination of the certificates involved in a securities transaction. Although good delivery is mostly a matter of street-side settlements between buying and selling brokers, it also applies to deliveries into the brokerage house from customers on sell orders. In any broker-to-broker transaction, the delivered securities must be accompanied by a properly executed **uniform delivery ticket**. The transfer agent is the final arbiter of whether a security meets the requirements of good delivery.

Round lots: stocks. A round lot for common stock is 100 shares or any multiple thereof (e.g., 200, 1,700, etc.). Odd lots are units of fewer than 100 shares or a combination of a round lot with an odd lot (e.g., 125, 333, etc.).

Round lots: bonds. A round lot for bonds is $1,000 face amount or multiples thereof (e.g., $5,000, $100,000, etc.). In general, there are no odd lot bonds (although some issuers in the past put out "baby bonds" in $100 denominations). Good delivery of fully registered bonds is limited to $100,000 face value. If the face value of a bond is not the normal $100 or $1,000, the parties to the transaction can agree to accept that value as being good delivery.

Ethics in the Securities Industry

Ethical Business Practices

The securities industry is a highly competitive business; at times, the participants' desire to succeed seems to outweigh all other considerations. Despite this enormous personal pressure to succeed, the industry is governed by a very strong code of ethics. There is agreement on what constitutes acceptable behavior, and those who engage in unacceptable behavior risk sanctions ranging from fines and reprimands all the way to expulsion from the industry. There are clear standards against which business behavior and practices are measured for fairness and equity.

A problem in evaluating ethical behavior in securities industry transactions is the speed at which the industry operates. Decisions are made in split seconds, transactions occur almost instantaneously and millions of pieces of paper are generated and handled daily. If there are questions about the propriety of any transaction or agreement, it is nearly impossible to address them before the fact. This has caused some concern in the investing population—that in the shortness of time available to conduct business, there is also a shortness of time for considering the ethical consequences of actions.

Securities industry regulators are very active in detecting and preventing unethical behavior. Investigators regularly examine activity at all levels—from large firms to investment advisers to registered reps to individual investors. Even the most junior of employees is expected to employ high standards of business ethics and commercial honor in dealing with the public, customers, the firm and the industry.

Corporate Ethics and Responsibility

The rules that guide relationships between members of the securities industry and all of the other participants are set by the states, NASAA, the NASD, the SEC, the MSRB and other regulatory bodies and exchanges throughout the country. The federal securities acts, state laws, NASAA's *Statement of Policy on Unethical Business Practices of Investment Advisers*, *NASD Manual*, *NYSE Constitution and Rules*, the various other legislative acts governing securities all contain guidelines for what is and what is not acceptable behavior. It is the responsibility of broker-dealers, investment advisers, registered reps and others in the securities industry to be familiar with and follow these guidelines.

There is more to corporate responsibility than complying with rules, however. The first responsibility of any company, including a broker-dealer, is to its stockholders. Broker-dealers must be profitable so as to provide the long-term stability and security needed for a strong, viable securities market.

One part of corporate responsibility for ethical behavior involves a commitment to self-regulation. Every broker-dealer firm has the responsibility of supervising all associated persons. Each firm must have a written procedures manual and must designate a supervisor (principal) who is responsible for enforcing the rules in the manual. The principal must review and approve all correspondence and keep a record of all securities transactions and correspondence. The member must regularly review the activities of all branch offices. Individuals within the firm who engage in unethical behavior must be detected and their behavior corrected, or they risk being removed from their jobs. Compliance departments generally are the center of member firms' continuing effort to self-police. Employees need to know that compliance with regulations is important to the firm, and that noncompliance is dealt with swiftly.

Through self-regulation, broker-dealers protect customers. Protecting customers includes ensuring they are fully informed about their investments, have access to the information they need to make good investment decisions, and receive value for the commissions and markup paid to brokers and dealers. Customers deserve fair and equitable treatment; without it, the industry would lose credibility with the public.

Employee Ethics and Responsibility

The various federal and state securities regulations, the NASD Rules of Fair Practice and other laws cover employees as well as broker-dealers. Those who work for a broker-dealer or investment adviser represent the firm in all that they do. Employees, both producers and nonproducers, are responsible for ensuring that their activities fall within the guidelines set by regulators and by their firms.

Many firms view the regulations as minimum standards, and set stricter policies for internal behavior. Employees are responsible for knowing their firm's particular policies as these relate to the job they do. Even a well-intentioned employee of a broker-dealer or investment adviser can sometimes run afoul of the regulations. For example, a customer might suggest that an employee deliver a security in person, saving the firm the time and expense of registration and registered-mail delivery. But in most firms, delivering securities in this fashion is strictly against policy, and any person doing so could be subject to dismissal. Shortcuts are rarely a good idea—policies and regulations protect the employee, the firm and the customer.

Employees also have a responsibility to the industry. Serving on industry committees, assisting with public education, and self-education are all part of service to the industry; other examples include representing the firm and the industry in community activities and attending industry conferences and seminars.

Customer Ethics and Responsibility

Practices that would tend to give select investors an unfair advantage over the general public are prohibited by regulations; a prime example of such practices is insider trading. It is the responsibility of the individual investor to abide by these regulations.

The customer also should make full and honest disclosure to the registered representative. This information is all the representative or investment adviser has on which to base recommendations. Such information also may be important in gaining permission to engage in specific kinds or sizes of trades. A customer who fails to disclose relevant information could jeopardize the career of the representative or investment adviser. Failure on the part of a customer to provide information is often the first signal to compliance departments of potential trouble.

Prohibited Practices

The following is a list of trading practices that broker-dealers are prohibited by the NASD (as well as by NASAA and other SROs) from engaging in at all times. The prohibitions apply to all dealings with customers.

Manipulative and Fraudulent Devices

Without exception, NASD member firms are strictly prohibited from using manipulative, deceptive or other fraudulent tactics or methods to effect a transaction or in an attempt to induce the sale or purchase of a security. In recent years, the SEC has stepped up both enforcement and penalties for violations of this rule. A customer may bring suit for damages under the act of 1934 within three years of the alleged manipulation and within one year of discovering it. There is no dollar limit placed on damages in lawsuits based on allegations of manipulation.

Outside Business Activity (Private Securities Transactions)

Associated persons are prohibited from being employed by a firm other than their own or engaging in private securities transactions without the knowledge and consent of their employing broker-dealers. A **private securities transaction** is any sale of securities outside the regular business of an associated person and his employing member. Violations of the private securities transaction regulations are often referred to as **selling away**.

Notification. If an associated person wishes to enter into such a transaction, or into outside employment, that person must:

- provide any offering documents to his employer
- provide prior written notice to his employer
- describe in detail the proposed transaction
- describe in detail his proposed role in the transaction
- disclose whether he has or may receive compensation for the transaction

If the transaction or business activity is to be entered into for compensation, the employing member may approve or disapprove the associated person's participation. If the member approves the participation, it is required to treat the transaction as if it is being done on its own behalf by entering the transaction on its own books and supervising the associated person during the transaction. If the member disapproves the transaction, the associated person may not participate in it.

If the associated person has not or will not receive compensation for the private securities transaction, the employing member must acknowledge that it has received written notification and may require the associated person to adhere to specified conditions during his participation.

Transactions that the associated person enters into on behalf of immediate family members and for which the associated person receives no compensation are excluded from the definition of private securities transactions. Also excluded are personal transactions in investment company and variable annuity securities.

Recommendations to Customers

Suitability and Investment Recommendations

Investment recommendations must be in keeping with customer needs and objectives. Customers should be guided to investments that make sense for them, not just for the broker. Every investment should be fully explained, and the explanation should include a discussion of the investment's risks. At no time should customers own an investment which could put them at risk beyond their financial capacity.

Because all investments involve trade-offs, the task of the registered rep is to select securities that will provide the right balance between investor requirements on the one hand and investment capabilities on the other.

Selecting suitable investments to meet investor needs is both an art and a science. The process is too complex to computerize; even the most sophisticated and expensive financial plans are only partially based on a computerized model. In the final analysis, recommending investments requires the finest computer in existence: the human brain. As a registered rep or an investment adviser, one of your key tasks is to recommend suitable investments that best match your clients' unique characteristics.

Fair Dealing

The NASD's Rules of Fair Practice and the laws of most states require broker-dealers, registered reps and investment advisers to inquire into a customer's financial situation before making any recommendation to purchase, sell or exchange securities. The representative must determine such things as the client's other security holdings, income, expenses and financial goals and objectives. The following activities are considered violations of the rules regarding fair dealing:

- recommending speculative securities without finding out the customer's financial situation and being assured that the customer can bear the risk;
- short-term trading of mutual funds;
- setting up fictitious accounts to transact business that otherwise would be prohibited;
- making unauthorized transactions or use of funds;
- recommending purchases that are inconsistent with the customer's ability to pay;
- committing fraudulent acts (such as forgery and the omission or misstatement of material facts); and
- trading mutual fund positions with the same or similar objectives for the purpose of generating commissions (switching).

Excessive Trading: Churning

The practice of engaging aggressively or excessively in trading a customer's account primarily to generate commissions, rather than to make money for the customer, is an abuse of fiduciary responsibility known as *churning*. Churning can take the form of both excessive frequency (trading in and out of corporate bonds in a retirement account on a weekly basis could be a form a churning) and excessive size (recommending securities purchases to a customer that are so large that they require the liquidation of established positions in order to complete). As one method of preventing such abuses, self-regulatory organizations require that all accounts in which a registered rep or investment adviser has discretionary authority be reviewed frequently by a principal of the member firm.

Influencing or Rewarding Employees of Other Firms

Under the Rules of Fair Practice, member broker-dealers are not permitted to distribute business-related compensation (either cash or noncash gifts or gratuities) to the employees of other member firms. However, an offeror may give associated persons (employees) of other firms some form of compensation (either cash or noncash, but not securities) without being in violation of the rules if:

1. the compensation is not conditional on sales or promises of sales;
2. it has the prior approval of the employing member; and
3. the total value of the compensation does not exceed the annual limit set by the various SROs (currently fixed at $100 per year).

Associated persons are permitted to accept compensation only from their employing member firms, so all such gifts and gratuities must be given directly to the employing member for distribution. The member firm is required to maintain records of all gifts, gratuities and compensation (both cash and noncash) distributed to its associated persons. The records must include the name of the offeror, the name of the associated person and the amount and nature of the gift.

Employment contracts. This rule does not apply to legitimate employment contracts in which an employee of one firm supplies or performs services for another firm. The leasing of another firm's employee is acceptable provided there is a written employment agreement with employment duties and compensation delineated and with written consent of the person's employer (a principal of that firm must approve the arrangement), the temporary employer and the employee.

Selling Dividends

If an investor purchases shares just before the dividend distribution, she is at a double disadvantage. Not only does the market value of the fund shares decrease by the amount of the distribution, but she also incurs a tax liability on the distribution. A registered representative is forbidden to encourage an investor to purchase shares prior to a distribution because of this tax liability, and doing so is known as **selling dividends**.

Breakpoint Sales

Breakpoint sales are those in which a customer unknowingly buys investment company shares in an amount just under a dollar bracket amount that would qualify the investment for a reduction in sales charges. As a result, the customer pays a higher dollar amount in sales charges, which reduces the number of shares purchased and increases the cost basis per share. Encouraging a customer to make purchases in such a manner, or remaining silent when a customer unknowingly requests such a transaction, is unethical and a violation of the Rules of Fair Practice.

Borrowing and Lending

Borrowing money or securities from a client. Registered reps and investment advisers are prohibited from borrowing money or securities from a client *unless* the client is a bank, broker-dealer or other financial institution that is in the business of lending money.

Loaning money or securities to a client. Registered reps and investment advisers also are prohibited from lending money or securities to clients. This prohibition against lending money does not include broker-dealers making margin loans or investment advisers lending money as part of their normal business practices.

Misrepresentations

Registered reps and investment advisers are prohibited from misrepresenting themselves or their services to clients or potential clients. Included in this prohibition are misrepresentations covering:

- qualifications, experience and education
- nature of services offered
- fees to be charged

It would also be considered a misrepresentation to either inaccurately state or fail to state a material fact regarding any of the above. Without a full and accurate view of the facts and circumstances surrounding a professional relationship, a client would have difficulty comparing the services of professionals in the business.

Reports Prepared by Others

Investment advisers and broker-dealers are prohibited from presenting reports, analyses or recommendations prepared by another person or firm to a client without disclosing the fact that they were not prepared by the adviser. An adviser or broker-dealer may base a recommendation on reports or analysis prepared by others (that is, the adviser may conduct research that involves work done by a third party), as long these reports are not represented as their own.

Conflicts of Interest

Investment advisers are required to disclose in writing to clients any areas in which the adviser's interests conflict or could potentially conflict with those of the client. Examples of such conflicts include:

- affiliation(s) between the adviser and any product suppliers;
- compensation arrangements connected with advisory services to clients that are in addition to compensation from such clients for such services; and
- charging a client a fee for providing investment advice when a commission for executing securities transactions based on that advice will be received by the adviser or his employer.

Prohibitions Against Guarantees and Sharing in Customer Accounts

Broker-dealers, investment advisers and registered reps must not guarantee any customer against a loss or guarantee that a gain will be achieved in his account. Except in limited circumstances, members, advisers and representatives are also prohibited from sharing in any profits or losses in a customer's account. An exception will be made if a joint account has received *prior* written approval, and the registered representative shares in the profits and losses only to the extent of his *proportionate contribution* to the account.

If the member firm authorizes such a **shared account**, any or all such sharing must be directly proportionate to the financial contributions made by each party. However, in the case of an account being shared by a member or associated person and a member of that person's immediate family, directly proportionate sharing of profits and losses is not mandatory.

Immediate family members include parents, mother- or father-in-law, husband or wife, children, or any relative to whom the officer or employee in question contributes financial support.

Misuse of Nonpublic Information

The act of 1934 established strict regulations concerning the use and misuse of nonpublic information. Every registered representative and broker-dealer must establish, maintain and enforce written policies and procedures devoted to the prevention of violations of the rules covering nonpublic (inside) information.

Information Obtained as a Fiduciary

Confidentiality of customer information. Customers expect and deserve a high level of confidentiality. Employees of broker-dealers and investment advisers may not divulge personal information about customers without the express permission of the customer. This includes such information as security positions, personal and financial details and trading intentions. The securities industry depends on the trust of its customers; the employee is responsible for meeting and keeping that trust.

Numbered accounts. If a customer wants to keep his securities trades confidential, he may have a designated account assigned a number or a letter rather than a name. This is permitted if the member has on file a signed statement from the customer claiming ownership of that account.

Confidentiality of issuer information. When a member broker-dealer serves an issuer as a paying agent, transfer agent, underwriter or in another similar capacity, the member has established a *fiduciary* relationship with that issuer. In this role, the member may obtain information of a confidential nature such as the name, address or other information regarding the ownership of the securities it handles. The member is prohibited from using the information it obtains through its fiduciary role unless it is specifically asked to and authorized to do so by the issuer of the securities. For example, a member firm acting as transfer agent for a corporation's common stock cannot solicit the owners of the stock for its own purposes, but it may contact them on behalf of the issuer if the issuer requests and authorizes such contact to be made.

Other Unethical Trading Practices

Artificial transactions. As with fictitious quotations, artificial transactions are another way some people try to stage a hot market for a stock. Artificial transactions of all types are strictly prohibited.

Transactions involving no change in beneficial ownership. Again, the idea is to create the impression of a hot market for a particular stock. Working in tandem, one customer enters an order to buy while a second person enters an order to sell the same stock, at the same time, under the same terms, through the same broker-dealer. The broker-dealer crosses the buy and sell orders and reports the trade on the Consolidated Tape, thus showing a trade where one really did not occur.

Broker-dealers are prohibited from entering orders for the purchase or sale of securities with the knowledge that contra orders for the same stock, in the same amount, at approximately the same price have been or will be placed for the same customer or for different parties working in concert.

Excessive trading by broker-dealers. When a broker-dealer, acting alone or in concert with public customers, suddenly increases its own trading in a particular issue, it may be accused of **excessive trading**. If the firm's transaction volume in a given stock is clearly out of proportion with the firm's financial resources, or is out of line with the stock's normal daily trading volume, it may be suspected of trading excessively in order to induce public trades.

Participating in rings or pools. Broker-dealers are prohibited from participating directly or indirectly in any pool, ring, syndicate or other joint account venture formed for the purpose of rigging or otherwise influencing market prices. The prohibition against indirect participation includes investments in so-called blind trusts, as well as aiding and abetting individuals intent on committing fraud by offering marketing and capital-raising services, financing programs or order execution services.

Influencing market prices. NASD member firms are prohibited from attempting to influence the market price of securities by paying for favorable reviews, articles or other mentions in newspapers or other financial publications. This prohibition does not apply to paid advertisements placed in these publications and marked as such.

Spreading false and misleading information. Broker-dealers are prohibited from using their positions as centers of influence and opinion makers to sway customers by promoting and disseminating false or misleading information contrived for the purpose of inducing people to buy or sell a particular stock.

Front-running prohibitions. "Front-running" refers to situations in which a broker-dealer holds a customer order to buy or sell (typically a large block of stock that is very likely to move the market up or down) and buys or sells for the firm's own account on the same side of the market as the customer before showing the customer's order to the market.

A broker-dealer, when holding a customer order to buy, is prohibited from buying stock for its own account at or below the price at which the customer's order is subsequently filled. Similarly, when holding a customer's order to sell, a broker-dealer is prohibited from selling stock for a firm trading account at or above the price at which the customer's order is subsequently filled.

Joint participation in hidden accounts. Broker-dealers are prohibited from holding any direct or indirect interest in any joint account in which trading in eligible (listed) securities is to take place, without disclosing the full particulars of such an account to the NASD.

Falsely stating or implying that a trade will influence the closing price. Broker-dealers are prohibited from asserting, or attempting to induce a customer to trade on the basis, that a transaction executed in the third market will influence the closing price of the stock as reported on the Consolidated Tape.

Freeriding and withholding. Hot issues are public offering securities that sell at an *immediate premium* over the public offering price (POP) in the secondary market. To determine whether an issue is hot, the NASD compares its price in the secondary market to the POP. If there is enough public or institutional interest (or indications of interest) in the issue and it has the potential to trade at an immediate premium to the POP, it is considered a hot issue.

A member's failure to make a bona fide offering at the POP is considered **freeriding and withholding** under the NASD's Rules of Fair Practice (ROFP).

It is a violation of NASD rules for any underwriter or selling group member—or any broker-dealer buying public offering securities from an underwriter or selling group member—to sell any hot issue security to any individual listed below:

- the underwriters;
- any NASD member broker-dealer;
- any person associated with an NASD member;
- supported family members of a person associated with an NASD member; or
- any person financially dependent on a person associated with an NASD member.

Under certain circumstances, limited amounts of a hot issue may be sold to restricted accounts if it can be proved that the person buys similar types of securities regularly and routinely (normal investment practice).

Criminal Penalties

The criminal penalties for violations of securities laws were increased through an amendment to the act of 1934. If a person is convicted of willfully violating federal securities regulations, or of *knowingly* making false or misleading statements in a registration document, that person can be fined up to $1,000,000, sentenced to prison for not more than ten years, or both; the maximum fine is $2,500,000 for other than a natural person.

Assistance to Foreign Authorities

The SEC is pledged to assist foreign regulatory authorities in the investigation of any person who has violated, is violating or is about to violate any laws or rules relating to securities matters.

10 Economics and Analysis

Key Terms

business cycle
Consumer Price Index (CPI)
contraction
deflation
depression
discount rate
expansion
federal funds rate
Federal Open Market Committee (FOMC)
fiscal policy
gross domestic product (GDP)
inflation
monetary policy
peak
prosperity
recovery
reserve requirement
trough

Overview

Economics and economic activity are studied by those who want to determine the overall health and vitality of a country's economy. In particular, economists employed within the securities industry try to measure and predict how the economy's ups and downs will affect various investment instruments and corporations in a range of industries.

Economics

There are few measurable factors with greater influence on the securities markets than the economy. Business cycles, changes in the money supply, actions of the Federal Reserve Board (FRB), and a host of complex international monetary factors affect securities prices and trading.

Business Cycles

Throughout the United States' history, periods of economic expansion have followed periods of economic contraction in a predictable long-term pattern called the **business cycle**. Long-term business cycles go through four stages:

1. expansion
2. peak
3. contraction
4. trough

Expansion, also known as **recovery**, is characterized by increases in business activity throughout the economy. When the **peak** of this activity increase is reached, economists call that state **prosperity**. As business activity begins an overall period of decline, the economy is said to be going through a **contraction**. To an economist, mild short-term contractions that last two to six consecutive quarters (6 to 18 months) are known as **recessions**. More severe contractions of longer duration may be deemed **depressions**. At the bottom of a contraction is a period in which business activity stops its decline and begins the long road back through expansion to prosperity. This bottom of the business cycle is known as a **trough**. Figure 10.1 illustrates the four stages of the business cycle.

The U.S. Commerce Department defines recession and depression somewhat more strictly than most economists do, primarily for political reasons. According to the U.S. Commerce Department, the economy is in a recession when a decline in real output of goods and services (the gross domestic product—GDP) lasts for

Figure 10.1 The Four Stages of the Business Cycle

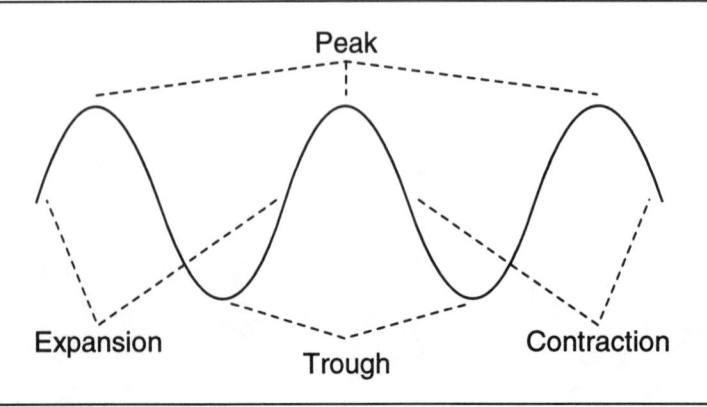

six months (two quarters) or more. It defines a depression as a severe downturn lasting for several years, with unemployment rates greater than 15%.

Although periods of prosperity inevitably are followed by hard times, and hard times in turn yield to prosperity, knowing when the economy is on an upward or a downward slope is not a simple matter. In the normal course of events, some industries or corporations will prosper as others fail. A long-term downward slope will be interrupted by temporary upturns that may or may not signal a return to prosperity, and vice versa. Economists take into account many factors when trying to determine where the economy is in the business cycle. Some of the signs of expansion that an economist will look for include:

- increases in industrial production
- bullish (rising) stock markets
- rising property values
- increased consumer demand for goods and services
- increasing GDP

Downturns in the business cycle tend to be associated with:

- rising numbers of bankruptcies and bond defaults
- higher consumer debt
- bearish (falling) stock markets
- rising inventories (a sign of slackening consumer demand in hard times)
- decreasing GDP

Gross Domestic Product

The annual economic output of a nation (all of the goods and services produced by the people, businesses and government units within it) is known as its *gross domestic product*. The United States' GDP includes personal consumption, government purchases (federal payrolls, defense spending, office supplies, etc.), gross private investment (including new buildings, machinery and inventories), foreign investments in the United States and the total value of exports. In periods of recession, the GDP decreases. During periods of expansion, the GDP increases.

C (Consumption) + **G** (Government spending) + **I** (Gross investment) = **GDP**

When comparing the GDP of one period with the GDP of another, a person must take into account changes in the relative prices of products that have occurred during the intervening time. Economists adjust GDP figures to **constant dollars**, rather than attempting to compare actual dollars. This allows economists and others who use GDP figures to compare the actual purchasing power of the dollars, rather than the dollars themselves. Otherwise, it would be nearly impossible to compare the GDP of recessionary periods (like the 1930s) with that of inflationary periods (like the 1970s).

Price Levels

Inflation. Inflation is a persistent and measurable rise in the general level of prices and generally is associated with periods of expansion and high levels of employment. Inflation itself is not bad, and mild inflation actually encourages economic growth. Gradually increasing prices tend to stimulate business investments, both domestic and foreign, and help maintain full employment and a growing GDP. It is when inflation reaches unacceptably high levels that it is considered detrimental to the economy. High inflation can cause hardships for many, particularly those on fixed incomes.

Increases in the inflation rate tend to drive up the rate of interest on new fixed income securities; this, in turn, drives down the prices of existing debt securities. Decreases in the inflation rate have the opposite effect: as the inflation rate drops, new debt is issued at lower rates and the prices of existing debt rise.

Deflation. Deflation is a persistent and measurable fall in the general level of prices. During periods of deflation, the production of goods and services exceeds the demand for them. Deflation usually occurs during recessions, when unemployment is on the rise.

Consumer Price Index. All prices do not change at the same rate. Some rise or fall more rapidly than others. The most prominent measure of price changes in general is the Consumer Price Index (CPI). The CPI measures the rate of increase or decrease in consumer prices for such things as food, housing, transportation, medical care, clothing, electricity, entertainment and services. The CPI is put out monthly by the U.S. Bureau of Labor Statistics and represents a composite of selected consumer items in selected cities over a one-month period.

Government Economic Policy

The President's and the federal government's policies on taxation and spending make up the country's **fiscal policy**. The government attempts to influence the country's economic health through its powers to tax and spend. The government will make decisions based on its fiscal policy that will have both direct and indirect impacts on aggregate supply and demand.

The Federal Reserve Board's policies on the size, movement and growth of the money supply compose its **monetary policy**. The FRB works through its influence on the banking system, the money supply, bank lending and interest rates. The actions the FRB can take to increase or decrease the money supply are part of its monetary policy.

The Federal Reserve Board and Monetary Policy

Monetary policy determines how the FRB acts to influence the money supply and, consequently, the economy. In 1913, Congress established the Federal Reserve System (Fed) to regulate the U.S. banking system and money supply. The Fed consists of twelve regional Federal Reserve Banks, 24 branch banks and hundreds of national and state banks that belong to the system. Under the direction of the FRB (which consists of seven members appointed by the President of the United States), the Fed performs the following functions:

- acts as an agent of the U.S. Treasury
- regulates the U.S. money supply
- sets reserve requirements for members
- supervises the printing of currency
- clears fund transfers throughout the system
- examines members to ensure their compliance with federal regulations

Indirectly, the FRB determines how much money is available for businesses and consumers to spend and is, therefore, one of the most powerful factors in the U.S. economy. The FRB affects the money supply through its use of three monetary tools:

1. changes in reserve requirements
2. changes in the discount rate (on loans to member banks)
3. open-market operations (buying and selling bonds)

Federal Funds

Commercial banks are required by the Federal Reserve Board to keep on deposit an amount of cash equal to a certain percentage of their depositors' money (called the **reserve requirement**). The term **"federal funds"** commonly is used to describe all money deposited by commercial banks at a Federal Reserve Bank, including any money in excess of the reserve requirement.

When a bank receives deposits or sells securities, that money increases its store of federal funds. When a bank makes loans or buys securities, its store of federal funds decreases. Small banks located away from the nation's money centers tend to have excesses of funds because their business usually involves taking in more money in local consumer deposits than they lend out in mortgages and other consumer loans. These small banks, with their excess federal funds on deposit, are in the position of being able to lend those federal funds.

Large banks located in the nation's money centers tend to send out more money in loans than they take in in deposits, due primarily to the fact that large corporations normally go to these money center banks when they need loans. As a result, large money center banks usually experience a net outflow of cash and have less federal funds than they need. These large banks, with their shortfalls of federal funds, need to borrow additional federal funds.

When a bank falls short of its reserve requirement, it may borrow the excess reserves (federal funds) of another member bank, normally as an overnight loan. Interest on these unsecured, overnight loans is computed at an annualized rate (360-day year) and paid by the borrower to the lender daily. The effective rate of interest is the daily average rate of interest costs as negotiated between the banks through the Federal Reserve System and is called the **federal funds rate**.

The federal funds rate fluctuates daily and is one of this country's most volatile rates. A rising rate usually indicates that member banks are more reluctant to lend their funds and, therefore, want a higher rate of interest in return. A higher rate usually is the result of a shortage of funds to lend and probably indicates that deposits, in general, are shrinking. A falling federal funds rate generally means that the lending banks are in competition to loan money and are trying to make their own loans more attractive by lowering their rates. A lower rate often results from an excess of deposits.

In addition to the effects local deposits and loans have on a bank's federal funds, there often are larger economic forces at work. The Federal Reserve can change the reserve requirement up or down and through this affect the money supply. The Treasury department may issue new securities, and banks may use their reserves to purchase them. Tax payments by individuals and businesses and the movement of money into or out of U.S. government accounts can affect the level of federal funds in reserve. Seasonal economic shifts may be more predictable than other economic factors, but they also affect the level of bank reserves.

Discount Rate

The Fed's second most important tool for affecting the money supply is raising and lowering the **discount rate**—the interest rate the Fed charges its members for certain very short-term loans. If a member has a reserve deficiency, it can borrow funds from its Federal Reserve district bank. This borrowing process is sometimes called *going to the discount window*.

The discount rate tends to remain close to the interest rate on U.S. Treasury bills. When the discount rate is only slightly below the T bill rate, banks that are short on reserves may borrow from the Federal Reserve instead of selling their own securities to meet reserve requirements. *Lowering* the discount rate tends to counteract a recessionary trend by making it easier for banks to increase their reserve funds. *Raising* the discount rate tends to counteract inflation by making it more difficult for member banks to increase their reserves.

Open-market Operations

The Federal Reserve's most important and flexible tool is **open-market operations**. When engaging in open-market operations, the Fed buys and sells U.S. government securities in the open market in order to expand and contract the money supply. The **Federal Open Market Committee (FOMC)** meets monthly to direct the government's open-market operations. The Fed enters its securities trades only with **primary dealers** (about 40 of the nation's largest banks and securities firms).

The Federal Open Market Committee (FOMC) trades U.S. government and agency securities in the secondary market. The FOMC will buy securities to inject reserves into the banks and will sell securities to drain reserves from the banks. This includes securities that are fully backed by the U.S. government, such as Treasury notes and GNMA certificates, and agency securities, such as those issued by the Federal Intermediate Credit Banks (FICBs), as well as some money-market securities such as bankers' acceptances. The Fed does not conduct open market operations with municipal securities.

When credit is tight and the Fed wants to expand (or *loosen*) the money supply, it buys securities. The seller usually is a bank, which receives direct credit in its reserve account. If the seller is not a bank, the Fed writes a check, which eventually is deposited in a commercial bank. This process increases the reserve of the banking system, permitting more loans (and effectively lowering interest rates). Thus, by buying securities, the Fed has pumped money into the banking system, expanding the money supply.

In times of inflation, when the Fed wants to contract (or *tighten*) the money supply, it sells some of its securities. The trade is charged against the buyer's (usually a dealer bank) reserve balance. This reduces the bank's ability to lend money, thereby tightening credit (and effectively raising interest rates). By selling securities, the Fed has pulled money out of the system, contracting the money supply.

When the Fed buys, bank excess reserves go up; when the Fed sells, bank excess reserves go down. When the Fed buys securities, it *expands* the money supply; when the Fed sells securities, it *contracts* the money supply. Because most of these transactions involve next-day payment, the effects on the money supply are immediate—making open-market operations the Fed's most efficient tool.

To expand credit during deflationary periods:	To tighten credit during inflationary periods:
Buy securities in the open market.	Sell securities in the open market.
Lower reserve requirements.	Raise reserve requirements.
Lower the discount rate.	Raise the discount rate.

Fiscal Policy

As the FRB manipulates the economy through monetary policy, the President and Congress attack economic problems through fiscal policy. The term "fiscal" refers to budgets (as in "fiscal year"), and "fiscal policy" refers to governmental budget decisions, which can include increases or decreases in:

- federal spending
- money raised through taxation
- federal budget deficits or surpluses

Fiscal policy is based on the assumption that by using the tools and policies at its disposal, the government can:

- reduce the rate of inflation by reducing aggregate demand for goods and services if price levels are excessive; or
- increase the rate of inflation by increasing aggregate demand if low inflation is causing unemployment and economic stagnation.

Congress uses fiscal policy just as the FRB uses monetary policy to control the severity of fluctuations in the economy. The condition of the economy prompts government intervention, and government actions, in turn, help shape the economy.

The Stock Market

Monetary policies frequently have considerable influence on the stock market. By raising margin requirements, the Federal Reserve Board can restrain speculation in stocks. Even more significant, the FRB's ability to control the money supply can influence stock prices. If the FRB increases the money supply, credit is easier to obtain. As credit becomes easier to obtain, interest rates drop, and lower interest rates tend to encourage bullish stock markets.

Similarly, lowering tax rates may stimulate spending by those individuals or businesses that now find themselves with more of their earnings to spend. Like easier credit, reductions in tax rates fuel bullish speculation in the stock markets. Raising taxes, of course, tends to have the opposite effect by reducing the amount of money available for business and consumer spending or for investment.

Interest Rates

The cost of credit (interest rates) depends on supply and demand. In periods of easy money, when the credit supply exceeds demand, interest rates fall. Conversely, interest rates tend to rise when the FRB is tightening the money supply and demand exceeds supply. By influencing the money supply, the FRB affects interest rates.

In general, decreasing interest rates are indicative of a healthy, stable economy. Increasing interest rates, on the other hand, indicate that economic problems exist. The FRB's actions are watched worldwide and often are used to gauge the health of the U.S. economy as a whole.

Disintermediation

Disintermediation is the flow of money from low-yielding accounts in traditional savings institutions (financial intermediaries) to higher yielding investments in the marketplace. Disintermediation occurs when the FRB tightens the money supply and interest rates rise.

Business Cycles

The power of the FRB to influence interest rates and expand credit has a direct impact on business. Monetary policy helps determine how much money is available for business investments. The FRB's power is considerable, but not absolute. Not all commercial banks are members of the Fed, and the FRB exerts little influence over international banking. Nevertheless, financial analysts, investors and the general public watch the FRB closely, knowing its policies influence business cycles.

Government spending and taxation (fiscal policy) also influence the shape of the business cycle. Increases in government spending, as politicians eagerly tell voters at election time, tend to be inflationary. Money that the government injects into the economy increases the demand for goods and services, thereby driving up prices. Lower government spending, naturally, has the opposite effect, reducing inflation and lowering employment.

11 Investment Recommendations and Taxation

Key Terms

call risk
capital gain
capital loss
capital risk
constant dollar plan
credit risk
dollar cost averaging
earned income
holding period return
legislative risk

liquidity risk
market risk
nonsystematic risk
original issue discount (OID)
passive income
portfolio income
present value
reinvestment risk
systematic risk
wash sale

Overview

Before you can make appropriate recommendations to your customers, you must understand their financial objectives, financial status and their investment constraints. This chapter will explore the different factors that go into making an investment decision and recommendation. Some of these factors are controllable or changeable, some are not. Helping a customer choose investments wisely is very important to any ongoing financial relationship.

Taxes have been levied upon the citizens of states, countries and kingdoms since political organizations began. As these economic and political structures evolved, so have tax structures. This constant development continues today.

Congress continually alters tax laws, and the Internal Revenue Service (IRS) constantly reinterprets those laws. Judicial decisions amend and sometimes reverse existing statutes. Investors tailor decisions to the current tax structures, but must remain flexible enough to change as the laws change. Taxes imposed by states and cities are less imposing than federal taxes. So investors spend more time and energy trying to understand federal taxes and to minimize their impact.

Know Your Customer

Financial Profile

The more you know about your customer's income, current investment portfolio, retirement plans, net worth and other aspects of his current financial situation, the better will be your recommendations. The more your customer knows about the risks and rewards associated with each type of investment, the better will be his investment decisions.

Customer's Balance Sheet

Before you enter the first trade for a new customer, it is important to find out as much about that person's financial status as you can. Individuals, like businesses, have a financial balance sheet—a snapshot of their financial condition at a point in time. You can determine the status of your customer's personal balance sheet by asking questions similar to those in the following list:

- What kinds of assets do you own? Do you own your home? A car? Collectibles? A second home?
- What are your liabilities? Do you make mortgage payments on your home? Do you make car payments? Do you have any other outstanding loans or regular financial commitments?
- Do you own any marketable securities? What types of investments do you currently hold?
- Have you established any long-term investment accounts? Do you have an IRA, a Keogh or a corporate pension or profit-sharing plan? Are you contributing to any annuities? What is the cash value of your life insurance?

Customer's Income Statement

An important part of an individual's financial status is his personal income statement. For many people, this income statement takes the form of a monthly, quarterly or annual budget that measures the person's (or family's) income and outgo. In order to make appropriate investment recommendations, you need to determine what your customer's income statement looks like.

Gather information about your customer's marital status, financial responsibilities, projected inheritances, pending job changes and the like. You can do this by asking questions similar to those in the following list:

- What is your total gross income? What is your total family income? How stable is this income? Do you see major changes taking place over the next few years?
- How much do you pay in expenses each month? Is this a relatively stable figure? Do you anticipate any change in this amount over the next few years?

- What is your net spendable income after expenses? How much of this is available for investment?

Other Financial Elements

After you have gathered information on your customer's personal balance sheet and income statement, you will want to learn:

- whether the person owns his own home;
- how much and what type of insurance he has;
- what his tax bracket is and what changes may occur in it over the next few years; and
- whether he has experienced any credit problems.

Nonfinancial Investment Considerations

Once you have explored your customer's financial status and all of your questions have been answered, you can begin to gather information on his nonfinancial status. These nonfinancial considerations frequently carry more weight than the financial information.

Some of the items you will want to ask your customer about include:

- age
- marital status
- number and ages of dependents
- employment
- employment of family members
- current and future family educational needs
- current and future family health care needs

Finally, no matter how much an analysis of a person's financial status tells you about his ability to invest, it is the customer's emotional acceptance of investing and his motivation to invest that will mold his portfolio. To understand better a customer's aptitude for investment, ask questions similar to the following:

- What kind of risks can you afford to take?
- How liquid must your investments be?
- How important are tax considerations?
- Are you seeking long-term or short-term investments?
- What is your investment experience?
- What types of investments do you currently hold?
- How would you react to a loss of 5% of your principal? 10%? 50%?
- What level of return do you consider good? Poor? Excellent?
- What combination of risks and returns would you feel comfortable with?
- What is your investment temperament?
- Do you get bored with stable investments?
- Can you tolerate market fluctuations?

Customer Investment Outlook

Contrary to what many investment professionals and most customers believe, people have many reasons for investing and many needs that must be met by their investments. By asking appropriate questions of your customers, you can uncover these reasons and needs—an important step because customers often do not know why they choose to invest the way they do. Most customers will claim that they invest so that their money will grow. By careful questioning, however, you may learn that because of tax status, income or other events, some growth investments are appropriate, while others are not.

Some of the basic financial objectives customers may have are discussed in the following sections.

Preservation of capital. For many people, their single most important investment objective is to preserve the capital they have worked so hard to accumulate. A person with this as his most important objective would not be willing to invest in most equity securities, for example. In general, when clients speak of *safety*, they usually mean preservation of capital from losses due to credit, or financial, risk. Financial risk is the danger of losing all or part of the principal amount a person has invested.

Current income. Many investors, particularly retirees and others on fixed incomes, want to generate additional current income from their investments. Corporate bonds, municipal bonds, government and agency securities, income-oriented mutual funds, some stocks (including utilities and real estate investment trusts—REITs), money-market funds, annuities and some direct participation programs (DPPs) are among the investments that can contribute current income through dividend or interest payments.

Capital growth. Growth refers to an increase in the value of an investment over time. This growth can come from increases in the value of the security, the reinvestment of dividends and income, or both. Investors seek growth in order to meet a variety of needs (retirement planning, funding a child's education, travel or a vacation home, to name a few). The most common growth-oriented investments are common stock and stock mutual funds.

Tax advantages. Current tax rates—even though they were raised by the Revenue Reconciliation Act of 1993—are not as high as they once were. Nevertheless, as is always the case, investors seek ways to reduce their taxes. Some products, like individual retirement accounts (IRAs) and annuities, allow interest to accumulate tax deferred (no taxes are paid until the investor withdraws money from the account). Other products, like many municipal bonds, offer tax-free interest income. (The tax advantages of municipal securities may vary depending on the state in which the investor resides.)

Portfolio diversification. An investor may have reasons based on other than personal or financial factors for choosing an investment. Investment professionals frequently encounter investors whose portfolios are concentrated in only one or a few securities or investments. Because such concentrations of investments expose these customers to much higher risks, portfolio diversification becomes an important objective. Typical of these customers are retirees with large profit-sharing distributions of one company's stock and investors with all of their money invested in CDs or U.S. government savings bonds.

Liquidity. Some people want immediate access to their money at all times. A product is liquid if the customer can sell it quickly at face amount (or very close to it) or at a fair market price without losing significant principal. Stock, for example, has varying degrees of liquidity (depending on many factors, including safety, number of shares outstanding and the market's perception of the issuer), while DPPs, annuities and bank CDs generally are considered illiquid. Real estate is the classic example of an illiquid product because of the time and money it takes to convert it into cash.

Speculation. Among the investment objectives a customer might have is the need to speculate—that is, gamble on higher than average returns in exchange for higher than average risks. Speculation is a legitimate investment objective, and most customers would be well advised to place at least some of their investable assets (typically 5% to 25%) in speculative, high-potential-return investments and securities.

Figure 11.1 illustrates the categories used in portfolio diversification.

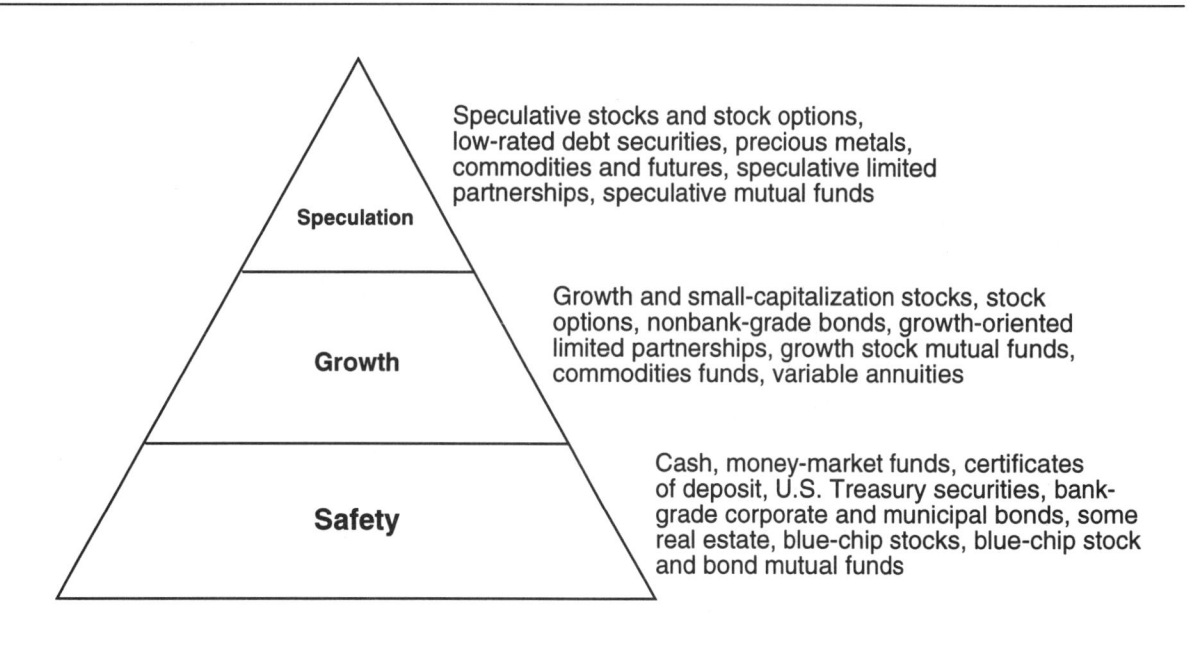

Figure 11.1 The Investment Pyramid

- **Speculation**: Speculative stocks and stock options, low-rated debt securities, precious metals, commodities and futures, speculative limited partnerships, speculative mutual funds
- **Growth**: Growth and small-capitalization stocks, stock options, nonbank-grade bonds, growth-oriented limited partnerships, growth stock mutual funds, commodities funds, variable annuities
- **Safety**: Cash, money-market funds, certificates of deposit, U.S. Treasury securities, bank-grade corporate and municipal bonds, some real estate, blue-chip stocks, blue-chip stock and bond mutual funds

Analyzing Financial Risks and Rewards

Suitability

Because all investments involve trade-offs, the task of the registered rep or investment advisor is to select securities that will provide the right balance between investor characteristics on the one hand and investment capabilities on the other.

Selecting suitable investments to meet investor needs is both an art and a science. The process is too complex to computerize; even the most sophisticated and expensive financial plans are only partially based on a computerized model. In the final analysis, recommending investments requires the finest computer in existence: the human brain. As an investment adviser, one of your key tasks is to recommend suitable investments that best match your clients' unique characteristics.

Unsuitable Trades

Occasionally a customer will ask a registered rep to enter a trade for a corporate security that the rep feels is unsuitable. It is the rep's responsibility to discuss the trade with the customer, and explain why that particular trade might not be suitable. If the customer insists on entering the transaction, the registered rep should have the customer sign a statement acknowledging that the rep recommended against the trade, and the rep should mark the order ticket "unsolicited." In any event, the account belongs to the investor to do with as he pleases—while the rep may attempt to counsel the customer against unsuitable trades, the customer has the right to enter into any transaction he chooses and to be given good service on all transactions.

Investment Risks

In general terms, the greater the risk assumed by the investor, the greater the potential for reward. There are several risks to consider in determining the suitability of various types of investments when building a financial portfolio.

Inflation Risk

Also known as **purchasing power risk**, inflation risk measures the effects of continually rising prices on investments. If an investment's yield is lower than the rate of inflation, the client's money will have less purchasing power as time goes on. A client who buys a bond or a fixed annuity may be able to purchase far less with the invested funds when the investment matures.

Capital Risk

Capital risk is the potential for an investor to lose all of her money or capital under circumstances unrelated to the financial strength of the issuer. For example, when options expire out-of-the-money, buyers lose all of their capital (the cost of the premium) even though the underlying security may be solvent.

Selection Risk

When all other factors have been accounted for and an investor chooses (or has recommended to her) an investment, there is always the possibility that the choice will be a poor one. Even when an industry is expected to outperform the market and an investment in a company within that industry seems to be a sure thing, the company chosen might be the one company that files for protection under bankruptcy laws. This is known as **selection risk**.

Timing Risk

As in most encounters with today's world, timing is everything. Even an investment in the soundest company with the most profit potential might do poorly simply because the investment was timed wrong. The risk to an investor of buying or selling at the wrong time and incurring losses or lower gains is known as **timing risk**.

Interest Rate Risk

Interest rate risk is associated with investments relating to the sensitivity of price or value to fluctuation in the current level of interest rates; it is also the risk that involves the competitive cost of money. This term is generally associated with bond prices, but it applies to all investments. In bonds, the price carries an interest risk because if bond prices rise, outstanding bonds will not remain competitive unless their yields and prices are adjusted to reflect the current market.

Reinvestment Risk

Because bond investors typically seek a steady flow of income, they risk not being able to reinvest their interest income or principal at the same rate. This is known as **reinvestment risk** and is of particular concern during periods of falling interest rates. If interest rates decline, it is extremely difficult for bond investors to maintain the same level of current income without increasing their credit or market risks. Zero-coupon bonds are not susceptible to reinvestment risk because periodic interest payments have been eliminated.

Market Risk

Both stocks and bonds involve some degree of **market risk**—that is, the risk that investors may lose some of their principal due to price volatility in the market. Stocks tend to be more volatile than bonds; stock prices can rise or fall dramatically due to changing investor demand.

Prices of existing bonds can fluctuate with changing interest rates. There is an inverse relationship between bond prices and bond yields: as bond yields go up, bond prices go down (and vice versa). In order to maintain a competitive yield, the market price of existing bonds drops as new bonds are issued with higher coupon rates.

All things being equal, deep discount bonds are more responsive to changes in market yields than bonds selling at par or at a premium. Compared to other bonds, deep discount bonds tend to appreciate faster as interest rates fall and drop faster as interest rates rise. The most deeply discounted bonds (zero-coupon bonds) are the most susceptible to market risk. Of course, clients will receive face value for their bonds at maturity. If they should sell their bonds before maturity, however, they risk losing some of their principal. This particularly affects clients who invest in bonds with long maturities. They have stable income, but risk losing some principal if they sell the bonds before maturity. Furthermore, if interest rates rise considerably after a bond is issued, the holder may be stuck with a low interest rate until the bond matures, which may be in 20 years.

For bonds with short maturities, the opposite is true. Their price remains fairly stable because investors generally will not sell them at deep discounts or buy them at high premiums. A client's income from short maturities, however, will vary with prevailing interest rates.

Credit Risk

Credit risk (also called **financial risk** or **default risk**) involves the danger of losing all or part of one's invested principal through failure of the issuer. Credit risk varies with the investment product. Bonds backed by the federal government or municipalities tend to be very secure and have low credit risk. Long-term bonds involve more credit risk than short-term bonds because of the increased uncertainty that results from holding bonds for many years. Preferred stocks generally are safer than common stocks. Mutual funds offer increased safety through diversification. On the other hand, penny stocks, nonbank-grade bonds and some options positions can be quite risky, yet right for some customers.

Bond investors concerned about credit risks should pay attention to the ratings. Two of the best known rating services that analyze the financial strength of thousands of corporate and municipal issuers are Moody's Investors Service and Standard & Poor's Corporation. To a great extent, the value of a bond depends on how much credit risk investors are taking. The higher the rating, the less likely the bond is to default and, therefore, the lower the coupon rate. Clients seeking the highest possible yield from bonds might want to buy bonds with lower ratings. The higher yields are a reward for taking more credit risks.

Liquidity Risk

The risk that a client might not be able to liquidate her investment at a time when she needs cash is known as **liquidity** (or **marketability) risk**. The marketability of the securities you recommend must be related directly to the client's liquidity needs. Government bonds, for instance, are marketed easily; on the other hand, DPPs are illiquid and extremely difficult to market. Municipal securities have a regional rather than a national market; therefore, they may be less marketable than more widely held securities.

Legislative Risk

Congress has the power to change existing laws affecting securities. The risk that such a change in law might affect an investment adversely is known as **legislative risk**. For example, by changing the tax consequences of passive income from DPPs, Congress affected the viability of many deep tax shelter programs. Similarly, a client who goes short against the box to postpone capital gains might be disappointed if Congress changes the taxation of such gains. When recommending suitable investments, you should warn clients of any pending changes in the law that may affect those investments.

Call Risk

Related to reinvestment risk, **call risk** is the risk that a bond might be called before maturity and investors will be unable to reinvest their principal at the same (or a higher) rate of return. When interest rates are falling, bonds with higher coupon rates are most likely to be called. Thus, investors will lose their steady stream of income. Investors concerned about call risk should look for call protection—a period of time during which a bond cannot be called. Most corporate and municipal issuers generally provide some years of call protection.

Analyzing Investment Returns

Regardless of whether an investor is pursuing aggressive investment strategies (those that entail high levels of risk in return for potential high rewards) or defensive investment strategies (those that emphasize preservation of capital and guaranteed returns), the key question remains: What returns have been made on the investment in securities?

Holding period return. The easiest (and most misleading) method is to compute the holding period rate of return. This involves calculating the total return from capital gains and dividend income without taking into consideration how long the investment was held. For example, assume an investor bought 100 shares of stock at $10 per share, sold them for $15 and received $100 in dividends. This is a 60% total return ($500 capital gains + $100 dividend income ÷ $1,000 initial investment = 60%).

A 60% return is fine if the holding period is a year or less. But if this investment were held for ten years or more, a 60% return would not be that impressive. (The investor might do better in a bank savings account, at 5 1/4% interest, offering guaranteed safety of principal and full liquidity.) Thus, the holding period return can be misleading because it fails to take into account the time value of money.

Present value. The concept of present value is based on the time value of money. Receiving a dollar today is preferable to receiving a dollar at some future date. Present value calculates today's value of a future payment or stream of payments, discounted at a given compound interest rate. For example, assume that a customer is offered a zero-coupon bond maturing in one year at $1,000. What price should the customer pay for the bond? Certainly not $1,000. Assume that the interest rate for this type of security is 5%. The price the customer would pay would be $1,000 divided by 1.05, or $952.38. This is the bond's present value.

Internal rate of return. A related concept is the internal rate of return (IRR). This theoretical investment value is most commonly used to calculate the potential return from an investment. The IRR is the discount rate at which the present value of future cash flows of an investment equals the cost of that investment. It is found by trial and error. When the present value of cash outflows (costs) equals cash inflows (returns), the investment is valued at the IRR and there will be no profits. When the IRR is greater than the investor's required rate of return, the investment is acceptable.

Portfolio Analysis

Portfolio Management Strategies

A **portfolio** is an individual's or business's combined holdings of stocks, bonds, cash equivalents, packaged investment products and other investment securities. Most portfolios are built over time, and their compositions change as purchases and sales of the underlying securities are made. By its very nature, a portfolio of securities offers the investor **diversification**.

Many things can influence the makeup of a portfolio, including both personal and market factors. An investor's portfolio changes as he grows older and his investment needs change. A portfolio of securities appropriate for a 25-year-old unmarried man may not be appropriate for a 45-year-old married man with two children in college or a 65-year-old woman facing retirement. Similarly, a portfolio built during a recessionary period with safety- and income-oriented bonds may be inappropriate at a later date when the economy is experiencing inflation and stocks are showing healthy growth.

Aggressive Investment Strategies

Investors willing to take risks with their capital in order to maximize the returns on their investment portfolios adopt what are known as *aggressive* investment strategies. Aggressive investors place a high percentage of their investable assets in equity securities in the belief that the stock markets will provide the best growth opportunities. These investors keep a much lower percentage in safer debt securities and cash equivalents that provide lower returns. Aggressive investors pursue aggressive policies to buy and sell securities, including:

- selecting stocks with high betas
- buying securities on margin
- using put and call option strategies
- employing arbitrage techniques

Defensive Investment Strategies

Not all investors are financially and temperamentally able to withstand the risks that accompany aggressive strategies. These investors are more likely to adopt *defensive* investment strategies in making their investment decisions. Defensive investors are willing to accept potentially lower total returns in order to minimize investment risk and preserve their capital. Investors who apply defensive strategies to their portfolios place a high percentage of their investable capital in bonds, cash equivalents and stocks that are likely to fare well in recessionary times, including stocks in energy, food, pharmaceuticals and other defensive industries.

Balanced Investment Strategies

Most investors adopt a combination of aggressive and defensive strategies when making decisions about the securities in their portfolios. A **balanced** (or **mixed**) **portfolio** will have securities of many types in it, including bonds, stocks, packaged products and cash equivalents. An investor who creates a balanced portfolio will have securities that provide a hedge against the market no matter what its course.

Modern Portfolio Theory

Modern portfolio theory is a fairly sophisticated approach to choosing investments that allows investors to quantify and control the amount of risk they accept and return they achieve in their portfolios. It differs from traditional securities analysis in that it shifts the emphasis away from analyzing the specific securities in the portfolio to determining the relationship between risk and reward in the total portfolio.

Systematic and Nonsystematic Risk

When investing in equity and debt securities, clients risk losing some of their principal due to fluctuations in market value. Analysts distinguish between **systematic risk** (risk common to all stocks or bonds) and **nonsystematic risk** (risk specific to a particular stock or bond).

Systematic risk. The tendency for security prices to move together is known as systematic risk. Investors who hold securities in their portfolio cannot avoid this risk, not even through diversification. In bull markets, the prices of individual securities tend to rise with the market. In bear markets, the prices of individual securities tend to decline, regardless of the financial condition of the company that issued the security.

Nonsystematic risk. Nonsystematic risk is associated with the underlying investment itself. Strikes, natural disasters, operating losses and many other factors may cause an individual security's price to decline when the market as a whole is rising. And the introduction of a new product line or an attempted takeover may cause an individual security to rise even when the market is declining. The larger and more diversified an investor's portfolio, the less subject it is to nonsystematic risk.

Risk Management Techniques

Diversification. While investors can do little to avoid systematic risk or inflation, they can temper nonsystematic risk. One important investment strategy is diversification. A portfolio can be diversified in many ways, including:

- type of instrument (equity, debt, packaged and so on)
- industry

- companies within an industry
- length of maturity
- investment rating
- geography

By mixing industries and types of assets, investors spread their risk. A particular event (deregulation of the airline industry, for example) will have less impact if an investor's portfolio consists of a wide assortment of securities than if the investor buys only airline stock.

Dollar cost averaging. A common defensive technique investors use to manage the risk in their portfolios is dollar cost averaging. To apply a dollar cost averaging strategy, an investor makes periodic purchases of a fixed dollar amount in one or more common stocks or mutual funds. In a fluctuating market, the average *cost* of the stock purchased in this manner is always less than the average market *price*. Dollar cost averaging is not a guarantee that the investor will not suffer a loss (and it would be fraudulent for a registered rep to imply so), but it does help control the cost of investing.

Constant ratio plan. The strategy behind a constant ratio plan is that securities should be bought and sold in such a manner as to keep the portfolio balanced between equity and debt securities. The investor initially sets an equity-to-debt ratio (as an example, 60% equity to 40% debt). Purchases and sales are then made as necessary to maintain the ratio between debt and equity securities.

Constant dollar plan. An often used defensive strategy is the constant dollar plan. This strategy's primary goal is to buy and sell securities so that a set dollar amount remains invested at all times. As an example of a constant dollar plan strategy, assume that a customer wants to keep her portfolio at a constant level of $100,000. Under a constant dollar plan, if the value of her portfolio reaches $110,000, the investor will liquidate $10,000 worth of securities. Conversely, if her portfolio slips to $95,000, she will buy $5,000 worth of securities. This forces the investor to sell when the market is high and buy when it is low.

By employing this technique, the client is selling as prices rise and buying as prices fall. A problem with this strategy is that in an extended bull market, the investor keeps liquidating more and more equities to stay at the constant dollar level. By doing so, she may not be taking advantage of the bull stock market.

Federal and State Taxation

Income Taxes

Federal income taxes are imposed on three types of income: earned, passive and portfolio.

Earned income. Earned income includes salary, bonuses and income derived from active participation in a trade or business.

Passive income. Passive income and losses come from rental property, limited partnerships and enterprises (regardless of business structure) in which the individual is not actively involved. For the general partner, income from a limited partnership is earned income; for the limited partner, such income is passive. Passive income is netted against passive losses in order to determine net taxable income.

TRA 1986 made a significant change in the treatment of passive losses from such investments. Passive losses may be used to offset passive income only.

Portfolio income. Portfolio income includes dividends, interest and net capital gains derived from the sale of securities. No matter what the source of the income, it is taxed in the year in which it is received.

Individual Federal Income Taxes

The basic design of the tax return is:

	Earned income
plus	Passive income (net against passive losses)
plus	Interest and dividends
plus/minus	Net capital gains/losses
	Adjusted gross income (AGI)
minus	Itemized deductions
minus	Standard deductions
minus	Personal exemptions
	Taxable income
times	Tax rate
	Tax liability

Income Tax Brackets

Personal income tax rates have tended to change in recent years as successive administrations lower and raise taxes. Recent tax rates have been 15%, 28%, 31% and 36%.

Actually, the rates are more complex than this. U.S. income tax tables are structured so that successively earned portions of one's income are taxed at progressively higher rates. For example, assume that a married couple filing jointly has a taxable income of $45,000 and that currently the cutoff between the two lowest tax brackets is $38,000. Then the couple would pay 15% on the first $38,000 of income and 28% on the remaining $7,000. Remember that these are hypothetical numbers and that the actual numbers change yearly because the tax brackets are indexed to inflation.

In addition, various surcharges and special taxes have been adopted by Congress that are designed to shift more of the federal tax burden to those in the highest income brackets. With these surcharges, some individuals pay up to an effective 39.6% tax rate.

Taxation and Investment Portfolios

Interest Income

Interest paid on debt securities is income to the bondholder. It may or may not be taxable, depending on the type of security. Based on the **doctrine of mutual reciprocity**, there is a reciprocal agreement between governments. The federal government does not tax state and municipal issues. In turn, state and local governments usually do not tax federal securities. Furthermore, the debt obligations of U.S. territories and political subdivisions (Puerto Rico, Guam, the Virgin Islands) are fully exempt from all taxation.

Corporate bonds. Interest income on corporate bonds is taxable by federal, state and some local governments.

U.S. government securities. Interest income on direct federal debt is exempt from state and local taxes, but is federally taxable. Direct debt includes U.S. Treasury bills, notes and bonds. The interest on T bills is the difference between the purchase price (below par) and the sale or maturity price.

Agency obligations. The interest income on most federal agency debt, like that on Treasury securities, is taxable by the federal government but is exempt from state and local taxes. However, some agency issues are fully taxable at all levels; these include:

- mortgage-backed securities of the Government National Mortgage Association (GNMA—Ginnie Maes);
- securities issued by the Federal National Mortgage Association (FNMA—Fannie Maes); and
- securities of the Inter-American Development Bank (IADB).

Tax-exempt Interest Income

Municipal securities. Interest on municipal bonds issued before August 7, 1986, and on municipal bonds with a public purpose issued after that date is exempt from federal taxes. Furthermore, interest from municipal obligations of U.S. territories (Puerto Rico, Guam, the Virgin Islands) is exempt from federal, state and local taxes.

Interest on a municipal bond or note may or may not be taxable for residents of the state in which the bond or note is issued. The tax status of municipal securities

Dividend Income

Dividend income received from stocks and mutual funds is taxed in the same manner as interest income received from debt securities.

Dividend income from mutual funds. Under Subchapter M of the Internal Revenue Code (IRC), a **regulated investment company** may gain exemption from taxation on income if 90% of that income is passed on to shareholders. Owners of mutual fund shares receive **dividend checks** that represent the pass-through of dividends and interest earned on the underlying portfolio. The tax consequences depend on what types of securities are in the underlying portfolio.

- Municipal bond mutual funds or unit investment trusts (UITs) distribute federally tax-free dividends to shareholders.
- Dividend distributions from taxable mutual funds (for example, a corporate bond fund or stock fund) are taxable in the year they are received by the investor. Reinvested dividends are considered constructively received and also are taxable in the year they are distributed.

Taxable on Receipt

Interest and dividends are taxable only in the year they are *received*. Investors do not owe taxes on dividends or interest declared or accrued until the year in which they actually receive the money.

Capital Gains (and Losses)

The sale of capital assets (securities, real estate and all tangible property) can result in a capital gain or a capital loss. A capital gain occurs when the difference between a capital asset's purchase price and its selling price is positive. If the difference is negative, it is a capital loss. Capital gains and losses are considered to have occurred in the year in which the trade date falls. For tax purposes, trades that occur at the end of the year but that settle in the next year are counted as having occurred in the trade year.

Adjusting Cost Basis

The cost basis of an investment is used to determine whether there is a taxable gain or tax-deductible loss when the asset is sold. Because many things affect the cost basis of an asset, the IRS allows the cost basis to be adjusted for such things as stock splits and stock dividends.

Capital gains. A capital gain occurs when capital assets (securities, real estate and tangible property) are sold at prices that exceed the adjusted cost basis. Usually, computing the capital gain or loss on an asset is a simple matter of comparing the purchase price with the selling price (less commissions).

Figure 11.2 Wash Sale Rule

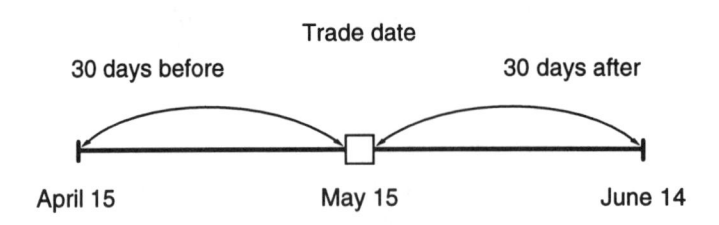

```
           30 days before    Trade date    30 days after

           |‾‾‾‾‾‾‾‾‾‾‾‾‾‾‾‾‾‾‾‾‾‾‾□‾‾‾‾‾‾‾‾‾‾‾‾‾‾‾‾‾‾‾‾|
              April 15         May 15          June 14
```

Capital losses. A capital loss occurs when capital assets are sold at prices that are less than the adjusted cost basis.

Net capital gains and losses. To calculate tax liability, taxpayers must first add all capital gains for the year. Then, they separately add all capital losses. Finally, they offset the totals to determine the net capital gain or loss for the year. If the result is a net capital gain, it is fully taxable at the same rate as earned income (up to a maximum rate of 28%). Net capital losses are deductible against earned income to a maximum of $3,000 per year. Any capital losses not deducted in a taxable year may be carried forward indefinitely to lower taxable income in future years.

Determining which shares to sell. An investor holding identical securities with different acquisition dates and different cost bases may determine which shares to sell. The IRS presumes that the first securities purchased are the first sold (first in, first out—FIFO) unless the investor specifically instructs otherwise.

Wash sales. Capital losses may not be used to offset gains or income if the investor sells a security at a loss and purchases the same (or a substantially identical) security within 30 days before or after the trade date establishing the loss. The sale at a loss and the repurchase within this period is a **wash sale**. (See Figure 11.2).

Substantially identical securities include stock rights, call options, the sale of short-term deep in-the-money puts, warrants and convertible securities of the same issue. The IRS compares three qualities of debt securities in determining whether they are substantially identical: the maturity, coupon and issuer. The bond is substantially identical if all three qualities of the bond sold at a loss and the newly purchased bond are the same.

The wash sale rule applies only to realized losses; it does not apply to realized gains. An investor may sell a stock to realize a gain and immediately repurchase it to reestablish her position.

Bonds Purchased at a Discount

Original issue discount. When corporate or municipal bonds are issued at a discount, it is normally because the coupon rate is not competitive with yields available on similar securities. The investor considers the difference between the discounted purchase price and the par value he will receive at maturity as additional income. If an **original issue discount (OID)** bond is sold before it matures, the cost basis of the bond is adjusted by **accreting** the amount of the discount annually as determined by the issuer (normally on a straight-line basis). If an OID bond is held until maturity, 100% of the discount will have been accreted and the investor will have no taxable capital gain.

Secondary market discount. The cost basis of a bond bought at a discount in the secondary market is not adjusted. If the bond is held to maturity, the investor will realize a capital gain. If the bond is sold again in the secondary market, the gain or loss is determined by the difference between the bond's purchase price and sale price.

Margin Expenses

Interest paid for securities margin loans is a tax-deductible expense. The one exception is interest expenses incurred in the purchase of municipal securities. Because the interest income is federally tax exempt, the IRS will not allow taxpayers to claim deductions for the interest expense on municipal securities.

Investors can deduct interest expenses for other securities to the extent they do not exceed their net investment income, which includes interest income, dividends and all capital gains.

◆ Review Questions

1. Which of the following characteristics best define(s) the term "growth"?

   A. Increase in the value of an investment over time
   B. Increase in principal and accumulating interest and dividends over time
   C. Investments that appreciate tax deferred
   D. All of the above

2. Credit risk involves

   A. safety of principal
   B. fluctuations in overall interest rates
   C. the danger of not being able to sell the investment at a fair market price
   D. inflationary risks

3. Which of the following investments is LEAST appropriate for a client who is primarily concerned with liquidity?

   A. Preferred stock
   B. Municipal bond mutual funds
   C. Bank savings accounts
   D. Direct participation programs

4. Bondholders face the risk that the value of their bonds may fall as interest rates rise. This is known as

   A. credit risk
   B. reinvestment risk
   C. marketability risk
   D. market risk

5. Which of the following constitutes a constant dollar plan?

   A. 60% equities, 40% fixed-income investments
   B. 40% equities, 60% fixed-income investments
   C. Fixed amount in the portfolio regardless of market price
   D. Fixed amount in fixed-income investments regardless of market price

6. Which of the following bonds are totally tax exempt?

   A. Hawaii GO bonds
   B. U.S. government bonds
   C. Puerto Rico GO bonds
   D. U.S. Steel bonds

7. Max Leveridge invests $5,000 in the following new issue:

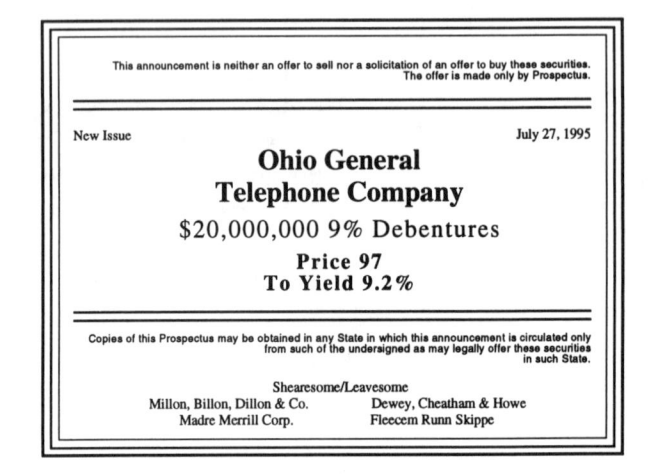

   > This announcement is neither an offer to sell nor a solicitation of an offer to buy these securities.
   > The offer is made only by Prospectus.
   >
   > New Issue   July 27, 1995
   >
   > **Ohio General
   > Telephone Company**
   >
   > $20,000,000 9% Debentures
   > Price 97
   > To Yield 9.2%
   >
   > Copies of this Prospectus may be obtained in any State in which this announcement is circulated only from such of the undersigned as may legally offer these securities in such State.
   >
   > Shearesome/Leavesome
   > Millon, Billon, Dillon & Co.   Dewey, Cheatham & Howe
   > Madre Merrill Corp.   Fleecem Runn Skippe

   The bonds are

   A. federal and state tax exempt
   B. state tax exempt
   C. federal and state tax exempt if purchased by an Ohio resident
   D. fully taxable

8. Income from all of the following securities is fully taxable at the federal, state and local levels EXCEPT

   A. Ginnie Maes
   B. Treasury bonds
   C. reinvested mutual fund dividends
   D. IADB securities

◆ Answers & Rationale

1. **A.** "Growth" refers to an increase in the value of an investment over time. This growth can come from increases in the value of the security, the reinvestment of dividends and income, or both.

2. **A.** Credit risk (also called *financial risk* or *default risk*) involves the danger of losing all or part of one's invested principal through failure of the issuer.

3. **D.** Direct participation programs or limited partnerships are illiquid investments because there is no immediate market for them.

4. **D.** Prices of existing bonds can fluctuate with changing interest rates. There is an inverse relationship between bond prices and bond yields: as bond yields go up, bond prices go down (and vice versa).

5. **C.** The primary goal of a constant dollar plan strategy is to buy and sell securities so that a fixed dollar amount remains invested at all times.

6. **C.** Puerto Rico GO bonds are exempt from federal, state and local taxes.

7. **D.** Ohio General Telephone Company bonds are corporate bonds, which are fully taxable.

8. **B.** Treasury bonds are not taxed at the state level.

12 Investment Company Products

Key Terms

ask price
asset allocation fund
balanced fund
bid price
bond fund
breakpoint
closed-end investment company
combination fund
diversification
dual-purpose fund
expense ratio
face-amount certificate (FAC)
family of funds
fixed dollar plan
growth fund
income fund

management company
money-market fund
mutual fund
nondiversified company
open-end investment company
preferred stock fund
publicly traded fund
sales load
75-5-10 test
specialized (sector) fund
tax-free bond fund
U.S. government fund
underwriting group
unit investment trust (UIT)
withdrawal plan

Overview

An investment company is a *corporation* or a *trust* through which individuals can invest in a large, diversified portfolio of securities by pooling their funds with other investors' funds. By investing through an investment company, individuals can gain some of the advantages large investors enjoy (diversification of investments, lower transaction costs, professional management and more) that the smaller investor might not otherwise be able to achieve.

This chapter describes the different types of investment companies and the distinguishing characteristics of each. The areas that will be highlighted include:

- how they are established and governed
- how they are structured
- what features and corresponding benefits they offer investors

Investment Company Offerings

An investment company is in the business of pooling investors' money and investing in securities for them. The management of an investment company attempts to invest and manage funds for people more effectively than the individual investors could themselves (given the limited time, knowledge of various securities markets and resources that most investors have). Investment companies operate and invest these pooled funds as a single large account jointly owned by every shareholder in the company.

The Investment Company Act of 1940

During the early decades of this century, Congress directed the Securities and Exchange Commission (SEC) to study investment trusts and investment companies, their corporate structure, their investment policies and their influence on the companies in which they invest. This study led to the passage of the Investment Company Act of 1940, providing for SEC regulation of investment companies and their activities. In declaring the necessity for federal legislation, the act of 1940 states:

"... investment companies are affected with a national public interest in that:

- the securities they issue constitute a significant percentage of all securities publicly offered;
- their process of issuing redeemable securities and their redemption of those securities is continuous; and
- the investing, reinvesting and trading of investment companies constitutes a significant percentage of all transactions in the securities markets of the nation."

Investment Company Purpose

Like corporate issuers, investment companies raise capital by selling shares to the public. Investment companies must abide by the same registration and prospectus requirements imposed by the Securities Act of 1933 on every other issuer, plus more. Because of what investment companies do with the capital they raise, they are subject to stringent regulations regarding the manner, means, methods and conditions under which their shares are sold to the public, which is the subject of the Investment Company Act of 1940, as amended.

Investment companies have one thing in common: they are all **portfolio intermediaries** in the business of pooling the public's money and investing it for them. In the public's mind, an investment company's portfolio managers should be able to outperform the average investor in the market, which is one of the reasons people invest in these managed funds.

Types of Investment Companies

The Investment Company Act of 1940 classifies investment companies into three broad types: face-amount certificate companies (FACs); unit investment trusts (UITs); and management investment companies, which are the most common. The various classifications of investment company are shown in Figure 12.1.

Face-amount Certificate Companies

A face-amount certificate is a contract between an investor and an issuer in which the issuer guarantees a payment of a **stated** (or **fixed**) sum to the investor at some set date in the future. In return for this future payment, the investor agrees to pay the issuer a set amount of money either as a lump sum or in periodic installments. If the investor chooses to pay for the certificate in a lump sum, the investment is known as a **fully paid face-amount certificate**. Issuers of these investments are called, naturally enough, face-amount certificate companies.

Figure 12.1   Classifications of Investment Company

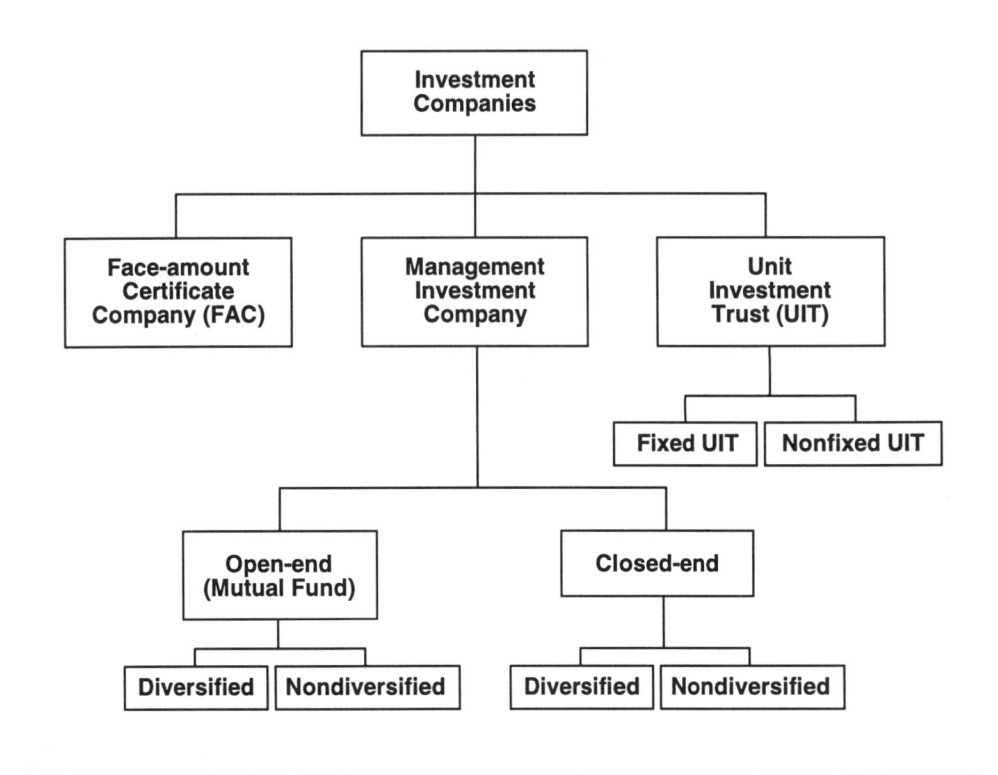

```
                    Investment
                    Companies
                        |
        ----------------+----------------
        |               |                |
   Face-amount     Management          Unit
   Certificate    Investment       Investment
   Company (FAC)   Company         Trust (UIT)
                       |                |
                       |          ------+------
                       |          |           |
                       |      Fixed UIT   Nonfixed UIT
                       |
              ---------+---------
              |                 |
          Open-end          Closed-end
         (Mutual Fund)
              |                 |
         -----+-----        ----+----
         |         |        |       |
    Diversified Nondiversified Diversified Nondiversified
```

Face-amount certificates may be backed by specific assets, such as U.S. government issues, VA and FHA mortgages, corporate debt issues or preferred stock. Usually, however, they are backed by bonds that mature when the certificates mature. In either case, principal and interest are guaranteed. When the value of the certificates is paid to the investor at maturity, the investment fund is exhausted.

Face-amount certificate companies continuously offer their shares (or investment contracts). A typical face-amount certificate contract will require the investor to make 20 semiannual payments of $1,000 each over a period of ten years (for a total investment of $20,000). In return, the company will guarantee that, at the end of ten years, it will return to the investor $25,000. Very few face-amount certificate companies operate today because of tax code changes.

Unit Investment Trusts

A UIT is an investment company organized under a trust indenture. The primary characteristics that set UITs apart from other types of investment companies are that UITs:

- do not have a board of directors
- do not employ an investment adviser
- do not actively manage their own portfolios (trade securities)

A UIT functions basically as a holding company for its investors. The managers of a UIT typically purchase an investment portfolio, consisting of other investment company shares or of fixed-income securities (such as government or municipal bonds). They then sell redeemable shares (also known as **units** or **shares of beneficial interest**) in this portfolio of securities. Each share represents the ownership of an *undivided interest* in the underlying portfolio. Since UITs are not managed, once any of the securities in the portfolio are sold, mature, or are otherwise liquidated, the proceeds must be distributed. Remember, UITs are organized without boards of directors and investment advisers; therefore, they are not able to reinvest proceeds or otherwise manage the trust's portfolio.

A UIT may be fixed or nonfixed. A typical fixed UIT may purchase a portfolio of bonds. When the bonds in the portfolio have matured, the trust is terminated. The nonfixed UIT is often used by investors interested in purchasing units on a contractual basis (a *contractual plan*). The trust may purchase shares of an underlying mutual fund for the nonfixed UIT portfolio.

Under the act of 1940, the trustee of a UIT is required to maintain a secondary market in the units, thus guaranteeing a measure of liquidity to the shareholders.

Management Companies

The most familiar type of investment company, to most people, is the **management company**. Management companies actively *manage* a portfolio of securities in accordance with the investment objectives stated in their prospectuses. The single most important distinction between different types of management companies is their status as either *closed-end* or *open-end*. Both closed- and open-end companies sell shares to the public; the difference between them lies in the type of securities they sell and where investors buy and sell their shares.

Closed-end Investment Companies

As with many corporations, when a closed-end investment company wants to raise capital for investments, it conducts a stock offering. For the initial offering, the company registers a fixed number of shares with the SEC and makes these shares available to the public for a limited time through an **underwriting group** (the broker-dealers chosen to handle the distribution). When all of the shares that the investment company has registered to sell have been distributed by the underwriters, the public offering period comes to a close. The fund's capitalization is basically fixed (unless an additional issue public offering is made).

Closed-end investment companies are more commonly known as **publicly traded funds**. After the stock is distributed, anyone who wants to buy or sell shares does so in the secondary market (either on an exchange or OTC). Supply and demand determine the price the investor will receive or will have to pay for shares. The **bid** price (or price at which an investor can sell) and the **ask** price (or price at which an investor can buy) for the shares of many larger investment companies are published daily in the financial pages of most major newspapers; these bid and ask prices reflect the open market's current valuation of their shares.

Open-end Investment Companies

An **open-end** investment company (or **mutual fund**), unlike the closed-end company, does not specify the exact number of shares it intends to sell; rather, it registers an open offering with the SEC. With this type of registration, the open-end investment company can raise an unlimited amount of investment capital by continuously selling new shares in its portfolio of investments. By the same token, when investors liquidate their holdings in a mutual fund, the fund's capital shrinks. Because the number of shares the company can offer is not limited, the offering in effect never "closes." Any person who wants to make an investment in—or increase his holdings in—the company buys shares directly from the company or its underwriters at the public offering price (net asset value plus a sales charge).

The shares that an open-end investment company sells fall into a special category known as **redeemable securities**. Instead of buying and selling shares on the open market (like the investors in a closed-end company), investors place their orders directly with the investment company's underwriters (broker-dealers). When investors choose to sell their shares, the company itself redeems them at their net asset value (NAV). For each share an investor sells back (or redeems) the company will send the investor her proportionate share of the company's net assets.

Table 12.1 provides a comparison of open-end and closed-end management companies.

Diversified and Nondiversified

Diversified. In the mutual fund business, advertising the fact that the fund is an open-end diversified management company is an important selling point. Diversification is a combination risk management technique and investment approach that makes mutual funds popular with many investors. But not all management companies feature diversified portfolios.

Table 12.1   Open-end vs. Closed-end Management Companies

Characteristic	Open-end	Closed-end
Capitalization	Unlimited; continuous offering of shares.	Fixed; single offering of shares.
Issues	Common stock only; no debt securities; permitted to borrow.	May issue common, preferred and debt securities.
Shares	Full or fractional shares.	Full shares only.
Offerings and trading	Sold and redeemed by the fund only. Continuous primary offering. Must redeem shares.	Initial primary offering. Secondary trading OTC or on an exchange. Does not redeem shares.
Pricing	NAV plus sales charge. Selling price is determined by a formula found in the prospectus.	CMV plus commission. Price is determined by supply and demand.
Shareholder rights	Dividends (when declared), voting.	Dividends (when declared), voting, preemptive.
Ex-date	Set by the board of directors.	Set by the exchange or the NASD.

Under the Investment Company Act of 1940, a management company will qualify as a diversified investment company if it meets the following **75-5-10** test:

- *75%* of total assets must be invested in securities issued by companies *other than the investment company itself* or its affiliates. Cash on hand and cash equivalent investments (short-term government and money market securities) are counted as part of the 75% required investment in outside companies.
- No more than *5%* of total assets can be invested *in any one corporation's* securities.
- No more than *10%* of an outside corporation's *voting class securities* (common stock) can be owned by the management company.

Figure 12.2 illustrates how a mutual fund's assets must be diversified. An example follows of the 75-5-10 diversification test being applied. Assume a management company (in this case, a mutual fund) has $100 million in assets.

- To qualify as a diversified management company, the fund must keep at least 75% ($75 million) of the $100 million invested in publicly held securities.
- To ensure adequate diversification, not more than 5% of the $100 million in total assets may be invested in any one publicly held corporation. The maximum investment allowed, in this case, is $5 million (5% of the fund's $100 million in total assets).
- The fund must not own more than 10% of any one company's voting-class common stock. If it is assumed that the total common stock outstanding for a particular company amounts to $40 million, the maximum investment the fund is allowed to make in the company's common stock is $4 million (10% of $40 million).

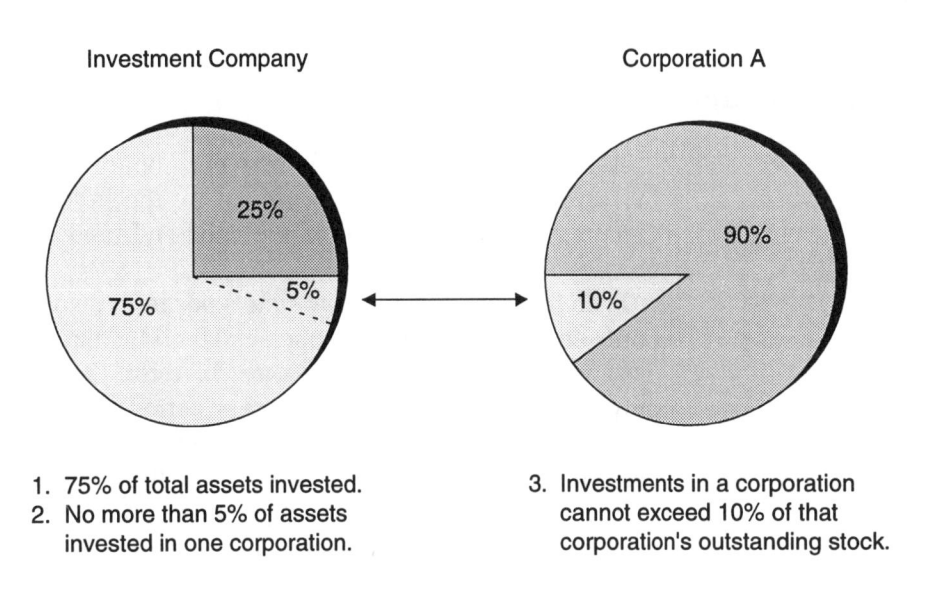

Figure 12.2 Diversified Management Company

Investment Company: 75%, 25%, 5%

Corporation A: 90%, 10%

1. 75% of total assets invested.
2. No more than 5% of assets invested in one corporation.
3. Investments in a corporation cannot exceed 10% of that corporation's outstanding stock.

Nondiversified. A nondiversified company, on the other hand, is any company that fails to meet one or more of these criteria. Some investment companies choose to invest their assets in such a way as to concentrate (or specialize) in a geographic area or industry. Investors may be familiar with investment companies specializing in natural resources, precious metals or gold mining stocks, to name a few specialties.

The fact that an investment company chooses to specialize in an industry does not make it a nondiversified company. Even if an investment company has made all of its investments in a single industry, it can still be considered diversified as long as it meets the 75-5-10 test.

Characteristics of Mutual Funds

The Mutual Fund Concept

A mutual fund is nothing more than a pool of investors' money that is invested in various securities as determined by the investment company's objective. Once an individual invests in the open-end fund, the money is thrown into the pool.

Each investor in the mutual fund's portfolio owns an **undivided interest** in the portfolio. All investors in the open-end fund are mutual participants; no one investor has a preferred status over any other investor. In other words, mutual funds issue only one class of common share; no preferred class of shares or debt can be issued. Each investor shares mutually with other investors in gains and distributions derived from the investment company portfolio.

Each investor's share in the performance of the fund's portfolio is based solely on the number of shares owned. These shares may be purchased in either full or fractional units, unlike corporate stock, which may be purchased in full units only. Because mutual fund shares can be fractional, the investor can think in terms of dollars rather than number of shares owned. For example, if XYZ Mutual Fund shares are $15 per share, a $100 investment will purchase 6.666 shares.

An investment company portfolio is elastic; that is, money is constantly being invested to purchase shares or paid out from the fund when shares are redeemed. The value of the mutual fund portfolio fluctuates as money is invested or redeemed and as the value of the securities held by the portfolio rises and falls. The investor's account value will fluctuate proportionately with the value of the mutual fund portfolio.

Advantages to Investors

Mutual funds (open-end investment companies) offer the investor several advantages. Of primary importance to fund investors is a mutual fund's *guaranteed marketability*. Guaranteed marketability is the ability to sell out of an investment. An open-end mutual fund must redeem shares presented to it by investors at the NAV within seven days (although the company may require a written request for redemption).

A second advantage offered to investors in mutual funds is professional portfolio management. Investment decisions for the funds are made by full-time professional advisers, a luxury few investors can afford when investing independently.

Finally, mutual fund shares offer diversification. Mutual funds provide a greater degree of diversification than most private investors are able to achieve independently. Other investor advantages include the following:

- A mutual fund's shares are held by a **custodian**, which ensures safekeeping.
- The investor has the ability to invest almost any sum he wishes any time he wants because investment companies continuously offer either full or fractional shares.
- Most funds allow a **minimum investment**, often $500 or less, to open an account, which is substantially less than the investment required by most other types of individual securities. Also, once an account is open, many funds allow additional investment for as little as $25.
- The investment company may allow investments at reduced sales charges by offering **breakpoints**. The investor may also qualify for breakpoints through a statement (letter) of intention or rights of accumulation.
- The fund may provide for **reinstatement** of investment. This privilege allows an investor to remove money from an account for emergencies and redeposit the money without paying a second sales charge. Certain rules apply:
    - Reinstatement must be provided for in the prospectus.
    - The investor has only 30 days to reinvest the money.
    - The investor cannot reinstate more than the amount withdrawn.
    - Reinstatement can be used only during the life of the investment.
- The investor retains **voting rights** similar to those rights extended to common stockholders, such as the right to vote for changes in the board of directors and management functions, including approval of the investment adviser, changes in the fund's investment objective, certain sales charges (12b-1 plans), liquidation of the fund and so on.
- Many funds offer **automatic reinvestment** of capital gains distributions and dividend distributions without a sales charge.
- The investor is able to **liquidate** a portion of his holding without disturbing the balance or diversification of the investment. To do so, he submits a written request with a signature guarantee.
- Tax liabilities for the investor are greatly simplified. Each year the fund must distribute to the investor a **Form 1099B** explaining taxability of distributions.
- The fund may offer various withdrawal plans allowing the investor choices of payment methods upon withdrawal from the fund.

Table 12.2 compares common stock and mutual fund shares.

Investment Objectives

Because the fund is operating with a pool of cash supplied by the shareholders, it is able to diversify to a greater extent than any individual could. The portfolio of a mutual fund may be invested in stocks, bonds or other investment securities. The investments can be diversified by company, industry or investment vehicle.

Table 12.2 Comparison of Common Stock and Mutual Fund Shares

Common Stock	Mutual Fund Shares
Form of ownership in a corporation	Form of ownership in an investment company
Unsecured	Unsecured
Dividends when declared	Dividends when declared
Dividends from corporate profits	Dividends from net investment income
Price of stock determined by supply and demand	Price of share determined by forward pricing—that is, the next price calculated as determined by the fund's pricing policy
Traded on an exchange or the over-the-counter market	Purchased from and redeemed with the investment company; no secondary trading
Sold in full units only	Can purchase full or fractional shares
First security issued by a public corporation	Only security issued by an investment company
High degree of financial risk	Lower degree of financial risk due to diversification of portfolio holdings
Carries voting rights	Carries voting rights
May carry preemptive rights	Does not carry preemptive rights
Gives holders residual rights to assets	Gives holders residual rights to portfolio assets
Not callable	Not callable
Ex-dividend: 4 business days prior to record date	Ex-dividend: typically the day after record date

Once an open-end investment company has decided on an objective, the portfolio can be invested to match the objective. The objective must be clearly stated in the investment company's prospectus and can be changed only by a majority vote of the fund's outstanding shares. The open-end investment company will state the objective in its prospectus. The potential investor can then shop around to find a mutual fund with an objective similar to the investor's own. With more than 5,000 mutual funds to choose from, finding a match is not difficult.

Diversified Common Stock Funds

Diversified common stock funds are probably the most typical of all investment companies. The portfolio will be made up of a wide range of common stocks.

Growth funds. Growth funds invest in equity securities of companies expected to increase in value more rapidly than the overall market. Growth companies tend to retain all or most of their earnings for research and development and reinvest profits in the company rather than pay out dividends. The objective may be long-term capital appreciation, where firmly established growth companies make up the portfolio, or aggressive growth, with the portfolio invested in newly emerging companies and technologies.

Income funds. An income fund stresses current yield, or income. The fund's objective may be accomplished by investing in equities of companies with long histories of dividend payments (utility companies, blue chip stocks and so on) or in investment-quality bonds. Such funds may sacrifice safety of principal for increased potential income (investing in lower grade corporate bonds, for example). The investor who selects income funds is more interested in current income than in potential growth.

Combination funds. A combination fund may attempt to combine the objectives of growth and current yield by diversifying its portfolio among companies showing long-term growth potential and companies currently paying high dividends.

Specialized (Sector) Funds

Many funds attempt to specialize in particular sectors of the economy or in specific industries. Usually, the funds have a minimum of 25% of their assets invested in their specialties. Examples include mutual funds investing in gold mining stock (gold funds), public utilities funds and portfolios that might be invested in nothing but low-grade (noninvestment-grade) bonds.

Other special situation funds buy for their portfolios securities of companies that may benefit from a change within the company or in the economy. Takeover candidates and other special situations are common investments. Sector funds offer high appreciation potential, but may also offer higher risks to the investor.

Balanced Funds

Many funds attempt to combine the objectives of growth and income by investing in different vehicles. Balanced funds invest in stocks for appreciation and bonds for income payments. Some funds take an even more conservative approach by balancing their investments between preferred stock and bonds. In a balanced fund, different types of securities are purchased according to a preset formula designed to be balanced. For example, a balanced fund's portfolio might contain 60% equity securities and 40% debt securities.

Asset Allocation Funds

These funds use the techniques of asset allocation in an attempt to provide a consistent return for the investor. These funds will split investments between stocks, bonds and money-market instruments or cash. The advisers of the funds will switch the percentage holdings in each asset category according to the performance, or expected performance, of that group.

For example, the fund may have 60% of its investments in stock, 20% in bonds and the remaining 20% in cash. If the stock market is expected to do well, the adviser may switch from cash and bonds into stock. The result may be a portfolio of 80% in stock, 10% in bonds and 10% in cash. On the other hand, if the stock market is in turmoil or there is uncertainty concerning the market, the fund may invest more heavily in cash, thus reducing its investments in stock.

Bond and Preferred Stock Funds

If income is a primary investment objective, it is often obtained by investing in bonds. Bond funds may also vary in their approach. Some funds invest solely in corporate bonds. Others, seeking enhanced safety, invest in government issues only. Still others seek capital appreciation by investing in lower rated issues (junk bonds) at high interest rates.

Tax-free (Tax-exempt) Bond Funds

Tax-exempt funds contain instruments such as municipal bonds or notes that produce income exempt from federal income tax. Municipal bond funds and tax-exempt money-market funds are common types of tax-exempt funds.

U.S. Government and Agency Security Funds

U.S. government funds purchase securities backed by the U.S. Treasury or issued by an agency of the U.S. government, such as Sallie Mae or Ginnie Mae. Investors in these funds seek current income and maximum safety.

Index Funds

Index funds are invested in a portfolio of securities that is selected to mirror a market index, such as the S&P 500. An index fund will buy and sell the securities in its portfolio in such a way that the portfolio maintains the same type and weightings of stock as the selected index. Index funds do not attempt to beat the performance of the underlying index by actively managing the portfolio. The fund's performance will track the underlying index's performance, and will rise and fall according to the movement of the market the index tracks.

Turnover of securities in an index fund's portfolio is kept to a minimum. As a result, a portfolio based on an index (a passive management strategy) generally has lower fund management costs than other types of funds.

Dual-purpose Funds

Dual-purpose funds are closed-end funds that meet two objectives. Investors seeking income purchase income shares and receive all the interest and dividends earned by the fund's portfolio. Other investors interested in capital gains purchase the gains shares and receive all gains on portfolio holdings. The two types of shares in a dual fund are listed separately in the financial pages.

Money-market Funds

Money-market funds are usually no-load, open-ended mutual funds, which means there are no sales charges to customers buying shares nor are there liquidation charges for customers selling shares. The management invests the fund's capital in money-market instruments that have high interest rates and short maturities, such as Treasury bills, Treasury bonds with a short time to maturity, commercial paper, bankers' acceptances and certificates of deposit (CDs). Interest rates on money-market funds are not fixed or guaranteed and change as frequently as daily. Interest earned by these funds is computed daily and credited to customers' accounts monthly. Many funds offer draft- (check-) writing privileges; however, checks must normally be written for amounts of $500 or more. The largest expense to investors is the management fee, which is usually around .5%.

The net asset value of money-market funds is set at $1.00 per share. Although this price is not guaranteed, the fund is managed so as to maintain it regardless of market changes. Thus, the price of money-market shares does not fluctuate in response to changing market conditions—that is, the NAV of these funds is not volatile.

Restrictions on money-market fund investments. Recent SEC rule changes have limited certain investments that can be made by money-market funds, and have required certain disclosures to investors. These changes and restrictions are:

- The front cover of the prospectus must prominently disclose that an investment in a money-market fund is neither insured nor guaranteed by the U.S. government and there is no assurance that the fund will be able to maintain a stable NAV. This statement must also appear in all literature used to market the fund.
- No more than 5% of the fund's assets may be invested in the securities of any one issuer.
- Investments are limited to securities with remaining maturities of not more than 13 months, with the average portfolio maturity not exceeding 90 days.
- Investments are limited to eligible securities determined to have minimal risk. *Eligible* securities are defined as securities rated by nationally recognized rating organizations (Standard & Poor's, Moody's, Fitch and so on) in one of the top two categories (no more than 5% of the portfolio in the second tier of ratings). Comparable unrated securities must adhere to the definition of "safety" as provided by the rating organizations. (Tax-exempt money-market funds are exempt from certain parts of the requirement to invest only in rated securities.)

Monetary policy and money-market funds. The primary purpose of the Federal Reserve Board is to establish monetary policy (i.e., setting reserve requirements for banks, setting the discount rate and using other tools to adjust money supply and interest rates). If the FRB changes the discount rate or increases reserve requirements for banks, the cost of money is either raised or lowered. FRB actions will act to influence interest rates, and as a result, will affect the rates payable (performance) on a money-market mutual fund. The NASD and SEC have broad regulatory powers over the operations of investment companies; however, actions by the FRB have the most impact on the yields of money-market funds.

Comparing Mutual Funds

The funds described previously by no means should be taken to represent the only types of funds available. Objectives will vary according to each fund. With the selection available, the investor should be careful to scrutinize each fund before making an investment.

When comparing funds, the investor should start by defining a personal investment objective. Once an objective has been determined, the investor can select from those funds that most closely parallel that objective. The investor will probably find that there are many investment companies with similar objectives; consequently, a further narrowing of the field will be required.

When comparing funds with similar objectives, the investor should scrutinize the information contained in the fund's prospectus. Items to compare include:

- performance
- costs
- portfolio turnover
- taxation
- services provided

Performance

The investor will want to review the performance of the fund over a period of time, as well as review how well the management of the fund has met the objectives set forth in the fund's prospectus. The Securities Act of 1933 requires that each fund list a history of its performance over the lesser of ten years or the fund's life. These histories are an invaluable source of information because they show the fund's performance in good years and in bad. The ten-year history must show what an investment made at the beginning of the period would have returned if held until the reporting date, which serves as a useful comparison between similar funds.

Naturally, the investor will also want to see how well the management of the fund has met the objectives set forth in the fund's prospectus. For example, a growth fund with a high dividend payout is a fund which has failed to follow through with its investment policy.

Costs

The cost of investing is a critical comparison to make. Sales loads, management fees and operating expenses reduce the return an investor can expect from the investment. Management fees and operating expenses are summarized in the fund's expense ratio.

Sales Loads

Historically, mutual funds have charged front-end loads of up to 8.5% of the money invested. This charge reduces the amount of money actually invested and "working" in the fund. Not all funds charge the maximum allowable. Many "low-load" funds are available charging between 2% and 5%. Additionally, funds may charge a load on the "back-end" upon withdrawal. Recently, funds have started charging an on-going fee under section 12b-1 of the Investment Company Act of 1940. These funds deduct a fee to pay for marketing and distribution costs from the assets managed annually. The type of sales charge a fund may apply is explained in detail later in this chapter.

Regardless of the method used, the sales charge is a cost and reduces the potential return to the investor. However, the charge pays for the services rendered by the offering company. The investor must decide if the cost is worth the service and performance provided.

Expense Ratio

The expense ratio of a fund relates the expenses of operating the fund, such as costs of administration and fees paid to the custodian, adviser or transfer agent, to the net assets of the fund (that is, the expenses of the fund divided by its average net assets). Typically, the more aggressive a fund, the higher its expense ratio. For example, an aggressive growth fund's expense ratio is expected to be higher than a AAA bond fund's expense ratio as a result of more frequent trading in the growth fund's portfolio.

Generally for stock funds, the expense ratio is between 1% and 1.5% of a fund's average net assets, for bond funds, the ratio is typically between 0.5% and 1.0%. Funds with expense ratios exceeding these norms are expensive to own. Unless the fund shows superior performance as a direct result of higher management fees, an individual investor is better off in a fund with a lower expense ratio. You will see that the cost of operating a fund reduces the money available to be distributed to shareholders.

Taxation

Investors in mutual funds pay taxes on gains received by the fund based upon the holding period of the security owned by the fund. Until recently, it did not matter whether a gain was long term or short term—it was taxed at the same rate. Now, however, there is a cap on tax rates for long-term gains. As a result, it's better to receive a long-term gain than a short-term gain.

Portfolio Turnover

Investors pay for the costs of the adviser buying and selling portfolio securities. These costs include commissions or markups (-downs) when a security is bought (sold). The measure used to identify these costs is the portfolio turnover rate. It is not uncommon for an aggressive growth fund to reflect a turnover rate of 100% or greater. In other words, the fund replaces its portfolio annually. If superior returns are achieved, the strategy is working—if not, the strategy is subjecting the investor to undue costs.

Portfolio turnover rates reflect a fund's holding period. If a fund has a turnover rate of 100%, it has held its securities, on average, for less than one year. All gains are therefore likely to be short term and subject to the maximum tax rate. On the other hand, a portfolio with a turnover rate of 25%, has an average holding period of four years and gains will likely be taxed at the long-term rate.

Services Offered

Funds today make investing easy. Services that mutual funds offer to investors include retirement accounts, investment plans, check writing privileges, telephone transfers, conversion privleges, combination investment plans, withdrawal plans and others. However, service costs money. The cost of services provided should always be weighed against the cost of services used.

Investment Company Registration

A company must register as an investment company with the SEC if:

- the company is in the business of investing, reinvesting, owning, holding or trading in securities; or
- 40% or more of the company's assets are invested in securities. (Government securities and securities of majority-owned subsidiaries are not used in calculating the 40% limitation.)

Registration of Investment Companies

Before a company may register as an investment company with the SEC, certain minimum requirements must be met. A management company (or any other type of investment company, for that matter) is not allowed to issue securities to the public unless it has:

- private capitalization (seed money) of at least $100,000
- 100 investors
- clearly defined investment objectives

If the investment company does not have 100 shareholders and $100,000 in assets, it can still register a public offering with the SEC provided that it can meet these requirements within 90 days of registration.

The company must clearly define an investment objective under which it plans to operate. Once defined, the objective, whether growth, income or whatever, may only be changed with a majority vote of the company's outstanding shares.

Open-end companies. In addition, the act of 1940 requires open-end companies to have the following:

- no more than one class of security
- a minimum asset-to-debt ratio of 300%

Because open-end management companies may issue only one class of security (common stock), they are permitted to borrow from banks. They cannot issue preferred stock or bonds, but may borrow money as long as the company's asset-to-debt ratio is not less than 3-to-1 (that is, debt coverage by assets of at least 300%).

SEC Registration and Public Offering Requirements

Management companies must file registration statements with the SEC, provide full disclosure and generally follow the same public offering procedures that other corporations and noninvestment companies follow when issuing securities. In filing for registration as an investment company with the SEC, a corporation must provide the following information in its registration form:

- the type of investment company it intends to be (i.e., open-end or closed-end);
- any plans the company has to raise money by borrowing;
- the company's intention (if any) to concentrate its investments in a single industry;
- any plans for investing in real estate or commodities;
- conditions under which investment policies may be changed by a vote of the shareholders;
- the full names and addresses of each affiliated person; and
- a description of the business experience of each officer and director during the preceding five years.

The investment company is considered registered upon the receipt of its notification of registration by the SEC. Once a corporation has met the above tests for registration as an investment company, the SEC allows it certain rights and places certain prohibitions on its activities. While operating as an investment company, corporations are strictly prohibited from:

- seeking to gain control of other companies
- acting in the capacity of a broker by trading securities for a commission
- acting as a bank, insurance company or savings and loan
- operating with fewer than 100 shareholders or less than $100,000 in assets

There are exceptions to these guidelines. Under the act, the following corporations are exempt from registration as investment companies with the SEC, even if more than 40% of their assets are invested in securities:

- underwriters and brokers
- banks, insurance companies and bank investment advisory accounts
- mortgage bankers
- security holders protective committees
- real estate investment trusts (REITs)

Continuous Public Offering Securities

The sale of open-end management company shares is treated by the SEC as a continuous public offering of shares, which means that the shares must be sold by prospectus only. All sales must be accompanied by a prospectus, which must be updated no less frequently than every 13 months. With publicly traded (closed-end) funds, only the initial public offering stock is sold with prospectus.

Purchasing mutual fund shares on margin. Because a mutual fund is continually issuing new shares, and it is considered a continuous primary offering, Regulation T prohibits the purchase of mutual fund shares on margin. Mutual fund shares may be used as collateral in a margin account, however, if they have been held fully paid for 30 days.

Registration of Investment Company Securities

In addition to filing as an investment company under the act of 1940, the investment company, like any other corporation, must register with the SEC any securities that it intends to issue. The registration of shares takes place under the Securities Act of 1933.

Registration Statement—Prospectus

The registration statement a corporation must file consists of two parts: part 1 is the prospectus, a copy of which must be furnished to every person to whom the securities are offered; and part 2 is the document containing information that need not be furnished to every purchaser, but that must be made available for public inspection. In general, the prospectus must contain any information that the SEC decides should be revealed in the best interest of the public. The fact that all publicly issued securities must be registered with the SEC does not mean that the SEC in any way *approves* the securities. For that reason, every prospectus must contain a disclaimer similar to the following on its front cover:

> These securities have not been approved or disapproved by the Securities and Exchange Commission nor has the commission passed upon the accuracy or adequacy of this prospectus. Any representation to the contrary is a criminal offense.

Securities Issued by Investment Companies

Common stock (equity securities). Investment companies, both open-end and closed-end, allow investors to participate in their portfolios by selling shares of the fund. The shares of common stock represent an undivided interest in the company's portfolio. The investor's interest in the portfolio is proportionate to the number of shares owned.

Open-end companies are not allowed to issue senior securities, such as bonds and preferred stock, but are permitted to borrow from banks. A 300% asset-to-debt coverage ratio applies to open-end companies borrowing from banks.

Bonds (debt securities). Only closed-end investment companies are permitted to issue debt securities (senior securities are issued under the Trust Indenture Act of 1939). A closed-end company may issue either bonds or debentures, provided that, after they have been issued, the company maintains an asset-to-debt coverage ratio of at least 300%.

As an example, if a closed-end investment company has $200 million in common stock outstanding, it can issue up to $100 million in bonds. After the bonds are issued, it will have $200 million in assets represented by the stock and $100 million in cash from the bond sale, for a total ratio of $300 million in assets to $100 million in debt (or 300% coverage). From another perspective, the company is allowed to issue bonds worth up to 50% of the value of its outstanding common stock.

Preferred stock (equity securities). A closed-end investment company can also issue preferred stock with the approval of its common shareholders. Restrictions similar to those covering the issuance of bonds exist, and the principal must become familiar with those restrictions.

In order to conduct an offering of preferred stock, the company must be able to maintain a 200% asset-to-preferred-stock coverage ratio. That is, the company can issue preferred stock in an amount equal to 100% of the value of its outstanding common stock. Any preferred stock that the investment company issues must be a cumulative preferred; the preferred stock must have the right to receive all scheduled dividends (including defaulted dividends) before any dividends are distributed to the common shareholders. After any distributions are made, the company must still maintain at least a 200% asset coverage.

Restrictions on Operations

Functions and Activities of Investment Companies

The act of 1940 sets out rules, restrictions and regulations under which investment companies must operate. These rules and regulations were written to protect the investor and have been amended and updated frequently. The SEC has been granted authority to prohibit a mutual fund from engaging in certain activities. Those activities which may be prohibited include:

- making securities purchases on margin
- selling securities short
- participation in joint investment or trading accounts
- acting as distributor of its own securities, except through an underwriter

Until the SEC issues rules and regulations prohibiting the activities described above, however, mutual funds may engage in these activities. It is clear that the fund must specifically disclose these activities and the extent to which it plans to engage in these activities in its prospectus.

Changes in the Registration Statement

Shareholders' Right to Vote

Whatever is stated in the prospectus as the management company's purpose for existence, its investment objectives, capital formation methods, organizational structure, shareholder services, and so on, can't be changed without a *majority of shares outstanding* being voted in favor of the changes.

Before any change can be made to the published bylaws or objectives of the fund, the approval of the shareholders is mandatory. In voting matters, it is the *majority of shares voted* for or against a proposition that counts, *not the majority of people voting*. Thus one shareholder holding 51% of all the shares outstanding can determine the outcome of a vote.

Among the changes that would require a majority vote of the shares outstanding are the following:

- changes in **borrowing** by open-end companies (open-end management companies are permitted to borrow cash from banks; closed-end companies are prohibited from borrowing money);
- **issuing or underwriting** other securities (closed-end companies are allowed to raise capital through the issuance of senior securities, either debt or preferred stock; open-end companies are prohibited from issuing senior securities);
- purchasing or underwriting **real estate**;
- making **loans**;
- change of **subclassification** (for example, from open-end to closed-end, or from diversified to nondiversified);
- change in **sales load policy** (for example, from a no-load fund to a load fund);
- change in the **nature of the business** (for example, ceasing business as an investment company); and
- change in **investment policy** (for example, from income to growth, or from bonds to small capitalization stocks).

In addition to the right to vote on these items, shareholders retain all rights normally accorded to the holders of any corporate stock.

Management of Investment Companies

Board of Directors

Like publicly owned corporations in general, a management company has a CEO, a team of officers and a board of directors, all in place to serve the interests of the investors. The officers and directors concern themselves with investment objectives, long-term strategy, portfolio funding and cash flow matters, accounting and business administration duties. But they themselves do not manage the investment portfolio. As with any other type of corporation, the shareholders of an investment company elect the board of directors to make decisions and oversee operations. The shareholders of a managed investment company must approve the election of the fund's board members, as well as any additions or replacements to the board.

The only exception to this rule is that any vacancies that occur after the initial election may be filled in any legal manner as long as at least two thirds of the directors have been elected by the shareholders. The board may be divided into classes, provided that no one class of directors is elected for a period shorter than one year or longer than five years.

The act of 1940 places restrictions on who is eligible to sit on the board of directors of an investment company. A section of the act, called **interlocking directorate** requires that at least 40% of the directors must be independent (noninterested persons). This means that no more than 60% of the board members may be interested persons, including attorneys on retainer, accountants and any persons employed in similar capacities with the company (see "Affiliated and Interested Persons" later). For example, if a fund has ten directors, at least four of the directors can hold no other position within the fund.

The second restriction is that no one may serve on a board of directors who has been convicted of either a felony (of any type) or of a misdemeanor involving the securities industry.

The third restriction to be aware of is that no person who has been either temporarily or permanently enjoined from acting as an underwriter, broker, dealer or investment company by any court can be elected to a term on a board.

Investment Adviser

Once an investment company is registered as such and has elected its board of directors, the board then contracts with an outside **investment adviser** (portfolio manager). The fund's investment adviser may be an individual or an investment advisory company. Once hired, the adviser is responsible for investing the cash and securities held in the fund's portfolio, implementing investment strategy, clearly identifying the tax status of any distribution made to shareholders as a result of activity in the fund's portfolio, and managing the day-to-day trading of the portfolio. Naturally, the adviser must adhere to the objective as stated in the fund's prospectus (only a majority vote of the shares can alter a fund's objective). The adviser cannot transfer the responsibility of portfolio management to anyone else. The simple fact that an investment adviser is elected does not relieve the directors of their responsibility of adhering to the fund's objective.

Investment advisers earn management fees for their services, typically a set annual percentage (such as .5% of the portfolio asset value being managed) which is paid from the net assets of the fund. In addition, if an investment adviser consistently outperforms a specified market performance benchmark, he will typically earn an incentive bonus. (But the sword is double-edged; if the adviser underperforms, his management contract may not be renewed.)

In choosing an investment adviser, the company must select the best, most qualified adviser it can find without regard to former, current or future ties or business the adviser might have with the company. To protect the shareholders of the investment company, the act of 1940 requires:

- a written contract, which must be approved initially by a vote of the shareholders, and approved annually thereafter by a vote of the shareholders and/or by the board of directors; and
- that the advisory contract has a *maximum life of two years,* during which time the contract must be *approved annually* by the directors and/or by a majority vote of the shares.

The **contract** must also include:

- a precise description of all compensation to be paid the investment adviser;
- a provision that the contract may be terminated by the board of directors or by a majority vote of the shares with 60 days notice;
- the stipulation that the contract will be terminated if the investment adviser assigns its contract to another person (note: *assignment* means any transfer of a controlling interest in the management group, of which the investment adviser is a part);
- the requirement that any such assignment be approved by the shareholders of the investment company; and
- the requirement that any amendment or renewal of the advisory contract be approved by a majority of the noninterested (independent) directors.

Similarly, the terms under which the principal underwriter handling the continuously issued and publicly offered shares will be compensated must also be in writing and approved by a majority of voting shares outstanding.

An investment company is prohibited from contracting with an investment adviser who has been convicted of a securities-related felony unless it has received an exemption from the SEC. In addition, an investment company is prohibited from lending money to its investment adviser.

Affiliated and Interested Persons

The act of 1940 and subsequent amendments identify certain categories of individuals and entities that have control over or may influence the operation of an investment company. The identification of these persons is critical, as the act regulates and places restrictions on their activities. The act broadly defines two classes of persons: affiliated and interested.

An **affiliated person** is in a *control* position within the company; in general, an affiliated person controls the investment company's operations. An **interested person** is in a position to *influence* the operations of an investment company.

Affiliated Persons

Anyone who could have any type of control over an investment company's operations is called an affiliated person. The act has set forth a series of regulations that effectively prohibit affiliated persons from using the control they have for their personal benefit. Those persons considered affiliated include:

- anyone with 5% or more of the outstanding voting securities of the investment company;
- any corporation in which the investment company holds 5% or more of its outstanding securities;
- any person (an individual or a corporate entity) controlled in whole or in part by the investment company;
- all officers, directors, partners and employees of the investment company;
- the investment adviser; and
- in the absence of a board of directors, the individual who deposits the assets of the UIT into the account at the custodial bank (also known as the depositor).

The act of 1940 places additional limits on the types of investments the fund may make if an affiliated person, such as a director, has an interest in the security. The fund may not invest in a security if an affiliated person owns *more than 1/2 of 1%* of the target company's outstanding stock. Because the director's influence over the fund is great, this restriction eliminates any question that an investment decision was made to benefit a director with large personal holdings in a target company.

Interested Persons

Introduced by the 1970 amendments to the act, the designation *interested person* broadens the category of people whose actions are restricted or regulated by the SEC. The list of restricted persons now includes broker-dealers, legal counsels and immediate family of affiliated persons, as well as anybody else whom the SEC wishes to designate as such. All of the following are considered interested persons:

- person associated with the investment company, its investment adviser or its principal underwriter, including the immediate families of any affiliated person;
- person employed by the investment company, the investment adviser or the principal underwriter;
- person who, within the last two years, has acted as legal counsel to any affiliated person;
- broker-dealer registered under the Securities Exchange Act of 1934; and
- any other person deemed to be interested by the SEC because of business dealings with the company, its investment adviser or its principal underwriter.

The directors of an investment company are specifically excluded from the definition of an interested person. The directors are, however, affiliated persons (see limitations of director membership in "Board of Directors" previously).

Restrictions

In addition to any other restrictions, an affiliated or interested person is prohibited from:

- borrowing money from the investment company; or
- selling any security or other property to the investment company or to any company controlled by the investment company.

Custodian Bank

As a means of safeguarding investors' assets, the act of 1940 requires each investment company to place its securities in the custody of a bank (with assets of at least $500,000) or a stock exchange member firm. The bank performs an important safekeeping role as custodian of the company's securities and cash and receives a fee for its services (which, like the adviser's fee, is paid from the net assets of the fund). Often, the custodian will handle most of the clerical functions the investment company might need. The custodian bank may, with the consent of the investment company, deposit the securities it is entrusted to hold in one of the systems for the central handling of securities established by the National Association of Securities Dealers, Inc. (NASD) or the New York Stock Exchange, Inc. (NYSE). These systems make it easier to transfer or pledge securities. Once securities are placed in the system, most such transfers can be accomplished with a simple bookkeeping entry rather than actual physical delivery of the securities.

Once a custodian bank has been designated by an investment company (and assets are transferred into its safekeeping), the bank is required to follow certain rules and regulations as specified by the act. The bank must:

- keep the investment company's assets physically segregated at all times;
- allow withdrawal only under the rules of the SEC; and
- restrict access to the account to certain officers and employees of the investment company.

The board of directors designates, by majority vote, which employees it wishes to have access to the account. As a further safeguard, the act specifies that at least two of these designated employees must be present each time the account is opened. The only other people the bank is permitted to allow access to the account are the independent public accountants verifying the securities and any authorized employees of the SEC.

The securities in the account must be verified by an independent public accountant at least three times a year. One accounting is performed for the annual report; the other two are held at the accountant's request without advance notice to the company.

Transfer Agent (Customer Services Agent)

The functions of the transfer agent are manifold; they include, among other duties, issuing and redeeming fund shares, handling name changes for the fund, sending out customer confirmations and sending out fund distributions.

The transfer agent can be the fund custodian or a separate service company. The fund pays the transfer agent a fee for these services.

Underwriter

The underwriter (often called the *sponsor* or *distributor*) markets fund shares, prepares sales literature and, in return, receives a percentage of the sales charge paid by the client. The underwriter's compensation is part of the sales load paid by the customer when shares are purchased. Sales fees are not part of the fund's expenses.

In general, open-end investment companies (issuers) may not also act as the distributor (underwriter). For example, the distributor for the JH Mutual Fund must be a separate and distinct entity from the JH Mutual Fund (even though it may be called JH Distributors). The underwriter (distributor) of funds receives a fee for selling and promoting the fund shares to the public. This fee is in the form of a sales charge. Except for offerings defined as *contractual plans*, sales charges cannot exceed 8.5%. The underwriter is hired as the head salesperson for the investment company. Obviously, this is an ongoing and important position. The board of directors will appoint an underwriter (sponsor, or distributor) to sell fund shares to the public. The open-end investment company will sell its shares to the underwriter at the current NAV but only as the underwriter needs the shares to fill customer orders. The underwriter is prohibited from maintaining an inventory in open-end company shares. The underwriter is compensated by adding a sales charge to the share's NAV when sales are made to the public.

Table 12.3 illustrates how a typical fund is organized.

Table 12.3 Organization of a Mutual Fund

Manager	Custodian/Transfer Agent	Underwriter
Makes investment decisions.	Holds assets.	Distributes shares.
Paid a percentage of NAV.	Issues and redeems shares.	Paid from sales charges.
Two-year initial contract.	Clerical duties.	Two-year initial contract.
Contract renewed annually.	Paid a fee by the fund.	Contract renewed annually.

Bonding of Directors and Employees

The investment company, as well as each officer or employee of an investment company who has access to the cash or securities of the company, must be bonded. The company may purchase separate bonds for each individual to be covered, or it may purchase a single bond that lists by name each employee to be covered within the company.

The amount of the bond must be determined by a majority of the noninterested directors at least once every twelve months. The SEC has set forth a schedule of minimum bonding requirements, determined by the investment company's gross assets at the end of the most recent fiscal quarter. A copy of the bond must be filed with the SEC. If a claim is made under the bond, the investment company must notify the SEC in writing of the nature and amount of the claim. The SEC must also be notified within five business days of the terms of a settlement of any such claim.

Officers and directors may be covered by the bond only for negligence. No bond protects an officer or director from acts of willful malfeasance, bad faith or gross negligence or reckless disregard of his duties in the conduct of his office.

Information Distributed to Investors

Prospectus

In an effort to simplify and enhance its readability, the prospectus distributed to investors may come in two parts: the prospectus (called an N1-A prospectus) and a statement of additional information. The prospectus must be distributed to an investor prior to or during any solicitation for sale. The statement of additional information may be obtained by the investor upon request from the fund.

The prospectus contains information on the fund's objective, investment policies, sales charges and management expenses, services offered and a 10-year history of per share capital changes (performance). The statement of additional information typically contains the funds consolidated financial statements including the balance sheet, statement of operations, income statement and portfolio list at the time the statement was compiled.

Financial Reports

The act of 1940 requires that shareholders receive financial reports at least semiannually (every six months). These reports must contain:

- the investment company's balance sheet;
- a valuation of all securities in the investment company's portfolio on the date of the balance sheet (a portfolio list);
- the investment company's income statement;
- a complete statement of all compensation paid to the board of directors and to the advisory board; and

- a statement of the total dollar amount of securities purchased and sold during the period.

It is the principal's responsibility to see that each of these reports is current and accurately reflects the state of the company at the end of the reporting period. In addition, the company must send a copy of its balance sheet to any shareholder who makes a written request for one at any time between semiannual reports.

The investment company must be audited at least annually and distribute an audited annual report to every investor once a year.

Additional Disclosure Requirements

The SEC, in a continuing effort to give investors more information on which to evaluate the performance of mutual funds, requires the fund to include in its prospectus or annual reports:

- a discussion of those factors and strategies that materially affected its performance during its most recently completed fiscal year;
- a line graph comparing its performance to that of an appropriate broad-based securities market index; and
- the name(s) and title(s) of the person(s) who are primarily responsible for the day-to-day management of the fund's portfolio.

Fund Performance

Fund management is required to discuss what happened to the fund during the previous fiscal year and why it happened. In its review, management is not obligated to evaluate the effectiveness of its strategies or investment techniques employed to achieve its performance.

Financial Highlights

A simplified "per share" table of condensed financial information must be provided in the prospectus. The table will enable an investor to track the operating performance of the fund on a per share basis from its beginning net asset value to its ending net asset value. A line graph comparison of the per share performance of the fund to an appropriate broad-based securities market index must be provided. For example, a broadly diversified common stock fund touting an 18% rise in share value may lose some of its appeal when compared to the S&P 500 which has risen 26% during the same time frame.

Disclosure of Advisers

Many investment advisers who have achieved stellar returns have attained celebrity status. Funds marketing their portfolios will advertise the fund as managed by the adviser "star," when in fact the fund is managed by a committee that may or may not include the personality advertised. To clarify and eliminate the potential for abuse, the prospectus must disclose the person(s) responsible for the day-to-day management of the fund's portfolio. Money-market and index funds are excluded from this requirement.

Mutual Fund Marketing, Pricing and Valuation

Methods of Marketing Mutual Fund Shares

A fund can use any number of methods to market its shares to the public. A discussion of some of the marketing methods used by various firms follows.

Fund to Underwriter to Dealer to Investor

An investor gives an order for fund shares to a dealer. The dealer then places the order with the underwriter. To fill the order, the fund sells shares to the underwriter at the current NAV. The underwriter sells the shares to the dealer at the NAV plus the underwriter's concession (or at the public offering price less the dealer's allowance or discount). The dealer then sells the shares to the investor at the full POP.

Fund to Underwriter to Investor

An investor gives an order for fund shares to the underwriter (the underwriter acts as the dealer and uses its own sales force to sell shares to the public). To fill the order, the fund sells shares to the underwriter at the current NAV. The underwriter then adds the sales charge and sells the shares to the investor at the full POP. The sales charge is split among the various salespersons (underwriter as dealer, registered reps and so on).

Fund to Investor

Some funds sell directly to the public without the use of an underwriter or a sales force and without a sales charge. If an open-end investment company distributes shares to the public directly—that is, without the services of a distributor—and the fund offers its shares for sale at no load (without a sales charge) the fund is called a **no-load fund**. The fund pays all sales expenses.

Fund to Underwriter to Plan Company to Investor

Organizations that sell contractual plans for the periodic purchase of mutual fund shares are called *plan companies*. The mutual fund shares are purchased by the plan company and held in trust for the individual purchasing shares under the periodic payment plan. The maximum sales charge for contractual plans is 9% over the life of the plan.

Sales at the Public Offering Price

Any sale of fund shares to a *customer* (a member of the general public who is *not* a member of the NASD) must be made at the **public offering price**. The route this sale takes (whether directly from the fund to the customer, from the fund through a dealer to the customer, etc.) is not important—the nonmember customer must be charged the POP. Only an NASD member acting as a dealer or an underwriter may purchase the fund shares at a discount from the issuer.

Determining the Value of Mutual Fund Shares

The act of 1940 requires mutual funds to calculate the value of the fund shares at least once per business day (because purchase and redemption prices are based on the NAV of the shares). Although funds may calculate the value more often, most wait until after the close of the NYSE (4:00 pm EST) before making their calculation.

Net Asset Value per Share

A fund's NAV is the price on which sales of new shares to investors is based. The actual price is referred to as the POP (ask price), which is equal to the NAV plus a sales charge. When a customer sells, the liquidation price is always equal to the current NAV. To determine the NAV per share, the custodian bank totals the value of all assets and subtracts all liabilities, which results in the total NAV of the fund. The *NAV per share* is determined by dividing the total net assets by the number of shares outstanding.

$$\text{Assets (Cash + Current value of securities)} - \text{Liabilities} = \text{NAV of fund}$$

$$\frac{\text{NAV of fund}}{\text{Number of shares outstanding}} = \text{NAV per share}$$

To illustrate, assume that a mutual fund has $47.6 million in total assets and $7 million in total liabilities, with 2.5 million shares outstanding. The NAV per share would be $16.24 ([$47.6 million – $7 million] ÷ 2.5 million shares = $16.24).

In working with NAV calculations, a fund's total assets include everything of value owned by the fund, not just the investment portfolio. This is why a mutual fund's NAV is analogous to a publicly owned corporation's book value.

Changes in NAV

The NAV can change daily because of changes in the market value of the fund's portfolio. If the number of shares remains constant while the portfolio value increases, the NAV will also increase. Likewise, if the value of the portfolio declines and the number of shares remains constant, the NAV will also decline.

The appreciation or depreciation of portfolio assets is also called *unrealized gain* or *loss*. For example, if the fund holds XYZ stock that it purchased for $100 per share and the market price of the stock increases to $110, the value of XYZ has appreciated. This appreciation is reflected in the fund's NAV. The gain is said to be unrealized because the fund did not sell the stock.

The events that may change a fund's NAV per share include but are not limited to:

- an *increase* in the NAV per share *if* portfolio securities increase in value or the portfolio receives income (interest on debt) from the securities held in the portfolio;
- a *decrease* in the NAV per share *if* portfolio securities decrease in value or portfolio income or gain is paid out to shareholders (dividends or gains distributions); and

- *no change* in the NAV per share *if* there is a sale (issuance) or redemption of fund shares or if there is a sale or purchase of portfolio securities (even if a previously unrealized gain or loss is realized). In these circumstances, the fund is exchanging securities for cash. The total net assets, therefore, remain unchanged.

An example may illustrate this last point more clearly. If the XYZ Mutual Fund has assets of $100 and ten shares outstanding, the NAV per share would be $10. If an investor wanted to purchase ten shares of XYZ Fund, excluding sales charges, the shares would cost $100. Now the fund has 20 shares outstanding, and because the fund receives the $100 for the shares purchased, it has assets of $200. The NAV per share remains at $10 ($200 ÷ 20 shares = $10 per share).

What has changed with this transaction is the proportionate ownership in the fund. Whereas prior to the sale of the new shares the ten shares outstanding represented a 100% ownership of the fund, ten shares now represent only a 50% ownership in the fund.

Sales Charges

As mentioned previously, the underwriter (or sponsor) is the key sales organization hired by the investment company. The underwriter is compensated for distributing the fund's shares by adding a sales charge to the NAV of the shares sold.

The NASD prohibits its members from assessing sales charges *in excess of 8.5%* of the POP on mutual funds purchases by customers. Broker-dealers are free to charge lower rates *if they specify these rates in the prospectus*, but they must never charge more than the 8.5% maximum.

Closed-end (publicly traded) funds do not carry a sales charge. The investor pays a brokerage commission to buy or to sell or a markup or markdown if a principal transaction is being executed.

All sales commissions and expenses are paid from the sales charges collected. Sales expenses include commissions for the managing underwriter, dealers, brokers and registered representatives, and all advertising and sales literature expenses. In most open-end investment companies, the underwriter is responsible for preparing sales literature because it is best equipped to prepare the literature in compliance with SEC rules and regulations.

There are three different methods used by mutual fund distributors to collect their fees for the sale of shares:

1. front-end loads (difference between purchase price and net invested)
2. back-end loads (contingent deferred sales loads)
3. 12b-1 sales charges (asset-based fees)

Classes of Fund Shares

Mutual funds offer several classes of shares that allow the investor the opportunity to select the type of sales charge when investing in a mutual fund. The most common class types are referred to as *Class A, Class B* or *Class C* shares.

- **Class A shares** have *front-end loads*—that is, the charge is paid at purchase; the charge is the difference between the purchase price and the net amount invested.
- **Class B shares** have *back-end loads*—that is, the charge is paid at redemption; the charge is a contingent deferred sales load.
- **Class C shares** have *level loads*—that is, the charge is an annually paid asset-based fee.

The class of share determines the type of sales charge only; all other rights associated with ownership of mutual fund shares remain the same across each class.

Front-end Loads

Front-end load sales charges are added to the NAV of the shares at the time the investor purchases the shares. Front-end loads are the most common way of paying for the distribution services provided by a fund's underwriter. The bulk of this section's discussion will describe the calculation of this payment—the difference between NAV and the public offering price (POP).

Back-end Loads

Back-end sales loads (contingent-deferred loads) are those charged at the redemption of mutual fund shares or variable contracts. The sales load is a *declining percentage charge* that is reduced *annually* (for example, 8% the first year, 7% the second, 6% the third, etc.) and that is applied to the proceeds of any shares sold in that year. The back-end load is usually structured so that it has dropped to zero after an extended holding period (up to eight years), and the sales load schedule is specified in the fund's prospectus.

For example, assume that ALF Mutual Fund charges a back-end load and reduces it annually according to the following schedule:

Percentage	Year
8%	One
7%	Two
6%	Three
5%	Four
3%	Five
1%	Six
0%	Seven

Assuming that the POP for ALF Mutual Fund shares is $10, an investment of $1,000 into the fund will purchase 100 shares. Should the investor decide to liquidate after six months (assuming there has been no change in NAV), the money returned will be $920 ($1,000 less the 8% back-end load of $80 equals $920). If the investor doesn't redeem the shares until the fifth year (again assuming there has been no change in NAV), he will receive $970 for the shares ($1,000 less the 3% back-end load of $30 equals $970).

12b-1 Asset-based Fees

An exception to the provision disallowing funds to act as distributors for their own fund shares is allowed under section 12b-1 of the securities acts. Under this section, a company may collect a fee for promotion, sale or another activity in connection with the distribution of its shares. The fee is determined annually as a flat dollar amount or as a percentage of the company's average total NAV during the year. There are certain requirements:

- The percentage of net assets charged must be reasonable (typically 1/2% to 1% of the net assets). This annual fee cannot exceed 8.5% of the offering price on a per-share basis.
- The fee must reflect the anticipated level of distribution services.

The payments represent charges that would have been paid to a third party (underwriter) had sales charges been negotiated for sales promotion, services and related activities.

Approval. The 12b-1 plan must be approved initially and reapproved at least annually by a majority of the outstanding voting securities, the board of directors and those directors who are not interested persons of the company.

Misuse of no-load terminology. To assert that a fund or contract being offered is a no-load fund or contract is a material misrepresentation if the fund indeed has a contingent deferred sales load or has an asset-based 12b-1 fee. To imply that a fund or contract with a deferred sales charge or 12b-1 fee is no-load violates the rules of fair practice; the violation is not alleviated by disclosures in the fund's or contract's prospectus.

Mutual Fund Pricing

Closed-end management companies (publicly traded funds) are bought and sold at market prices either on an exchange or in the OTC market—the same as corporate stock. Historically, closed-end funds trade below their book value, which is referred to as *NAV* when speaking of investment company securities.

In contrast, open-end management company shares (mutual funds) are bought through broker-dealers that are authorized distributors of the fund and are sold as public offering securities at a fixed price (based on the NAV plus a sales charge). On the other side of the market, if a customer holding mutual fund shares wants to sell, normally the shares are tendered for redemption (at current NAV) rather than sold in the open market. Many mutual fund principal underwriters will buy shares from customers who want to sell in OTC transactions as an accommodation. But the price on such transactions is always based on the current NAV, not on an open market price.

Pricing Management Company Shares

The formula for determining the POP of mutual fund shares is:

$$NAV + Sales\ charge = Offering\ price$$

The sales charge represents the money received by the underwriter for distributing fund shares. The charge collected includes the underwriter's concession and dealer discounts (if any) and pays for sales literature and advertising. The basic formula for determining the sales charge on mutual fund shares is:

$$\text{Offering price} - \text{NAV} = \text{Sales charge}$$

A mutual fund prospectus must contain a formula that explains how the fund computes the NAV and how the sales charge is added. The prospectus should also explain how often the fund makes these calculations. Often, a rep will know only the NAV and sales load of a mutual fund share. To determine the POP, divide the NAV by the complement of the sales load (100% – SL%). The formula is as follows:

$$\frac{\text{Net asset value}}{100\% - \text{Sales charge \%}} = \text{Public offering price}$$

It is important to use this formula because the sales charge is always based on the POP, not on the NAV.

For example, if a fund's NAV is $10 per share and the sales charge is 7%, to calculate the POP divide the NAV by the complement of the sales load (100% – 7% = 93%, or .93); an NAV of $10 divided by 93% equals a POP of $10.75. In another example, if the NAV is $20 per share and the sales charge is the maximum 8.5%, the POP will be: $20 ÷ (100% – 8.5%) = $21.86.

Because of the possible high front-end sales charge, investment in mutual funds is recommended as a long-term investment. Short-term trading is considered an unsuitable practice.

Computing the Sales Charge Percentage

When the NAV and the POP are known, the sales charge percentage included in the POP can be determined this way:

$$\text{POP} - \text{NAV} = \text{Sales charge (\$ amount)}$$

$$\frac{\text{Sales charge (\$ amount)}}{\text{POP}} = \text{Sales charge \%}$$

For example, if the POP is $43.70 and the NAV is $40 per share, the sales charge percentage is calculated as follows:

$$\$43.70 - \$40.00 = \$3.70 \text{ Sales charge \$ amount}$$

$$\$3.70 \div \$43.70 = 8.5\% \ (8.46\%) \text{ Sales charge \%}$$

Reductions in the Permitted Maximum Sales Charge

The permitted maximum sales charge is reduced from 8 1/2% if certain provisions are not offered by the investment company. To qualify for the maximum 8 1/2% sales charge, the investment company must offer all of the following:

- automatic reinvestment of income distributions at net asset value (no sales charge);
- a scale of reduced sales charges for lump-sum investments; and
- rights of accumulation.

Dividend reinvestment. Dividend reinvestment must be made available to any person who requests such reinvestment at least ten days prior to the record date for the distribution. The company does have the right to limit the availability of dividend reinvestment to holders of securities with a minimum stated value (minimum not to exceed $1,200).

Quantity discounts. If quantity discounts are not made available to any person in terms at least as favorable as the schedules established for rights of accumulation, the maximum sales charge on any transaction will also be reduced.

Rights of accumulation. Rights of accumulation or discounts for cumulative purchases must be made available to any person for a period of not less than ten years from the date of first purchase according to a schedule established by the act of 1940. If rights of accumulation are not made available under terms at least as favorable as in the established discount schedules, the maximum sales charge on any transaction will be reduced accordingly.

Sales Charges and Quantity Discounts

Like most other businesses, open-end investment companies encourage large investments by offering discounts. The principle of *economy of scale* would dictate that the purchaser of one pair of shoes will pay more per pair than the purchaser of 1,000 pairs of shoes. The same is true for mutual fund share purchases. There may be one sales charge percentage for investing $500 and a different sales charge percentage for investing $100,000, so that the sales charge would be considerably less per dollar of investment for the person investing $100,000.

Breakpoints

The schedule of discounts offered by a mutual fund is called the fund's **breakpoints**. Breakpoints are available to any person. The term "person," for this purpose, has a very loose definition. For example, most investment companies consider a family unit to be one person. However, a father and his 35-year-old son would not be considered a family unit qualifying for reduced sales charges because only minor children may be included in the family unit. Moreover, investment clubs or associations formed for the purpose of investing do not qualify for breakpoints. The following is an example of a breakpoint schedule:

Purchases		Sales Cost
$1 to $9,999	=	8 1/2%
$10,000 to $24,999	=	7 1/2%
$25,000 to $49,999	=	7%
$50,000 plus	=	6 1/2%

There are several ways an investor can qualify for breakpoints. As discussed, a large lump-sum investment would be one method. Mutual funds offer additional incentives for the investor to continue to invest and qualify for breakpoints, namely the statement of intention and rights of accumulation.

Statement of Intention (Letter of Intent)

Investors who do not have a large enough amount of money to invest at their initial purchase to qualify for a breakpoint may file a **letter of intent (LOI)**. In the LOI, they indicate their intent to invest the additional funds necessary to reach the breakpoint at some time during the next 13 months.

The LOI is a unilateral contract that is binding on the fund only. The customer must complete the investment in order to qualify for the reduced sales cost, and the fund will hold the extra shares purchased from the reduced sales load in escrow. If the client deposits the money to complete the LOI, he receives the escrowed shares. Appreciation and reinvested dividends do not count towards the contract amount.

Assume a mutual fund offers breakpoints as follows:

Investment		Sales Charge
$1 to $9,999	=	8 1/2%
$10,000 to $24,999	=	7%
$25,000 to $49,999	=	6 1/2%

A client investing $9,000 is just short of the $10,000 breakpoint. In such a situation, a letter of intent may be an option. This statement of intention, promising to invest an amount qualifying for the breakpoint (in this case, an additional $1,000) within 13 months from the date of the letter, will allow the investor to qualify currently for the reduced sales charge.

If at the end of the 13-month period the client has not completed the letter, she will be given the choice of sending a check for the difference in sales charges or cashing in enough of the escrowed shares to pay the difference.

Backdating the Letter

Because most investment companies are eager for people to become large investors, a fund often permits the client to sign a letter of intent as late as the 90th day after a purchase. The letter of intent is then backdated to the date of the original purchase. This means that if a client decides to sign the letter of intent after 60 days, she will have 11 months in which to complete the letter. The LOI may be backdated by up to 90 days to include prior purchases, but may not cover more than 13 months in total.

Rights of Accumulation

Rights of accumulation, like letters of intent, allow the investor to qualify for reduced sales charges. The client may qualify for reduced loads any time the aggregate value of shares previously purchased and shares currently being purchased in the account is over a breakpoint. For the purpose of qualifying for breakpoints, the investment company will base the quantity of securities owned on:

- the current value of the securities at either NAV or POP;
- total purchases of such securities at the actual offering price; or

- the higher of current NAV or the total of purchases made to date (typically how it is valued).

Assume an investment company offers breakpoints as follows:

Investment		Sales Charge
$1 to $9,999	=	8 1/2%
$10,000 to $24,999	=	7%
$25,000 to $49,999	=	6 1/2%

A client who originally invested $10,000, the value of which is currently $15,000, now wishes to invest an additional $10,000. Under rights of accumulation, the client will be charged 6 1/2% on the additional $10,000 investment. The original sales charge on the initial investment is not adjusted. Most funds set no limitations on the amount of time during which an investor can qualify for breakpoints under rights of accumulation.

Combination Privilege

Funds that have the same principal underwriter may grant an investor the privilege of combining separate investments in two or more funds under the same management towards a breakpoint. In this way, the investor would qualify for a reduced sales charge on his total investments.

For example, John Jones has invested $10,000 in the XYZ growth fund for retirement and $10,000 in the XYZ income fund for his children's education. The underwriter may offer John the privilege of combining the two separate investments into one investment totaling $20,000 for the purpose of calculating the sales charge. If the fund offers this privilege, it will be stated in the fund's prospectus.

Notifying Shareholders of Reductions in Sales Load

A mutual fund that grants any reduction in sales load to shareholders must notify all shareholders of this at least once a year.

Breakpoint Sales

To some registered reps, these larger sales represent reduced commissions, and a very few attempt to avoid the drop in their payout by encouraging investors to split their investments into smaller amounts. The NASD prohibits registered reps from the practice of selling investment company shares in dollar amounts just below the point at which the sales charge is reduced *in order to make the higher commission* (known as a **breakpoint sale**).

The NASD considers this practice contrary to just and equitable principles of trade; it is the responsibility of all parties concerned, particularly the principal, to see that such practices are eliminated.

Exchanges Within a Family of Funds

Sponsors frequently offer more than one fund and refer to these multiple offerings as their **family of funds**. One way that sponsors encourage customers to place additional money in their funds is by offering exchange (conversion) privileges within the family of funds.

Exchange privileges allow an investor to convert the value of shares held in one fund for an equal value of those of another in the same family. Some funds allow an investor to make this exchange with a phone call. The advantage to the investor of making an exchange within a family of mutual funds is that it is often accomplished without incurring an additional sales charge. (Keep in mind that any exchange of funds is considered a sale for tax purposes.)

Mutual funds may be purchased at NAV under a no-load exchange privilege. As with any other aspect of securities sales, certain rules apply:

- Any purchases may not exceed the proceeds generated by the sale (or redemption) of the other fund.
- The redemption may not involve a refund of sales charges.
- The sale (or exchange) must take place within 30 days after the redemption.
- The sales personnel and dealers must receive no compensation of any kind from the reinvestment.

Redemption of Fund Shares

By law, an open-end investment company must redeem shares tendered to it *within seven days* of receipt of a *written request* for redemption (or, if the fund certificates are held by the customer, the date the certificates and instructions to liquidate arrive at the custodian bank). The customer's signature on the written request must be guaranteed. The price at which shares are redeemed is the NAV, which must be calculated at least once per business day. There are times when the redemption requirement may be suspended:

- the NYSE is closed other than for a customary weekend or holiday closing;
- trading on the NYSE has been restricted;
- an emergency exists that would make disposal of securities owned by the company not reasonably practical; or
- the SEC has ordered the suspension of redemptions for the protection of the securities holders of the company.

Otherwise, the fund must redeem shares upon request.

Forward pricing. The redemption price is the NAV next calculated after the investment company receives the redemption request (known as **forward pricing**). For example, if a request to redeem shares were received by the fund today, that redemption request would be held until the fund next calculates the NAV per share. If the request were received after today's calculation had been made, the redemption would occur at the next calculation. (Forward pricing applies to the purchase of fund shares as well.) The fund may charge the investor a redemption fee, which is usually from 1/2 of 1% to 2% of the NAV.

With closed-end (publicly traded) funds, the NAV has no direct bearing on the market price because that price is determined by open market supply and demand. The NAV of a closed-end fund is one of many measuring tools for evaluating whether the current market price of the fund's shares are overvalued or undervalued.

Repurchase

Under a repurchase agreement, the principal underwriter will accept a wire order from the broker-dealer, and the transaction is completed at the next determined NAV. The dealer may charge a fee for repurchase above and beyond any redemption fee charged by the fund. Repurchase allows the investor to redeem shares immediately. Repurchase is offered by many companies but may be suspended or discontinued at any time.

Cancelation of Fund Shares

Once an open-end investment company share has been redeemed, it is destroyed. Unlike other corporate securities that may be transferred to other owners, mutual fund shares are not resold; they are canceled. An investor purchasing mutual fund shares receives new shares.

Mutual Fund Purchase and Withdrawal Plans

Types of Mutual Fund Accounts

Open Account

When opening an account with an open-end investment company, the client will make an initial deposit of at least the minimum required by the fund. At this point, the account is open, and the client will determine if fund share distributions are to be received in cash or reinvested. If the client elects to receive distributions in cash rather than reinvesting them, his proportionate interest in the mutual fund will be reduced each time a distribution is made. The client can make additional investments to an open account at any time and without limit as to dollar amount—that is, no such limit is set by law, although each fund may set its own minimums.

For example, John Fredericks chooses to receive all distributions in cash, while Mary Jones elects to reinvest her distributions in shares. Both start with 100 shares. The next time a dividend distribution is made, Mary purchases more shares. Assuming an NAV of $10 and a dividend distribution equal to $1, Mary receives ten shares, and John receives $100 in cash. Now Mary owns 110 shares, while John's account remains at 100 shares. Compared to Mary, John now has a lower proportionate ownership in the fund.

Accumulation Plans

Voluntary accumulation plan. A voluntary accumulation plan allows the client to deposit regular periodic investments on a voluntary basis in preset amounts. The plan is designed to help the client form regular investment habits while still offering some flexibility.

Under a voluntary accumulation plan, the client opens an account and voluntarily commits to additional periodic investments. Voluntary accumulation plans may require a minimum initial purchase and minimum optional additional purchase amounts. Many funds offer automatic withdrawal from customer checking accounts to simplify contributions. Most voluntary accumulation plans set up dividend and gains distributions on an automatic reinvestment basis, and most offer reduced sales charges as money accumulates. Because the plan is voluntary, should the client miss a payment, the fund can in no way penalize him. The plan may be discontinued at any time by the client.

Contractual accumulation plan. A contractual plan differs from a voluntary plan in that the investor signs an agreement to invest an agreed upon dollar amount over a specified period of time. Although called a contractual plan, the agreement is binding on the company only; the investor cannot be held to the contract.

Contractual plans may issue periodic plan certificates and use either of two methods of calculating sales charges. The choice is made by the investment company and is indicated in the prospectus. The Investment Company Act of 1940 allows a maximum of 9% in sales charges by contractual plans, although for large investments, the investor may qualify for lower sales charges by meeting breakpoint minimums.

Lump-sum accounts. Lump-sum accounts are also called regular accounts. The investor buys shares in the fund by depositing the entire amount he intends to invest all at once.

Periodic Payment Plans (Contractual Plans)

Periodic payment plans, also called *contractual plans*, enable the investor who would like to accumulate a sum of dollars over a fixed period of time to invest in a mutual fund on a periodic basis (usually monthly). A contractual plan allows an individual to invest an amount that is typically less than permitted under most minimum investment requirements of open-end funds. An investor may begin a contractual plan for as little as $20 per month, compared to typically higher minimum initial investments in an open-end fund. The investor will sign an agreement stating that she intends to invest a fixed number of dollars over a defined period of time. This agreement is not binding on the investor. The term "contractual plan" is really a misnomer because the agreement is unilateral; only the company is bound by the provisions. Finally, because sales charges are so heavy initially in these plans, some states do not allow their sale.

Characteristics of Contractual Plans

Separate products/separate prospectuses. When a contractual plan is sold, two interrelated sales are taking place. First, the customer is agreeing to make periodic payments to a contractual plan company (which is primarily a sales development company). Evidence of this agreement takes the form of a plan certificate issued by the contractual plan company. Second, as periodic payments are made by the customer, the plan company uses the money to buy shares in the mutual fund.

Contractual plan companies are organized as **UITs**. The customer's monthly payments to the plan buy dollar-denominated units that are credited to the customer's plan account. The dollars represented by these units, in turn, are invested in full and fractional shares issued by the mutual fund. The customer's units represent an undivided interest in the pool of underlying mutual fund shares.

Thus, there is a double sale—the sale of units in the plan account and the sale of shares in the fund. Therefore, two prospectuses exist.

Plan custodian. Plan companies also have their own plan custodian. The plan custodian has many of the same duties and functions as the investment company transfer agent. For instance, the plan company custodian is responsible for:

- safekeeping assets underlying the plan (held by the custodian, not by the investor);
- issuing a confirmation form to the customer designating the number of shares owned;

- taking care of any assignments or transfer of fund shares; and
- sending out the letter notifying the customer of the free-look period (45-day letter).

Front-end Load and Spread Load

Front-end load. Contractual plans may operate under one of two federal securities acts. The Investment Company Act of 1940 allows the company to charge up to 50% of the investor's deposits in the first year. These act of 1940 plans are known as **front-end load plans**. The seller is allowed to charge a maximum sales charge equal to 9% of the total payments stipulated in a contractual plan, as follows:

- 50% of the total payments made during the first twelve months (first year) may be deducted and applied against total sales charges due over the life of the plan. This 50% deduction must be applied evenly to twelve monthly payments.
- Over the remaining life of the plan, deductions for sales charges may be calculated in any reasonable manner (typically prorated over the payments remaining to the plan completion date).

If a person invests $100 a month under a front-end load plan ($1,200 the first year), the company could collect $600 in sales charges the first year.

Spread load. The Investment Company Act Amendments of 1970, which amends the 1940 act, allows the company to charge up to 20% of the investor's deposit in any one year as long as the average charge over the first four years does not exceed 16% annually. This arrangement is known as a **spread-load plan**.

- Over the *first four years* of the plan, *an average of 16%* of all payments made by the investor may be deducted and applied against the total sales charges called for over the life of the plan.
- In *each* of the *first four years*, the sales charge rate and dollar amount deducted for the year must be *uniformly applied* to each month's payment rather than bunched up and deducted from the first few months' payments.
- The rates at which sales charge deductions are made during each of the first four years are left to the seller's discretion, subject to the restriction that *the first year's deduction cannot exceed 20%* and the average over the four-year period cannot exceed 16%.

Table 12.4 shows how the spread load might be scheduled.

Table 12.4 Sales Charge Rates

	Plan A	Plan B	Plan C
First year	20%	20%	20%
Second year	19%	18%	16%
Third year	18%	16%	15%
Fourth year	7%	10%	13%
Four-year average	16%	16%	16%

If a person invests $100 per month under a spread-load plan, the company might charge $240 the first year (20%), $228 the second year (19%) and $216 the third year (18%). The sales charge in the fourth year would be limited to 7%, or $84, because the average charge per year cannot exceed 16%. (Total sales charges of $768 equal 16% of the total amount contributed, $4,800.)

Whether the plan company operates under the act of 1940 or the act of 1970, the maximum sales charge allowable is 9% over the life of the plan. For example, if a client plans to invest $100 per month for ten years, her total investment over the life of the plan would equal $12,000. The maximum sales charge would be $1,080 (9% of $12,000). The main difference between the two acts is the method of reaching this maximum sales charge, either up front (50% front-end load) or spread out (20% spread-load plan).

Table 12.5 shows a comparison of contractual plans.

Investor Right to Terminate a Plan

Under the provisions of the Investment Company Act of 1940, a periodic payment plan (either front end or spread load) must allow for the investor who reconsiders her purchase decision. The following opportunities must be made available to investors.

Right of withdrawal (45-day free look). The fund's custodian bank must furnish the investor with a written notice detailing the total sales charges that will apply over the life of the plan and must send that notice *within 60 calendar days* of the date a contractual plan certificate is issued to the customer.

The customer, if so inclined, may surrender the certificate and terminate the plan *within 45 days* from the mailing date of the custodian's written notice. If the customer does, in fact, surrender the certificate within that time, he is entitled to:

- a 100% refund of all sales charges paid to date, *plus*
- the current value of the investment.

The current value of the fund shares being liquidated at NAV may result in a profit or loss on the investment, depending on the NAV at the time of purchase and the current NAV.

Table 12.5   Comparison of Contractual Plans

Terms	1940 Act (Front-end)	1970 Act (Spread-load)
Max. sales charges (life)	9%	9%
Max. sales charges in any one year	50%	20%
Max. sales charges over four years	No limit set	16% average per year
45-day free-look letter	Refund of current NAV plus any sales charges	Refund of current NAV plus any sales charges
Termination within first 18 months	Refund of NAV plus any sales charges in excess of 15% of total payments	Refund of NAV only

Right to refund (18-month partial refund period). In a front-end load plan, the right to refund provides that if a customer requests termination of a front-end load plan within the *first 18 months* from the issuance date of the periodic payment plan certificate, she is entitled to a refund of:

- all sales charges paid to date *in excess of 15% of the total (gross) payments* made to date, *plus*
- the current value of the investment, which is liquidated at current NAV (and may result in a profit or loss).

To illustrate how the sales charge refund works, assume that a customer bought a front-end load contractual plan that called for monthly payments of $100 for 15 years. After making twelve monthly payments, the customer decides to terminate the plan. From each of twelve $100 monthly payments, a 50% deduction for sales charges is made.

Total payments:	12 at $100	=	$1,200
Total deductions:	12 at $50	=	$600
Total investment:	12 at $50	=	$600

The customer refund consists of:

$ 600	Total sales charge deductions
– 180	15% of total payments ($1,200)
$ 420	Refund of sales charges
+ 600	Current market value of investment (assuming no gain or loss in NAV)
$1,020	Total refund due customer

As a second example, assume a client invests $100 a month for ten months in a contractual plan under the act of 1940. The client's current account value (NAV) is $750 when he terminates the plan. The refund provisions under the act of 1940 require the plan company to return the current value of the client's account ($750) plus all sales charges deducted in excess of 15% of the amount invested ($100/month × 10 months = $1,000). The client has invested $100 per month, of which $50 is a sales charge. Over ten months, the company has collected a total of $500 as a sales charge. The company may keep only $150 (15% of $1,000) and must return the balance of $350 ($500 – $150). Therefore, the client will receive a total refund of $1,100 ($750 NAV + $350 sales charge refund).

The right to refund policy also applies if the investor abandons the plan prior to the end of the 18-month refund period. Abandonment means that the customer simply stops making the monthly payments called for in the contract. In such instances, the custodian bank must take steps to notify the customer that payment is overdue and that the person's account may be closed.

Notice of right to refund. If a contractual plan has reached its *fifteenth-month anniversary* and the investor has missed *three or more* monthly payments, the custodian (or the plan company) must issue a **right to refund notice** to the investor. The custodian has 30 calendar days from the fifteenth-month anniversary date to mail the notice to the delinquent customer.

If the contractual plan is *past* its fifteenth-month anniversary date but has *not passed the eighteenth month*, and the customer now misses a payment (or has missed two payments in the past and now misses a third), the custodian must send a right to refund notice as promptly as possible.

Partial withdrawals. Plan companies may also allow for partial liquidation or withdrawal in the event of an emergency. The amount withdrawn may be reinvested at no additional cost or at a very reduced sales charge.

Plan Completion Insurance

With some funds, the client may purchase a decreasing term policy at group rates to ensure completion of the accumulation plan. The custodian is named as the insurance beneficiary. At the death of the participant, the fund custodian receives the insurance proceeds to complete the purchase of fund shares, which are distributed to the survivors.

Dollar Cost Averaging

One method of purchasing mutual fund shares (and a basic advantage of contractual plans, which are discussed in a later section) is called **dollar cost averaging**, an investment method that requires a person to contribute money to be invested in regular amounts over a period of time. This form of investing allows the investor to purchase more shares when prices are low and fewer shares when prices are high. In a fluctuating market, the average cost per share over a period of time will be lower for the investor than the average price of the shares for the same period. If prices are declining, however, this will not ensure the investor a profit. The following example illustrates how average price and average cost may vary with dollar cost averaging:

Month	Amount Invested	Price per Share	No. of Shares
January	$ 600	$ 20	30
February	600	24	25
March	600	30	20
April	600	40	15
Total	$2,400	$114	90

The average price per share equals $114 (the sum of the prices) divided by 4 (the number of purchases), which is $28.50 per share. The average cost per share equals $2,400 (the total investment) divided by 90 (the total number of shares purchased), which is $26.67 per share.

Withdrawal Plans

In addition to lump-sum withdrawals (where a client requests that all of the shares he owns be sold and the proceeds distributed to him), mutual funds also offer **systematic withdrawal plans**. Not all mutual funds offer withdrawal plans, but those that do may offer plans based on a fixed-dollar, -percentage, -share or -time withdrawal.

Fixed dollar. A client may request the withdrawal of a fixed amount of money periodically. The fund will then liquidate enough shares to send that sum. The amount of money liquidated could be more or less than the earnings for the account during that period. If the amount requested is greater than the account's earnings, a portion of the principal will be liquidated.

Fixed percentage or fixed share. Under a fixed-percentage or fixed-share withdrawal plan, either a fixed number of shares or a fixed percentage of the account will be liquidated each period. The proceeds, whatever the dollar amount may be, are sent to the shareholder.

Fixed time. Under a fixed-time withdrawal plan, clients liquidate their holdings over a fixed period of time. For example, if a client wishes to receive the proceeds monthly for ten years, the fund will send an initial check equal to 1/120th of the client's current account value. Because the client has fixed the time, this type of withdrawal plan is considered self-exhausting; that is, for the above example, the client's account will be liquidated in ten years.

Regardless of the plan or plans offered by the fund, most open-end companies require a minimum amount of money to be invested before the plan may begin. Additionally, most funds discourage continued investment once withdrawals begin. (Withdrawals are at NAV; investments are at POP.)

Withdrawal plans are normally a free service offered by the open-end investment company.

Withdrawal Plan Sales Literature

Withdrawal plans are not guaranteed. With fixed-dollar plans, only the dollar amount to be received each period is fixed; all other factors (such as the number of shares liquidated or the time the plan will last) are variable. For a fixed-time plan, only the period of time is fixed; the amount of money the investor receives varies each period, and so on. Because withdrawal plans are not guaranteed, the SEC is very concerned that the benefits are not misrepresented.

- The registered rep can never promise the investor a guaranteed rate of return.
- The registered rep must stress to the investor that it is possible to exhaust the account by overwithdrawing.
- The registered rep must state that during a down market it is possible that the account will be exhausted if even a small amount is withdrawn.
- The registered rep must not use charts or tables unless the SEC specifically clears their use.

Mutual Fund Distributions and Taxation

Distributions from Mutual Funds

There are several economic advantages to mutual fund ownership. Gains can be realized through the sale of the fund's portfolio securities themselves, and if the gains from the portfolio are reinvested or unrealized, the fund shares themselves will reflect the appreciation, and the shareholder can sell the fund shares for a gain. Appreciation of share values is not the only return possible from mutual fund investment; current income is often the stated objective. This income is paid in the form of dividends.

Net Investment Income

Dividend distributions. The investment company may pay **dividends** to each shareholder in much the same way corporations pay dividends to stockholders. Dividends are paid from the net investment income of the mutual fund.

To calculate **net investment income**, the fund totals dividends received from common and preferred stock held in the portfolio and adds all interest income received from bonds and other debt instruments. The sum of dividends and interest equals the gross investment income of the fund. From gross investment income, the fund subtracts its expenses for operation (adviser's fee, custodial fee, utilities, salaries, accounting costs and so on). The result is net investment income.

Keep in mind that costs associated with selling shares to the public, such as advertising expenses and sales concessions and commissions, are collected as part of the sales load. These fees are not part of the fund expenses when calculating net investment income.

Calculating fund yields. Net investment income is dividends and interest received on portfolio securities, less operating expenses. The dividend paid from the net investment income is divided by the current offering price to calculate yield. All yield quotations must disclose the:

- general direction of the stock market for the period in question
- NAV of the fund at the beginning and the end of the period
- percentage change in the fund's price during the period

Current yield calculations may be based only on income distributions for the preceding twelve months. Gains distributions are considered misleading and, therefore, may not be included in the yield calculations.

Should the board of directors declare a dividend, the dividend is paid from net investment income to shareholders according to their interest in the fund. Most mutual funds distribute dividends quarterly, although monthly and even daily dividends are not uncommon. The mutual fund must disclose the source of the dividend payment if it is from other than retained or current income (for example, if it is the result of a short-term gain).

Ex-dividend date. Unlike the ex-dividend date for other corporate securities, the ex-dividend date for mutual funds is set by the board of directors. There is no four-day requirement, as for other corporate securities. Normally, the ex-dividend date for mutual funds is the day after the record date.

Capital Gains Distributions

Capital gains distributions are derived from the activities of the investment adviser trading securities held in the fund's portfolio. It is hoped that the investment adviser will be purchasing stock that may appreciate in value. At the appropriate time, the adviser may sell the stock for a gain. If the fund has held the stock for a period of at least one year, the gain is a capital gain. The investment company may retain the gain for further investment or may distribute the gain to shareholders in proportion to the number of shares owned. Capital gains distributions (long term) may not be made more frequently than once per year.

Any distribution of gains from an open-end investment company will be long term. Short-term gains are considered income distributions and will be identified and distributed as dividends.

Selling dividends. If an investor purchases fund shares just before the ex-dividend date, she is at a double disadvantage. Not only does the market value of the fund shares decrease by the amount of the distribution, but the investor also incurs a tax liability on the distribution. A registered representative is forbidden to encourage investors to purchase fund shares prior to a distribution because of this tax liability, and doing so is known as **selling dividends**.

Reinvestment of Dividend and Gains Distributions

Dividends and capital gains are distributed in cash. However, the shareholder may elect to reinvest the cash distributions to purchase additional shares of the mutual fund. This reinvestment of distributions is called *automatic reinvestment* and is similar to compounding interest at a bank; the reinvested distributions purchase additional shares, which then begin earning dividends or sharing in gains distributions.

Dividends may be systematically reinvested by customers at less than the POP, and can be used to purchase full and fractional shares as long as:

- shareholders who are not already participants in the reinvestment plan are given a separate opportunity to reinvest each dividend;
- the plan is described in the prospectus;
- the issuer of the securities bears no additional costs beyond those that would have been incurred in the normal payout of dividends; and
- all shareholders are notified of the availability of the dividend reinvestment plan at least once every year.

The mutual fund may apply a reasonable charge against each dividend reinvestment, and may require the shareholder to request the reinvestment at least 10 days prior to the record date.

If the company wishes to establish a plan through which investors can reinvest their capital gains distributions (as opposed to their dividends) at a discount to the POP, the following rules apply:

- The plan must be described in the prospectus.
- All participants must be given a separate opportunity to reinvest capital gains at each distribution.
- All participants must be notified at least once a year of the availability of the distribution reinvestment plan.

Whether the distributions are taken in cash or reinvested to purchase additional shares, they are taxable to the shareholders. Distributions from net investment income are taxed as ordinary income. Long-term capital gains are taxed at the ordinary income tax rate.

Source of distributions. The fund must disclose the source and character of distributions, either from income or from capital transactions, as each distribution is made. Form 1099B is sent after the close of the year and details tax information related to distributions for the year.

Realized and Unrealized Appreciation

As stated earlier, the fund's investment adviser may sell stock that has appreciated in value, creating a gain. The gain may be distributed to shareholders, or it may be reinvested to purchase other securities for the fund portfolio. Should the adviser decide to hold the appreciated stock, the NAV of the fund shares will reflect this appreciated value. If the shareholder now decides to sell his appreciated mutual fund shares at a gain, his tax liability will depend on the difference between the original cost for the shares and the appreciated selling price.

The gain, whether long or short term, will be taxed at the investor's ordinary income tax bracket. The investor does not receive a 1099B for shares sold; the recordkeeping requirements are the responsibility of the investor.

If the shareholder does not sell the appreciated fund shares, the gain, whether long or short term, is unrealized. There is no income tax liability.

Advertising Returns

Although in reality an investor's total return from a mutual fund investment will include income distributions, gains distributions and share appreciation, advertising return based on the sum of all distributions and appreciation is considered misleading. Current yield calculations may be based only on income distributions for the past twelve months, divided by the current price of the share.

$$\text{Dividend return} \div \text{Current price} = \text{Current yield}$$

For example, if the XYZ Mutual Fund has a current offering price of $10 and over the past twelve months has distributed dividends totaling $1 and gains totaling $.75, the current yield for this fund is only 10%, not 17.5%.

Taxation of Mutual Funds

Investment Income: IRC Subchapter M

As a corporation or trust, the mutual fund is responsible for taxes on income earned from the securities held in the company's portfolio. Of concern to the investor, the taxation of income at the fund's level subjects the investment income to a tax liability on three levels: the corporate level of the individual company; the investment company; and the investor upon receiving the distribution.

Conduit (pipeline) theory. Triple taxation of investment income may be avoided if the open-end investment company qualifies under Subchapter M of the Internal Revenue Code (IRC). If a mutual fund acts as a conduit, or pipeline, for the distribution of net investment income, the fund may qualify as a *regulated investment company* and be subject to tax only on the amount of investment income retained by the company. The investment income distributed to shareholders escapes taxation at the investment company level. Subchapter M requires that the investment company distribute at least 90% of its net investment income to shareholders. If the company distributes 89%, the company is liable for tax on 100% of net investment income.

The definition of net investment income under IRC Subchapter M is interest and dividend income minus expenses. Gains are not included in the calculation of net investment income.

Capital Gains

If the investment company distributes capital gains to the mutual fund shareholder, the shareholder is responsible for taxes. If the investment company retains a capital gain and reinvests the gain in other securities, the shareholder is still liable for tax on the gain.

The investment company designates to the shareholder of record a proportionate share of the undistributed capital gain. This amount is included on the shareholder's 1040 as reportable income. The regulated investment company pays tax on amounts designated to shareholders, but the tax paid is treated as an advance payment by the shareholder. Because the tax rates on gains differ for corporate and individual taxpayers, the tax due from the shareholder is changed, as is the shareholder's cost basis in the fund portfolio.

Fund Share Liquidations to the Investor

Once the investor has decided to liquidate holdings (sell the shares) in the open-end investment company, he will have to establish his cost base in the shares in order to calculate tax liability.

A simple definition of cost base is: that amount of money invested that has already been taxed. Upon liquidation, cost base represents a return of capital and is not subject to a tax liability. The difference between cost base and the current value of the investor's shares represents his taxable gain (or loss if cost base is greater than the current value of the shares).

Valuing fund shares. The cost base of mutual fund shares includes the total cost of the shares, including sales charges, plus any reinvested investment income and capital gains. The cost base is compared to the amount of money received from the sale of the shares. If the amount received is greater than the cost base, the investor will report a taxable gain. If the amount received is less than the cost base, the investor has a reportable loss.

$$\text{Total value of fund shares} - \text{Cost base} = \text{Taxable gain}$$

Capital Losses

An investor can claim up to $3,000 in net losses to offset ordinary income in any one year. If the investor has more than $3,000 in losses, the amount exceeding the $3,000 limit can be carried forward to offset income in following years. The $3,000 limitation applies to net losses, long and short term. Short-term and long-term losses are deducted against ordinary income dollar for dollar.

For example, an investor with a $2,000 short-term loss and a $2,000 long-term loss could offset $3,000 of taxable income. The short-term loss is used first and, therefore, $1,000 of the long-term loss would be carried forward and applied in future years. There is no limit on the amount of loss that can be carried forward, nor on the number of years over which it is applied.

Wash sales. The IRS will disallow a loss if the investor repurchases a substantially identical security within 30 days before or after the sale of the security in which the loss was claimed. Substantially identical securities would include warrants, options, convertible securities or any security that might be exchanged for or represents the investor's original holding.

Accounting Methods

Should the investor decide to liquidate on a per-share basis, the calculation of cost base can be accomplished by electing one of two accounting methods: first in, first out (FIFO) or share identification. If the investor fails to choose, the IRS assumes the investor is liquidating shares on a FIFO basis.

Share Identification

Probably the more frequently used and advantageous method of determining cost on a per-share basis is share identification. The investor keeps track of the cost of each share purchased. Upon selling the shares, the investor decides which shares to liquidate. He then identifies the cost base of each share liquidated in whichever order provides the necessary tax benefit. Share identification is the most flexible of the two methods. For example, if the investor needs to report a loss, those shares with a higher cost base than the current NAV could be liquidated; if he can absorb a taxable gain, lower cost base shares could be liquidated.

Other Mutual Fund Taxation Considerations

Withholding tax. If an investor neglects or fails to include her tax ID number when purchasing mutual fund shares, the fund is required to withhold 20% of the distributions to the investor as a withholding tax.

Cost basis of shares transferred. The basis of property inherited is either stepped up or stepped down to its fair market value (FMV) at the date of the decedent's death. No adjustment of basis is necessary for the period prior to the decedent's death.

For example, Jane Jones inherited $10,000 worth of mutual fund shares from her father. At her father's death, the NAV of the shares was $11,500. Jane's basis in the shares is the FMV, or $11,500.

Dividend exclusions. The Tax Reform Act of 1986 (TRA 1986) repealed the dividend exclusion for individual taxpayers and reduced the corporate dividend exclusion to 70%.

Taxation of investment returns. The taxation of investment returns can be summarized as follows:

Income distributions:	taxed as ordinary income
Capital gains distributions:	taxed as long-term capital gains
Profit or loss on sale:	short- or long-term gain or loss; cost basis

Exchanges within a family of funds. Even though there is no sales charge on the exchange, for tax purposes, the IRS considers a sale to have taken place and the customer has some tax liability under IRS regulations. This tax liability can be significant, and shareholders should be aware of this potential cost of conversion.

Tracking Investment Company Securities

Investment company prices, like those for individual securities, are quoted daily in the financial press. However, because of the various methods used to calculate sales charges as described below, the financial press uses several footnotes to explain the type of sales charge used by the mutual fund issuer. The registered representative must understand the presentation and meaning of the footnotes associated with investment company quotes so that he can accurately describe the quotes to the investing public. An example of mutual fund quotations and associated footnotes is shown in Figure 12.3.

Most newspapers carry daily quotes of the NAV and POP for most major mutual funds. The bid price of a mutual fund is its NAV; the ask (offer) price is the NAV plus the sales charge (POP). The offer price includes the NAV plus the *maximum* sales charge, if any. The "NAV Chg." column reflects the change to NAV from the previous day's quote.

Let's look at the family of funds called ArGood Mutual Funds. ArGood Growth Fund is a part of this group; its net asset value, offering price and the change in its net asset value per share are listed. As stated previously, when there is a difference between the NAV and the offering price, the fund is a load fund. A no-load fund is usually identified by the letters "NL" in the Offer Price column. Look at the Best Mutual funds; they are a family of no-load funds.

The final column shows the change in the net asset value of a share since the last trading date. A plus (+) indicates an upward move and a minus (–) indicates a downward turn.

Figure 12.3 Mutual Fund Quotations as They Might Appear in a Newspaper

Mutual Fund Quotations
Tuesday, September 13, 1998

Price ranges for investment companies, as quoted by the National Association of Securities Dealers. NAV stands for net asset value per share. The offering price includes net asset value plus maximum sales charge, if any.

	NAV	Offer Price	NAV Chg.		NAV	Offer Price	NAV Chg.
ArGood Mutual Funds				**FastTrak Funds**			
CapApp	4.80	5.04	+ .02	App	13.79	14.44	– .01
Grwth	6.87	7.21	+ .02	CapAp	22.13	23.17	+ .15
HiYld	10.28	10.79	+ .01	Grwth	18.33	19.24	– .10
TaxEx	11.62	12.20	– .04	**Z Best Invest**			
Best Mutual				Grth p	14.81	15.59	– .03
Balan	12.32	NL	– .06	HiYld p	9.25	9.74	+ .03
Canada	10.59	NL	– .04	Inco p	7.95	8.37	– .04
US Gov	10.49	NL	– .02	MuniB p	8.11	8.54	– .03

e- Ex-distribution. f- Previous day's quote. s- Stock split or div. x- Ex-dividend. NL- No load.
p- Distribution costs apply, 12b-1plan. r- Redemption charge may apply.

From this information, you will be able to calculate the sales charge of any mutual fund. For example, find the FastTrak group of funds. The first entry is App. Remember the formula for calculating the sales charge:

$$\text{Sales charge} = \text{Public offering price} - \text{NAV}$$
$$= \$14.44 - \$13.79 = \$0.65$$

$$\text{Sales charge \%} = \text{Sales charge} \div \text{Public offering price}$$
$$= \$0.65 \div \$14.44 = 4.50\%$$

You will also be able to watch the movements of the fund's share value.

Stock guides such as Standard & Poor's include summaries of mutual funds for the year. Figure 12.4 shows a portion of a table taken from the *1991 Standard & Poor's Stock Guide;* you can use it to evaluate different mutual funds.

To the right of the third fund listed on the table, Alliance Fund, you will find the following information:

- **Principal objective of the fund**. "G" means Alliance is a growth fund. Other objectives might be income, return on capital, or stability; they are listed in the footnotes below the table.
- **Type of fund**. Alliance Fund is a "C," or common stock fund. Other types are also listed in the footnotes; they are:

B	– balanced		FL	– flexible
BD	– bond		H	– hedge
C	– common		L	– leverage
CN	– Canadian		P	– preferred
CT	– common, tax shelter		SP	– specialized
CV	– convertible bond and preferred stock		TF	– tax free

Figure 12.4   Standard & Poor's Mutual Fund Summary for 1991

Fund	Prin. Obj.	Type	Dec 31, 1991 Total Net Assets (MILS)	Cash & Equiv (MILS)	Net Assets per Share % Chg. from Prev. Dec 31 At Dec. 31 1989	1990	1991	Max. Sales Min. Unit	Chg. %	$10,000 Invested 12-31-81 Now Worth	Price Record 1991 High	Low	NAV Per Sh as of 12-31-91 NAV per Shr.	Offer Price
Acorn	G	C	525.8	47.0	+ 3.9	+30.1	+15.4	$4,000	None	29,603	47.71	37.61	47.71	47.71
ALFA Securities	G	C	672.6	22.9	+33.5	+41.1	+21.6	$1,000	None	32,518	24.75	19.62	24.47	24.47
Alliance Fund	G	C	948.2	19.0	– 5.2	+29.5	+ 8.9	$250	5.5	24,661	9.67	6.96	9.45	10.00
Alliance Tech	G	C	200.8	10.0	–16.4	+26.1	+12.0	$250	5.5	....	36.47	23.44	34.24	36.23
Amer Balanced	IS	B	202.0	24.0	+ 7.7	+27.1	+15.8	$500	8.5	27,889	12.61	10.92	12.32	13.46
Amer Cap Corp Bond	IS	BD	136.0	16.0	+ 9.2	+24.6	+10.8	$500	8.5	23,457	7.51	7.12	7.12	7.48
Amer Cap Mun Bond	I	TF	187.0	7.0	+10.0	+22.0	+15.9	$500	4.75	22,897	21.74	18.53	19.14	20.09
Analytic Opt Equity	GI	C	85.7	11.7	+ 6.6	+15.5	+10.2	$5,000	None	20,662	15.59	13.88	15.45	15.45
Axe-Houghton Bond	SIR	B	204.5	4.0	+ 5.8	+31.6	+21.5	$1,000	None	27,766	12.16	10.26	11.93	11.93
Axe-Houghton Stock	G	C	93.4	2.0	–15.0	+31.1	+10.8	$1,000	None	28,394	11.46	8.25	11.13	11.13

Principal Objective: G-Growth; I-Income; R-Return on Capital; S-Stability; E-Objectives treated Equally; P-Preservation of Capital; Listed in order of importance. Type: B-Balanced; BD-Bond; C-Common; CV-Conv Bond and Prefd Stock; FL-Flexible; GB-Long-term Gov't; GL-Global; H-Hedge; L-Leverage; P-Preferred; PM-Precious Metals; O-Options; SP-Specialized; TF-Tax Free; ST-Short-term investments.

- **Total net assets.** This column lists total net assets at market value—that is, assets minus liabilities. Alliance Fund has total net assets of $948.2 million.
- **Cash and equivalents.** This column includes cash and receivables, short-term government securities and other money-market instruments less current liabilities. Cash and equivalents are part of the total net assets.
- **Percentage change in net assets per share.** These columns show the performance of a fund over a specific period—in this case, from the previous December 31st. For example, on December 31, 1990, Alliance Fund had a 29.5% increase in net asset value per share since December 31, 1989.
- **Minimum unit.** This is the minimum initial purchase of shares. For Alliance Fund, it is $250.
- **Maximum sales charge.** Alliance Fund charges 5.5%. If a fund is a no-load fund, there is no sales charge.
- **Current worth of $10,000 invested December 31, 1981.** This column provides a gauge of a fund's performance over several years. In this case, $10,000 invested in Alliance Fund on December 31, 1981, would have more than doubled, growing to $24,661.
- From the **price record** columns, you can learn the **percentage of appreciation of a share** from its low price of the year. To determine the percentage of appreciation, subtract the low price from the latest NAV per share, and then divide the difference by the low price. For example, during 1991 Alliance Fund sold at a low of 6.96. If on June 30, 1991 (the current date), its NAV per share was 9.67, the appreciation would be computed as follows:

$$\begin{array}{rr} \text{NAV} & 9.67 \\ \text{Low} & -6.96 \\ \hline & 2.71 \end{array}$$

$2.71 \div 6.96 = 38.93\%$ Appreciation

- **NAV per share.** This column shows the current NAV per share, as well as the current POP.

After some practice at reading the tables of mutual funds, you will be able to distinguish the differences between the three management companies.

Q: Which of the following is most likely to be: (1) a closed-end fund, (2) an open-end fund, and (3) a no-load fund?

	Fund	NAV	Offer Price
A.	IDS Fund	$ 5.84	$ 6.05
B.	Midwest Fund	$ 8.50	$ 8.20
C.	Apollo Fund	$10.10	$10.10

A: The IDS Fund is most likely an open-end fund because the offering price is higher than the NAV.

The Midwest Fund must be a closed-end fund because the offering price is less than the NAV. The fund is selling at a discount from its NAV.

The Apollo Fund is a no-load fund because the NAV and the offering price are the same, indicating that there is no sale charge. (There is a possibility that it is a closed-end fund that is trading for neither a discount nor a premium.)

◆ Review Questions

1. "Mutual fund" is a popular name for
   A. all investment companies
   B. open-end investment companies
   C. closed-end investment companies
   D. any company that invests pooled funds

2. What kind of investment company has no provision for redeeming outstanding shares?
   A. Open-end company
   B. Closed-end company
   C. Unit investment trust
   D. Mutual fund

3. The essential difference between an open-end fund and a closed-end fund is
   A. the method of determining book value
   B. that closed-end funds are closed to secondary trading
   C. capitalization
   D. There is no difference.

4. An investor looking for current income would be LEAST interested in
   A. bond funds
   B. preferred stock funds
   C. common stock funds
   D. gains shares in a dual-purpose fund

5. Money-market funds usually offer which of the following?
   I. Daily interest calculations
   II. Check-writing privileges
   III. No-load funds
   IV. Long-term growth potential
   A. I and II
   B. I, II and III
   C. I, II and IV
   D. II, III and IV

6. The custodian of a mutual fund usually does which of the following?
   A. Approves changes in investment policy
   B. Holds the cash and securities of the fund and performs related clerical functions
   C. Manages the fund
   D. Cleans the fund's properties and carries out related duties

7. Which type of mutual fund is sold at net asset value?
   A. Open-end
   B. Closed-end
   C. Front-end load
   D. No-load

8. In order for a company to charge the maximum sales charge of 8 1/2%, it must offer all of the following EXCEPT
   A. automatic reinvestment of dividends and capital gains at NAV
   B. breakpoints
   C. automatic reinvestment at POP
   D. rights of accumulation

9. If a mutual fund is quoted at $16.56 NAV and $18.00 POP, the percentage of sales charge is
   A. 7 1/2%
   B. 7 3/4%
   C. 8%
   D. 8 1/2%

10. A no-load fund may be redeemed at
    A. NAV minus sales charge
    B. POP minus sales charge
    C. NAV plus sales charge
    D. NAV

◆ Answers & Rationale

1. **B.** The term "mutual fund" is used exclusively for open-end investment companies.

2. **B.** Closed-end investment companies do not redeem their own shares. Once a closed-end fund has sold all of its shares in its initial public offering, investors can buy and sell shares only in the open market.

3. **C.** A closed-end fund issues a set number of shares in an initial public offering to raise capital. Open-end funds raise capital through an open-ended offering in which they continuously issue new shares.

4. **D.** A dual-purpose fund issues two types of shares—income shares and gains shares. Owners of income shares receive any income that the fund distributes. Owners of gains shares receive the benefits of the fund's capital gains.

5. **B.** Money-market funds invest in short-term debt instruments that do not offer potential for long-term growth or capital gains.

6. **B.** The bank or other financial institution hired by the fund to act as its custodian is charged with all of the clerical functions related to holding the fund's cash and securities.

7. **D.** No-load funds are sold at their net asset values (i.e., without sales charges or commissions).

8. **C.** A firm that offered automatic reinvestment at the public offering price would not be offering its investors any special advantage.

9. **C.** The sales charge is calculated as a percentage of the public offering price.

10. **D.** A no-load fund is bought and sold at its net asset value.

13 Retirement Planning

Key Terms

deferred compensation plan
defined benefit plan
defined contribution plan
Employee Retirement Income
  Security Act of 1974 (ERISA)
individual retirement account (IRA)
Keogh plan
payroll deduction plan

Pension Reform Act
profit-sharing plan
qualified plan
rollover
spousal account
top-heavy Keogh
vesting

Overview

An important goal for most investors is to provide themselves with retirement income. Many individuals accomplish this through corporate retirement plans. Others set up their own plans. Still others have both individual and corporate retirement plans. Whether set up by a corporation or by an individual, these plans are called "qualified plans" if contributions to them are tax deductible under IRS rules; otherwise, they are "nonqualified plans."

The Employee Retirement Income Security Act

The Employee Retirement Income Security Act (ERISA) was passed by Congress in 1974; it is the most comprehensive employee benefits legislation enacted to date. ERISA was intended to protect participants in corporate pension plans across the country against the abuse and misuse of pension funds. ERISA guidelines for the regulation of retirement plans include:

- **Participation**. If a company has a retirement plan, employees must be covered within a reasonable time, defined by ERISA as no more than three years.
- **Funding**. Funds contributed to the plan must be segregated from other corporate assets. The plan's trustees have a fiduciary responsibility to invest prudently and manage funds in a way that represents the best interest of all participants.
- **Vesting**. Employees must be entitled to their entire retirement benefit amount within a certain time period, even if they are no longer with the employer.
- **Communication**. The retirement plan must be in writing, and employees must be kept informed of plan benefits, availability, account status and vesting procedure.
- **Nondiscrimination**. A uniformly applied formula determines benefits and contributions of all employees. Such a method ensures equitable and impartial treatment.

ERISA is frequently referred to as the **Pension Reform Act**, but it actually regulates almost all types of employee benefit plans and personal retirement plans. Congress wrote the ERISA legislation in four distinct parts, referred to as **titles:**

- **Title 1** is administered by the Department of Labor. It deals with the protection of employee benefit rights.
- **Title 2** is administered by the Internal Revenue Service (IRS). It is composed of amendments to the Internal Revenue Code's pension and benefits sections.
- **Title 3** deals primarily with the division of responsibilities among all of the agencies administering the new pension laws.
- **Title 4** concerns itself with pension plan termination insurance provisions and established the Pension Benefit Guaranty Corporation (PBGC).

Although far-reaching in its scope, ERISA does not require any employer to establish a pension plan for its workers. Those employers who do choose to establish such a plan, however, must abide by the regulations set forth under ERISA and must meet certain strict standards. These standards reflect ERISA's major goals:

- that pension plan participants are not required to satisfy unreasonable age and service requirements before becoming eligible for plan participation (these are addressed by ERISA's participation provisions);
- that persons who work for a specified minimum period of time under a pension plan are assured of at least some benefits at retirement age (these are ERISA's vesting provisions);
- that adequate money will be there to pay all employee-earned pension benefits when they are due (these are dealt with under ERISA's funding provisions);

- that plan sponsors meet their duties and responsibilities by handling their plan's funds prudently (covered by ERISA's fiduciary responsibility provisions);
- that employees and their beneficiaries know both their rights and their obligations under the plans (ERISA's reporting and disclosure provisions);
- that spouses of pensioners are afforded better coverage and protection (through ERISA's joint and survivor provisions);
- that the benefits of workers in certain defined benefit pension plans are protected in the event of plan termination (through ERISA's plan termination insurance provisions); and
- that tax laws relevant to pensions and their distribution are made more equitable (through various provisions of Title 2 of the Internal Revenue Code).

Corporations usually choose to organize their plans under the standards set forth by ERISA. They do this because of the favorable tax treatment that both employer sponsors and employee plan participants are eligible for. The most important tax advantages for ERISA-qualified pension plans are:

- The employer is entitled to take a current income tax deduction for contributions made to the plan.
- The employees do not have to include in their current year's gross income any of their employer's contributions to their retirement plan. All contributions to the plan are tax deferred until they are distributed.
- Any income earned (or capital gains achieved) by the investments in the participant's account are not taxed to the plan participant until they are distributed or withdrawn.
- Distributions from the retirement plan may be eligible for special income and estate tax treatment at the time of withdrawal.

Individual Retirement Accounts

Individual retirement accounts (IRAs) were created by Congress in 1974 as a way of encouraging people to save towards their retirement. All employed individuals, regardless of whether they are covered by a qualified corporate retirement plan, may open and contribute to an IRA.

Tax Benefits

The Economic Recovery Tax Act of 1981 (ERTA) allowed all IRA participants to fully deduct the amount contributed to their IRAs from their taxable income. TRA 1986 changed the deductibility limits, lowering them for individuals who are covered by other qualified plans. If an individual is not actively participating in other qualified plans, however, the full amount of the contribution to the IRA is still deductible.

For an individual covered by another plan, the portion deductible is determined by that person's income level. For individuals whose gross income exceeds $35,000 or couples whose combined gross income exceeds $50,000, there is no allowable deduction. This is true for married couples even if only one partner is covered by a company-sponsored plan.

Participation in an IRA

Any taxpayer reporting income for a given tax year may participate in an IRA. However, the person's income must be earned income—that is, from the performance of personal services (as in a job) and not passive income (as from investments). The taxpayer may not participate if she has reached the age of 70 1/2 during the tax year. Contributions to an IRA may be made up to April 15th on the year following the tax year.

IRA Contributions

The maximum annual IRA contribution that an employed individual can make is subject to the following limitations:

- for an individual account, 100% of earned income or $2,000, whichever is less; and
- for a spousal account, 100% of earned income or $2,250 (divided between two accounts), whichever is less.

The IRS allows an individual who has an unemployed spouse to contribute to a separate retirement account established for the nonworking spouse (known as a **spousal account**). The contribution may be divided between the two accounts in any way as long as the total contribution is not more than $2,250 and no more than $2,000 is contributed to either account.

The maximum contributions described may or may not be tax deductible, depending on whether the taxpayer is participating in an employer-sponsored retirement plan. IRA tax deductions are summarized in Table 13.1.

IRA owners are always *100% vested* in their contributions to their accounts. This means that they are entitled to withdraw the full amount at any time, although they may incur penalties and will be liable for any taxes due on the amount withdrawn. The retirement account belongs to the account owner—and can be shared with the employee's spouse or passed into the owner's estate at his death.

Nonparticipating (noncovered) employees. If the taxpayer is not actively participating in an employer-sponsored pension or profit-sharing plan (including Keogh and simplified employee pension plan coverage), the person may continue to make tax-deductible contributions to a self-funded, personal IRA up to the annual contribution limits specified in Table 13.1.

Participating (covered) employees. If the taxpayer is actively participating in an employer-sponsored pension or profit-sharing plan (including Keogh and simplified employee pension plan [SEP] coverage), the person's total earnings for the year will determine the extent to which self-funded, personal IRA contributions will be tax deductible.

In essence, the tax deduction gradually fades away as the taxpayer's adjusted gross income (AGI) climbs. IRA contributions, as investments, continue to offer tax deferral on income and capital-compounding opportunities, even if the tax-deductible contribution aspect of an IRA is reduced or eliminated.

Excess Contributions

Annual IRA contributions in excess of the maximum are subject to a 6% penalty tax if the excess is not removed by the time the taxpayer files the tax return. The penalty is applied until the excess is removed from the account.

Table 13.1 IRA Tax-deductible Contributions

Tier	Taxpayer's Adjusted Gross Income (AGI)	Allowable Tax Deduction
1	Single, less than $25,000 Married, less than $40,000	Contribution is 100% tax-deductible.
2	Single, from $25,000 to $35,000 Married, from $40,000 to $50,000	Allowable deduction reduces at the rate of 10% per $1,000 income over $25,000 ($40,000 if married).
3	Single, more than $35,000 Married, more than $50,000	No portion of the contribution is tax deductible.

IRA Custodians and Investments

Taxpayers are free to appoint an IRA custodian of their choice, selecting from a range of financial service vendors, securities broker-dealers, banks and savings institutions, insurance carriers, credit unions and mutual fund distributors.

IRA Investments

Permissible investments. IRA investments may include stocks, bonds, UITs, mutual funds, limited partnerships, government securities, U.S. government-issued gold and silver coins, annuities and many others.

Investments chosen for an IRA (as for any retirement plan) should be carefully evaluated for the amount of risk they entail compared to the return they offer. Because contributions to an IRA are limited to an annual dollar amount, an account owner may not be able to replace money that is lost in a risky investment or a down market. Risk should not be the only factor considered, however, when recommending investments for an IRA. Because an IRA may serve as a significant source of retirement funds, it is important that the account be managed for adequate long-term growth. Most option-based strategies are deemed inappropriate for retirement accounts because options are short-term, wasting assets (no residual value at expiration) that often entail high risks. Uncovered (naked) option writing is among the riskiest of strategies, and is generally not permitted in a retirement account.

Depending on where a person is in his earnings-cycle and how close his projected retirement date, growth-oriented stocks and mutual funds may be the best choice even though they carry with them the higher risks associated with investments in the stock market.

Ineligible investments. There are certain investments that are considered ineligible for use in an IRA. Collectibles (antiques, gems, rare coins, works of art, stamps, etc.) are not acceptable IRA investments. Life insurance contracts (*cash value*, *term* and *decreasing term* insurance with no cash surrender value) may not be purchased in an IRA.

IRA Rollovers

Individuals may take possession of the funds and investments in a qualified plan in order to move them to another qualified plan, but may do so not more than once a year. Such a rollover into another account must be completed within *60 calendar days* of the original funds' withdrawal from the qualified plan. For example, if an individual changes employers, the amount in his pension plan may be distributed to him in a lump-sum payment. He may then deposit the distribution in an IRA rollover account, where the amount deposited retains its tax-deferred status. Only the taxable portion (before-tax contributions and earnings) of the account may be rolled over. Any portion not rolled over is considered a distribution and is subject to ordinary income tax.

Withholding

Effective for distributions made after 1992, if an individual elects to roll over assets from a qualified plan to an IRA or other qualified plan, the payor of the distribution must retain 20% of the distribution as a withholding tax. The option to forgo withholding is not available to the participant. If the individual elects a direct transfer, there is no withholding on the amount directly transferred.

IRA Transfers

Transfers of funds between qualified retirement accounts differ from rollovers in that the account owner never actually takes physical possession of the funds; the money or investments are sent directly from one IRA custodian to another. There is no limit to the number of times per year a person can transfer investments between qualified plans, provided the assets in the accounts do not pass through the hands of the taxpayer.

IRA Withdrawals

IRA earnings are tax deferred until the money is received, usually at retirement. Withdrawals may not begin without penalty before age 59 1/2 and must begin by the year after the year in which the account owner reaches age 70 1/2 (as an example, if the IRA owner reaches 70 1/2 on January 1, 1995, he would have to begin withdrawals by December 31, 1996).

Withdrawals may be made in a lump sum, in varying amounts or in regular installments. Withdrawals, except those that result from contributions made with aftertax dollars (that is, nonqualified contributions), are taxable as ordinary income. Early withdrawals incur a 10% penalty unless they occur because of the individual's death or disability. A 50% penalty is applied to accounts not meeting minimum Internal Revenue Code (IRC) distribution requirements after age 70 1/2.

Taxation on IRA Distributions

Taxpayers may elect to start receiving income from their IRAs at age 59 1/2, or postpone distributions to as late as the year after the year in which the taxpayer reaches age 70 1/2, at which age distribution becomes mandatory. All distributions are treated as taxable income in the year in which received. Under ERISA, when an employee retires IRA payments can be made to the employee or jointly to the employee and spouse. In the event that the account owner dies, payments may continue to be made to a designated beneficiary; a person's rights to accumulated IRA benefits do not stop at the death of that person.

Lump-sum distributions from an IRA are possible, but they afford the taxpayer no advantage because the full amount is taxable as ordinary income for the current tax year.

Taxation on Nondeductible Capital Withdrawals

IRA investors who are covered by an employer-sponsored qualified plan and report AGI over $25,000 ($40,000, if married) may continue to make annual contributions either wholly or partly nondeductible to a self-funded IRA. If so, because aftertax dollars were used to fund the IRA contribution, the same dollars can be returned to the taxpayer without being taxed.

IRA Abuses and Tax Penalties

There are three situations in which a taxpayer's IRA activity will lead to penalties being levied by the IRS.

1. Excess contributions over the maximum annual limits will subject the taxpayer to a tax penalty of *6% of the excess amount*.
2. Early withdrawals (prior to the minimum IRA disbursement age of 59 1/2) will be subject to a *tax penalty of 10%*, in addition to the full amount of the early withdrawal being treated as ordinary income (death and permanent disability are the only exceptions to this rule).
3. Failure to start distributions by the year after the year in which the taxpayer reaches age 70 1/2 (the maximum age for continuing contributions and the mandatory start-up age for receiving distributions) will cause the IRS to impose a special penalty on the taxpayer. Based on actuarial tables, funds that should have been (but were not) disbursed starting at age 70 1/2 will compose a dollar base for calculating a 50% tax penalty.

Keogh (HR-10) Plans

For anyone who is self-employed or owns a small business or professional practice, a Keogh plan offers virtually the same tax advantages and retirement coverage found with corporate retirement programs.

Keogh Plan Eligibility

Keogh plans are intended for self-employed individuals and owner-employees of nonincorporated business concerns or professional practices.

Included in the self-employed category are independent contractors, consultants, free-lancers and anyone else who files and pays self-employment social security taxes.

The term "owner-employee" refers to sole proprietors who rely on their business for their livelihood. The term also applies to partnership establishments in which each partner works for the partnership as an employee, and also owns a stake in the business.

Income must be earned. As required in IRAs, full-time or part-time income must be earned income from personal services, not passive income from investments or other unearned sources.

Business must show a profit. Owner-employees of businesses or professional practices must show a gross profit to qualify for a tax-deductible contribution to a Keogh plan. If there is no business profit, no contribution is allowed.

Plan must be nondiscriminatory. Owner-employees who have full-time employees on their payrolls must provide for these people's retirement security under a Keogh plan in the same manner and to the same extent that the owner-employee's retirement security is provided.

Contributions

Tax-deductible

The Keogh planholder is permitted to make tax-deductible *cash* contributions of up to 25% of earned (after-contribution) income or $30,000, whichever is less. As with IRAs, a person may make contributions to a Keogh until he has reached age 70 1/2.

After-contribution income. In computing the 25% contribution limit for a business owner or self-employed person, it is important to remember that the limit is based on the owner's income remaining *after* the contribution is made.

For example, if the business's gross income is $100,000 and a Keogh contribution is planned at the 25% maximum, multiply the $100,000 precontribution income by 20% to calculate the maximum Keogh contribution of $20,000. Next, subtract the $20,000 contribution from the $100,000 gross income, which yields an after-contribution net income of $80,000. By dividing the $20,000 contribution by the

$80,000 net income, you will see that the $20,000 Keogh contribution represents 25% of after-contribution income.

Nontax-deductible

In addition to tax-deductible contributions, individuals with Keogh retirement plans may make nondeductible contributions of up to 10% of their income. The interest, dividends and growth attributable to such a nondeductible contribution accumulate tax-free until the owner withdraws them.

Top-heavy Keoghs ($200,000 Maximum Salary Base)

To help prevent inequities in dollar amount contributions made at the same rate (when one employee earns $10,000 and another earns $500,000), the maximum salary level on which Keogh contributions may be based is $200,000.

Employee Eligibility

Employee coverage. If the owner of a sole proprietorship or the partners in a partnership have common law employees (meaning payroll employees), these people must be covered under the employer's Keogh plan at the same rate of annual contribution as the owner. However, employee participation in an employer's Keogh plan is subject to the following employee eligibility rules:

- **Full-time employees.** All employees who receive compensation for at least 1,000 hours of work per year.
- **Tenured employees.** All employees who have completed one or more years of continuous employment or who have been employed continuously from the start-up date of the Keogh plan if less than three years have elapsed.
- **Adult employees.** By law, employees under the age of 21 can be excluded from Keogh plan coverage.

Keogh Plan Employee Vesting Requirements

Vesting refers to the waiting period that employees must work through before contributions made by an employer become the employee's property without penalty or conditions attached. ERISA/IRS rules set minimum employee vesting requirements.

In general, an employee must be fully vested after 5 years of full-time service. However, a Keogh plan may elect an alternative vesting schedule which allows the individual to begin vesting (accruing ownership) after the third year of employment and become fully (100%) vested upon completion of 7 years of full time service.

Comparison of Qualified Retirement Plans

HR-10 (Keogh) plans and IRAs are both tax-deferred retirement plans designed to encourage individuals to set aside funds for retirement income.

The principal similarities between Keoghs and IRAs are as follows:

- **Age limits.** Anyone under age 70 1/2 and who is otherwise eligible may contribute to a Keogh or to an IRA plan.
- **Tax deferral of income contributed to plans.** Taxes are deferred on the amount of contribution until the individual begins to receive distributions.
- **Tax-sheltered.** Investment income from dividends, interest and capital gains is deferred until distribution.
- **Cash-only contributions.** An investor may contribute cash to a plan, but not stocks, bonds or other securities.
- **Distributions.** Retirement income distributions can begin as early as 59 1/2 or as late as the year after the year in which the taxpayer reaches 70 1/2, as is true of IRAs. The tax penalties for early withdrawals or failure to start withdrawals are the same as with IRAs.
- **Penalties for early withdrawal.** The individual pays income tax on the amount withdrawn during the year, plus a 10% penalty. Early withdrawals without penalty are permitted in the event of death or disability, and from the voluntary, nondeductible contributions.
- **Rollovers and transfers.** Retirement benefits from IRAs and Keoghs may be rolled over once every twelve months. The rollover must be completed within 60 days.
- **Available payout options.** Lump-sum distributions (which are eligible for five-year income averaging) or regular, periodic payouts are both permissible.
- **Beneficiary(ies).** Upon the planholder's death, payments are made to a beneficiary—rights to the cash and securities accumulated in the account do not end with the death of the owner.

The differences between Keoghs and IRAs are shown in Table 13.2.

Table 13.2 Differences Between Keogh Plans and IRAs

Characteristic	Keogh Plans	IRAs
Permissible investments	Most equity and debt securities, U.S. government-minted precious-metal coins, annuities and cash-value life insurance.	Most equity and debt securities, U.S. government-minted precious-metal coins and annuities.
Nonpermissible investments	Term insurance and collectibles.	Term insurance, collectibles and cash-value life insurance.
Change of employer	Lump-sum distribution can be rolled over into an IRA within 60 days.	Does not apply.
Penalty for excess contribution	Excess is not deductible.	6% penalty.
Taxation of distributions	Taxed as ordinary income.	Taxed as ordinary income.

Corporate Retirement Plans

All corporate pension and profit-sharing plans must be established under a trust agreement. A trustee will be appointed for the plan and will have a fiduciary responsibility towards the plan and the beneficial owners—the planholders.

Defined Contribution and Defined Benefit

All qualified retirement plans fall into one of two categories. Those that shelter contributions of otherwise taxable income without promise of specific future benefits are called **defined contribution plans**. Those that promise a specific retirement benefit but do not specify the level of current contributions are called **defined benefit plans**. Before covering specific plan provisions, it is important to understand the distinctions between these two approaches.

Defined contribution plans. There are many types of plans that are considered defined contribution plans. These include profit-sharing plans, money-purchase pension plans, thrift plans, 401K plans, stock bonus plans and target (assumed) benefit pension plans (though target benefit plans have many characteristics of the defined benefit approach, they are considered defined contribution plans).

All of these plans share a basic feature: the provisions cover amounts going into the plan currently or the plan's current allocation. These plans identify the participants' interest and vested balance. Funds then accumulate to some future event, generally retirement, when the values may be withdrawn. The future final accumulation or account balance depends on the total of the amounts contributed, interest and dividends earned and increase in value (asset appreciation). Whatever cash value finally exists at the date of surrender determines the payout.

Defined benefit plans. In contrast, the phrase "collecting a pension" usually describes a defined benefit pension plan. Defined benefit plans are designed to provide a specified benefit for their participants. For example, such a plan may provide a fixed dollar amount of monthly income at normal retirement. Although these plans may also provide benefits in the event of early retirement, death or disability, the key concept remains: definitely determinable benefits are provided at some future date. No matter what is actually earned on the underlying assets, the promised benefit is paid under the terms of the contract. In a similar manner, these plans use actuarial assumptions including mortality, turnover and interest to derive the appropriate current outlay necessary to fund the future benefits.

Contributions and Benefit Limitations

Defined Contribution Plans

Under defined contribution plans, limits are placed on the contributions made to the plan. Employers sponsoring these types of plans are limited to the *lesser* of:

- 25% of the compensation of plan participants; or
- $30,000 for annual contribution deductions to the plan.

Defined Benefit Plans

In order to define the plan's benefit, several formulas are commonly used:

- The retirement benefit may be expressed as a flat or fixed dollar amount paid monthly—for example, $150 per month for life (a flat dollar amount).
- The benefit may be provided based on a percentage of compensation—for example, a monthly life income equal to 20% of the participant's highest five consecutive years' earnings divided by 60 (flat percentage, final average).

A defined benefit pension plan is one that provides a specified or formulated benefit at normal retirement age. Amounts reasonable and necessary to provide such benefits are deductible by the employer. Under these types of plans, limitations are placed on the benefits that can accrue to the participant, but not the cost of the contributions to the plans. These benefit limitations take three forms, and all apply:

1. **Replacement of earnings**. In general, a plan may not provide a final benefit that exceeds 100% of the participant's average compensation for the final three years.
2. **Dollar amount**. To partially limit the tendency of retirement plans to favor highly compensated individuals, the law imposes a ceiling on the annual dollar amount a defined benefit pension plan can provide. This dollar limit is indexed to inflation and changes from year to year.
3. **Dollars considered**. When calculating a participant's benefit, only the first $200,000 of compensation a participant earns can be taken into account.

Payment of Benefits

The ultimate purpose of any qualified plan is to provide future retirement or savings benefits. Although the method of paying benefits varies with the underlying plan, payouts can be of any amount and are not limited by Social Security or any other payments received by the account owner.

Normal Retirement Provisions

The latest date that an employer can provide for normal retirement under a qualified plan is the *later* of:

- the participant's reaching age 65; or
- the tenth anniversary of commencement of participation in the plan.

Early Retirement Provisions

Not all employees will want to work until age 65. For example, a plan could specify early retirement at age 55 and the completion of a minimum period of service, such as 10 or 15 years. Where the consent of the employer is required, the early retirement benefit cannot exceed the benefit that the employee would be entitled to if she terminated employment with a vested interest.

Taxation of Distributions

Distributions are taxed at the employee's ordinary income rate at the time of distribution.

Profit-sharing Plans

A profit-sharing plan is a plan established and maintained by an employer to allow employees to participate in the profits of the business. The benefits of participation can come in the form of current cash paid directly to the employee; they can be deferred into an account for payment at a future time, such as retirement, death or separation from service; or they can be a combination of both approaches. Obviously, cash benefits paid directly to an employee are bonuses and do not fit the definition of a qualified plan; therefore, this discussion will center around profit-sharing plans that defer benefits to a future date.

Unlike other qualified plans, a profit-sharing plan does not have to entail a definite predetermined contribution formula. Contributions can be made on a discretionary basis; for example, they can be determined annually by a company's board of directors, based on how the business fared during the year. Profit-sharing plans that do include a definite contribution formula generally express contributions as a fixed percentage of profits. In either event, to ensure permanency and maintain qualification, a profit-sharing plan must have "substantial and recurring" contributions according to the Internal Revenue Code (IRC).

A prime reason why an employer will install a profit-sharing plan is to offer an incentive to the participating employees to perform more productively and efficiently. If this is the intent of the employer, its profit sharing should contain a contribution formula so that employees will receive a fixed percentage of profits rather than have the profit share arbitrarily decided by the board of directors. The formula should substantially reward employees for their efforts in good years.

A profit-sharing plan also can be financially attractive to a company. The privilege to skip contributions in years of low profits is particularly appealing to small and medium-sized corporations.

For reference, a profit-sharing plan is a defined contribution plan, although, as noted, the employer's annual contribution is usually not a fixed annual amount, nor is it necessarily prescribed by formula. This plan is extremely popular because it offers the greatest amount of investment and contribution flexibility. It is also relatively easy to install, administer and communicate to employees.

Thrift and 401K Plans

One special feature offered by thrift and 401K defined contribution plans is that they permit an employer to make *matching contributions* up to a set percentage of the employee's contributions. Both the employee's basic and the employer's matching contributions are made pre-tax.

Nonqualified Corporate Retirement Plans

A nonqualified plan is an employee benefit provided by an employer that does not meet the standards required for qualified plan status. The plan does not require advance approval from the IRS or Department of Labor. As a result, the plan does not receive advantageous tax treatment. On the other hand, a nonqualified plan is not bound to comply with the nondiscrimination rules the way a qualified plan is. The employer may make a nonqualified benefit available to certain classes of employees and exclude others. This is drastically different from the manner in which a qualified plan must operate.

Nonqualified plans are not subject to the same stringent reporting and disclosure requirements as are qualified plans. This means the employer that sponsors the nonqualified plan need not adhere to strict guidelines regarding the specific information that must be communicated to employees about the benefit plan. However, nonqualified plans still must be in writing and communicated to the participants of the plan.

Taxation

Contributions to nonqualified plans are not exempt from current income tax. With nonqualified plans, the tax is paid on the amount of contribution in the year the contribution is made (whether the contribution is made by the employer or directly by the employee). Contributions made by the company on behalf of the participant are not deductible until paid to the participant.

If the plan is funded, taxes on any earnings within the plan itself may or may not be deferred. Deferral of tax on plan earnings depends on the investment vehicle used to fund the plan. For example, earnings are tax deferred in a plan using an annuity as an investment vehicle, whereas earnings are taxed currently in a plan using a mutual fund as an investment vehicle. The investment vehicle determines whether the tax on earnings is deferred, not the plan.

Types of Plans

Payroll Deduction Plans

Payroll deduction programs are just what the name implies. The employee authorizes a deduction from his check on a weekly, monthly or quarterly basis. The money is deducted after taxes are paid and may be invested in any number of investment vehicles at the employee's option.

One of the vehicles an individual may choose to fund the payroll deduction plan is an annuity. By itself, the annuity is considered a nonqualified retirement plan for the individual, but because of the tax benefits offered by the annuity (the product, not the plan), growth in the contract is deferred.

Deferred Compensation Plans

Deferred compensation plans represent a *contractual agreement* between a firm and an employee by which the employee agrees to defer receipt of current compensation in favor of a payout at retirement (or at the employee's disability or death) when it is assumed that the employee will be in a lower tax bracket. The agreement underlying a deferred compensation plan will usually include the following:

- list of the conditions and circumstances under which some or all of the benefits may be forfeited (a contract may specify that an employee gives up all benefits if the employee moves to a competing firm—sometimes known as a *golden handcuffs* clause);
- statement to the effect that the employee is not entitled to any claim against the assets of the employer until retirement, death or disability; and
- disclaimer that the agreement may be void if the firm suffers a business failure or bankruptcy.

Directors of the company are not considered employees for purposes of establishing eligibility for a deferred compensation plan, and as a result, may not participate in the plan.

Business failure. Generally, the employee enjoys no benefits from the program until retirement. One problem with such programs is that in the event the business fails, the employee is nothing more than a general creditor of the business; there is no guarantee the employee will receive the deferred payment.

Funding. Deferred compensation plans are typically unfunded, in which case the deferred compensation is paid from the operating assets of the firm. However, the plan may be funded, in which case the employer sets up an account to fund the program.

Taxation. Regardless of whether the plan is funded, the employer does not receive a deduction for contributions until payments are made to the employee. The income tax on the earnings of the program, if funded, is paid by the employer. Upon retirement, the employee will receive the deferred payment as ordinary income.

Annuity Plans

An annuity is a contract between an individual and an insurance company, usually purchased for retirement income. Investors, called annuitants, contribute money to an annuity plan either in a lump sum or as periodic contractual payments. At some future time (specified in the contract), the owner of the annuity plan will begin receiving regular income distributions.

Owners of variable annuities, like owners of mutual fund shares, have the right to vote on changes in investment policy and the right to vote for the investment adviser every two years. They may elect the board of managers, which oversees the management of the portfolio.

Types of Annuity Contracts

Annuity contracts are classified into three kinds, depending on the type of payment the annuity makes:

1. fixed annuities
2. variable annuities
3. combination and other annuities

Fixed Annuities

Guaranteed return. A fixed annuity has a guaranteed rate of return. When the individual elects to begin receiving income, payout is determined by the value of the account and the annuitant's life expectancy (based on mortality tables). Payment from a fixed annuity remains constant throughout the annuitant's life. Because the minimum return in a fixed annuity is guaranteed by the insurance company and no risk is borne by the annuitant, a fixed annuity is considered an insurance product. Because of this insurance aspect, a salesperson must have an insurance license to sell fixed annuities.

Risks. Although his principal and interest are not at risk, an investor with a fixed annuity risks loss of purchasing power because of inflation. For example, an individual who annuitized a contract in 1953 may have been guaranteed monthly payments of $375. Decades later, that amount may provide insufficient income on which to live. By assuming the financial risk of fluctuating payments, the investor increases the chances that these payments will keep pace with inflation.

Variable Annuities

The investor who wants to minimize inflation risks associated with fixed annuities purchases a variable annuity contract. The money deposited in a variable annuity is invested primarily in a portfolio of equity securities (which stand a better chance of keeping pace with inflation than do investments in fixed income securities). The annuitant, however, participates in both the greater potential gain and the greater potential risk associated with equity securities (as compared to debt securities). Although the investor hopes the securities will increase in value, payouts may vary considerably as the value of the annuity units fluctuates with the value of those securities.

Comparison of Fixed and Variable Annuities

Table 13.3 compares the principal features of fixed and variable annuities.

Separate Account

The contributions made by investors to a variable annuity are kept in a **separate account** from the insurance company's general funds. If the funds in the separate account are used to purchase securities directly, the separate account is considered a *management company* under the Investment Company Act of 1940. If the funds in the separate account are used to purchase shares in a mutual fund that is managed by someone other than the issuer of the variable annuity, the separate account is considered a *unit trust* under the act of 1940. A separate account may begin operations as long as the insurance company has a net worth of $1,000,000 or the separate account has a net worth of $100,000.

Because the risk is borne by the investor rather than the insurance company, the variable annuity must be registered under the Investment Company Act of 1940. In addition to having a valid insurance license in each state in which they do business, variable annuity salespeople must be registered with the SEC and NASD.

Direct and indirect investment. If the annuity money is invested directly into a separate account operated as a mutual fund, the separate account must register as a mutual fund. The value of the contract holder's investment in the separate account is an undivided interest in the securities held in the separate account, called *accumulation units*.

Table 13.3 Comparison of Fixed and Variable Annuities

Fixed	Variable
Guaranteed fixed payments	Variable payments
Guaranteed interest rate	Variable rate of return
Investment company risk assumed by insurance company	Investment risk assumed by annuitant
Portfolio of fixed-income securities	Portfolio of equities, debt or money-market instruments
General account	Separate account
Vulnerable to inflation	Resistant to inflation
Subject to insurance regulation	Subject to insurance and securities regulation

Table 13.4 Comparison of Mutual Funds and Variable Annuties

Mutual Funds	Variable Annuities
Investment company	Insurance company
Shares	Units
Redeemed by issuer	Redeemed by issuer
Price based on formula	Price based on formula
Investment objectives varied	Investment objectives primarily growth and income
Board of directors	Board of managers
No guarantees	Few guarantees

The separate account will purchase shares of one or more mutual funds and hold the shares in trust. The variable annuity money collected then purchases an *undivided interest* in the mutual fund shares purchased and held in the separate account. With *indirect investment*, the separate account does not manage the securities but only holds mutual fund shares purchased in trust for the benefit of the contract holder. With direct investment, the contract holder's money is invested in a portfolio of individual securities actively managed by the separate account.

Comparison of Mutual Funds and Variable Annuities

Table 13.4 compares the principal features of mutual funds and variable annuities.

Variable Annuity Payments

Variable annuity payments are not fixed at a certain amount, but are determined by mortality tables and the value of the underlying securities in the annuitant's portfolio. Variable annuity plans do not guarantee the amount of payment because the insurance company does not (and cannot) guarantee the performance of the separate account.

Initial payout is used to determine the number of annuity units in the account; future payouts are determined by the fluctuating value of the annuity unit. An investor who annuitized a variable annuity in 1953 and began with monthly payments of $375, for example, may now be receiving $1,275 per month.

Combination Annuities

Some insurance companies offer a combination annuity wherein the investor contributes to both a fixed account and a variable account. The result is a guaranteed return on the fixed annuity portion and a possible higher return on the variable annuity portion. The fixed annuity appeals to the individual who wants or needs a guaranteed payment, the variable annuity appeals to the individual who wants payments to keep pace with inflation and the combination annuity attempts to provide for both objectives.

Purchasing Annuities

The pay-in period for an annuity is also known as the **accumulation stage**. The insurance company attempts to make it easy for the annuity owner to accumulate money in an annuity by offering a number of purchase options.

Deferred annuities. Annuities may be purchased with a lump-sum investment with payment of benefits deferred until the annuitant elects to receive them. This type of investment is referred to as a **single premium (payment) deferred annuity**.

A person can also purchase an annuity by making several smaller payments—known as **periodic payments**—over a period of time. The contract holder can invest money on a monthly, quarterly or annual basis. A contractual plan may also be offered by the insurer for investment. If the investor elects this form of regular payments, the annuity is referred to as a **periodic payment deferred annuity**.

Immediate annuities. Investors may also purchase immediate annuities. In an immediate annuity contract, an investor purchases the annuity by depositing a single lump sum. The insurance company then begins to pay out the annuity's benefits immediately (usually within 60 days).

Sales Charges on Variable Annuities

Although variable annuities are subject to slightly different rules and restrictions on sales charges, they are administered in basically the same manner as mutual funds and UITs. In general, the following are the maximum sales charges allowed.

Periodic-payment Annuities

For periodic-payment annuities the maximum sales charge is 8.5% of the total payments made to the contract for the lesser of the payment period or twelve years.

Single-payment Annuities

For single-payment annuities, the maximum sales charge must be related to the amount of the purchase payment. The company must allow for a reducing scale as follows:

- first $25,000, 8.5% of payment
- next $25,000, 7.5% of payment
- over $50,000, 6.5% of payment

If sales charges are not stated separately from other deductions (administrative fees, mortality expense fees and so on), then the total of all deductions (excluding premium taxes and insurance premiums) from the purchase payment will be treated as the sales charge and must meet the above percentages.

Contractual Plans

Contributions to annuities may be made in installments under the provisions of a contractual plan. Installment contributions are usually made under one of two kinds of contractual plans: front-end load or spread-load. Contractual plans have a maximum sales charge of 9% over the life of the plan.

Accumulation Stage

During the accumulation stage of an annuity contract, the terms of the contract are quite flexible. For example, if an investor misses a periodic payment, there is no danger of forfeiting any of the preceding investments. The client can terminate the contract at any time while in the accumulation stage of the contract. In an attempt to prevent termination of contracts, insurance companies often allow certain loan privileges. The contract holder may borrow from the account without having to cancel the contract. Cancelation of the contract or a loan received from the contract is considered a withdrawal and subject to tax.

Variable Annuity Sales and Redemption Practices

All applications and purchase payments must be promptly transmitted to the issuer of the variable annuity contract without exception. The insurance company must make prompt payments on any partial or total redemptions requested by contract holders in accordance with the terms of the contract.

Redemption

Members may not participate in the offering, distribution or sale of variable annuity contracts with any insurance company that does not make prompt payments as required by law.

Sales Agreements

If a principal underwriter is selling variable contracts through another broker-dealer, both parties must be NASD members and there must be a sales agreement in effect between the parties.

A key provision that must be included in every variable annuity sales agreement is the stipulation that all commissions must be returned if the contract is tendered for redemption by the investor within seven business days after the company's acceptance of the contract application.

Annuity Payout Options

Annuities also offer several payout options of the money accumulated in the annuity contract. The investor may elect to leave the money in the annuity to accumulate, or the investor can withdraw the accumulated moneys in a lump sum. The contract owner may also withdraw the accumulated funds periodically. Typically, the contract owner **annuitizes** the contract. Selecting from payment options offered by the insurance company, the contract holder or annuitant turns the accumulation account over to the insurance company, which offers periodic payments to the annuitant for an agreed upon period.

This decision to annuitize the contract should not be taken lightly, because once the payment option is elected, the contract holder may not alter it, change it, or elect a different payout mode. The annuity options available are described below.

- **Life annuity/straight life**. Clients receive monthly benefit checks over their lifetime. There are no added options or benefits, and with this option, the annuitant receives the largest monthly payout.
- **Life annuity with period certain**. Clients receive payments for life, with a certain period of time guaranteed. If the investor dies before the expiration of the *period certain*, payments go to the annuitant's named beneficiary. If the annuitant lives beyond the period certain, payments continue until the annuitant's death. As an example, assume a client purchases a life annuity with a ten-year period certain. The insurance company guarantees payments for the life of the annuitant or for ten years, whichever is longer. If the annuitant lives for only one year after payments begin, the company will continue to make payments to the annuitant's beneficiary for nine more years. If the annuitant dies after receiving payments for 13 years, payments would cease at death.
- **Joint life with last survivor**. In this option, two people are covered by the annuity and can receive payments. A husband and wife might own an annuity jointly with a last survivor clause. The contract will continue to pay as long as one of the annuitants remains alive. The payment may be the same as when both were alive, or it may be reduced for the surviving annuitant, depending on the contract. This option may include more than two annuitants, in which case payments would cease at the death of the last survivor.
- **Unit refund annuity**. This plan pays the annuitant until her death. If the investor dies before receiving an amount equal to the value of the account, the beneficiary receives the money remaining in the account.
- **Life contingency**. This is an annuity with a death benefit that applies during the accumulation stage. A full contribution will be made to the account if the owner dies and the payout will be made to the beneficiary.

Annuity Accounting

Accumulation Units

An accumulation unit is an accounting measure that represents the investor's share of ownership in the separate account. The value of an accumulation unit is determined in a manner identical to that used to determine the value of shares in a mutual fund. The unit value changes with the value of the securities held in the separate account and the total number of accumulation units outstanding. When the contract is annuitized, accumulation units are converted into annuity units.

Annuity Units

An annuity unit is a measure of value used only during the payout period of an annuitized contract. It is an accounting measure that determines the amount of each payment to the annuitant.

The number of annuity units is calculated when the owner annuitizes the contract—that is, when payout begins. The value of the unit fluctuates with the value of the separate account portfolio. The number of units credited to the annuitant's account is based on this initial unit value and other variables, such as the payout option selected, accumulated value of the annuitant's account, age and sex of the individual and assumed interest rate.

Assumed Interest Rate

The assumed interest rate (AIR) is a basis for projecting earnings for the variable annuity. The rate provides an earnings target for the separate account and is usually conservatively estimated. Table 13.5 shows an example of AIR compared to actual earnings and the impact on account performance.

An AIR is used to project the value of an account through the annuitant's age at death, as forecasted by mortality tables. Based on this value, the insurance company projects its distributions to the annuitant. It is also used when determining the number of annuity units. The higher the AIR, the higher the projected value of units and the greater the initial payment. The reverse, of course, is also true.

Effects of investment returns on annuity payouts. The AIR does not guarantee a rate of return. It is a tool for adjusting the value of an annuity unit to changes in the investment return of the portfolio of the separate account. A change in value of an annuity unit changes the amount of annuity payments. The annuitant always receives a payment equal to the value of one annuity unit times the number of units in the annuitant's account. Table 13.6 shows the effect of investment return on annuity payout.

Fluctuating payments. After the insurance company determines the number of annuity units used in calculating the payment, the amount of each payment equals the number of units multiplied by the current value of the annuity unit. The number of annuity units used to calculate future payment remains the same. However, because the value of the units depends on the performance of the separate account, if the value fluctuates, the annuitant's payments may also fluctuate.

Table 13.5 AIR Compared to Actual Earnings

Assume the AIR is 5% and the initial check is $400.

Period	1	2	3	4	5	6
Actual earnings	5%	6%	5%	6%	3%	5%
Change from AIR	0	+1	0	+1	−2	0
Payout	$400	$410	$410	$420	$410	$410

Table 13.6 Effects of Investment Returns on Annuity Payouts

IF the realized rate of return:	THEN the value of the annuity unit:	AND the payout in relation to the previous payout:
increases above AIR	increases	increases
decreases below AIR	decreases	decreases
stays the same as AIR	stays the same	stays the same

If an insurance company chooses an AIR that is too high, subsequent payments will continually decrease because the projections are not met by actual portfolio performance. If the AIR is too low, payments will most likely continually increase as projected returns are surpassed.

Taxation of Annuities

Contributions to annuities are made with aftertax dollars. Because contributions have already been taxed, the amount of the contribution is not taxable when the account is annuitized (that is, the investor is receiving retirement income). As with other investments, the money invested in an annuity represents the investor's cost base. The primary advantage of an annuity as an investment is that the growth of the contract is not taxed in the year in which it occurs. Tax on interest received or capital growth of the contract is deferred until the owner withdraws money from the contract. On withdrawal, the amount in excess of the investor's cost base is taxed as ordinary income.

Lump-sum withdrawals are taken out on a LIFO (last in, first out) basis. This means earnings are removed before contributions. If the investor receives a lump-sum withdrawal before age 59 1/2, the portion withdrawn is taxed as ordinary income (to the extent of earnings) and would be subject to an additional 10% penalty. The penalty does not apply, however, if the amount withdrawn is due to death or disability or is part of a life-income option plan with fixed payments. After age 59 1/2, taxes are payable on the earnings portion of the withdrawal only.

Tax treatment for annuitized payments differs. The cost basis in the contract for a nonqualified plan is divided by the number of years of life expectancy (from mortality tables). That dollar figure is considered the nontaxable amount of each year's payments. Distributions over and above the cost basis are taxable at ordinary income rates.

Table 13.7 summarizes the tax treatment of annuity contracts.

Table 13.7 Tax Treatment for the Variable Annuity Contract Holder

		Tax Treatment
Accumulation Period:	Earnings (realized capital gains and net investment income)	Tax deferred
	Early withdrawal or surrender of contract	Interest earnings always withdrawn first, so withdrawal is taxable as ordinary income to the extent that cash surrender value exceeds investment in contract.
	Death	Benefits over investment value are taxable as ordinary income to the beneficiary.
Annuity Period:	Return of cost	Not taxable
	Investment gain	Taxable as ordinary income

Qualified Annuity Plans

Tax Advantages

Qualified annuity plans offered under sections 403(b) and 501(c)3 of the Internal Revenue Code, sometimes referred to as *tax-deferred annuities* (*TDAs*) or *tax-sheltered annuities* (*TSAs*), are designed for long-term savings only. To ensure this objective, TDAs (like IRAs and other retirement plans) are subject to tax penalties if the savings are withdrawn before the participant retires. TDAs are entitled to the following tax advantages:

- Contributions to a TDA are excluded from a participant's gross income.
- A participant's earnings in his TDA accumulate tax free until distribution.

Income exclusion. If an eligible employee elects to make annual contributions to a TDA, those contributions are excluded from the employee's gross income for that year. The amount of the contribution is not reported as income, with the end result being that the employee pays less current income taxes.

Tax-free accumulation. Though most participants in a TDA program would cite the taxable income reduction feature as their greatest tax benefit, the advantage of tax-free accumulation of plan assets ranks a very close second. Earnings in a TDA accumulate tax free and do not increase the participant's taxable income until the total dollars are withdrawn at retirement, usually when that person is at a lower tax rate than during his working years.

Investments

Prior to the passage of ERISA, tax-deferred annuity plans had but one source of investment—the annuity contracts from a life insurance company. Now, mutual funds, stocks, bonds and CDs are also available as investment vehicles. As a result of this expansion of permissible investments, banks, brokerage houses, savings and loans and credit unions also offer these plans.

Eligibility Requirements

In order for an employer to be eligible to establish a TDA, the employer must qualify under one of the following classifications:

- public educational 403(b) institutions
- tax-exempt 501(c)3 organizations
- church organizations

Public educational 403(b) institutions. In order to qualify as a public educational institution, the organization must be state supported or a political subdivision or an agency of the state. The key word here is *state*. Private school systems have a separate set of qualifying rules, as explained in the next section. These state-run educational systems include:

- elementary schools
- secondary schools
- colleges and universities
- medical schools

Individuals who are employed by the above school systems in the following job classifications may enroll in a TDA plan:

- teachers and other faculty members;
- administrators, managers, principals, supervisors and other members of the administrative staff;
- counselors;
- clerical staff and maintenance workers; and
- individuals who perform services for the institution, such as doctors or nurses.

Tax-exempt 501(c)3 organizations. As stated earlier, 501(c)3 organizations are tax-exempt entities and are specifically cited in the IRC as being eligible to establish a TDA for their employees. Typical 501(c)3 organizations include:

- private colleges and universities
- trade schools
- parochial schools
- zoos and museums
- research and scientific foundations
- religious and charitable institutions
- private hospitals and medical schools

Church organizations. So as not to confuse the situation, the 501(c)3 organizations listed above have to be determined by the IRS to be nonprofit organizations. A church organization as an employer has been defined by the IRS to mean a church, an association of churches or an elementary or secondary school that is controlled by a church or an association of churches. Employees in this grouping who are eligible for a TDA plan usually consist of ordained ministers, priests or missionaries of the church. Clerical or administrative staff of a church organization are not eligible to participate in a TDA plan.

Definition of an Employee

Only employees of qualified employers are eligible to participate in a TDA plan. Independent contractors, by contrast, are not eligible. By all accounts, it is the employer's responsibility to determine an individual's status or definition.

Eligibility. Similar to other qualified plans, all TDAs, whether employer contribution or employee elective deferral, must be made available to each employee who has:

- reached age 21; and
- completed one year of service.

An employee must meet *both* of these requirements to be eligible to participate in a TDA.

Plan Requirements

Following the simplified course set forth by the enabling Congressional legislation, TDAs must meet only two plan requirements:

1. The plan must be in writing, through a plan instrument, trust agreement or both.
2. The employer must remit plan contributions to an annuity contract, a mutual fund or another approved investment.

Employee elective deferrals. Under an employee elective deferral TDA program, the employer has no contributions to make and little, if any, paperwork. The only requirement is that the employer and employee must enter into a written agreement that specifies the amount or percentage of pay to be deducted, the timing of the deduction (e.g., weekly, monthly, quarterly, etc.) and whether the amount to be deducted is to be a reduction in salary or an agreement to forego a pay increase.

The salary reduction agreement between the employer and employee must be in writing and legally binding upon both parties. The IRS will not accept verbal or informal arrangements. Compensation covered under the agreement must be for compensation earned after the date of the agreement and can only cover a period of one year. A new agreement must be entered into each year. Additionally, the employee is not allowed to contribute money to the TDA out of his personal funds. All employee contributions must come as a result of salary reductions, per the agreement.

Contribution Limits

Employer contribution plans. Employer contributions to a TDA can be made solely on behalf of the covered employee or in conjunction with an employee deferral. As one might expect, because TDAs are qualified plans, they are governed by many of the same rules discussed throughout this section.

Personal contributions. Elective employee deferrals to a TDA cannot exceed $9,500 per year. This $9,500 limit also applies if an individual is participating in two or more TDA plans.

Employer contributions. Employer contributions to a TDA are subject to the same maximums that apply to all defined-contribution plans: the lesser of 25% of the participant's compensation or $30,000 per year.

Catch-up provisions. The primary reason for what are known as *catch-up provisions* is to allow employees who had low contributions during the early stages of their careers to catch up later with higher contributions. The catch-up provisions are available only to those TDA participants who have completed 15 years of service.

Taxation of Distributions from a TDA

Distributions from a TDA must follow the same rules as all qualified plans. Because the employee's deferrals to the TDA were made with pretax dollars, any lump sum, installment or annuity payment will be subject to ordinary income rates in the year it is received. A normal distribution can start at age 59 1/2. A premature distribution is subject to a 10% penalty tax unless the distribution is made for an allowable reason (death or disability of the participant, etc.). Delayed distributions must start by April 1st of the year following the year in which the participant becomes 70 1/2 or they will be subject to the excess accumulation tax of 50%. Once delayed distributions begin, they must be paid annually by December 31st of each tax year following the initial distribution.

Variable Life Insurance

A life insurance policy is designed to provide financial compensation to the policy owner's beneficiaries in the event of the policy owner's death. Many types of life insurance contracts are available; each type serves a different need. We will focus on those contracts that employ separate accounts to fund the death benefit and that are considered "securities" as defined by the Securities Act of 1933.

Conventional Life Insurance

Term Life Insurance

Term life insurance is the simplest type of life insurance contract. It provides insurance protection for a specified period (or **term**) and pays a benefit only if the insured dies during that period. Some term policies provide coverage for a specified number of years (for example, a five-year term policy protects the insured from the date of issue until the end of the fifth year). Other term policies provide coverage until the insured reaches a specified age (for example, a term to 65 policy protects the insured from the date of issue until the insured reaches age 65).

Descriptions of three common types of term life insurance follow:

- **Level term insurance** provides a death benefit that does not change over the policy's term.
- **Decreasing term insurance** provides a death benefit that decreases gradually over the policy's term.
- **Increasing term insurance** provides a death benefit that increases gradually over the policy's term. The benefit can be increased by specific dollar amounts or by a percentage of the original benefit, or it may be tied to a cost-of-living index, such as the Consumer Price Index.

Term Life Premiums

The premium of an insurance plan reflects, in part, the risk the insurer accepts when it issues the policy. With life insurance, the age of the insured is a significant risk factor. The probability of death increases with age, so the premiums increase with age. Moreover, the rate of increase accelerates at greater ages. Few people could afford the premium rates that would be charged at higher ages; therefore, insurance companies offer term insurance plans on a level-premium basis: the premiums are calculated and charged so that they remain level throughout the policy's term period.

Whole Life Insurance

Also known as *permanent* or *cash value* insurance, whole life insurance (WLI) provides protection for the "whole of life." Coverage begins on the date of issue and continues to the date of the insured's death, provided the premiums are paid.

The benefit payable is the face amount of the policy, which remains constant throughout the policy's life. The premium is set at the time of the policy's issue and it, too, remains level for the policy's life.

Cash Values

Unlike term insurance, which provides only a death benefit, whole life insurance combines a death benefit with an accumulation, or savings, element. This accumulation, commonly referred to as the policy's **cash value**, increases each year the policy is kept in force.

Whole Life Premiums

The premiums for whole life insurance are based on the assumption that the insured will be paying them until age 100. At age 100, the cash value of the policy would have accumulated to the point that it equals the face amount of the policy. Thus, the premium payable for a whole life policy is calculated, in part, on the basis of the number of years between the insured's age at issue and age 100.

Universal Life Insurance

Universal life insurance (ULI) is a variation of whole life insurance, but it is considerably more flexible. Unlike whole life, ULI allows the policy owner to determine the amount and frequency of the premium payments and to adjust the policy face amount up or down to reflect changes in needs. ULI is technically defined as term insurance with a **policy value fund**. Even though the policy owner may pay a level premium, as the insured ages an increasing share of that premium goes to pay the mortality charge. As premiums are paid and cash values accumulate, interest is credited to the policy's cash value account. As long as the cash value account is sufficient to pay the monthly mortality and expense costs, the policy continues in force, whether or not the owner pays the premium. Of course, premium payments must be large enough and frequent enough to generate sufficient cash values. If the cash value account is not sufficient to support the monthly deductions, the policy terminates.

At stated intervals (and usually upon providing evidence of insurability), the policy owner can increase the face amount of the policy. The policy owner can also request a decrease in the face amount. A corresponding increase (or decrease) in premium payment is not required as long as the cash value account can cover the mortality and expense costs. By the same token, the policy owner can elect to pay more into the policy, thus adding to the cash value account—subject to certain guidelines that control the relationship between the cash values and the policy's face amount.

Variable Life Insurance

Variable life insurance (VLI) has many of the characteristics of whole life (sometimes known as *traditional*) insurance. The main difference is the manner in which the reserves are invested. In traditional whole life insurance, the reserves are invested by the insurer in conservative investments (for example, bonds, real estate, mortgage loans and so on). Because of the low risk of such investments, the insurer can guarantee the policy's cash value and the nonforfeiture options that are based on that cash value. Traditional life insurance reserves are held in the insurer's **general accounts**.

With variable life insurance, the policy owner chooses how the reserves will be invested (for example, in common stocks, bonds, money-market accounts or other securities). Consequently, the cash value fluctuates with the performance of the investment portfolio, and the performance is not guaranteed. VLI reserves are held by the insurer in special **separate accounts** and can be invested in riskier (and potentially higher yielding) investments than can general account reserves.

As with traditional whole life insurance, the cash values of a variable life policy become part of the policy's death benefit. Depending upon investment results, of course, the variable life death benefit will increase or decrease; however, a minimum death benefit equal to the face amount of the policy is guaranteed.

Table 13.8 compares the characteristics of variable life and whole life policies.

Scheduled Premiums

A scheduled-premium (or fixed-premium) VLI contract is—as stated earlier—issued with a minimum guaranteed death benefit. (The premiums for some variable life contracts are flexible—discussed later, under "Variable Universal Life.") The amount of the death benefit of a scheduled-premium VLI contract is determined at issue, and evidence of insurability is required. The premium is calculated according to the policy owner's age and sex and the face amount (guaranteed amount) of the policy at issue. Once the premium has been determined and the expenses have been deducted, the net premium is invested in a separate account selected by the policy owner.

Table 13.8   Comparison of Variable Life and Whole Life Policies

Variable Life	Whole Life
Premium is level and fixed.	Premium is level and fixed.
Premium is payable for life.	Premium is payable for life.
A minimum death benefit is guaranteed; benefit may fluctuate above minimum amount.	Death benefit is guaranteed and fixed; it remains level.
Cash value is not guaranteed; depends on performance of separate account.	Cash value is guaranteed.
Premiums are held in separate account(s).	Premiums are held in general account.
Reserves are maintained in general account.	Reserves are maintained in general account.
Expenses are paid from investment income.	Expenses are paid from investment income.

Charges and Expenses

Charges and expenses are deducted either from the gross premium or from the separate account. The charges and expenses must be reasonable and as described in the VLI contract. When and how they are collected is important because it affects the amount of premium that may be invested in the separate account and the investment return of the separate account.

Deductions from Premium

Deductions from the gross premium normally reduce the amount of money credited to (invested in) the separate account. The greater the deductions, the less money available for the investment base in the separate account. Charges deducted from the gross premium include:

- administrative fee
- sales load
- state premium taxes

The administrative fee is normally a one-time charge to cover the cost of processing the application.

Deductions from the Separate Account

Deductions from the separate account normally reduce the investment return payable to the policy owner. Charges deducted from the separate account include:

- mortality risk fee
- expense risk fee
- investment management fee
- cost of insurance

The mortality risk fee covers the risk that the policy owner may live for a period shorter than assumed. The expense risk fee covers the risk that the costs of administering and issuing the policy may be greater than assumed.

The investment management fee and the cost of insurance are the charges that have the greatest impact on the investment return payable to the policy owner. The investment management fee covers the services relating to investment selection and the operation of the separate account assets; the fee is normally a fraction of 1% of the assets managed.

The cost of insurance is deducted from the policy owner's benefit base (that amount equaling the investment in the separate account). The cost is based on the policy owner's attained age, using mortality tables, and the insurance amount at risk (face amount plus variable amount less cash value). The cost of insurance is normally deducted annually, at the policy anniversary.

Assumed Interest Rate and Variable Death Benefit

The death benefit payable under a VLI policy equals the guaranteed death benefit plus the variable insurance amount. The variable insurance amount is based on a cumulative total of net investment return for the policy in all prior years, and it may be positive or negative. The death benefit must be calculated at least annually.

The effect that a change in earnings has on the contract's death benefit depends on a comparison of actual account performance and the performance assumed by the insurance company. This latter is called the *assumed interest rate* (AIR), and is usually set at 3% to 4%. When the insurance company estimates the premium levels necessary to fund the contract, it assumes the separate account will earn this rate so as to generate the funds necessary for paying the guaranteed benefits. If the separate account returns are greater than the AIR, additional funds will be available to the policy owner. These extra earnings will be reflected in an increase in death benefit, an increase in cash value, or an increase in both. If the separate account returns equal the AIR, actual earnings will meet estimated expenses, resulting in no change in benefit levels. Should the separate account returns be less than the AIR, the death benefit of the contract may decrease; however, it may never fall below the amount guaranteed at issue.

An increase in account earnings, even if the account is earning more than the AIR, may not automatically increase the death benefit of the contract. If the account returns have been less than the AIR for several months, these negative earnings will have been recorded by the insurance company. The death benefit will not increase until the account has earned a greater amount (earnings above AIR) to offset the earlier negative performance.

Cash Value

The policy owner's cash values reflect the investments held in the separate account. Because insurance is regulated at the state level, the individual policy's cash value must be calculated at least *monthly* (state law).

The cash value, like the death benefit, may increase or decrease depending on the performance of the separate account. If performance has been negative, the cash value may decrease to zero, even if the contract has been in force for several years. The cash value cannot be negative, but the insurance company will keep track of negative performance. Therefore, like the death benefit, the cash value may not increase until prior negative performance has been offset.

Loans

Like traditional whole life insurance, VLI contracts allow the insured to borrow the cash value that has accumulated in the contract. There are, however, certain restrictions. Usually the insured may borrow only a percentage of the cash value. The minimum percentage that must be made available is 75% (after the policy has been in force for three years). Because the contract value varies, the insured's ability to borrow is reduced to allow for cash value fluctuations (negative cash values may lead to contract termination). Of course, if the death benefit becomes payable during the period that a loan is outstanding, the amount of the loan will be deducted from the proceeds payable.

Should an extreme decline in account value occur during the period of a loan, the policy owner will be liable for maintaining a positive net cash value in the account. If the loan amount exceeds the contract's net cash value, the policy owner must repay enough of the loan to restore the cash value to a positive amount. The insurance company will notify the policy owner when the account falls below the required amount. If a positive cash value is not restored within 31 days, the insurance company has the right to terminate the contract.

Contract Exchange

During the early stage of ownership, a policy owner has the right to exchange a VLI contract for a traditional fixed-benefit WLI contract. The length of time this exchange privilege is in effect varies from company to company, but under no circumstances can the period be less than 24 months (federal law).

The exchange is allowed without evidence of insurability. If a contract is exchanged, the new WLI policy will have the same contract date and death benefit as the minimum guaranteed in the VLI contract. The premiums will equal the amounts guaranteed in the new WLI contract as if it were the original contract.

Sales Charges and Refunds

The separate accounts that fund VLI contracts are defined under the Investment Company Act of 1940 as *periodic payment plans*. As such, they normally operate as either front-end load or spread-load plans.

Sales Charges

The sales charges on a fixed-premium VLI contract may not exceed 9% of the payments to be made over the life of the contract. The "life" of the contract means the lesser of 20 years or the life expectancy of the insured.

In determining the sales charge as a percentage of premium, certain costs are first deducted from the premium. The remaining amount represents the sales load. The costs that are first deducted are:

- necessary additions to the cash value taken from the premium payment
- administrative fees
- policy risk fees
- premium taxes
- deductions for dividends if the contract is participating

Refund Provisions

The refund provisions under VLI contracts differ from the refund provisions of the Investment Company Act of 1940. The insurer is required to extend a free look to the policy owner for 45 days from the execution of the application, or for 10 days from the time the policy is received or a letter notifying the policy owner of the free look right is mailed, whichever is longer.

During the free look period, the policy owner may terminate the policy and receive *all* payments made (unlike other periodic payment plans, where the sales charge and current net asset value are refunded, which may be more or less than the payments made).

The refund provisions extend for two years from issuance of the policy. If within the two-year period the policy owner terminates participation in the contract, the insurer must refund the cash value of the contract (the value calculated after receipt of the redemption notice) plus all sales charges deducted in excess of 30% in the first year of the contract and 10% in the second year. After the two-year period has lapsed, only the cash value need be refunded; the insurer retains all sales charges.

Voting Rights

Contract holders receive one vote per $100 of cash value funded by the separate account. If the insurance company votes the shares, it must vote according to the proxies received from the contract holders. As with other investment company securities, changes in investment objectives and other matters of substance can only be accomplished by a majority vote of the separate account's outstanding shares.

Variable Universal Life

Variable universal life (VUL) is a flexible-premium variable life product. Sometimes referred to as *universal variable life,* VUL combines certain characteristics of a variable life policy, such as a death benefit and cash value that vary according to the performance of the separate account, and certain characteristics of universal life, principally that the policy owner may adjust the premium payments and death benefit according to changing needs. He also can steer the investments underlying one or more separate accounts funding the VUL policy.

Subject to underwriting limitations, the policy owner may elect the premium payment schedule and, as long as the policy's cash value is sufficient to meet current charges, he can adjust the premium payments. Thus, policy lapse is not linked to the cash value of the contract. The cash value and, indirectly, the death benefit, are linked to the investment performance of the separate account. Like VLI policies, VUL policies are subject to state and federal regulation.

Table 13.9 compares the characteristics of variable life and variable universal life policies.

Table 13.9 Comparison of Variable Life and Variable Universal Life Policies

Variable Life	Variable Universal Life
Premiums are fixed as to timing and amount.	Premiums are discretionary as to timing and amount.
Fees and charges are deducted from premium payments.	Fees and charges are deducted from cash value.
Policy lapses are due to failure to pay premium.	Policy lapses are due to insufficient cash value.
Initial minimum death benefit is guaranteed based on premiums; adjustments are not allowed.	Death benefit may equal policy's face amount or face amount plus cash value; face amount cannot be less than a predetermined percentage of cash value (100% to 250%).
Investment experience does not affect premiums due.	Investment experience affects duration of policy; that is, earnings must be enough to pay for face amount.
Premiums and minimum death benefits are fixed.	Policy owner may directly adjust death benefit with additional premium or less premium, subject to policy minimums and underwriting requirements (insurability).

◆ Review Questions

1. Each of the following is an example of a qualified retirement plan EXCEPT a(n)
   A. deferred compensation plan
   B. individual retirement account
   C. pension and profit-sharing plan
   D. defined benefit plan

2. Under ERISA, payments upon retirement can go to the
   I. employee only
   II. employee jointly with the employee's spouse
   III. employee, and at the employee's death, to a designated beneficiary
   IV. employee's designated beneficiary

   A. I only
   B. I, II and III only
   C. IV only
   D. I, II, III and IV

3. Which of the following plans requires the services of an actuary?
   A. Profit-sharing
   B. Defined benefit
   C. Defined contribution
   D. Pension

4. Regulations regarding how contributions are made to tax-qualified plans relate to which of the following ERISA requirements?
   A. Vesting
   B. Funding
   C. Nondiscrimination
   D. Reporting and disclosure

5. A qualified profit-sharing plan has all of the following features EXCEPT
   A. the contribution is tax deductible to the employee
   B. the contribution is not reportable by the employer
   C. the contribution is taxable upon payment at retirement
   D. upon retirement the beneficiary may average out the income

6. The amount paid into a defined contribution plan is set by the
   A. ERISA-defined contribution requirements
   B. trust agreement
   C. employer's age
   D. employer's profits

7. When an employee's contribution to an employer-sponsored qualified pension plan is distributed to the employee, it is
   A. returned tax free
   B. taxed at a reduced rate
   C. taxed at the beneficiary's ordinary tax rate
   D. taxed at the current capital gains rate

8. Corporate pension plans have all of the following features EXCEPT that payments
   A. cannot exceed Social Security benefits
   B. can be tied to Social Security benefits
   C. will depend on length of service and salary
   D. will depend on an employee's value to the company

9. Corporate profit-sharing plans must be in the form of a(n)
   A. trust
   B. conservatorship
   C. administratorship
   D. beneficial ownership

10. Under Keogh plan provisions, a "full-time employee" would be defined as one working at least how many hours per year?

    A. 100
    B. 500
    C. 800
    D. 1,000

◆ Answers & Rationale

1. **A.** No IRS approval is required to initiate a deferred compensation plan for employees. All qualified retirement plans need IRS approval.

2. **D.** Under ERISA, benefits do not die with the employee, but can be passed on to a beneficiary.

3. **B.** Because the payout is set and the contributions must cover the benefits adequately, the calculations are performed by an actuary based on the employee's life expectancy.

4. **B.** *Vesting* describes how quickly rights to a retirement account turn over to an employee. *Nondiscrimination* refers to employee coverage by the plan. All retirement plans must meet ERISA's fiduciary responsibility reporting and disclosure requirements. Only *funding* covers how an employer makes contributions to (or funds) a plan.

5. **A.** Qualified retirement plans are tax deductible to the employer, not to the employee.

6. **B.** The retirement plan's trust agreement will contain a section explaining the formula(s) used to determine the contributions to a defined contribution plan.

7. **A.** Employee contributions to a qualified retirement plan are made with aftertax dollars. Therefore, because the employee already paid taxes on this money, it will be returned tax free. All earnings attributable to those dollars, as well as all employer-contributed money, will be taxed at the employee's ordinary income rate at the time of distribution.

8. **A.** Payments made to an employee at retirement can be of any amount and are not limited by Social Security payments. All of the other statements are true.

9. **A.** All corporate pension and profit-sharing plans must be set up under a trust agreement. The plan's trustee has fiduciary responsibility for the plan.

10. **D.** "Full-time" is defined as 1,000 hours or more per year, regardless of the number of days, weeks or months worked. In other words, to be considered full time, a person must work at least 50% of the 2,000 hours that a normal employee works in a year.

14. U.S. Government and State Rules and Regulations

Key Terms

blue-sky laws
Insider Trading Act of 1988
investment adviser
Investment Advisers Act of 1940
SEC Release IA-1092
Securities Investor Protection Corporation (SIPC)

Overview

The securities industry is regulated by legislation at the federal and state levels. Securities regulations are designed to protect investors by requiring proper disclosure of information and establishing procedures that safeguard against fraud and misrepresentation.

The major pieces of federal legislation are the Securities Act of 1933 and the Securities Exchange Act of 1934; this chapter introduces the later acts that expanded or amended these basic regulations.

The securities laws at the state level are known as *blue-sky laws*. The blue-sky laws deal with issues such as registration requirements for securities, broker-dealers and representatives. The Uniform Securities Act is model legislation that most states have adopted, with each state adapting the act to its specific requirements.

The Investment Advisers Act of 1940 and SEC Release IA-1092

Release IA-1092 was written to help clarify the application of the Investment Advisers Act of 1940 to financial planners and other financial professionals who provided investment advice as part of their services. The SEC, together with the North American Securities Administrators Association, developed IA-1092 to provide uniform interpretation and application of federal and state advisers laws, and to define the phrase "in the business of" as it applies to investment advisers.

Registration of Investment Advisers

Any person who falls within the definition of investment adviser (and does not qualify for one of the exclusions) is required to register with the SEC as such under the act of 1940. The person may also be required by the state in which he does business to register as an investment adviser in that state, even if he is exempt from registration with the SEC.

Definitions

A familiarity with the terms established by the Investment Advisers Act of 1940 (also known as the *advisers act*) and SEC Release IA-1092 is important to an understanding of the act itself. Most of the definitions used in the act are similar to those established by other federal securities acts. This section will concentrate on the definitions that are significantly different from those used in other acts, as well as definitions that are unique to the advisers act.

Investment adviser. Any person who (1) provides investment advice, (2) is in the business of providing investment advice, and (3) is compensated for providing investment advice is considered an "investment adviser." It is immaterial whether the advice is given directly (such as during face-to-face financial planning) or indirectly (such as through an investment newsletter, analysis, report or on-line computer service).

If the person giving the advice holds himself out as an investment adviser or receives any compensation for giving investment advice, the person is considered to be "in the business" of giving investment advice and is required to register under the act.

Compensation for investment advice can take the form of a(n):

- advisory fee
- total services fee
- commission
- any combination of the above

The payments may be considered compensation even if not paid directly by the person receiving the investment advice. Compensation can come from another source, such as commissions generated from sales of the products the investment adviser has recommended.

The definition of "investment adviser" does *not* include:

- banks and bank holding companies;
- publishers of any bona fide newspaper, newsmagazine or business or financial publication of general and regular circulation;
- brokers or dealers (or their associated persons and registered reps) whose giving of investment advice is incidental to the conduct of the broker-dealer's business and who receive no special compensation for the advice;
- persons who advise on U.S. government securities; or
- persons whose giving of investment advice is incidental to their professions, such as:
    - lawyers
    - accountants
    - engineers
    - teachers

The federal definition of *investment adviser* differs in two ways from the state definition. The act of 1940 allows an exclusion for those people whose advice is limited to government securities, but they are not allowed an exclusion under the state definition. Conversely, the act of 1940 does not allow an exclusion for IA representatives, while the state definition does exclude them.

Insider Trading and Securities Fraud Enforcement Act of 1988

Policies and Procedures

The Insider Trading and Securities Fraud Enforcement Act of 1988 expanded the definition of, and the liabilities and penalties for, the illicit use of nonpublic information established by the Securities Exchange Act of 1934. Insiders (including officers, directors and 10% shareholders) may now be held liable for more than just transactions in their own accounts. The act recognizes the fiduciary responsibility of the insider to the issuer, to the stockholders and to others who might be affected by trades made with insider knowledge. Investors who have suffered monetary damage because of insider trading now have legal recourse against the insider and against any other party who had control over the misuse of nonpublic information.

An insider is any person who has access to nonpublic information about a corporation. Insiders may not use inside information as a basis for personal trading until that information has been made public. The SEC can levy a penalty of up to three times the amount of profit made (or loss avoided) if inside information is used. Any individual who is a corporate insider and owns securities in that corporation must file a statement of ownership with the SEC. Inside information is any information that has not been disseminated to, or is not readily available to, the general public. To determine whether information is nonpublic, the SEC considers the method by which the information is released to the public and the timing of trades relative to when other people also have the information.

Written supervisory procedures. All broker-dealers must establish **written supervisory procedures** specifically prohibiting the use of material nonpublic information by all persons interested in, affiliated with or in any way engaged in the securities-related activities of the broker-dealers. Once these procedures are established, broker-dealers must actively maintain and enforce them.

SEC investigations. The SEC has the right to investigate any person who has violated or is suspected of violating any of the provisions of the Insider Trading Act. The Commission also has the right to require anyone who has violated the act or is suspected of a violation to file a written statement with the SEC covering all of the facts and circumstances relating to the suspected violation.

The Commission also has the right to exempt anyone involved in a violation of the act from prosecution if it decides that it would be in the public interest to do so or that it would be necessary for the protection of investors.

Securities Investor Protection Corporation

SIPC, created by the Securities Investor Protection Act of 1970, is an independent government-sponsored corporation (not an agency of the U.S. government). SIPC members pay assessments into a general insurance fund that is used to meet customer claims in the event a broker-dealer fails. All broker-dealers registered with the SEC (other than banks that are registered municipal securities dealers) must be SIPC members. Exempt from membership are:

- broker-dealers handling exclusively open-end investment company shares or unit trusts;
- broker-dealers handling exclusively variable annuities or insurance; and
- investment advisers.

The SIPC fund. SIPC collects from its members an annual assessment based on a percentage of a member's gross revenues from the securities business. Members must pay their assessments. Any member that fails to pay its assessments to SIPC is prohibited from engaging in the brokerage business.

Customer Account Coverage

Separate Customers

Individuals. Under SIPC rules, each *separate customer account* is entitled to coverage up to SIPC limits. In general, "separate customer accounts" are defined as those accounts with *unique beneficial owners*. Usually, if the account name is different it is considered a different customer and is entitled to full and separate coverage.

Claims by broker-dealers, general partners of the broker-dealers, officers of the broker-dealers, subordinated lenders, control persons of the broker-dealers and owners of more than 5% of the equity of the firms are not allowed.

Executors and administrators. All accounts held on behalf of a single deceased person, even through different executors and estate administrators, are combined in a single account for claim purposes.

Corporations and partnerships. Each corporate and partnership account is entitled to separate customer status—separate from the accounts of its directors, partners and owners.

Trust accounts. If a trust is fully qualified and has on file all necessary trust documents, it is considered a separate customer.

Joint accounts. If two or more joint accounts exist with the same beneficial owners, all of the accounts are combined in a single account for claim purposes.

Coverage limits. Customer accounts are covered to a *maximum of $500,000*, with *cash claims* not to exceed *$100,000*. Only claims for securities and cash are covered; claims resulting from open positions in commodity futures contracts do not fall under SIPC coverage. Each customer may enter a claim up to the $500,000 coverage limit. This limit is applied to all accounts in that customer's name (for instance, John Doe's cash account and his margin account would be considered one account). Examples of coverage limits are shown in Table 14.1.

Table 14.1 Examples of Customer Coverage Limits

John Doe—Cash account John Doe—Margin account	1 customer	= $500,000 coverage
John and Mary Doe—Joint account	1 customer	= $500,000 coverage
John Doe as Custodian for Jane Doe	1 customer	= $500,000 coverage

15 Other SEC and SRO Rules and Regulations

Key Terms

advertising
associated person (AP)
Code of Arbitration Procedure
Code of Procedure (COP)
District Business Conduct
 Committee (DBCC)
form letter
generic advertising

NASD Manual
National Association of Securities
 Dealers (NASD)
regular complaint procedure
Rules of Fair Practice (RFP)
sales literature
summary complaint procedure
Uniform Practice Code

Overview

As an amendment to the Securities Exchange Act of 1934, the Maloney Act permitted the establishment of self-regulatory organizations to oversee broker-dealers transacting business. The exchanges—the CBOE, the NASD, the MSRB and others—all serve that self-regulatory function by developing and enforcing rules and overseeing a portion of the securities industry.

Registration and Regulation of Broker-Dealers

Securities Exchange Act of 1934

Broker-dealers that transact securities business with customers or with other broker-dealers must apply and be approved for registration with the SEC. A broker-dealer may be exempted from this registration requirement if it does securities business intrastate only, does not use the mails (or other means of interstate commerce) and does not effect transactions on a national securities exchange.

SEC sanctions against broker-dealers. The SEC has at its disposal a number of sanctions that can be used against a broker-dealer that violates SEC regulations. The SEC is entitled to:

- censure (a public reprimand of a firm or a person associated with a firm);
- limit activities, functions or operations (curtailment of brokerage or investment banking activity);
- suspend (a broker-dealer's registration or an associated person's license to do business in the securities industry for up to one year);
- revoke registration (of a broker-dealer—closing the firm—or an associated person) if it believes this action to be in the public interest;
- fine (in its own administrative proceedings); or
- seek civil monetary penalties (through the courts for violations of federal securities laws).

An associated person also can be suspended, censured, restricted in his activities, fined or barred from association with a broker-dealer. If the SEC has barred an associated person, no broker-dealer may allow that person to associate with it without the express permission of the Commission. If an associated person is suspended by a member firm, the firm must report the suspension to the exchanges where the firm is a member.

Although a broker-dealer's registration with the SEC is required, the broker-dealer may not claim that this registration in any way implies that the Commission has passed upon or approved the broker-dealer's financial standing, business or conduct. The SEC will consider any broker-dealer making such a claim or statement guilty of misrepresentation and fraud under the act of 1934.

Fingerprinting

Registered broker-dealers are required to have fingerprint records made for all of their employees, directors, officers and partners, and are required to submit those fingerprint cards to the U.S. attorney general for identification and processing. Certain employees of broker-dealers (typically clerical and ministerial) are exempt from the fingerprinting requirement if they:

- are not involved in securities sales;
- do not handle or have access to cash or securities or to the books and records of original entry relating to money and securities; and
- do not supervise other employees engaged in these activities.

NASD Bylaws

The SEC and members of the securities industry foresaw the need for an independent self-regulatory securities industry association to supervise the activities of the OTC market. Working together, they provided for the creation of a national association through Section 15A of the Securities Exchange Act of 1934, the 1938 Maloney Act (named for its sponsor, the late Sen. Francis T. Maloney of Connecticut). The **National Association of Securities Dealers (NASD)** filed its registration statement with the SEC in 1939 and has been operating as the OTC industry's SRO ever since.

The NASD is an industry association, similar in many ways to other accredited rule-making professional associations, such as the American Bar Association. Just as it is virtually impossible to practice law without being a member in good standing of the ABA, it is also difficult to engage in investment banking and securities business without being a member of the NASD.

The NASD is one of eight SROs functioning under the oversight of the SEC. Each SRO is accountable to the Commission for enforcing federal securities laws, as well as supervising securities practices within an assigned field of jurisdiction. The largest of these SROs, and their jurisdictions, are the following:

- **National Association of Securities Dealers (NASD).** Regulates all matters related to investment banking (securities underwriting) and trading in the OTC market and the conduct of NASD member firms and associated persons.
- **New York Stock Exchange (NYSE).** Regulates all matters related to trading in NYSE-listed securities and the conduct of NYSE member firms and associated persons.
- **Municipal Securities Rulemaking Board (MSRB).** Regulates all matters related to the underwriting and trading of state and municipal securities (the MSRB regulates but does not have enforcement powers—it depends on other SROs for the enforcement of its rules).
- **Chicago Board Options Exchange (CBOE).** Regulates all matters related to writing and trading standardized options and related contracts listed on that exchange.

Administration of the NASD

Membership Corporation

The NASD is a membership corporation (membership corporations do not issue capital stock) incorporated under the laws of the State of Delaware. As they do in all states, the incorporation laws of the State of Delaware require that the applicant state the objectives or purposes of the enterprise being established. The purposes and objectives of the NASD are to:

- promote the investment banking and securities business, to standardize principles and practices, to promote high standards of commercial honor and to encourage the observance of federal and state securities laws;
- provide a medium for communication among its members, and between its members, the government and other agencies;
- adopt, administer and enforce the NASD's Rules of Fair Practice and rules designed to prevent fraudulent and manipulative practices, as well as to promote just and equitable principles of trade; and
- promote self-discipline among members and to investigate and adjust grievances between the public and members and between members.

Districts. The NASD has divided the United States into districts in order to facilitate operation. Each district elects a district committee to administer NASD codes and rules. A committee has a maximum of twelve members who serve for three years.

Every year, each district committee appoints a **District Business Conduct Committee (DBCC)**, which handles the trade practice complaints that arise in the district. On the national level, the executive committee of the NASD, made up of members of the Board of Governors, manages NASD affairs between meetings of the Board.

NASD Dues, Assessments and Other Charges

Assessments. The NASD is self-supporting. It assesses member firms' registered reps and applicants to raise money to meet its expenses. The NASD's Board of Governors determines the amount of assessments, which is subject to change.

Article III of the NASD Bylaws outlines the assessments and charges that members of the NASD must pay. The annual fee charged to members includes the following:

- basic membership fee
- assessment based on gross income
- fee for each principal and registered representative
- charge for each branch office

In addition, the NASD exacts fees for administering licensing exams, for registering personnel and branch offices and for various other filings, reports, services and assessments. Failure to pay dues is a rule violation that can result in the suspension or revocation of membership.

Use of the NASD's Corporate Name

Members of the NASD are prohibited from using the name of the Association in any manner that would suggest that the member's registration with the NASD means that the Association has passed upon or approved its financial standing, business or conduct. Use of the name of the Association is permissible if it is stated as "Member of the NASD" and if it is not given greater prominence than the name of the member. Any other use of the Association's name is prohibited without the express prior permission of the NASD.

NASD Manual

To fulfill its role as a regulatory body, the NASD has outlined its policies in the *NASD Manual*. The manual describes the following four sets of basic rules and codes by which the OTC market is regulated:

1. **Rules of Fair Practice**. This sets out fair and ethical trade practices that must be followed by member firms and their representatives when dealing with the public.
2. **Uniform Practice Code**. This established the Uniform Trade Practices, including settlement, good delivery, ex-dates, confirmations, don't know (DK) procedures and other guidelines for broker-dealers to follow when they do business with other member broker-dealer firms.
3. **Code of Procedure**. This describes how the NASD hears and handles member violations of the Rules of Fair Practice.
4. **Code of Arbitration Procedure**. This governs the resolution of disagreements and claims between members, registered reps and the public; it addresses monetary claims, not violations of the Rules of Fair Practice.

NASD Membership and Registration

The NASD's Board of Governors has the authority to adopt rules, regulations and membership eligibility standards as it sees fit. At present, the following membership standards and registration requirements are in place.

Broker-Dealer Registration

Any broker-dealer that is registered as such with the SEC is eligible and may apply for membership in the NASD. Any person who effects transactions in securities as a broker, a dealer or an investment banker also may register with the NASD, as may municipal bond houses, many of which are not required to be registered with the SEC if they deal exclusively in exempt securities. Application for membership in the NASD specifically carries the applying firm's agreement to:

- comply with the rules and regulations of the Association;
- comply with federal securities laws; and
- pay dues, assessments and other charges in the manner and amounts fixed by the Association.

All membership applications are referred to the NASD district office in the district in which the applying firm has its home office. There the application is reviewed, and the district committee (made up of representatives from member firms in the local region) sets up a premembership interview, during which the committee covers the applicant's capital, recordkeeping, familiarity with NASD rules and capability of properly conducting a securities business.

If the firm's qualifications are passed on by a district committee, the firm can be accepted into membership in the Association.

Branch Offices

Registration. For those broker-dealers that maintain and staff branch office systems, each such office must be registered with the NASD. In addition, the NASD must be notified promptly in writing of the opening or closing of any branch.

Vote of branch offices. On business matters brought before any of the district committees' attention, each NASD member firm is entitled to one vote in each district in which the firm has one or more branch offices. But the firm has only one vote per district regardless of the number of branches that might be located within a specific district. This one-vote-per-district rule also applies to the district in which the firm is headquartered.

Executive representative. At a national level, each member firm is entitled to appoint an executive representative to voice the firm's opinions, vote on matters and act in the firm's interest on business and political issues brought before the NASD in Washington, D.C. Each firm may appoint only one executive representative, and this individual must be a member of the firm's top management as well as a registered principal. The firm may have other officers, directors, partners or executives serving on various advisory panels or holding office with the NASD in Washington, D.C.

Associated Person Registration

Any person who is or becomes associated with an NASD member firm and who intends to engage in the investment banking or securities business must be registered with the NASD as an associated person. Anyone applying for registration with the NASD as an associated person (either as a registered representative or as a registered principal) must have a member firm as a sponsor.

Failure to register personnel. Failure on the part of a member firm to register an employee who performs any of the functions of a registered rep may lead to disciplinary action by the NASD.

Registration Rules and Regulations

Qualifications investigated. Prior to submitting an application (a U-4 Form) to enroll any person with the NASD as a registered representative, the member firm is obligated to investigate and ascertain the person's business reputation over the previous ten years, good character, educational institutions attended (and whether the person graduated), qualifications and experience. As part of the application completion process, the member firm must certify that an investigation has been made and that the candidate's credentials are in order.

Registered persons changing firms. NASD registration is *nontransferable*. If a registered person leaves one member firm to join another firm, he must terminate registration at the first firm on a U-5 Form (triggering the termination process described below) and reapply for registration with the new employing member firm (on a U-4 Form). If a person has terminated his registration with one firm, he must register with another firm within two years or he will be required to requalify for his license.

Continuing commissions. An individual must be registered in order to sell most nonexempt securities. Persons not registered may not receive commissions on securities sales. A registered representative who leaves a member firm (upon retirement, for example) may continue to receive commissions on business he placed while employed. There must, however, be a contract to this effect before the representative leaves the firm. Heirs of a deceased representative also may receive continuing commissions on business placed by the representative if a contract exists.

Notification of disciplinary action. A member firm must notify the NASD if one of its registered reps or any other associated person in the firm's employment is subjected to disciplinary action by one of the following:

- national securities exchange or association
- clearing corporation
- commodity futures market regulatory agency
- federal or state regulatory commission

The notification must include the name of the individual and the nature of the action (e.g., fine, censure, suspension).

Member firms also must notify the NASD of disciplinary action taken by the firm itself against a registered rep or another associated person and the nature of the action (suspension, termination, limitation of business activity, withholding of commissions, or fines imposed in excess of $2,500).

Terminations. If an associated person voluntarily ends her employment with a member, her NASD registration ceases 30 calendar days from the date written notice is received by the NASD from the employing member firm. Whenever employment of any registered person (principal or representative) is terminated, the member firm must notify the NASD in writing (on a U-5 Form) within 30 calendar days. The NASD will assess a late filing fee if the deadline is not met.

Terminating reps under investigation. If a registered representative or another associated person is under investigation for federal securities law violations or has disciplinary action pending against him from the NASD or any other SRO, a member firm may not terminate its business relationship with this person until the investigation or disciplinary action has been resolved. However, the NASD will backdate the effective date of the person's termination as a registered representative.

Exemptions from Registration

Certain people in the securities industry and some employees of members are not required to register with the Association as associated persons.

Foreign associates. Non-U.S. citizens employed by NASD member firms (usually in Canadian or overseas branch offices) are not subject to registration and licensing with the Association. This does not include U.S. citizens living and working in overseas or Canadian branch offices, however. Each exempted foreign associate must agree not to engage in securities business in any country or territory under the jurisdiction of the United States and not to do business with any U.S. citizen or national or resident alien.

Clerical and ministerial personnel and corporate officers. A member firm's employee whose function is purely clerical or ministerial does not have to register with the Association. Corporate officers who are not involved with the investment banking business of the member also are exempt from registration.

Employees in other specific functions. Employees who are registered with an exchange as a floor member (and who work or trade only on the floor) or who transact business only in exempted securities or commodities are exempt from registration.

Qualifications Examinations

As part of the registration process, an individual applying to become an associated person must prove her competency by passing the appropriate licensing examination(s). Each representative and principal registration requires that the applicant pass a qualifications examination (the NASD can waive this requirement, although the applicant's circumstances have to be unusual or extraordinary). The exams are strictly regulated and highly confidential; there are severe penalties for reproducing, copying or reporting to another person any information on any exam.

Registered Representatives

For NASD registration, examination and licensing purposes, all associated persons engaged in the investment banking and securities business are considered registered representatives, including any:

- assistant officer who does not function as a principal;
- individual who supervises, solicits or conducts business in securities; and
- individual who trains people to supervise, solicit or conduct business in securities.

Anyone who is not already registered as a principal and who is not engaged strictly in clerical work or brokerage office administration must register as a representative and pass the appropriate licensing examination. In addition to registering with the NASD, registered reps and broker-dealers must register with the State Securities Administrator in each state in which they intend to do business.

There are several categories of registration available to associated persons, each differing by the type of security sold or business in which the person will be engaged.

Limited Representative License

Some NASD representative qualifications exams qualify a person to sell only certain specified securities products. These limited representative licenses include the following.

Series 6. The Series 6 Investment Company/Variable Contract Products Limited Representative license entitles a representative to sell mutual funds and variable annuities and is used by many firms that are engaged primarily in the sale of insurance-related products. It can serve as a prerequisite for the Series 26 principal examination.

Series 63. In order to sell an issue in any state, the broker-dealer, the registered reps and the security itself must each be registered in that state. Registering an issue in a state is known as *blue-skying* the issue. In order to sell securities in any of the 41 states that currently require state-level representative registration, a registered rep must pass the Series 63 Uniform Securities Agent State Law Exam and be registered in that state. The typical blue-sky laws have provisions for revoking the license of a broker-dealer or salesperson.

Ineligibility and Disqualifications

NASD membership will be denied to any broker-dealer and status as an associated person will be refused to any firm or individual candidate who fails to meet the Association's eligibility standards with regard to training, experience, competence or any other qualification the Board of Governors finds necessary or desirable.

Statutory disqualification. Disciplinary sanctions by the SEC or another SRO can be cause for statutory disqualification of NASD membership. A broker-dealer or an individual applying for registration as an associated person will be rejected (or, if already accepted, will have his registration revoked) and must be treated as a nonmember if the firm or person:

- has been and is expelled or suspended from membership or participation in any other SRO;
- is under an SEC order denying, suspending or revoking the broker-dealer's SEC registration or barring the individual from association with a broker-dealer; or
- has been found to be the cause of another broker-dealer or associated person being expelled or suspended by another SRO or the SEC.

Any of the following also will disqualify an applicant for registration:

- misstatements willfully made in an application for membership or registration as an associated person;
- a felony conviction (either domestic or foreign) within the previous ten years or a misdemeanor charge involving securities or money within the past ten years—misdemeanor charges involving securities or money include a range of white-collar crimes, such as larceny, extortion, forgery, counterfeiting, embezzlement, bribery and misappropriation of funds and securities, in addition to violations of federal securities laws, securities fraud, public deceptions and market manipulation; and
- court injunctions prohibiting the firm or individual from acting as an investment adviser, an underwriter or a broker-dealer or in other capacities aligned with the securities and financial services industry.

The NASD's disqualification criteria are similar to those of the SEC.

NASD Definitions

Associated person (AP) of a member. Any employee, manager, director, officer or partner of a member broker-dealer or another entity (issuer, bank, etc.) or any person controlling, controlled by or in common control with that member. Syn: registered representative.

Broker. (1) An individual or a firm that charges a fee or commission for executing buy and sell orders submitted by another individual or firm. (2) The role of a broker firm when it acts as an agent for a customer and charges the customer a commission for its services. (3) Any person who is engaged in the business of effecting transactions in securities for the accounts of others and who is not a bank. Syn: agent.

Completion of the transaction. The point at which a customer pays any part of the purchase price to the broker-dealer for a security she has purchased or delivers a security she has sold. If the customer makes payment to the broker-dealer before the payment is due, completion of the transaction occurs when the broker-dealer delivers the security.

Customer. Any person who is not a broker, dealer or municipal securities dealer.

Dealer. (1) The role of a brokerage firm when it acts as a principal in a particular trade. A firm is acting as a dealer when it buys or sells a security for its own account and at its own risk and then charges the customer a markup or markdown. (2) Any person who is engaged in the business of buying and selling securities for his own account, either directly or through a broker, and who is not a bank is considered a dealer. Syn: principal.

Investment banking (securities) business. The business carried on by a broker, dealer or municipal or government securities dealer of underwriting or distributing new issues of securities as a dealer or of buying and selling securities on the order and for the benefit of others as a broker.

Member. (1) Of the NYSE: One of the 1,366 individuals owning a seat on the New York Stock Exchange. (2) Of the NASD: Any broker or dealer admitted to membership in the NASD.

Security. Under the act of 1934, any note, stock, bond, investment contract, profit-sharing or partnership agreement, certificate of deposit, option on a security or other instrument of investment commonly known as a *security*.

Statutory disqualification. Any person who has been expelled, barred or suspended from association with a member of an SRO; has had her registration suspended, denied or revoked by the Commission; has been the cause of someone else's suspension, barring or revocation; has been convicted of certain specified crimes; or has falsified any application or report that she is required to file with or on behalf of a membership organization.

Codes of Procedure and of Arbitration Procedure

Code of Procedure

The NASD's Code of Procedure was developed as a guide to settling complaints that arise between and among members and associated persons.

It is the task of the District Business Conduct Committees (DBCCs) of the NASD to determine whether a charge or complaint is valid, and if so to take appropriate disciplinary action against the offending member firm or associated person.

Sources of complaints. The overwhelming majority of complaints are filed by NASD examiners who audit each member firm's books on a regular basis, bringing any evidence of wrongdoing to the attention of the DBCC in the district in which the firm is headquartered.

When a customer, another member firm or one of the NASD's own committees lodges a complaint, one of the first steps in the proceedings is to have an NASD examiner investigate the accused member's premises and inspect the books in an effort to substantiate or discredit the complaint.

Complaint resolution process. The first official action occurs when the DBCC notifies the accused member in writing, advising it as to the specifics of the complaint, identifying who has filed the complaint and requesting a response from the accused member within 20 calendar days of the date of receipt.

Request for hearing. When the regular complaint proceeding is chosen, typically the member firm (or associated person) will either deny the charge of rule violation or make an offer of settlement. The complainant, in turn, may accept the offer or continue the proceedings by demanding a formal hearing. The respondent also can demand a hearing.

Venue. Once a complaint has been filed, it usually is scheduled to be heard before a district committee located in the district in which the member has its home office, or in the district in which the branch office is located (if the complaint is limited to the activities of or at a single branch). The complaint may be brought before a committee in a different district if the request is made in writing, if all the parties agree to the change in venue and if the National Business Conduct Committee determines that the move is appropriate.

Hearing panels. NASD disciplinary hearings are informal proceedings. A hearing panel is convened that consists of members of the DBCC, all of whom are associated persons with member firms and, therefore, peers of the respondent. Hearing panels, at times, also may consist of members of the NASD's Market Surveillance Committee.

Decision of the committee. In due course, the presiding DBCC will pass on the merits of the charge, either upholding a rule violation or dismissing the complaint. Either way, the DBCC will issue a written decision and announce the sanctions being imposed on the member firm or associated person as disciplinary action (assuming the rule violation was upheld).

The DBCC's decision becomes final after 45 calendar days (the first business day after expiration of the 45-calendar-day period). Similar to court decrees issued in civil suits, a 45-day waiting period from the issuance of the DBCC's decision to the final date is necessary to accommodate possible appeal proceedings.

Summary complaint. Very often, a DBCC will issue a summary complaint as an advance step to the more formal time-consuming regular complaint resolution process. In a summary complaint, the complainant usually has sufficient evidence on hand to support the complaint that a violation has occurred. So strong might the complainant's case be that the respondent may have no choice but to plead no contest.

If amenable to the settlement terms stated in a summary complaint, the member firm or associated person named in the complaint signs and returns a *letter of acceptance, waiver and consent*. In signing, the firm or the individual (or both) agrees to forfeit the right to appeal and possible redress and to honor the sanctions or other disciplinary actions and penalties cited in the summary complaint. The maximum penalty that can be imposed under a summary complaint is $2,500 per respondent, plus public censure.

A respondent has ten business days from the date of receipt of a summary complaint to decide on a course of action—either pay the penalty or refuse the settlement terms, which means the initiation of a regular complaint proceeding.

Penalties. If the DBCC finds that a rule violation has occurred, one or more of the following sanctions (disciplinary actions) may be imposed once the decision becomes final:

- censure of the member firm or associated person named in the complaint;
- fine imposed on the member firm or associated person;
- suspension of the member firm's or associated person's NASD registration;
- expulsion of the member firm or associated person; or
- barring of the member firm or associated person from association with all members.

Appeal and review. A respondent in receipt of the DBCC's findings in favor of the complainant has 15 calendar days from the date of receipt to appeal the decision to the NASD Board of Governors. This 15-day deadline runs concurrently with the 45-day waiting period for the DBCC's decision to become final.

The NASD Board of Governors functions two ways with respect to appeals and reviews. The Board may opt to review and possibly overturn the decision of the DBCC. If so, the Board must announce its intentions and begin the review proceedings before the 45-calendar-day period expires.

In other instances, the Board may act in response to an appeal filed by the member firm or associated person named in the original complaint. When this is the case, the Board must decide whether to review the DBCC's decision, and if a review is deemed appropriate, it must start the proceedings before the 45-day period expires.

If the Board of Governors elects to review, it will render its decision in writing, and 45 calendar days later, this decision becomes final.

Settlement procedure. The respondent may offer to make a settlement at any time during the proceedings, but such offer might not be accepted.

Payment of fines and costs. All fines levied as penalties for rule violations against a member firm or an associated person must be paid promptly after the date of the DBCC's decision or, if that decision was appealed, after the final date of the Board of Governors' decision.

Appeal to SEC. If either the complainant or the respondent feels aggrieved by the decision of the NASD Board of Governors, application can be made to the SEC for a review.

Civil suits. If, at any point in the complaint proceedings, the respondent feels aggrieved by the DBCC's decision, by the Board of Governors' decision upon review or by the SEC's decision, recourse to the civil courts for redress is always possible. If an SEC decision is appealed, the federal (U.S.) appellate court must be used.

Code of Arbitration Procedure

The **Code of Arbitration Procedure** should not be confused with disciplinary proceedings under the Code of Procedure. Although disputes may arise that touch on possible violations of the Rules of Fair Practice (without a specific complaint being charged by either party), the arbitration process is geared primarily towards resolving problems and financial losses that usually can be traced to misunderstandings and faulty communications or to the failure of one person to live up to another person's expectations (Uniform Practice Code violations).

Arbitration is a valuable process in that it offers participants a relatively easy method of settling disputes at a cost that is usually significantly lower than the cost of settling a dispute through the courts.

Matters eligible for submission. Any dispute, **statement of claim** or controversy may be submitted to the NASD's National Arbitration Committee for resolution and settlement. Disputes or statements of claims eligible for arbitration must be submitted within six years of the occurrence.

Required submissions. Internal disputes between member firms and between associated persons must be submitted for resolution and settlement via arbitration. Respondents have 20 calendar days in which to answer a claim.

Arbitration involving customers. Customers are under no obligation to submit any matter of dispute or claim to the NASD's Board of Arbitration. For them, arbitration is strictly optional; although a customer can take a member firm or an associated person before an arbitration panel on demand, neither a member firm nor an associated person can demand that a customer submit to arbitration. The customer must consent to arbitration in writing.

No redress through the courts. All parties to an NASD arbitration proceeding must understand that they are forfeiting the freedom to bring suit against one another in the civil courts while the arbitration proceeding is in progress, unless otherwise directed by law. Findings under the Code of Arbitration are binding on all parties involved in the dispute.

NASD National Arbitration Board. The NASD maintains a pool of arbitrators consisting of industry people and representatives of the public. From this pool, arbitration panels are convened as needed to appraise evidence, evaluate pleadings, render judgments and determine awards.

Simplified industry arbitration. Disputes not involving customers can be submitted for resolution under simplified industry arbitration procedures provided the dollar amount of the claim does not exceed $10,000. Claims of $10,000 or less are heard by a panel of three arbitrators. The arbitrators will review evidence and pleadings from both sides of the dispute and render a decision, usually without the need for a hearing. All awards under simplified industry arbitration are made within 30 business days from the date the arbitration panel declares the disputed matter closed.

Simplified customer arbitration. Once again, a customer cannot be forced into arbitration by a member firm or an associated person; such arbitration must be at the insistence of the customer. As with simplified industry arbitration, the dollar amount in dispute must not exceed $10,000.

Arbitration awards. All awards granted by an arbitration panel will be in writing and signed by a majority of the arbitrators. Because such an award can be entered as a judgment against the respondent in any court of competent jurisdiction, the NASD's Director of Arbitration will attempt to serve copies of the award on all parties to the proceedings via registered or certified mail. In all cases, the arbitration panel will attempt to render an award within 30 business days from the date the disputed matter is declared closed.

Failure to act under arbitration procedures. Any member firm or associated person who fails to submit required matters for arbitration, fails to submit evidence or give testimony in conjunction with a matter under arbitration or fails to honor an award issued by an arbitration panel will be in violation of the Rules of Fair Practice.

Amendments to the Code of Arbitration

The NASD has implemented amendments that make the Code of Arbitration Procedures uniform with those of other SROs. The major changes are as follows:

- Disputes subject to arbitration now include the business of members (excluding insurance), as well as securities-related disputes.
- All parties have the right to challenge arbitrators, and arbitrators have the obligation to convey potential conflicts of interest.
- The number of arbitrators increases from three to five only when the amount in dispute exceeds $30,000.
- Parties may agree to arrange private settlements or to withdraw from arbitration without panel approval.

Table 15.1 summarizes the Code of Arbitration Procedure and the Code of Procedure.

Table 15.1 Summary of the Codes of Arbitration and Procedure

	Code of Arbitration (Dispute Settlement)	Code of Procedure (Disciplinary Action)
Description	Used to resolve disputes, claims and controversies that arise in the course of business, none of which are violations of NASD rules and regulations.	Used in conjunction with formal complaints that a member firm or an associated person violated specific NASD rules and regulations.
Monetary Redress	Used to recover monetary damages allegedly suffered by the claimant as the result of disputed acts, practices or omissions by a member firm or an associated person.	Used to fine and punish a member firm or an associated person for NASD rule violations as charged in the complaint if the charges are upheld.
Primary Complainant or Claimant	Customer in dispute with a member firm or an associated person; associated person in dispute with a member firm or another associated person; member firm in dispute with another member firm or an associated person.	NASD DBCC (or Board of Governors) lodging a complaint against a member firm or an associated person based on findings of misconduct, or on reasonable grounds for same, as determined by NASD auditors/examiners.
Outcome of Proceedings	If panel of arbitrators rules in favor of the complainant, awards for monetary damage will be made.	

Communications with the Public

Although the terms are often used interchangeably by the public, the NASD and the NYSE expect principals and representatives to be able to recognize the difference between "advertising" and "sales literature."

Advertising and Sales Literature

Advertising. "Advertising" includes copy and support graphics and/or other support materials intended for:

- publication in newspapers, magazines or other periodicals;
- radio or television broadcast;
- prerecorded telephone marketing messages and tape recordings;
- videotape displays;
- signs or billboards;
- motion pictures and filmstrips;
- telephone directories; or
- *any other use of the public media.*

Sales literature. "Sales literature" is *any written communication distributed to customers* (or to the public in general) or available to people upon request. It must always be preceded or accompanied by a prospectus. Sales literature includes materials such as:

- circulars;
- research reports;
- market letters;
- form letters;
- options worksheets;
- performance reports and summaries;
- text prepared and used for educational seminars;
- prepared scripts for public interest radio and television interview programs; and
- reprints and excerpts from any advertisement, sales literature or published news item or article.

Sales literature can be distributed in either written or oral form. Standardized sales pitches, telephone scripts and seminar tapes are all classed as sales literature, and are therefore subject to the same regulations that apply to printed literature.

Form letters. The principal and registered rep will encounter two basic types of **form letters** and must know the difference for the NASD exam. One type of form letter appears as two or more substantially identical sales letters. The second type of form letter, more common with today's word-processing capabilities, is a sales letter that contains sections or statements that are identical in essence to statements made or contained in other sales letters. In either case, a letter becomes a form letter if it is sent to more than 25 persons within any 90 consecutive days. As with all other forms of sales literature, these must be approved in advance by the principal and maintained in a file for a period of *three years* from the date of their first use.

Generic advertising (Rule 135a). Generic (or institutional) advertising is a special type of advertising that is used to promote securities as an investment medium but that does not make reference to any particular security. The rules that regulate generic advertising are similar to those that govern tombstones, except that they specifically mention investment company advertising. Institutional advertising uses general terms and phrases and often includes information about:

- the securities offered by investment companies
- the nature of investment companies
- services offered in connection with the described securities
- explanations of the various types of investment companies
- descriptions of exchange and reinvestment privileges
- where the public can write or call for further information

All generic advertisements must contain the name and address of the registered sponsor of the advertisement. Even more important, an institutional or generic advertisement can be placed only by a firm that actually offers the type of security or service described. For example, a discount brokerage firm would not be permitted to advertise no-load mutual funds if it does not sell them.

Tombstones (Rule 134 advertisements). Rule 145 makes it unlawful to solicit stockholders unless a prospectus accompanies the solicitation. An underwriter is limited in what he can publicly state about a security in registration when advertising or otherwise gathering indications of interest for an upcoming public offering. Under Rule 134, advertising copy and other sales materials will not be deemed a prospectus (which means they need not be filed with the SEC as part of the registration statement) if the body copy is limited to the following:

- the name of the issuer of the securities being offered (or the name of the person or company whose assets are to be sold in exchange for the securities being offered);
- a brief description of the business of the person making the offer;
- the date, time and place of the meeting at which stockholders are to vote on or consent to the proposed transaction (exchange of securities or sale of assets);
- a brief description of the planned transaction (material facts and financial information); or
- any legend or disclaimer statement required by state or federal law.

Advertisements that meet these restrictions are more commonly known as *tombstones* or *Rule 134 advertisements*. Any advertising copy in a tombstone must also contain the following disclaimers:

- that the registration statement has been filed by the issuer but is not yet effective;
- that the communication does *not* represent an offer to sell the securities described—securities are sold **by prospectus only**;
- the name and address of the person (or firm) to contact for a prospectus; and
- that a response to this advertisement does not obligate the prospect to a buying commitment of any kind (i.e., that it represents only an **indication of interest**).

Advertisements and other promotional materials created in support of open-end investment company securities being sold on a continuous new-issue offering basis are also covered by this rule.

NASD Rules Concerning Public Communications

Many rules and regulations regarding securities transactions were conceived and written into law in order to offer the general public some form of protection from unscrupulous investment professionals. In recognition of the power of the various media to persuade people, the NASD and the SEC strictly enforce all of the rules and regulations designed to protect the public.

The two main problems addressed by the NASD's code of professionalism in advertising and sales literature are omissions and distortions of material facts. In general, all communications from a member to the public must be based on principles of fair dealing and good faith. The communication should provide a sound basis for evaluating the facts in regard to the product, service or industry promoted. Exaggerated, unwarranted or misleading statements or claims are strictly prohibited.

In an attempt to guide members in creating and producing advertising and sales literature that meet the Association's professional standards, specific requirements apply.

Identification. In general, sales literature (including market letters and research reports) must identify: the name of the member firm; the person or firm that prepared the material if copy was prepared outside; and the date the material was first used.

If the literature cites price or market performance data that are not current (or any other noncurrent information), that fact should be stated in the material. Copy created for paid advertising need carry only the name of the member firm.

Customer Recommendations

Because of the inherently close relationship between recommending securities and receiving a commission from their sale, it is easy to see how unethical salespeople could manipulate the relationship to their advantage. It is the principal's responsibility to see that this does not happen.

Disclosure requirements. Proposals and written presentations that include specific recommendations (sales literature) must have reasonable bases to support the recommendations, and the member firm must provide these in the proposal or other written document, or offer to furnish them upon request. In any event, the member should have reasonable grounds for believing that a security is a suitable investment for a customer before recommending its purchase.

A recommendation typically takes the form of a simple summary of what the customer said her investment needs were and what she wants to accomplish, coupled with an explanation of the recommendation being made and how it relates to the customer's needs and wants.

When, in recommending a security to a customer, a firm uses material referring to the performance of past recommendations, it must reveal certain information. In particular, it must disclose:

- the price (or price range) of the recommended security at the date and time that the recommendation is made;
- the general direction of the market;
- the availability of information supporting the recommendation;
- any recommendations made of similar securities within the past twelve months (including the nature of the recommendations—buy, sell or hold);
- whether the firm intends to buy or sell any of the recommended security for its own account;
- whether the firm is a market maker in the recommended security;
- whether the firm or its officers or partners own options, rights or warrants to buy the recommended security;
- whether the firm managed or co-managed a public offering of the recommended security or any other of the same issuer's securities during the past three years; and
- all recommendations (gainers and losers) made by the firm over the period of time in question.

The time span covered in the list of recommendations must run through consecutive periods, without skipping periods in an attempt to hide particular recommendations or negative price performance data.

The above is the type of information a knowledgeable investor can use to determine whether a recommendation is appropriate for his situation. In addition to meeting these requirements, the firm making the recommendation must not:

- imply that there are any guarantees accompanying the recommendation;
- compare the recommended security to dissimilar products;
- make fraudulent or misleading statements about the recommended security; or
- make any predictions about the future performance or potential of the recommended security.

Recommending Mutual Funds

Whenever an investment company or a broker-dealer develops advertisements or sales literature for a mutual fund, it must comply with all of the rules designed to protect the public. It is the principal's duty to see that all public communications containing recommendations are developed in accordance with these rules and that the registered reps using them to sell investment products use them properly.

When recommending mutual funds to clients as investments and when using advertisements or sales literature developed for those investments the broker-dealer should:

- use charts or graphs showing the fund's performance covering a period of time long enough to reflect variations in value under different market conditions, generally a period of at least ten years;
- reveal the source of the graphic;
- separate dividends from capital gains when making statements about the fund's cash returns;

- not state that a mutual fund is similar to or safer than any other type of security (including government bonds, insurance policies or annuities, or corporate bonds);
- reveal the fund's highest sales charge, even if the client appears to qualify for a breakpoint; and
- not make any fraudulent or misleading statements or omissions of facts.

Periodic Investment Plans

Mutual fund plans that fall into the periodic payment category (frequently sold in this manner to receive the benefits of dollar cost averaging) cannot be described in advertisements or sales literature without the disclosure that:

- a profit is not assured;
- they do not provide protection from losses in a declining market;
- the plan involves continuous investments regardless of market fluctuations; and
- the investor should consider his financial ability to continue purchases during periods of declining prices.

Other Communication Prohibitions

Claims and opinions couched as facts and conclusions. It is unprofessional and a violation of these regulations to pass off opinions, projections and forecasts as guarantees of performance or as scientific evidence.

Testimonials. Testimonials and endorsements by celebrities and public opinion influencers related to specific recommendations or investment results must not be misleading or suggest that past performance (or the personal experience of the person providing the testimonial) is an indication of future performance. If the member firm paid a fee or other compensation to the person for the testimonial or endorsement, this fact must be disclosed.

If a broker-dealer assembles a sales piece about a particular investment company that includes testimonials by one or more customers, the sales piece must include the following information and/or caveats:

- Past performance is not indicative of future performance.
- If the company compensated the person who made the testimonial, this must be stated.
- If the testimonial implies that the person is making the statement based on special experience or knowledge, the advertisement must state the person's qualifications.

The NASD would consider it highly improper if, for example, a member included a testimonial by "Doctor Henderson" about the investment potential of its new Medical Technology Fund if the doctor's degree was in landscaping.

Offers of free service. It is unprofessional to use offers of free service (or free investment reports and topical news) if, in fact, the respondent must assume obligations of one sort or another. Reports, analyses or other services offered to the public must be furnished entirely free and without condition or obligation.

Other rules. The following is a list of rules regarding unprofessional practices:

- A communication must not state or imply that research facilities are more extensive than they actually are.
- Hedge clauses, caveats and disclaimers must not be used if they are misleading or inconsistent with the content of the material.
- If periodic investment plans are being promoted, the material must caution that such plans do not ensure a profit. Also, if dollar cost averaging is mentioned in connection with systematic investment plans, it must be pointed out that this concept is valid only if accompanied by investor persistence and continuous access to fresh capital over the long term.
- Ambiguous references to the NASD or other SROs must not be made with the aim of leading people to believe that a broker-dealer is acting with the endorsement and approval of the Association (or one of the other SROs). If the name or logo of the NASD is used in a member's sales literature, it must not appear in a typeface larger or more prominent than the one used for the member's own name.
- If advertisements or sales literature includes price performance information in the form of charts, graphs or statistical tables prepared by or obtained from outside sources, the source of the data must be disclosed.

Use of Members' Names

General standards. All advertising and sales literature must contain the name of the NASD member, and no material fact is to be omitted if the omission causes the advertisement or literature to be misleading. As a result, all advertising and sales literature must:

- clearly and prominently disclose the name of the NASD member;
- when multiple entities and products are being offered, clearly describe the relationship between the NASD member and the named entities and products;
- clearly disclose the relationship of an individual and NASD member when an individual is named in the communication;
- not use or refer to nonexistent degrees or designations; and
- not use degrees or designations in a misleading manner.

Specific Requirements

Fictional names. Fictional names and/or DBA (doing business as) designations are permitted if the name is filed with the NASD and the SEC on form BD and is the name used to designate the member. However, for states requiring the use of a DBA (cannot file under BD name), the member must disclose that the DBA is used in the particular state or states for that reason in addition to identification of the name under which it is filed with the NASD and SEC. Whenever possible, the NASD urges the member to use a name (DBA or other) acceptable for all advertising and sales literature.

Generic names. The NASD permits members to use an altered version of a firm name as an "umbrella" identification for purposes of promoting name recognition. A generic, or umbrella, name can be used as long as:

- it is displayed with the NASD member name also being prominently displayed;
- its relationship with the member name is clear (i.e., the information describes the link or separation between the member and the generic name); and
- there is no implication that the generic or umbrella name is the broker-dealer.

Other designations. Members may designate a portion of their business using such terms as "division of," "service of" or "securities offered through" only if a bona fide division exists. The member name must be clearly designated and the division be clearly identified as a division of the member.

For use by nonmember firms, the nonmember must clearly and prominently display the name of the member firm and the relationship to the member. Additionally, the securities function must be clearly identified as a function of the member and not as a function of the nonmember.

Hiring New Registered Representatives

Recruitment Advertising

Companies that run advertisements to attract new registered reps are regulated by the same Rules of Fair Practice that cover companies advertising investment products. The advertisements must be truthful, informative and fair in representing the opportunities in the industry and must not contain exaggerated or unwarranted claims.

The advertisements may not emphasize the salaries of top-paid salespeople without revealing that they are not representative, and they may not contain any other statements that may be misleading or fraudulent.

Broker-dealers are permitted, in this one instance, to run blind advertisements (that is, advertisements that do not list the company's name).

Interviews

Once a company starts interviewing potential employees, it is the principal's responsibility to see that both the industry and the job opportunity are represented honestly. Any discussions of the business must present both the upside and the downside of the position and should not misrepresent the average employee's compensation. Every job has potential, but starting out an interview by saying, "Let's talk about $100,000 a year," is unethical and misleading and is therefore in direct contravention of the NASD rules.

Review of NASD Regulations

The following summarizes the NASD regulations regarding advertising and sales literature:

1. All advertising and sales literature must be approved by a principal prior to use.
2. All advertising and sales literature must be kept in a separate file for a minimum of three years.

3. All advertising and sales literature concerning registered investment companies must be filed within ten business days of first use by any member acting as a principal underwriter for the securities.
4. New members must file all advertising they produce or distribute during their first year at least ten days prior to first use with the NASD.
5. The NASD may (if it deems it necessary) require any member to resume filing all of its advertising and sales literature prior to use.

Legal Recourse of Customers

The Securities Exchange Act of 1934, and the acts of 1933 and 1940, all contain sections prohibiting the use of any fraudulent or manipulative device in the selling of securities to the public.

The rules make it unlawful for any person to use the mails or any facilities of interstate commerce to "... employ, in connection with the purchase or sale of any security ... any manipulative or deceptive device ... in contravention of such rules and regulations as the Commission may prescribe as necessary."

In essence, this passage states simply that an act is unlawful if the SEC says it is, and the enforcement of the intent of the act is not to be limited by the letter of the law.

Any client may sue for damages if he believes that the broker-dealer employed any form of manipulative or deceptive practices in the sale of securities. The client must bring the lawsuit within three years of when the manipulative act occurs and within one year of his discovery of the manipulation or deception.

◆ Review Questions

1. The NASD Uniform Practice Code was established to
   A. require that practices in the investment banking and securities industry be just, reasonable and nondiscriminatory between investors
   B. eliminate advertising and sales literature that the SEC considers to be in violation of standards
   C. provide a procedure for handling trade complaints from investors
   D. maintain similarity of business practices among member organizations in the securities industry

2. "Freeriding and withholding" refers to
   A. distributing new issues valued at amounts exceeding the cost
   B. purchasing securities with the intent of selling them before the settlement date
   C. a member of an underwriting or a selling group's failing to make a public offering of a security at the public offering price
   D. none of the above

3. Disciplinary decisions of the NASD Board of Governors and appellate and review procedures are matters covered in the
   A. SEC Bylaws
   B. Rules of Fair Practice
   C. Code of Procedure
   D. Uniform Practice Code

4. The purpose of the Rules of Fair Practice is to
   A. provide a means of handling trade complaints from investors
   B. provide a means of communication between member firms
   C. require that business practices be similar among all members
   D. promote fair and ethical trade practices for member firms to use when dealing with the public

5. The Code of Arbitration is for
   A. handling violations of the Rules of Fair Practice
   B. ensuring just and equitable practices of fair trade
   C. establishing uniform trade practices
   D. handling disagreements and claims between member firms, registered reps and the public

◆ Answers & Rationale

1. **D.** The NASD Uniform Practice Code covers settlement, good delivery, ex-dates, confirmations and DK procedures, and contains guidelines for broker-dealers to follow when they do business with other member broker-dealers.

2. **C.** When a member firm participates in a new-issue distribution, the Rules of Fair Practice state that the member must make a bona fide offering at the POP. Failure to do so is considered "freeriding and withholding."

3. **C.** The Code of Procedure outlines the methods for handling trade practice complaints when a violation of the Rules of Fair Practice is involved.

4. **D.** The NASD drafted the Rules of Fair Practice as a comprehensive set of guidelines and rules that require member firms (and registered representatives) to use just and equitable practices of trade. The main goal of the rules is to protect the customer by preventing fraud, market manipulation and unreasonable charges and commissions.

5. **D.** The Code of Arbitration provides procedures for settling disputes, claims and controversies that arise between broker-dealers, registered representatives and the public.

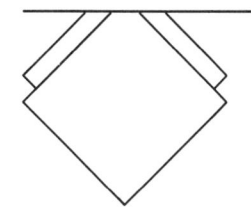

Glossary

abandon The act of not exercising or selling an option before its expiration.

Accelerated Cost Recovery System (ACRS) *See* Modified Accelerated Cost Recovery System (MACRS).

accordion loan A broker's collateral loan that requires the brokerage firm to deposit additional securities into a single loan account and enables it to withdraw more money; only one loan need be maintained. *See also* broker's loan, call loan.

account executive *See* registered representative.

accredited investor As defined in Rule 502 of Regulation D, an accredited investor is any institution or individual meeting minimum net worth requirements for the purchase of securities qualifying under the Regulation D registration exemption.

An *accredited investor* is generally accepted to be one who:
- has a net worth of $1 million or more; or
- has had an annual income of $200,000 or more in each of the two most recent years (or $300,000 jointly with a spouse) and who has a reasonable expectation of reaching the same income level in the current year.

accretion of bond discount An accounting process whereby the initial cost of a bond purchased at a discount is increased to reflect its basis as the bond's maturity date approaches.

accrual accounting A method of reporting income when earned and expenses when incurred, as opposed to reporting income when received and expenses when paid. *See also* cash basis accounting.

accrued interest Interest that is added to the contract price of a bond transaction. This interest has accrued since the last interest payment up to but not including the settlement date. Exceptions are income bonds, bonds in default and zero-coupon bonds.

accumulation unit An accounting measure (net asset value) that represents a contract owner's proportionate unit of interest in a separate account (the portfolio) during the accumulations (deposit) period. *See also* separate account.

acid test ratio A more stringent test of liquidity than current ratio, calculated by adding the sum of cash, cash equivalents and accounts and notes receivable and dividing that sum by total current liabilities. *See also* current ratio.

acquisition fee The total of all fees and commissions paid by any party in connection with the selection or purchase of property by a program. Included in the computation of such fees or commissions shall be any real estate commission, acquisition fee, development fee, selection fee or construction fee of a similar nature. Acquisition expenses include such items as legal and appraisal expenses, settlement costs, title insurance and any development fee paid to a person not affiliated with a sponsor in connection with the actual development of a project after acquisition of the land by the program. The cost is added to the basis in the asset for the purpose of depreciation and calculating gain or loss on sale.

ACRS *See* Accelerated Cost Recovery System.

ACT *See* Automated Confirmation Transaction service.

active crowd That section of the NYSE that trades actively traded bonds. (*Syn.* free crowd)

actual The physical commodity being traded, as opposed to the futures contracts on that commodity.

adjacent acreage Producing or nonproducing oil or gas leases located within the area of an existing well site. Adjacent acreage may prove valuable for continued development of the original oil or gas prospect.

adjusted basis Basis adjusted by additions and subtractions to reflect deductions taken with respect to the property and capital improvements to the property. Adjusted basis is used to compute gain or loss on the sale or another disposition of property.

adjusted gross income (AGI) Gross income minus allowable deductions for trade and business expenses.

adjustment bond *See* income bond.

administrator A person authorized by a court of law to liquidate the estate of an intestate decedent. The official or agency administering the securities laws of a state.

ADR *See* American depositary receipt.

ad valorem tax A tax based on the value of real property or personal property. Property taxes are the major source of revenues for local governing units. *See also* assessed value, mill rate.

advance/decline line A technical analysis tool representing the total of differences between advances and declines of security prices. The advance/decline line is considered the best indicator of market movement as a whole.

advance refunding A new municipal bond is issued, the proceeds of which will be used to refinance an existing issue prior to the existing issue's maturity or call date. The proceeds of the new issue will be invested, and the principal and interest earned will be used to pay the principal and interest of the securities being refunded. *See also* defeasance. (*Syn.* prerefunding)

advertisement Any material designed for use by newspapers, magazines, radio, television, telephone recording or any other public medium to solicit business. The firm using advertising has little control over the type of individuals being exposed to the advertising. *See also* sales literature.

advisory board Under the Investment Company Act of 1940, an advisory board serves to advise an investment company on matters concerning its investments in securities, but does not have the power to make investment decisions or take action itself. An advisory board must be composed of persons who have no other connection with, and serve no other function for, the company.

affiliate 1) Any person directly or indirectly owning, controlling or holding with power to vote 10% or more of the outstanding voting securities of another person; also, any officer, director or partner of another entity for which such person acts in such capacity. When used with respect to a member or sponsor, affiliate means any person who controls, is controlled by or is under common control with such member or sponsor and includes any partner, officer or director (or any person performing similar functions) of such member or sponsor or a person who beneficially owns 50% or more of the equity interest in, or has the power to vote 50% or more of the voting interest in, such member or sponsor. 2) Affiliate under the Investment Company Act of 1940 is anyone who could have any type of control over an investment company's operations, which includes anyone with 5% or more of the outstanding voting securities of the investment company or any corporation in which the investment company holds 5% or more of its outstanding securities.

agency basis Securities sold through normal broker transactions and executed through a national dealer market. The broker is acting for the accounts of others.

agency issue A debt security issued by an authorized agency of the federal government. Such issues are backed by the issuing agencies themselves, not by the full faith and credit of the U.S. government (except GNMA and Federal Import Export Bank).

agency transaction A transaction in which the broker-dealer is acting for the accounts of others by buying or selling securities on behalf of customers; also, securities sold through normal broker transactions, executed through a national dealer market.

agent 1) An individual acting for the accounts of others; any person licensed by a state as a life insurance agent. (*Syn.* broker). 2) An agent is a securities salesperson who represents a broker-dealer or issuer when selling or trying to sell securities to the investing public. This individual is considered an agent whether he actually receives or simply solicits orders. In other words, an agent is a registered representative or anyone who receives an order while representing a broker-dealer.

The term "agent" is defined in the Uniform Securities Act so that it can be legally determined who must register in the state as an agent. If an individual does not fall into the classification of agent as defined by the law, then the registration process is not necessary. An individual is not considered an agent if he represents any of the following exempt *issuers* or exempt *securities:*

- U.S. government;
- municipality;
- Canadian government, Canadian province or municipality;
- any foreign government with which the U.S. maintains diplomatic relations;
- U.S. banks, savings institutions or trust companies;
- commercial paper with maturities of nine months or less; or
- investment contracts issued in connection with an employee's stock purchase, savings, pension, profit-sharing or similar benefit plan.

An individual is also not considered an agent if he represents an issuer in an exempt transaction. The following are considered exempt transactions:
- isolated nonissuer transactions;
- transactions between an issuer and its underwriters;
- transactions with savings institutions or trust companies; and
- transactions with an issuer's employees, partners or directors if no commission is paid directly or indirectly for the soliciting.

An individual is not considered an agent merely because he is a partner, officer or director of a brokerage firm. If the partner, officer or director of a brokerage firm limits his activities to managerial functions and does not attempt to effect purchases or sales, that person is not considered an agent.

aggregate indebtedness (AI) 1) An accounting of all money (liabilities) a broker-dealer is obligated to pay out to customers, other broker-dealers, banks and other lenders, business suppliers and vendors, and anyone who does business with or works for the firm. Liabilities that are excluded from aggregate indebtedness include those that are secured by fixed assets and other amounts payable that are secured by the firm's own securities (Rule 15c3-1). 2) Customer net margin debit balances.

aggressive investment strategy A method of investing a person uses when trying to get the maximum return on a portfolio by timing purchases and sales to coincide with expected market movements and by varying the structure of the portfolio in line with these expected market moves.

AGI *See* adjusted gross income.

agreement among underwriters If an underwriting syndicate is being formed to help with an issue, the syndicate manager's responsibilities include drawing up an agreement among underwriters. This agreement sets forth the terms under which each member of the syndicate will participate and states the duties and responsibilities of the manager of the underwriting.

AIR *See* assumed interest rate.

allied member A general partner of an NYSE member firm who is not an NYSE member, an owner of 5% or more of the outstanding voting stock of an NYSE member corporation or a principal executive director or officer of a member corporation. Allied members do not own seats on the NYSE.

all or none offering (AON) All-or-none underwriting is one form of best-efforts underwriting. The underwriter agrees to sell all the shares (or a prescribed minimum) or none of them. This type of agreement may be used when the issuer requires a minimum amount of capital to be raised. If the minimum is not reached, the securities sold and the money raised are returned. Commissions will not be paid unless the offering is completed.

all or none order (AON) An order in which the floor broker is instructed to execute an entire order in one transaction (no partial executions).

allowance A deduction from the invoiced amount allowed by the seller of goods to compensate the buyer for losses or damage. *See also* quality allowance.

alternative minimum tax (AMT) An alternate tax computation that includes certain tax preference items that are added back into adjusted gross income for determining the AMT. The AMT is paid if it is higher than the regular tax liability for the year. The tax is currently 28%, or 26% for amounts less than $175,000. The regular tax and the amount by which the AMT exceeds the regular tax are paid.

AMBAC The AMBAC Indemnity Corporation offers insurance on the timely payment of interest and principal obligations of municipal securities. Bonds insured by AMBAC usually receive an AAA rating from the rating services.

American depositary receipt (ADR) A negotiable receipt for a given number of shares of stock in a foreign corporation. An ADR is bought and sold in the American securities markets just as stock is traded.

American Stock Exchange AUTOAMOS The American Stock Exchange uses the Automatic AMEX Options Switch (AUTOAMOS) system for options orders. AUTOAMOS can be used to electronically route day, GTC and marketable limit orders from brokers to AMEX specialists and execution reports from the specialists back to the brokers. AUTOAMOS automatically executes trades for the four to six most active stocks of the *Standard & Poor's 100 Index* options. AUTOAMOS accepts options orders from brokers for up to 20 contracts.

American Stock Exchange AUTOPER The American Stock Exchange uses the Automatic Post Execution & Reporting (AUTOPER) system for equity orders. AUTOPER can be used to electronically route day, GTC and marketable limit orders from brokers to AMEX specialists and execution reports from the specialists back to the brokers. AUTOPER accepts both odd- and round-lot equity orders from brokers for up to 2,000 shares.

amortization Paying off debt (principal) over a period of time in periodic installments. *Amortization* is also defined as the ratable deduction of certain capitalized expenditures over a specified period of time.

amortization of bond premium An accounting process whereby the initial price of a bond purchased at a premium is decreased to reflect the basis of the bond as it approaches maturity.

AMT *See* alternative minimum tax.

annuitant A person who receives the distribution of an annuity contract.

annuitize To change an annuity contract from the accumulation period to the distribution of the funds.

annuity A contract between an insurance company and an individual, which generally guarantees lifetime income to the person on whose life the contract is based in return for either a lump sum or a periodic payment to the insurance company. *See also* deferred annuity, fixed annuity, immediate annuity, variable annuity.

annuity unit The accounting measure used to determine the amount of each payment to an annuitant during payout of the annuity.

AON *See* all or none offering, all or none order.

AP *See* associated person.

appraisal A written opinion of the value of a property prepared by an independent appraiser qualified to appraise that particular type of property.

appreciation The increase in value of an asset.

approved plan *See* qualified retirement plan.

arbitrage Effecting sales and purchases simultaneously in the same or related securities to take advantage of a market inefficiency; also, two assets improperly priced relative to one another. *See also* market arbitrage, security arbitrage.

arbitrageur One who engages in arbitrage.

ask The current price for which a security may be bought, as in the OTC market. For mutual funds, the asked price includes any sales charge that is added to the net asset value. *See also* public offering price. (*Syn.* bid, offer, quote)

assessed value The value of property as appraised by a taxing authority for the purpose of levying taxes. Assessed value may equal market value or a stipulated percentage of market value.

assessment An additional amount of capital that a participant may be called upon to furnish beyond the subscription amount. Assessments may be mandatory or optional, are limited to the original subscription amount and must be called within twelve months.

asset Anything that an individual or a corporation owns.

assignee A person who has acquired a beneficial interest in one or more units from a third party but who is neither a substituted limited partner nor an assignee of record.

assignee of record An assignee who has acquired a beneficial interest in one or more units, whose ownership of such units has been recorded on the books of the partnership and whose ownership is the subject of a written instrument of assignment, the effective date of which assignment has passed.

assignment 1) A document accompanying or part of a stock certificate that is signed by the person named on the certificate for the purpose of transferring the certificate's title to another person's name. 2) The act of identifying and notifying an account holder that an option held short in that account has been exercised by the option owner. *See also* stock power.

assistant representative/order processing *See* Series 11.

associated person of a member (AP) Any employee, manager, director, officer or partner of a member broker-dealer or another entity (issuer, bank, etc.) or any person controlling, controlled by or in common control with that member is considered an associated person of that member.

assumed interest rate (AIR) The rate of investment return that would be required to be credited to a variable life insurance policy—after deducting charges for taxes, investment expenses and mortality and expense guarantees—to maintain the variable death benefit equal at all times to the amount of death benefit. This does not include incidental insurance benefits, which would be payable under the plan of insurance if the death benefit did not vary according to the investment experience of the separate account.

A base for projecting payments from a variable annuity, the AIR is not a guarantee. AIRs offered by companies vary. Naturally, the higher the assumption, the higher the initial benefit and vice versa. The importance of the AIR as a base for projection rests with the fact that, once selected, the account must earn that rate to maintain the initial benefit level.

at-the-close A customer's order that specifies it is to be executed at the close of the market or of trading in that security. If the order is not executed at-the-close, it is canceled. The order does not have to be executed at the closing price. *See also* at-the-open.

at-the-money An option in which the underlying stock is trading precisely at the exercise price of that option. *See also* in-the-money, out-of-the-money.

at-the-open A customer's order that specifies it is to be executed at the open of the market or of trading in that security. If the order is not executed at-the-open, it is canceled. The order does not have to be executed at the opening price. *See also* at-the-close.

auction market A market in which buyers enter competitive bids and sellers enter competitive offers simultaneously. The NYSE is an auction market. (*Syn.* double auction market)

audited financial statement A financial statement of a program, a corporation or an issuer (including the profit and loss statement, cash flow and source and application of revenues statement, and balance sheet) that has been audited by an independent certified public accountant.

authorized stock The number of shares of stock that a corporation is permitted to issue. This number is stipulated in the corporation's state-approved charter and may be changed by a vote of the corporation's stockholders.

authorizing resolution The document enabling a municipality or state government to issue municipal securities. The resolution provides for the establishment of a revenue fund in which receipts or income is deposited.

AUTOAMOS *See* American Stock Exchange AUTOAMOS.

Automated Confirmation Transaction (ACT) service The ACT service is a postexecution, on-line transaction reporting and comparison system developed by the NASD. ACT's primary purpose is to make reconciliation and matching telephone-negotiated trades easier for member firms, thereby increasing the efficiency of the firms' back office operations.

AUTOPER *See* American Stock Exchange AUTOPER.

back away The failure of an over-the-counter market maker to honor a firm bid and asked price.

backwardation *See* inverted market.

balanced fund A type of mutual fund whose stated investment policy is to have at all times some portion of its investment assets in bonds and preferred stock as well as in common stock. Therefore, there is a balance between the two classes, equity and debt. *See also* mutual fund.

balance of payments An international accounting record of all payments made from one nation to another; *balance* means that a particular country has taken in as much foreign currency as it has paid out in its own currency.

balance sheet A report of a company's financial condition at a specific time.

balloon maturity A maturity schedule for an issue of bonds wherein a large number of the bonds come due at a prescribed time (normally at the final maturity date). This kind of maturity schedule is a type of serial maturity. *See also* maturity date.

BAN *See* bond anticipation note.

banker's acceptance A money market instrument used to finance international and domestic trade. A banker's acceptance is a check drawn on a bank by an importer or exporter of goods and represents the bank's conditional promise to pay the face amount of the note at maturity (normally less than three months).

bank guarantee letter The document supplied by an approved bank in which the bank certifies that a put writer has sufficient funds on deposit at the bank to equal the aggregate exercise price of the put.

base grade The standard grade of a commodity on which a futures contract is based.

basis 1) The cost of property. 2) The difference between the spot or cash price of a commodity and a futures contract price of the same commodity. Basis is usually computed between the spot and the nearby futures contract.

basis point Equal to 1/100 of 1% of yield (e.g., 1/2% = 50 basis points).

basis quote The price of a security quoted in terms of the yield that the purchaser can expect to receive.

bearer bond *See* coupon bond.

bear market A market in which prices of securities are falling or are expected to fall.

bedbug letter *See* deficiency letter.

benefit base The amount to which the net investment return is applied.

best efforts offering Acting as an agent for the issuer, the underwriter puts forth its best efforts to sell as many shares as possible. The issuer pays the underwriter a commission for those shares sold. The underwriter has no liability for unsold shares, as in the case of a firm commitment agreement.

beta coefficient A means of measuring the volatility of a security or portfolio of securities in comparison with the market as a whole. A beta of 1 indicates that the security's price will move with the market. A beta higher than 1 indicates that the security's price will be more volatile than the market. A beta of less than 1 means that it will be less volatile than the market as a whole.

bid An indication by an investor, a trader or a dealer of a willingness to buy a security or commodity. *See also* offer. (*Syn.* quotation, quote)

bid form The form submitted by underwriters in a competitive bid on a new issue of municipal securities. The underwriter states the interest rate, price bid and net interest cost to the issuer.

bid price *See* net asset value.

blind pool A direct participation product that does not state in advance the specific properties in which the general partners will invest the partnership's money. (*Syn.* unspecified property program)

block trade A trade of 10,000 or more shares.

blue chip stock The issues of normally strong, well-established companies that have demonstrated their ability to pay dividends in good and bad times.

Blue List, The A daily trade publication for the secondary market that lists the current municipal bond offerings of banks and brokers nationwide.

blue-sky To qualify a securities offering in a particular state.

blue-sky laws The nickname for state regulations governing the securities industry.

board of directors A unit that governs the NYSE, composed of 20 members who are elected for a term of two years by the general membership of the NYSE; also, individuals elected by stockholders to establish corporate management policies. A board of directors decides, among other items, if and when dividends will be paid to stockholders.

Board of Governors The body that governs the NASD, composed of 27 members elected by both the general membership and the Board itself.

board order A customer's order that becomes a market order as soon as the market touches or breaks through the order price. Board orders to buy are placed below the current market. Board orders to sell are placed above the current market. (*Syn.* market-if-touched order)

bona fide quote A quote from a dealer in municipal securities that is willing to execute a trade under the terms and conditions stated at the time of the quote. *See also* firm quote.

bond An evidence of debt issued by corporations, municipalities and the federal government. Bonds represent the borrowing of money by a corporation or government. A bond is a legal obligation of the issuing company or government to repay principal at the maturity of the bond. Terms of the repayment and any interest to be paid are stated in the bond indenture. Bonds are issued with a par value ($1,000) representing the amount of money borrowed. The issuer promises to pay a percentage of the par value as interest on the borrowed funds. The interest payment is stated on the face of the bond at issue.

bond anticipation note (BAN) A short-term debt instrument issued by a municipality to be paid from the proceeds of long-term debt issued.

bond attorney An attorney retained by a municipal issuer to give opinions concerning the legality of a municipal issue. *See also* legal opinion of counsel. (*Syn.* bond counsel)

Bond Buyer, The **indexes** Index, published by *The Bond Buyer*, of yield levels of municipal bonds. The indexes are indicators of yields that would be offered on AA and A general obligation bonds with 20-year maturities and revenue bonds with 30-year maturities.

bond counsel *See* bond attorney.

bond fund A type of mutual fund whose investment policy is to provide stable income with a minimum of capital risks. It invests in both bonds and preferred stock and may invest in corporate, government or municipal bonds. *See also* mutual fund.

bond quote A corporate bond that is quoted on a percentage of par with increments of 1/8, where a quote of 99 1/8 represents 99.125% of par

($1,000), or $991.25. Bonds may also be quoted on a yield to maturity basis.

bond ratio The percentage of a company's invested capital that is provided by long-term debt financing. It is found by dividing the face value of the outstanding bonds by the invested capital. (*Syn.* debt ratio)

bond swap A technique used by investors in municipal bonds that involves the sale of a bond or bonds at a loss and the simultaneous purchase of entirely different bonds in a like amount, with comparable coupons or maturities.

book-entry security A security sold without delivery of a certificate. Evidence of ownership is maintained on records kept by a central agency, such as the Treasury on the sale of Treasury bills. Transfer of ownership is recorded by entering the change on the books.

book value per bond *See* net tangible assets per bond.

book value per share A measure of the net worth of each share of common stock that is calculated by subtracting intangible assets and preferred stock from total net worth and then dividing by the number of shares of common outstanding. (*Syn.* net tangible assets per common share)

branch office A branch office is any location identified by any means to the public as a location in which the member conducts an investment banking or securities business. An office is considered a branch office if:
- the member firm pays all or a substantial portion of the operating expenses (especially rent) involved in maintaining the space, either in a commercial or residential setting;
- the location is identified to the general public as an office of the member through any kind of signage or listing in a directory;
- the location is advertised in any way; or
- it is listed in any publication (trade or otherwise, including telephone directories) as a designated office of the firm.

breadth-of-market theory A technical theory that forecasts the strength of the market based on the number of issues that advance or decline in a particular trading day. (*Syn.* advance/decline line)

breakeven call spread Breakeven is calculated by adding the net premium to the lower strike price.

breakeven long hedge Breakeven occurs when the market price of a stock equals the purchase price of the stock plus the premium paid for the put.

breakeven point The market price that a stock must reach for the option buyer to avoid a loss if he exercises. For a call, it is the strike price plus the premium paid. For a put, it is the strike price minus the premium paid.

breakeven point straddle Two breakeven points on straddles that are calculated by adding and subtracting the total premium from the exercise price on the straddle.

breakeven put spread Breakeven for a put spread is calculated by subtracting the net premium from the higher strike price.

breakeven short hedge The short sales price minus the premium paid to buy the call.

breakout The movement of a security's price through an established support or resistance level.

breakpoint The schedule of discounts offered by a mutual fund for lump-sum or cumulative investments.

breakpoint sale The sale of mutual fund shares in quantities just below the level at which the purchaser would qualify for reduced sales charges. This violates the NASD Rules of Fair Practice.

broad tape The news wires from which price and background information on securities and commodities markets can be gathered.

broker 1) An individual or firm that charges a fee or commission for executing buy and sell orders submitted by another individual or firm. 2) The role of a broker firm when it acts as an agent for a customer and charges the customer a commission for its services.

The term "broker-dealer" is defined in the Uniform Securities Act so that it can be determined who must register in the state as a broker-dealer. If the person does not fall under the definition of broker-dealer as defined by the law, then the registration process is not necessary.

The following persons would not be classified as broker-dealers:
- agents (registered representatives);
- issuers;
- banks, savings institutions or trust companies; or
- persons who have no place of business in the state and who: (a) effect securities transactions in the state exclusively through the issuers of the securities, other broker-dealers or financial institutions (banks, savings institutions, trust companies, insurance companies, and investment companies), or (b) do not during any period of 12 consecutive months direct more than 15 solicitations into the state to persons other than those specified above.

brokerage house *See* commission house.

broker fail *See* fail to deliver.

broker's broker A specialist handling orders for a commission house broker; also, a floor broker on an exchange or a broker-dealer in the over-the-counter market acting on behalf of (as an agent for) another broker in executing a trade. *See also* correspondent broker-dealer.

broker's loan A money loan made to a brokerage firm by a commercial bank or another lending institution for financing a margin account debit balance. *See also* call loan, loan for set amount.

bucketing The act of accepting customer orders and using firm or other customer positions or orders to offset them without executing them immediately through an exchange.

bulletin board *See* OTC bulletin board.

bullion Ingots or bars of gold assayed at .995 fine or higher.

bull market A market in which prices of securities are moving or are expected to move higher.

bunching orders The act of combining odd-lot orders from different clients into a round lot so as to save the clients the odd-lot differential.

business day A day on which the NYSE is open for business (trading).

buyer's option A settlement contract that calls for delivery and payment according to the number of days specified by the buyer. *See also* seller's option.

buy-in The procedure that occurs when the seller of a security fails to complete a contract to sell according to its terms. The buyer can close the contract by buying the securities in the open market and charging them to the account of the seller who failed to complete the contract.

buying a hedge The purchase of futures options as a means of protecting against an increase in commodities prices in the future. *See also* long hedge, short hedge, selling a hedge.

buying power The dollar amount of securities that a client can purchase using only the special memorandum account balance and without depositing additional equity.

cabinet crowd *See* inactive crowd.

calendar spread The spread between options with the same exercise price but different expiration dates. (*Syn.* horizontal spread)

call An option contract giving the owner the right to buy stock at a stated price within a specified period of time.

callable bond A type of bond issued with a provision allowing the issuer to redeem the bond prior to maturity at a predetermined price. *See also* call price.

callable preferred stock A type of preferred stock carrying the provision that the corporation retains the right to call in the stock at a certain price and retire it. *See also* call price, preferred stock.

call buyer An investor who pays a premium for an option contract and receives the right to buy, during a specified time, the underlying security at a specified price.

call date The date after which the issuer of a bond has the option to redeem the issue at par or at par plus a premium.

call loan A collateralized loan of a brokerage firm having no maturity date that may be called (terminated) at any time and having a fluctuating interest rate recomputed daily. Generally the loan is payable on demand the day after the loan has been contracted. If not called, the loan is automatically renewed for another day. *See also* broker's loan, loan for set amount.

call loan rate The rate of interest a brokerage firm charges its margin account clients on their debit balances.

call price The price paid (usually a premium over the par value of the issue) for preferred stocks or bonds redeemed prior to maturity of the issue.

call protection This provision limiting the right to call an issue is normally stated in terms of time (five years, ten years, etc.) from the original issue before the issuer may exercise the call provision. *See also* call provision.

call provision The written agreement between an issuing corporation and its bondholders or preferred stockholders, giving the corporation the option to redeem its senior securities at a specified price before maturity and under specified conditions.

call spread The result of an investor buying a call on a particular security and writing a call with a different expiration date, different exercise price or both on the same security.

call writer An investor who receives a premium and takes on, for a specified time, the obligation to sell the underlying security at the specified price, at the call buyer's discretion.

cancel former order (CFO) An instruction by a customer to cancel a previously entered order.

can crowd *See* inactive crowd.

capital Accumulated money or goods used to produce income.

capital appreciation A rise in the market prices of assets owned.

capital asset Broadly defined to include all property held by a taxpayer, whether or not connected with her trade or business. However, there are a number of exceptions to this definition, the most important of which excludes a taxpayer's stock in trade, inventory or property held by the taxpayer primarily for sale to customers in the ordinary course of her trade or business.

capital contribution The gross amount of investment in a program by a participant or all participants, not including units purchased by the sponsors.

capital cost Any cost required to be capitalized for income tax purposes, such as the cost of acquiring leaseholds, geological and geophysical exploration costs, the cost of acquiring tangible property and equipment and the cost of real property.

capital gain The gain (selling price minus cost basis) on an asset. *See also* capital loss, long-term gain.

capitalization The sum of a company's long-term debt, capital stock and surpluses. *See also* capital structure. (*Syn.* invested capital)

capitalization ratio A ratio revealing the percentage of bonds, preferred stock or common stock to total capitalization.

capitalize An accounting procedure whereby the taxpayer records an expenditure as a capital asset on its books instead of charging it to expenses for the year.

capital loss The loss (cost basis minus selling price) on an asset. *See also* capital gain, long-term loss.

capital market That segment of the securities market that deals in instruments with more than one year to maturity—that is, long-term debt and equity securities.

capital stock The total stated value or par value of all outstanding preferred stock and common stock of a corporation.

capital structure The composition of long-term funds (equity and debt) a company has as a source for financing. *See also* capitalization, invested capital.

capital surplus The money a corporation receives in excess of the stated value of the stock at the time of sale. *See also* par value. (*Syn.* paid-in surplus)

carrying broker *See also* clearing broker.

carrying charge Any cost associated with holding or storing a commodity, including interest, insurance, rents and so on.

carrying charge market The situation that exists when the difference in price between delivery months of a commodity in the futures markets covers all interest, insurance and storage costs. (*Syn.* contango, normal market)

carryover Any part of the supply of a commodity (particularly crop production) carried over from one year to the next.

cash account An account in which a client is required to pay in full for securities purchased not later than the seventh business day from the trade date.

cash and carry market *See* cash market.

cash assets ratio The most stringent test of liquidity, this ratio is calculated by adding the sum of cash and cash equivalents and dividing that sum by total current liabilities.

cash basis accounting An accounting method whereby revenues and expenses are accounted for when received or paid, rather than earned or incurred. *See also* accrual accounting.

cash commodity The actual, physical good being traded, rather than a futures contract on that good.

cash dividend A cash payment to a company's stockholders out of the company's current earnings or accumulated profits. The dividend must be declared by the board of directors.

cash equivalent A security that is extremely liquid and can be readily converted into cash (e.g., Treasury bill, certificate of deposit and money-market fund).

cash flow The money received by a business minus the money paid out. Cash flow is also equal to net income plus depreciation or depletion.

cashiering department The department within a brokerage firm that delivers and receives securities and money to and from other firms and clients of the firm. (*Syn.* security cage)

cash market Transactions between buyers and sellers of commodities that entail immediate delivery of and payment for a physical commodity. *See also* futures market. (*Syn.* cash and carry market)

cash price The market price for goods to be delivered and paid for immediately.

cash securities equivalent Any Treasury bill, certificate of deposit, money market fund and so on that is extremely liquid and readily converted into cash.

cash transaction A securities settlement contract that calls for delivery and payment on the date of the trade, due by 2:30 pm EST (or within 30 minutes of the trade if made after 2:00 pm) in New York. (*Syn.* cash trade)

casing A heavy steel pipe cemented to the wall of the hole drilled to reinforce a well when it reaches a certain depth.

catastrophe call The redemption of a bond due to disaster (e.g., a power plant built with proceeds from an issue burns to the ground). *See also* mandatory call.

CBOE *See* Chicago Board Options Exchange.

CCC *See* Commodity Credit Corporation.

CD *See* negotiable certificate of deposit.

CEA *See* Commodity Exchange Authority.

certificate of deposit *See* negotiable certificate of deposit.

CFO *See* cancel former order.

CFTC *See* Commodities Futures Trading Commission.

change The change from the previous day's settlement price.

chartist A securities analyst who uses charts and graphs of the past price movements of a security to predict its future movements. *See also* technical analysis.

Chicago Board Options Exchange (CBOE) The first national securities exchange for the trading of listed options.

Chicago Board Options Exchange ORS The Chicago Board Options Exchange (CBOE) uses the Order Routing System (ORS) to collect, store, route and execute public customer (nonbroker-dealer) orders. ORS automatically routes option market and limit orders of up to 2,000 contracts to the CBOE member firm's floor booth, to the floor brokers in the trading crowd, to the order book official's electronic book or to RAES.

Chicago Board Options Exchange RAES Market orders and executable limit orders of ten or fewer contracts received by ORS are sent to the Retail Automatic Execution System (RAES). Customer orders sent through RAES receive instantaneous executions (fills) at the prevailing market quote and are confirmed almost immediately to the originating firm.

Chinese wall The wall through which insider information must not pass from corporate advisers to investment traders, who could make use of the information to reap large profits.

Christmas tree The assembly of valves, gauges and pipes at the wellhead of an oil or gas well.

churning Excessive trading in a customer's account. The term suggests that the registered representative ignores the objectives and interests of clients and seeks only to increase commissions. (*Syn.* overtrading)

class All options of the same type (e.g., all calls or all puts) on the same underlying security. *See also* series, type.

clearing agency The purpose of a clearing agency is to act as an intermediary between the sides in a securities transaction, receiving and delivering payments and securities. Any organization that fills this function, including a securities depository but not including a Federal Reserve Bank, is considered a clearing agency.

clearing broker A broker-dealer that clears its own trades, as well as trades of introducing brokers. A clearing broker-dealer can hold customers' securities and cash. (*Syn.* carrying broker)

Clearing Corporation Refers to the Clearing Corporation of the Chicago Board of Trade, through which transactions in futures and option contracts are settled, guaranteed, offset and filled. The Clearing Corporation positions itself between the buyer and the seller in a contract, becoming the buyer for all sellers and the seller for all buyers. It settles all transactions at the end of each business day and is the guarantor of all contracts.

clearinghouse 1) An agency of a futures exchange, through which transactions in futures and option contracts are settled, guaranteed, offset and filled. The clearinghouse may be an independent corporation or exchange-owned. 2) A member firm of the Clearing Corporation. *See also* Clearing Corporation.

close The price of the last transaction for a particular security on a particular day. The midprice of a closing trading range.

closed-end lien A provision of a bond issue preventing the issuer from issuing additional bonds having an equal claim to the same collateral or revenues.

closed-end management company A management investment company operated in much the same manner as a conventional corporation. The closed-end fund will issue a fixed number of shares for sale (fixed capitalization). The shares may be of several classes. Shares are bought and sold in the secondary marketplace; the fund does not offer to redeem shares. The market price of the shares is determined by supply and demand and not by their net asset value. The shares may be traded on an exchange or over-the-counter market.

closed-end pledge *See* junior lien debt.

closing date The date designated by the general partners when sales of units in a program cease. Typically the offering period is for one year.

closing purchase transaction The act of closing out an opening sale by buying options of the same series.

closing range The relatively narrow range of prices at which transactions take place in the closing minutes of the trading day.

closing sale transaction The transaction that takes place when an investor who owns an option closes out the position in that option by selling it.

CMV *See* current market value.

COD *See* collect on delivery.

Code of Arbitration The Code of Arbitration provides a method of handling securities-related disputes or clearing controversies between members, public customers, clearing corporations or clearing banks. Any claim, dispute or controversy subject to arbitration is required to be submitted to arbitration.

Code of Procedure The Code of Procedure is the NASD's procedure for handling trade practice complaints. The NASD District Business Conduct Committee (DBCC) is the first body to hear and judge complaints. Appeals and review of DBCC decisions are handled by the NASD Board of Governors.

collateral trust bond A form of debt backed by stocks or bonds of another issuer. The collateral is held by a trustee for safekeeping. (*Syn.* collateral trust certificate)

collateral trust certificate *See* collateral trust bond.

collection ratio A rough measure of the length of time accounts receivable have been outstanding. It is calculated by multiplying the receivables by 360 and dividing that amount by the net sales. For municipal bonds, the collection ratio is calculated by dividing taxes collected by taxes assessed.

collect on delivery (COD) *See* delivery vs. payment.

combination An option position that represents a put and a call on the same stock in which the investor has neither purchased a straddle nor sold a straddle.

combined account A customer account that has cash and long and short margin positions in different securities.

combined distribution *See* split offering.

commercial bank An institution that accepts deposits and makes business loans.

commercial paper An unsecured, short-term promissory note issued by well-known businesses chiefly for financing accounts receivable. It is usually issued at a discount reflecting prevailing market interest rates. Maturities range up to 270 days.

commingling The failure to clearly identify and segregate securities (carried for the account of any customer) that have been fully paid or that are excess margin securities.

commission broker A member eligible to execute orders for customers of her member firm on the floor of the Exchange. (*Syn.* floor broker)

commissioner The commissioner of insurance of the state.

commission house A registered member firm of a given commodity exchange that handles customer accounts and transactions on that exchange. (*Syn.* brokerage house, futures commission merchant, wire house)

Committee on Uniform Securities Identification Procedures (CUSIP) A committee that assigns identification numbers and codes to all securities, to be used when recording all buy and sell orders.

Commodities Futures Trading Commission (CFTC) The federal regulatory agency established by the Commodities Futures Trading Commission Act of 1974 to administer the Commodities Exchange Act. The five CFTC commissioners are appointed by the President (subject to Senate approval).

commodity Any bulk good traded on an exchange or in the cash (spot) market, such as metals, grains, meats, and so on.

Commodity Credit Corporation (CCC) A government-owned and -sponsored corporation that aids American agriculture through price support programs, controlling supplies and controlling foreign sales.

Commodity Exchange Authority (CEA) The predecessor of the Commodities Futures Trading Commission established by the U.S. Department of Agriculture to administer the Commodities Exchange Act of 1936.

commodity pool operator (CPO) An individual or organization involved in the solicitation of funds for the purpose of pooling them to invest in commodities futures contracts.

commodity trading adviser (CTA) An individual or organization that makes recommendations and issues reports on commodities futures or options trading for a fee.

common stock An equity security that represents ownership in a corporation. This is the first security a corporation issues to raise capital. *See also* equity, preferred stock.

competitive bidding The submission of sealed bids by rival underwriting syndicates that want the privilege of underwriting the issue of securities. Competitive bidding normally is used to determine the underwriters for issues of general obligation municipal bonds and is required by law in most states for general obligation bonds of more than $100,000. *See also* negotiated underwriting.

completion of the transaction The point at which a customer pays any part of the purchase price to the broker-dealer for a security he has purchased or delivers a security that he has sold. If the customer makes payment to the broker-dealer before the payment is due, the completion of the transaction occurs when the broker-dealer delivers the security.

compliance department The department within a brokerage firm that oversees the trading and market-making activities of the firm. It ensures that the employees and officers of the firm are in compliance with the rules and regulations of the SEC, exchanges and SROs.

concession The allowance (profit) that an underwriter allows a broker-dealer that is not a syndicate member. The broker-dealer will purchase the security at the public price minus the concession. (*Syn.* reallowance)

confidence theory A technical theory that analyzes the confidence of investors by comparing the yields on high-grade bonds to the yields on lower rated bonds.

confirmation A bill or comparison of trade that is sent or given to a customer on or before the settlement date. *See also* duplicate confirmation.

congestion A narrow price range within which a commodity's price trades for an extended period of time.

consent to lend agreement *See* loan consent agreement.

Consolidated Quotation System (CQS) The NASD offers a quotation and last-sale reporting service for NASD members that are active market makers of listed securities in the third market. As a quotations collection system, CQS is used by market makers willing to stand ready to buy and sell the securities for their own accounts on a continuous basis but that do not wish to do so through an exchange.

CQS is part of the Nasdaq market-making system. Quotation display service is available to all Nasdaq subscribers (at a fee), while quotation input service is available only to those members that are registered to do business in third market stocks. NASD members that are registered market makers may enter quotes into CQS through the Nasdaq system.

Consolidated Tape The Consolidated Tape system (also known as the Consolidated Ticker Tape) is a service of the NYSE designed to deliver real-time reports of securities transactions to subscribers as they occur on the various exchanges. Subscribers to the Tape can choose to receive transaction reports in either of two ways: over the high-speed electronic line (directly linked to their Quotrons® or other types of terminals); or through the low-speed ticker (visible report) line—the type of report commonly seen as quotes racing across a sign at a brokerage counter.

The Tape distributes reports over two different networks that subscribers can tap into through either the low-speed or the high-speed lines. *Network A* reports transactions in NYSE-listed securities (stocks, warrants, rights and so on) wherever they are traded. As an example, a transaction involving NYSE-listed IBM that occurs on the Pacific Stock Exchange will be reported on Network A. *Network B* carries reports of AMEX-listed securities transactions as well as reports of transactions in regional exchange issues that *substantially meet* AMEX listing requirements. Transactions in these securities must be reported within 90 seconds for inclusion on the Consolidated Tape.

consolidation The narrowing of the trading range for a commodity or security. Technical analysts consider consolidation an indication that a strong price move is imminent.

constant dollar plan An investment technique where a constant sum of money is invested regardless of the price fluctuation in a security. The objective is to average out the prices of securities purchased.

constant ratio plan A method of investment in which an investor tries to maintain a predetermined ratio of debt to equity and makes purchases and sales to maintain the desired ratio.

construction fee A fee for acting as general contractor to construct improvements on a program's property either initially or at a later date.

Consumer Price Index (CPI) A measure of inflation or deflation based on price changes in consumer goods and services.

contango *See* normal market.

contingent-deferred sales load A sales load that is charged upon redemption of mutual fund shares or variable contracts; also called a *back-end load*.

The load is charged on a declining basis annually, usually reduced to zero after an extended holding period (up to eight years).

contra broker The broker on the other side of a transaction.

contract One unit of trading in futures.

contract grade The exchange-authorized grade of a commodity that can be delivered against a contract.

contractionary policy A fiscal policy that has as its end the decrease (contraction) of the money supply.

contract market A Commodities Futures Trading Commission–designated exchange on which a specified commodity can be traded.

contract month The designated month in which a particular futures contract may be satisfied by making delivery (the contract seller) or taking delivery (the contract buyer).

contractual plan For mutual funds, a type of accumulation plan in which the investor makes a firm commitment to invest a specific amount of money in the fund during a specific time. *See also* front-end load, mutual fund, spread-load option. (*Syn.* penalty plan, prepaid charge plan)

contract unit The unit of delivery specified in a futures contract.

control (controlling, controlled by, under common control with) The possession, direct or indirect, of the power to direct or cause the direction of the management and policies of a person, whether through the ownership of voting securities, by contract other than a commercial contract for goods or nonmanagement services, or otherwise, unless the power is the result of an official position with or corporate office held by the person. Control shall be presumed to exist if any person, directly or indirectly, owns, controls, holds with the power to vote, or holds proxies representing more than 10% of the voting securities of any other person. This presumption may be rebutted by a showing made to the satisfaction of the Commissioner that control does not exist in fact. The Commissioner may determine, after furnishing all persons in interest notice and the opportunity to be heard and after making specific findings of fact to support such determination, that control exists in fact, notwithstanding the absence of a presumption to that effect.

control (of securities) Securities are considered in the possession or under the control of a broker-dealer if they are in the broker-dealer's physical possession, are in an alternate location acceptable to the SEC, or are in transit for a period of time that does not exceed standards set by the SEC.

control person Includes: 1) a director, an officer or another affiliate of an issuer, or 2) a stockholder who owns at least 10% of any class of a company's outstanding securities.

control security Any security owned by a director, an officer or another affiliate of the issuer or by a stockholder who owns at least 10% of any class of a company's outstanding securities. Who owns the security is the factor that determines that specific securities are control securities, not the securities themselves. Public offerings of control securities must comply with SEC Rule 144.

conversion The conversion of income taxable at ordinary income rates into gain taxable at long-term gains rates.

conversion parity The state of having two securities (one of which can be converted into the other) of equal dollar value.

conversion price The amount of par value exchangeable for one share of common stock. This term really refers to the stock price and means the dollar amount of the bond's (or preferred stock's) par value that is exchangeable for one share of common stock.

conversion privilege *See* exchange privilege.

conversion rate *See* conversion ratio.

conversion ratio The number of shares per $1,000 debenture (or preferred stock) that the holder would receive if the debenture were converted into shares of common stock. *See also* debenture. (*Syn.* conversion rate)

conversion value The total market value of common stock into which a debenture (or preferred stock) is convertible. *See also* convertible bond, debenture.

convertible bond A type of debt security (usually in the form of a debenture) that can be converted into (exchanged for) equity securities of the issuing corporation, that is, common and preferred stock. *See also* debenture.

convertible preferred stock A type of preferred stock that offers the holder the privilege of exchanging (converting) the preferred stock for (into) common stock at specified prices or rates. Dividends may be cumulative or noncumulative. *See also* cumulative preferred stock, noncumulative preferred stock, preferred stock.

cooling-off period The period (a minimum of 20 days) between the filing date of a registration statement and the effective date of the registration. In practice, this period varies in length.

copartnership account An account in which the individual members of the partnership are empowered to act on behalf of the partnership as a whole.

Corporate Securities Limited Representative *See* Series 62.

corporation A form of business organization in which the organization's total worth is divided into shares of stock, each share representing a unit of ownership. By law, the corporation has certain rights and responsibilities. It is characterized by a continuous life span and by the limited liability of the owners.

correspondent broker-dealer A broker-dealer that performs services (transactions) for another broker-dealer in a market or locale in which the first broker-dealer has no office.

cost basis Money on which taxes have been paid. A return of cost basis is a return of capital and not subject to tax.

cost depletion A method of depletion whereby the capitalized cost of the producing property is written off over the property's life by an annual deduction. The annual deduction takes into account the number of known recoverable units to arrive at a cost-per-unit figure. The allowance is then determined by multiplying this figure by the number of units sold.

cost of carry All out-of-pocket costs incurred by an investor while holding an open position in a security, including margin costs, interest costs, opportunity costs and so on.

cost-push inflation A type of inflation caused by higher production costs (e.g., wages).

coterminous Municipal entities that share the same boundaries (e.g., a school district and a fire district), which can issue debt separately. *See also* overlapping debt.

country basis The local cash (or spot) market price in comparison to the nearby futures price at the Chicago Board of Trade. (*Syn.* local basis)

coupon bond A bond without the name of the owner printed on its face and with coupons representing semiannual interest payments attached. Coupons are submitted to the trustee by the holder to receive the interest payments. (*Syn.* bearer bond)

coupon yield *See* nominal yield.

covenant A promise or restriction of an issue made part of a trust indenture (bond contract). Examples include rate covenants that establish a minimum revenue coverage for a bond; insurance covenants that require insurance on a project; and maintenance covenants that require maintenance on a facility constructed by the proceeds of a bond issue.

cover 1) Futures purchased to offset a short position. 2) Being long actuals when shorting futures.

coverage For revenue bonds, a measure of safety for payment of principal and interest. Coverage is the multiple of earnings that exceed debt service plus operating and maintenance expenses payable for a time period.

covered call writer An investor who writes a call and owns some other asset that guarantees the ability to perform if the call is exercised.

covered put writer An investor who writes a put and owns some other asset that guarantees the ability to perform if the put is exercised.

CPI *See* Consumer Price Index.

CPO *See* commodity pool operator.

CQS *See* Consolidated Quotation System.

CR *See* credit balance.

cracking spread A spread established with long crude oil futures and short heating oil or gasoline futures. *Cracking* is the term used to describe the process by which crude oil is turned into distillates.

credit An amount applied against the amount of tax due. Every dollar of tax credit reduces the amount of tax due dollar for dollar.

credit agreement An agreement signed in conjunction with a margin agreement, outlining the conditions of the credit arrangement between broker and client.

credit balance (CR) The amount of money remaining in a client's account after all commitments have been paid in full. *See also* debit balance. (*Syn.* credit record, credit register)

credit record *See* credit balance.

credit register *See* credit balance.

credit risk Like financial risk, credit risk involves the safety of one's principal. The term is generally associated with bonds, and the risk is that the issuer will default in the payment of either principal or interest. (*Syn.* default risk)

credit spread The difference between the value of two options when the value of the option sold exceeds the value of the option bought; the opposite of a debit spread.

cross hedge The act of hedging a futures contract risk with a different but related commodity.

cross-reference sheet A compilation of the guideline sections, referenced to the page of the prospectus, partnership agreement or another exhibit, and a justification of any deviation from the guidelines.

cross trade A manipulative practice where customers' buy and sell orders are offset against each other off the floor of the Exchange and the resultant transaction is not recorded with the Exchange.

crush spread A spread established with long soybean futures and short soybean oil and meal futures (*crushing* is the term used to describe the process by which soybeans are turned into oil and meal).

CTA *See* commodity trading adviser.

cum rights Stock trading with rights. *See also* ex-rights.

cumulative preferred stock A type of preferred stock that offers the holder any unpaid dividends in arrears. These dividends accumulate and must be paid to the holder of cumulative preferred stock before any dividends can be paid to the common stockholders. *See also* noncumulative preferred stock, preferred stock.

cumulative voting rights A voting procedure that permits stockholders to cast all of their votes for any one director or to cast their total number of votes in any proportion they choose.

current assets Assets that are in the form of cash or are expected to be converted into cash within the next twelve months in the normal course of business.

current liabilities A corporation's debt obligations due for payment within the next twelve months.

current market value (CMV) The current market price of the securities in an account, based on the closing prices on the previous business day. (*Syn.* long market value)

current price *See* offering price.

current ratio A measure of liquidity that is calculated by dividing total current assets by total current liabilities. (*Syn.* working capital ratio)

current yield The annual dollar return on a security (interest or dividends) divided by the current market price of the security (bonds or stock).

CUSIP *See* Committee on Uniform Securities Identification Procedures.

custodian The institution or person responsible for protecting the property of another. Mutual funds have custodians responsible for safeguarding certificates and performing clerical duties. *See also* mutual fund custodian.

custodian of a minor One who manages a gift of securities to a minor under the Uniform Gifts to Minors Act; also, someone who takes charge of an incompetent's affairs.

customer Any person who is not a broker, dealer or municipal securities dealer is considered a customer.

customer protection rule *See* Rule 15c3-3.

customer statement A statement of a customer's account showing positions and entries. The SEC requires that a customer statement be sent quarterly, but customers generally receive them monthly.

cycle A particular set of months of maturities for listed options (e.g., January, April, July and October make up a cycle).

dated date The date on which interest on a bond issue begins to accrue.

day order An order that is canceled if it is not executed on the day it is entered.

day trader A trader in securities or commodities who opens all positions after the opening of the market and offsets or closes out all positions before the close of the market on the same day.

DBCC *See* NASD District Business Conduct Committee.

dealer The role of a brokerage firm when it acts as a principal in a particular trade. A firm is acting as a dealer when it buys or sells a security for its own account and at its own risk and then charges the customer a markup or markdown. Any person who is *engaged in the business* of buying and selling securities for her own account either directly or through a broker, and who is not a bank, is considered a dealer. (*Syn.* principal)

debenture A debt obligation backed by the general credit of the issuing corporation. *See also* convertible bond.

debit balance (DR) The amount of money a client owes a brokerage firm. *See also* credit balance.

debit record *See* debit balance.

debit register *See* debit balance.

debt ratio The percent of debt in relation to total capitalization of a corporation. *See also* capitalization ratio. (*Syn.* bond ratio)

debt security An evidence of debt issued by corporations, municipalities and the federal government.

debt service The annual amount needed to pay interest and principal (or the scheduled sinking fund contribution) on an outstanding debt.

debt-to-equity ratio The ratio of total debt to total stockholder's equity.

declaration date The date on which a company declares an upcoming dividend.

declining balance method of depreciation A uniform rate is applied each year to the unrecovered cost or another basis of the property. No salvage value is taken into account in determining the annual allowances under this method. Normally a switch to straight-line depreciation occurs in order to maximize the deduction available.

deduction An item or expenditure subtracted from gross income and adjusted gross income to arrive at taxable income, thus reducing the amount of income subject to tax.

deed of trust *See* trust indenture.

default 1) The failure to pay interest or principal promptly when due. 2) The failure to perform on a futures contract as required by an exchange.

default risk *See* credit risk.

defeasance A corporation or municipality removes debt from its balance sheet by issuing a new debt issue or creating a trust to be funded by assets, typically U.S. government securities that will generate enough cash flow to provide for the payment of interest and principal on the debt issue removed from the balance sheet (refunded). *See also* advance refunding, prerefunding.

defensive industry An industry that is relatively unaffected by business cycles, such as the food industry or the utility industry.

defensive issue An issue of an established company in an industry relatively unaffected by business cycles. (*Syn.* defensive stock)

defensive stock *See* defensive issue.

defensive strategy An investment method whereby an investor seeks to minimize the risk of losing principal (e.g., the policy of making purchases and sales according to predetermined objectives without regard for market changes).

deferred annuity An annuity contract that guarantees payment of income, installment payments or a lump-sum payment will be made at an agreed upon future time. *See also* annuity.

deficiency letter A list of additions or corrections that must be made to a registration statement before the SEC will release an offering to the public. The SEC sends a deficiency letter to the issuing corporation. (*Syn.* bedbug letter)

deflation A persistent fall in the general level of prices.

delivery The change in ownership or control of the actual commodity in exchange for cash in settlement of a futures contract.

delivery month The month specified for delivery in a futures contract.

delivery point The location or facility (storage, shipping, etc.) to which a commodity must be delivered in order to fulfill a commodities contract.

delivery vs. payment (DVP) A transaction settlement procedure in which the securities are delivered to the buying institution's bank in exchange for payment of the amount due. (*Syn.* collect on delivery)

delta A term used to describe the responsiveness of option premiums to a change in the price of the underlying asset. Deep in-the-money options have a delta near 1; these show the biggest response to futures price changes. Deep out-of-the-money options have very low deltas.

demand The consumers' desire and willingness to pay for a good or service.

demand-pull A type of inflation resulting from an excessive money supply that increases the demand for goods (i.e., too much money chasing too few goods).

depletion An allowance deducted as an expense to enable the recovery of the cost of a natural resource (coal, oil, gas, quarries, etc.). Two methods of depletion are allowed: cost depletion and percentage depletion.

depreciation An expense allowed for the recovery of the cost of qualifying property; with currency exchange rates, a decrease in the value of a particular currency relative to other currencies. *See also* Modified Accelerated Cost Recovery System.

depreciation expense A noncash expense charged against earnings to recover the cost of an asset over its useful life. Depreciation (recovery) is a bookkeeping entry that does not require the outlay of cash.

designated order An order of a specified minimum size to be executed by (and commissions paid to) a dealer designated by a client (generally in reference to municipal bond transactions). The size of the order establishes its priority for subscription to an issue. *See also* member order, presale order.

development fee A fee for the packaging of a program's property, including negotiating and approving plans, and undertaking to assist in obtaining zoning and necessary variances and financing for the specific property either initially or at a later date.

development well A well drilled within an area of proven oil or gas reserves.

DI *See* disposable income.

diagonal spread The simultaneous purchase and sale of options of the same class but with different exercise prices and expiration dates.

dilution A reduction in earnings per share of common stock. Dilution occurs through the issuance of additional shares of common stock and the conversion of convertible securities.

direct debt The percentage of an issuer's debt evidenced by outstanding bonds and notes.

direct participation program (DPP) A program that provides for flow-through tax consequences, regardless of the structure of the legal entity or the vehicle for distribution. These programs include but are not limited to oil and gas programs, real estate programs, agricultural programs, cattle programs, condominium securities, Subchapter S corporate offerings and all other programs of a similar nature, regardless of the industry represented by the program or any combination thereof.

Direct Participation Programs Limited Representative *See* Series 22.

discount The difference between the price paid for a security and the security's face amount at issue.

discount bond A bond selling below par. *See also* premium.

discount rate The interest rate charged to member banks that borrow from the nine Federal Reserve Banks.

discretionary account An account in which the principal (beneficial owner) has given a registered rep authority to make transactions in the account at the registered rep's discretion. The registered rep may use discretion about price (buy or sell), time and choice of securities (bought or sold). Orders must be marked "DE" (discretion exercised) or "DNE" (discretion not exercised).

disposable income (DI) The sum that people divide between spending and personal savings.

disproportionate sharing arrangement In a disproportionate sharing arrangement, the sponsor will share costs of the program but will receive a disproportionately higher percentage of the revenues. One arrangement would have the sponsor paying 10% of program costs and receiving 25% of revenues. The sponsor shares in dry hole costs, and investors share in both deductible and nondeductible costs.

distant contract Of two or more futures contracts, the contract with the longest time remaining to expiration. *See also* nearby contract. (*Syn.* distant delivery)

distant delivery *See* distant contract.

distributable cash from operations The funds provided by operations after debt service and less the partnership management fee (cash flow).

distribution Any cash or other property distributed to holders and general partners that arises from their interests in the partnership. It does not include any payments to the general partners or agent(s) for partnership expenses.

diversified common stock fund *See* growth fund.

diversified management company A management company that has at least 75% of its total assets in cash, receivables or securities invested, no more than 5% of its total assets invested in the voting securities of any company, and no single investment representing ownership of more than 10% of the outstanding voting securities of any one company.

divided account *See* Western account.

dividend A distribution of the earnings of a corporation. Dividends may be in the form of cash, stock or property (securities owned by a corporation). The board of directors must declare a dividend. *See also* dividend yield.

dividend exclusion An arrangement whereby a corporation may exclude from its taxable income 70% of dividends received from domestic preferred and common stocks. The Tax Reform Act of 1986 repealed the dividend exclusion for individual investors. Formerly the Internal Revenue Code allowed an investor to exclude up to $100 of dividend income from taxable income ($200 on a joint return).

dividend payout ratio A ratio used to analyze a company's policy of paying cash dividends, calculated by dividing the dividends paid on common stock by the net income available for common stockholders.

dividend yield The annual percentage of return that an investor receives on either common or preferred stock. The yield is based on the amount of the annual dividend divided by the market price (at the time of purchase) of the stock. *See also* current yield, dividend.

DJIA *See* Dow Jones Industrial Average.

DK *See* don't know.

DNR *See* do not reduce order.

dollar bonds A term used to describe municipal bonds that are quoted and traded on a basis of dollars rather than yield to maturity. Term bonds, tax-exempt notes and Public Housing Authority bonds are dollar bonds. Municipal serial bonds are quoted on a yield-to-maturity basis.

dollar cost averaging For mutual funds, a system of buying fixed dollar amounts of securities at regular fixed intervals, regardless of the price of the shares. This method may result in an average cost that is generally lower than the average price of all prices at which the securities were purchased.

do not reduce order (DNR) An order that stipulates that the price of limit or stop orders should not be reduced as a result of cash dividends.

don't know (DK) An acronym for "don't know," indicating a lack of information about a transaction or a record of transaction between broker-dealers.

double auction market *See* auction market.

double-barreled bond A municipal revenue bond backed by the full faith and credit of the issuing municipality, as well as by pledged revenues. *See also* general obligation bond, revenue bond.

double declining balance depreciation A form of accelerated depreciation in which a corporation writes off more of the value of an asset in its early years.

Dow Jones Industrial Average (DJIA) The most widely used market indicator, composed of 30 large, actively traded issues.

down tick *See* minus tick.

Dow theory A technical market theory that seeks to interpret long-term trends in the stock market by analyzing the movements of the Dow Jones Industrial Averages.

DPP *See* direct participation program.

DR *See* debit balance.

dry hole Any well that is plugged and abandoned without being completed or that is abandoned for any reason without having produced commercially for 60 days.

dual purpose fund A type of closed-end investment company that offers two classes of stock: income shares and capital shares. Income shares entitle the holder to all net dividends and interest paid to the fund on both income and capital shares but do not allow the holder to participate in any capital appreciation. Capital shares entitle the holder to profit from the growth of all the securities held by the fund. *See also* closed-end management company.

due bill A printed statement showing the transfer of a security's title or rights or showing the obligation of a seller to deliver the securities or rights to the purchaser. The due bill is used as a demand for dividends due a buyer when the transaction occurs before the ex-dividend date.

due diligence The careful investigation by the underwriters that is necessary to ensure that all material information pertinent to an issue has been disclosed to the public.

due diligence meeting A meeting between an issuing corporation's officials and representatives of the underwriting group held to discuss details of the pending issue of securities. These details include the registration statement and the preparation of prospectuses.

duplicate confirmation A copy of a client's confirmation that a brokerage firm sends to an agent or an attorney if the client requests it in writing. Clients must receive copies unless they specify in writing that they do not wish to receive them. *See also* confirmation.

DVP *See* delivery vs. payment.

early warning A broker-dealer is in early warning if its net capital falls to less than 120% of the required minimum or if the firm's ratio of aggregate indebtedness to net capital (AI:NC) exceeds 12:1. When a broker-dealer is in early warning, its FOCUS reporting requirements are stepped up until three months after it is out of early warning.

earned income Income that is derived from personal services, such as wages, salary, tips, commissions and bonuses. *See also* unearned income.

earned surplus *See* retained earnings.

earnings per share (EPS) The net income available for common stock divided by the number of shares of common stock outstanding.

earnings per share fully diluted The earnings per share calculated assuming that convertible securities (convertible preferred stock, convertible bonds) have been converted. (*Syn.* primary earnings per share)

Eastern account Liability for the distribution of an issue of securities is undivided, and each member of the underwriting syndicate is responsible for a proportionate share of any securities remaining unsold. *See also* Western account.

economic risk The risk related to international developments and domestic events.

EE savings bond A nonnegotiable government debt issued at a discount from face value. The difference between the purchase price and the value of the bond upon redemption determines the interest rate. Currently EE bonds pay a variable rate of interest linked to 85% of the rate paid on five-year treasury securities.

effective date The date the registration of an issue of securities becomes effective. The underwriter confirms sales of the newly issued securities after this date.

efficient market theory A theory based on the assumption that the stock market processes information efficiently. This theory postulates that new information, as it becomes known, is reflected immediately in the price of stock and, therefore, stock prices represent fair prices.

elasticity The responsiveness of consumers and producers to a change in prices. A large change in demand or production resulting from a small change in price for a good would be considered an indication of elasticity. A small or no change in production or demand following a change in price would be considered an indication of inelasticity.

Employee Retirement Income Security Act (ERISA) A 1974 law governing the operation of most private pension and benefit plans. The law eased pension eligibility rules, set up the Pension Benefit Guaranty Corporation and established guidelines for the management of pension funds.

endorsement The signature on the back of a certificate by the person named on the certificate as owner. Owners must endorse certificates when transferring them to another person's name.

EPS *See* earnings per share.

equipment note or bond *See* equipment trust certificate.

equipment trust *See* equipment trust equity.

equipment trust certificate A debt obligation backed by equipment. The title to the equipment is held by an independent trustee (usually a bank), not the company. Equipment trust certificates are generally issued by transportation companies such as railroads. *See also* New York plan. (*Syn.* equipment note or bond, equipment trust)

equity The ownership interest of common and preferred stockholders in a corporation; also, the client's net worth in a margin account; also, what is owned less what is owed. *See also* common stock, margin account, preferred stock.

equity financing When stock (common or preferred) is sold to individuals or institutions and, in return for the money paid, the individuals or institutions receive ownership interest in the corporation.

equity interest When used with respect to a corporation, *equity interest* means common stock and any security convertible into, exchangeable for or exercisable for common stock. When used with respect to a partnership, *equity interest* means an interest in the capital or profits or losses of the partnership.

equity security The SEC defines an equity security as any:
- stock or similar security;
- certificate of participation in any profitsharing agreement;
- preorganization certificate, subscription, transferable share, voting trust certificate or certificate of deposit for an equity security;
- limited partnership interest, interest in a joint venture or certificate of interest in a business trust;
- convertible security, warrant or rights certificate that carries the right to subscribe to an equity security; or
- put, call or other option that offers the privilege of buying or selling an equity security.

If the market price of the security in question trends or tracks with the price of the common stock, it is an equity security.

ERISA *See* Employee Retirement Income Security Act.

escrow receipt The certificate provided by an approved bank that guarantees that the indicated securities are on deposit at that bank and will be delivered if the option is exercised.

Eurobond A bond issued by a government or corporation in a particular country and denominated in that country's currency but sold outside that country.

Eurodollar U.S. currency held in banks outside the United States.

excess equity The amount of money in a margin account that is in excess of the federal requirement. (*Syn.* margin excess, Regulation T excess)

exchange Any organization, association or group of persons that maintains or provides a marketplace in which securities can be bought and sold. An exchange does not have to be a physical place, and several strictly electronic exchanges do business around the world.

exchange distribution A block trading procedure in which a block of stock is crossed on the floor of the exchange with no prior announcement on the broad tape.

exchange-listed security In order for a security to be traded by exchange members on an exchange, it has to be listed on that exchange. Once it is accepted for listing, it is admitted to full trading privileges on that exchange. Listed securities can also be traded in the over-the-counter market (which is known as third-market trading).

exchange offer An offer to exchange one type of security for another.

exchange privilege The ability of an investor who has invested in one fund to transfer to another fund under the same sponsor without incurring an additional sales charge. (*Syn.* conversion privilege)

exchange rate The price at which one country's currency can be converted into that of another.

ex-date The first day buyers are not entitled to receive distributions previously declared. The ex-date is usually four business days before the record date. (*Syn.* ex-dividend date)

ex-dividend date *See* ex-date.

executor A person authorized to manage a brokerage account for an estate. An executor's authority is established by the last will of the decedent.

exempt security A security exempt from the registration requirements (although not from the antifraud requirements) of the Securities Act of 1933 (e.g., U.S. government and municipal securities).

exempt transaction Exempt transactions are those transactions exempted from registration and advertising requirements under the Uniform Securities Act. Examples of exempt transactions include the following:
- isolated nonissuer transactions;
- nonissuer transactions in outstanding securities (normal market trading);
- transactions with financial institutions (banks, savings institutions, trust companies, insurance companies, pension or profit sharing plans, broker-dealers, etc.);
- unsolicited transactions;
- fiduciary transactions;
- private placement transactions;
- transactions between an issuer and its underwriters; and
- transactions with an issuer's employees, partners or directors if no commission is paid directly or indirectly for the soliciting.

Exemption from the act's registration and advertising requirements does not mean that a transaction is exempt from the act's antifraud provisions.

exercise To implement the rights of an option or a warrant (e.g., a call holder exercises a call by implementing the right to buy 100 shares of the underlying stock at the agreed-upon price).

exercise price The price per share at which the holder of a call, an option or a warrant may buy (or the holder of a put may sell) the underlying security. (*Syn.* strike price, striking price)

ex-legal trade A municipal issue trading without a legal opinion of counsel accompanying the bond. An ex-legal trade must be designated as such at the time of the trade.

expansionary policy A fiscal policy that has as its end the increase (expansion) of the money supply.

expense ratio A ratio used to compare the efficiency of a mutual fund. The ratio is calculated by dividing expenses of operation by the fund's net assets.

expiration date The specified date on which an option becomes worthless and the buyer no longer has the rights specified in the contract.

ex-pit transaction A trade executed outside the normal exchange trading ring or pit.

exploratory well A well drilled either 1) in search of a new and as yet undiscovered pool of oil or gas or 2) with the hope of substantially extending the limits of a pool already developed.

ex-rights Stock purchased without rights. *See also* cum rights.

ex-rights date The date on or after which stocks will be traded without subscription rights.

ex-warrants The date on or after which the buyer of a security is no longer entitled to warrants that will be distributed to the security's owners.

FAC *See* face-amount certificate company.

face-amount certificate company (FAC) The certificates (debt instruments) issued by an investment company that obligate it to pay an investor a stated amount of money (the face amount) at a specific time. The investor pays into the certificate in periodic payments or in a lump sum.

face value *See* par value, principal.

fail to deliver Any situation where the broker-dealer on the sell side of a transaction or contract has not delivered the securities specified in the trade to the broker-dealer on the buy side.

fail to receive Any situation where the broker-dealer on the buy side of a transaction or contract has not received the securities specified in the trade from the broker-dealer on the sell side.

Fannie Mae *See* Federal National Mortgage Association.

farm out An agreement whereby the owner of a leasehold or working interest agrees to assign his interest in certain specific acreage to the assignees, retaining such interest as an overriding royalty, offset acreage or another type of interest, subject to the drilling of one or more specific wells or another performance as a condition of the assignment.

FCM *See* futures commission merchant.

FDIC *See* Federal Deposit Insurance Corporation.

feasibility study A study to determine whether a proposed municipal project will generate sufficient funds to cover operation of the project and debt service. A feasibility study is generally required before the issuance of a municipal revenue bond.

Fed, the *See* Federal Reserve System.

Fed call *See* margin call.

federal call *See* margin call.

Federal Deposit Insurance Corporation (FDIC) The federal agency established in 1933 to provide deposit insurance for member banks and to conduct business activities to prevent bank and thrift failures.

federal funds The reserves of banks and certain other institutions greater than the reserve requirements or excess reserves. These funds are available immediately.

federal funds rate The interest rate charged by one institution lending federal funds to another.

federal margin *See* margin call.

Federal National Mortgage Association (FNMA) A publicly held corporation whose common stock is traded on the NYSE. FNMA purchases conventional mortgages and mortgages guaranteed by the Federal Housing Administration, Department of Veterans Affairs and Farmers Home Administration. (*Syn.* Fannie Mae)

Federal Open Market Committee (FOMC) A committee that makes decisions concerning the Fed's open market operations. *See also* open market operations.

Federal Reserve Board (FRB) A seven-member group appointed by the president (subject to approval by Congress) to oversee operations of the Federal Reserve System.

Federal Reserve System (Fed) The central bank system of the United States. Its chief responsibility is to regulate the flow of money and credit. (*Syn.* The Fed)

FGIC *See* Financial Guaranty Insurance Corporation.

fictitious quotation A bid or an offer of which the interdealer quotation system is unaware.

fidelity (surety) bond 1) A bond required by NYSE Rule 319 for all employees, officers and partners of member firms to protect clients against acts of misplacement, fraudulent trading and check forgery. 2) Every member firm required to join the Securities Investor Protection Corporation (that is, any firm doing business with the public) must purchase and maintain a blanket fidelity bond that indemnifies against losses due to acts such as check forgery, lost securities or fraudulent trading. The minimum coverage must not be less than $25,000, with substantially higher coverage amounts necessary based on the size of the firm and the scope of its business operations.

fiduciary A person legally appointed and authorized to represent another person and act on her behalf.

FIFO *See* first in, first out.

filing date The day on which a registration statement is filed with the SEC.

fill or kill order (FOK) An order that instructs the floor broker to fill the entire order immediately or kill (cancel) the entire order. A partial fill is not acceptable.

final prospectus The prospectus delivered by an issuing corporation that includes the price of the securities, the delivery date, the underwriting spread and other material information.

Financial and Operational Combined Uniform and Single Report *See* FOCUS Report

Financial Guaranty Insurance Corporation (FGIC) An insurance company that offers insurance on the timely payment of interest and principal on municipal issues and unit investment trusts.

financial risk The risk associated with the safety of one's principal related to the ability of an issuer of a security to meet principal, interest or dividend payments.

firm commitment underwriting When the underwriter offers to sell the entire issue of securities to be offered by the issuer. The underwriter is acting as a dealer and will pay the issuer as such in a lump sum for the securities. The underwriter assumes all financial responsibility for any unsold shares.

firm quote The actual price at which a trading unit (such as 100 shares of stock or five bonds) of the security may be bought or sold.

first in, first out (FIFO) An accounting method for assessing a company's inventory in which it is assumed that the first goods acquired are the first to be sold. Also used to designate the order in which sales or withdrawals from an investment are made to determine cost basis for tax purposes. *See also* last in, first out.

fiscal policy The federal tax and spending policies set by Congress or the White House.

Fitch Investors Service, Inc. A rating service for corporate bonds, municipal bonds, commercial paper and other debt obligations.

5% markup policy The NASD's general guideline for the percentage markup, markdown and commissions on securities transactions.

fixed annuity (annuity guaranteed) An annuity contract in which the insurance company makes fixed dollar payments to the annuitant for the term of the contract (usually until the annuitant dies). The insurance company guarantees both earnings and principal amount. *See also* annuity. (*Syn.* fixed dollar annuity, guaranteed dollar annuity)

fixed asset A tangible, physical property owned by a corporation that is used in the production of the corporation's income.

fixed dollar annuity *See* fixed annuity.

fixing The act of trading in a new security for the purpose of stabilizing its price above the established public offering price. (*Syn.* pegging)

flat A term used to describe bonds traded without accrued interest. The bonds are traded at the agreed upon market price only.

flexible premium policy Any variable life insurance policy other than a scheduled premium policy.

floating debt Any obligation payable on demand or having a very short maturity.

floor broker (*Syn.* commission broker)

floor trader An exchange member who enters transactions only for his own account from the floor of the exchange. (*Syn.* local)

flower bond A type of Treasury bond that can be used to settle estate taxes. Flower bonds tend to trade at discounts due to their low coupon rates.

flow of funds The priority for payment of revenues collected.

flow-through A term used to describe the way income, deductions and credits resulting from the activities of a business are applied to individual tax and expenses returns as though each incurred the income and deductions (expenses) directly. *See also* limited partnership.

FNMA *See* Federal National Mortgage Association.

FOCUS Report Broker-dealers are required to file periodic Financial and Operational Combined Uniform and Single (FOCUS) Reports with the SEC at both the Commission's Washington office and the broker-dealer's regional SEC office. General securities broker-dealers are required to file a FOCUS Report Part I monthly and a FOCUS Report Part II quarterly. Introducing broker-dealers are required to file a FOCUS Report Part IIA quarterly, but are not required to file a monthly report.

FOK *See* fill or kill order.

FOMC *See* Federal Open Market Committee.

forced conversion A process used by a corporation that strongly encourages a convertible bondholder to exercise the conversion option. Often conversion is forced by calling the bonds when the market value of the stock is higher than the redemption price offered by the corporation. *See also* redemption.

foreign associate A non-U.S. citizen employed by an NASD member firm, usually in a Canadian or an overseas branch office is not subject to registration and licensing with the Association. This does not include U.S. citizens living and working in overseas or Canadian branch offices, however.

Each exempted foreign associate must agree not to: 1) engage in the securities business in any country or territory under the jurisdiction of the United States, or 2) do business with any U.S. citizen, national or resident alien.

foreign currency The currency of a country other than the one in which the investor resides. Options and futures contracts trade on numerous foreign currencies.

foreign fund *See* specialized fund.

Form 3 A form used by officers, directors and principal stockholders to file an initial statement of beneficial ownership of equity securities. The form is filed with the exchange(s) on which those securities trade (although if there is more than one exchange listing the securities, the issuer can designate the one exchange with which it will file its reports).

Form 4 A form used to report changes in the beneficial ownership of a corporation.

Form 8K A form nicknamed "the current report" by the SEC and filed only when events (or transactions) of consequence occur. For example, Form 8K is used to report:
- changes in the control of a company
- changes in a company's name or address
- the commencement of bankruptcy
- a change of auditors
- resignations of members of the board
- mergers or acquisitions
- changes in assets

Form 10C A form used by issuers of securities that are quoted on Nasdaq. An issuer would use a 10C to report a change in its name and changes of more than 5% in the amount of securities it has outstanding (more than a 5% increase or decrease from the last report).

Form 10K An annual audited report that covers essentially all the information in the original registration statement. The report is due within 90 days of year end.

Form 10Q A quarterly report containing unaudited financial data. Certain types of nonrecurring events that arise during the quarterly period, such as significant litigation, must be reported on Form 10Q. This report is due 45 days after the end of each of the first three fiscal quarters (i.e., May 15th, August 14th and November 14th of each year).

forward contract A cash market transaction in which a future delivery date is specified. Forward contracts differ from futures contracts in that the terms of forward contracts are not standardized and are not traded in contract markets.

forward market The nonexchange trading of commodities specifying delivery at some future date.

forward pricing When pricing mutual fund shares, the valuation of the portfolio occurs at least once per day, and orders to purchase or redeem shares are completed at the valuation following the order placement.

fourth market The trading of securities directly from one institutional investor to another without the services of a brokerage firm, primarily through the use of INSTINET. (*Syn.* INSTINET)

fractional share A portion of a whole share of stock. Fractional shares used to be generated when corporations declared stock dividends, merged or voted to split stock. These days it is more common for corporations to issue the cash equivalent of fractional shares to investors. Mutual fund shares are frequently issued in fractional amounts.

fraud The deliberate concealment, misrepresentation or omission of material information or the truth to deceive or manipulate another party for unlawful or unfair gain.

FRB *See* Federal Reserve Board.

free credit balance Cash balances (customer funds) in customer accounts. Broker-dealers are required to notify customers of their free credit balances at least quarterly. *See also* Rule 15c3-2.

free crowd *See* active crowd.

free-look letter (45-day letter) A letter to clients explaining the sales charge and operation of a contractual plan. The letter must be sent within 60 days of the sale. During the free-look period, the client may terminate the plan without paying a sales charge. *See also* contractual plan.

freeriding The illegal extension of credit for the purpose of trading securities.

freeriding and withholding A violation of the NASD Rules of Fair Practice, freeriding and withholding is the failure of a member participating in the distribution of a new issue to make a bona fide public offering at the public offering price for an issue that is hot. A hot issue is one that opens in the secondary market at a premium to the public offering price.

front-end load 1) The fees and expenses paid by any party for any service rendered during the program's organization or acquisition phase, including front-end organization and offering expenses, acquisition fees and expenses and any other similar fees designated by the sponsor. 2) A system of sales charge for contractual plans that permits up to 50% of the first year's payments to be deducted as a sales charge. Investors have a right to withdraw from the plan, but there are some restrictions if this occurs. *See also* contractual plan, sales charge.

frozen account An account requiring cash in advance to buy and securities in hand to sell.

Full Disclosure Act Another name for the Securities Act of 1933.

full faith and credit bonds *See* general obligation bond.

full trading authorization The authorization for someone other than the customer to have full trading privileges in her account, which includes making purchases, sales and withdrawals.

fully registered A bond registered as to both principal and interest.

functional allocation A sharing arrangement formulated around the types of costs that exist in an oil and gas program. Investors are responsible for intangible costs, and the sponsor is responsible for tangible (capitalized) costs. The revenue-sharing arrangement reflects the percentage of the costs in the program.

fund With mutual funds, the entity responsible for the general administration and supervision of the investment portfolio.

fundamental analysis A method of securities analysis that tries to evaluate the intrinsic value of a particular stock. It is a study of the overall economy, industry conditions and the financial condition and management of a particular company.

funded debt All long-term financing of a corporation or municipality, that is, all outstanding bonds maturing in five years or longer.

funding The conversion of floating debt into bonded debt. *See also* floating debt, funded debt.

fund manager With mutual funds, the entity responsible for investment advisory services. *See also* mutual fund.

funds statement A financial statement that analyzes why a company's working capital increases or decreases.

fungibility Having the same value or quality. A security that is freely transferable with another security and can be used in place of the security traded is considered a fungible security.

futures Exchange-standardized contracts for the purchase or sale of a commodity at a future date.

futures commission merchant (FCM) An individual or organization engaged in the solicitation or acceptance of orders and the extension of credit for the purchase or sale of commodities futures.

futures contract A standardized, exchange-traded contract to make or take delivery of a particular type and grade of commodity at an agreed upon place and point in the future. Futures contracts are transferable between parties.

futures exchange A centralized facility for the trading of futures contracts.

futures market A continuous auction market in which participants buy and sell commodities contracts for delivery at a specified point in the future. Trading is carried on through open outcry and hand signals in a trading pit or ring. *See also* cash market.

general account All assets of an insurer other than assets in separate accounts whether or not established for variable life insurance.

general obligation bond (GO) A type of municipal bond backed by the full faith, credit and taxing power of the issuer for payment of interest and principal. (*Syn.* full faith and credit bond)

general partner (GP) A partner in a partnership who is personally liable for all debts of the partnership and who partakes in the management and control of the partnership.

general partnership (GP) An association of two or more entities forming to conduct a trade or partnership business. The partnership does not require documents for formation, and the general partners are joint and severally liable for the partnership's liabilities.

General Securities Representative *See* Series 7.

Ginnie Mae *See* Government National Mortgage Association.

GNMA *See* Government National Mortgage Association.

GNP *See* gross national product.

GO *See* general obligation bond.

good delivery A security that is negotiable in compliance with the contract of the sale and ready to be transferred from seller to purchaser.

good faith deposit A deposit by underwriters bidding for a municipal issue required to ensure performance by the low bidder. This requirement is stipulated in the official notice of sale sent to prospective underwriters; the amount required is usually 2% to 5% of the bid.

good till canceled order (GTC) An order that is left in force until it is executed or canceled. (*Syn.* open order)

Government National Mortgage Association (GNMA) A wholly owned government corporation that issues several types of securities backed by the full faith and credit of the U.S. government. (*Syn.* Ginnie Mae)

government security An obligation of the U.S. government, backed by the full faith and credit of the government, and regarded as the highest grade or safest issue (i.e., default risk-free). The U.S. government issues short-term Treasury bills, medium-term Treasury notes and long-term Treasury bonds.

GP *See* general partner, general partnership.

GPM *See* gross processing margin.

grade The specified quality of a commodity.

grantor The writer or seller of an option or a contract.

gross income All income of a taxpayer, from whatever source derived.

gross national product (GNP) The total value of goods and services produced in a society during one year. This includes consumption, government purchases, investment and exports minus imports.

gross proceeds The aggregate total of the original invested capital of the original and all of the additional limited partners.

gross processing margin (GPM) The difference between the cost of soybeans and the revenue from the resultant meal and oil after processing.

gross revenue pledge The pledge that debt service is the first payment to be made from revenues received from a municipal project. *See also* net revenue pledge.

gross revenues All revenues from the operation of properties owned by a partnership. The term "gross revenues" typically does not include revenues from interest income or from the sale, refinancing or another disposition of partnership properties.

group net order An order received by an underwriting syndicate for the benefit of the syndicate.

Commissions (takedowns) are paid to members according to their participation in the syndicate.

growth fund A type of diversified common stock fund that has capital appreciation as its primary goal. It invests in companies that reinvest most of their earnings for expansion, research or development. The term also refers to growth income funds that invest in common stocks for both current income and long-term growth of both capital and income. *See also* diversified common stock fund, mutual fund.

growth stock A relatively speculative issue, often paying low dividends and selling at high price-earnings ratios.

GTC *See* good till canceled order.

guaranteed Securities that have a guarantee, usually from a source other than the issuer, as to the payment of principal, interest or dividends.

guaranteed bond A debt obligation in which a company other than the issuing corporation guarantees payment of interest and principal on the bond.

guaranteed dollar annuity *See* fixed annuity.

guaranteed stock Generally a preferred stock that has divided payments guaranteed by a corporation other than the issuing corporation but that remains the stock of the issuing corporation. Guaranteed stock is considered a dual security.

guarantor *See* writer.

guardian A person who manages a gift of securities to a minor under the Uniform Gifts to Minors Act; also, a person who takes charge of an incompetent's affairs.

haircut The formula used to calculate the discounted value of securities in a broker-dealer's possession in the computation of net capital.

head and shoulders A technical trading pattern that has three peaks resembling a head and two shoulders. The stock moves up to its first peak (the left shoulder), drops back, then moves to a higher peak (the top of the head), drops again but recovers to another, lower peak (the right shoulder). A head and shoulder formation after a substantial rise would indicate a market reversal. An inverted head and shoulders would indicate an advance.

heating oil #2 fuel oil.

hedge 1) The act of investing to reduce the risk of a position in a security (typically the risk of adverse price movements), normally by taking a protecting position in a related security. 2) The protective position taken.

high The highest price a security or commodity reaches during a specified period of time.

holder *See* long.

holding company A company organized to invest in and manage other corporations.

holding period A time period that starts the day after a purchase and ends on the day of the sale.

horizontal spread *See* calendar spread.

hot issue An issue that sells at a premium over the public offering price. *See also* freeriding and withholding.

house maintenance call *See* maintenance call.

house requirement The minimum amount of equity that a client must maintain in a margin account according to the particular firm's rules (most firms have a higher maintenance requirement than that set by the NYSE).

Housing Authority bond A type of municipal bond issued by local public housing authorities to redevelop and improve certain areas. (*Syn.* Public Housing Authority bond)

HR-10 plan *See* Keogh plan.

hypothecation The pledging of clients' securities as collateral for loans. Brokerage firms hypothecate clients' securities to finance their margin loans to customers.

IDB *See* industrial development bond.

identified share The particular share from a multiple position of the same security that a client identifies as being the share that he wants delivered for sale.

immediate annuity An annuity contract purchased for a lump sum (single premium) that starts to pay immediately following its purchase. *See also* annuity.

immediate family Includes a parent, a mother-in-law or father-in-law, husband or wife, children or any relative to whose support the sponsor, member or person associated with the member contributes directly or indirectly.

immediate or cancel order (IOC) An order instructing the floor broker to execute immediately. Any portion of the order that remains unexecuted is canceled.

inactive crowd That section of the NYSE that trades inactive, infrequently traded bonds. (*Syn.* cabinet crowd, can crowd)

incidental insurance benefit Any insurance benefit in a variable life insurance policy, other than the variable death benefit and the minimum death benefit, and including but not limited to any accidental death and dismemberment benefit, disability income benefit, guaranteed insurability option, family income benefit or fixed-benefit term rider.

income bond A debt obligation that promises to repay bond principal in full at maturity. Interest on these bonds is paid only if the corporation's earnings are sufficient to meet the interest payment and if the interest payment is declared by the board of directors. These bonds are usually traded flat. *See also* flat. (*Syn.* adjustment bond)

income fund A type of mutual fund that seeks to provide a stable current income from investments by investing in securities that pay interest. *See also* mutual fund.

income statement A financial statement that summarizes a corporation's revenues and expenses for a specific fiscal period.

indication of interest (IOI) An investor's expression of conditional interest in buying an upcoming securities issue after the investor has reviewed a preliminary prospectus. An indication of interest is not a commitment to buy.

individual retirement account (IRA) A qualified tax-deferred retirement plan for employed individuals that allows a contribution of 100% of earned income up to a maximum of $2,000 per year. Some or all of the contribution may be tax deductible, depending on the individual's compensation level and coverage by other qualified retirement plans. *See also* qualified retirement plan.

industrial development bond (IDB) A municipal security issue, the proceeds from which a state or municipal authority uses to finance construction or the purchase of facilities to be leased or purchased by a private company. The bonds are backed by the credit of the private company and often are not considered an obligation of the issuing municipality.

industrial revenue bond *See* industrial development bond.

industry fund *See* specialized fund.

inflation An increase in the general level of prices.

inflation risk *See* purchasing power risk.

initial margin requirement The amount of equity a customer must deposit when making a new purchase in a margin account. The Regulation T requirement is currently 50% for equity securities. The NYSE and NASD initial requirement is an equity of $2,000 but not more than 100% of the purchase cost. *See also* margin.

initial public offering (IPO) A company's initial public offering, sometimes referred to as "going public," is the first sale of stock by the company to the public.

inside information Material and nonpublic information obtained or used by a person for the purpose of trading in securities.

inside market For any given over-the-counter stock at any given point during trading hours, the inside market is the best bid (highest) price at which stock can be sold in the interdealer market and the best ask (lowest) price at which the same stock can be bought.

insider Any person who has nonpublic knowledge (material information) about a corporation. Insiders include directors, officers and stockholders who own more than 10% of any class of equity security of a corporation.

INSTINET An electronic system owned by Reuters Holdings PLC that offers its subscribers a means of trading over 10,000 American and European securities without using a broker-dealer or going through an exchange. INSTINET collects price quotations from exchange-based market makers and Nasdaq and displays the best bid and asked for each security. INSTINET is registered as a broker-dealer with the SEC. (*Syn.* fourth market)

institutional account An institutional account is an account held for the benefit of others. Examples of institutional accounts include banks, trusts, pension and profit-sharing plans, mutual funds and insurance companies. An institutional order can be of any size.

institutional investor A person or organization that trades securities in large enough share quantities or dollar amounts that it qualifies for preferential treatment and lower trade costs (commissions). Institutional investors are covered by fewer protective regulations because it is assumed that they are more knowledgeable and better able to protect themselves.

in-street-name account An account in which the customer's securities are held in the name of the brokerage firm. *See also* street name.

intangible asset An asset that is not physical, such as a copyright or good will.

intangible drilling development expense An expense in the drilling operations for oil and gas, such as labor, fuel or other nontangible costs. These costs may be expensed in the year incurred or capitalized and depleted at a later date.

interest coverage ratio A ratio describing the safety of a corporate bond. The ratio is calculated by dividing operating income by interest expense. The ratio reveals the multiple of income-to-interest expense; the higher the multiple, the less risk there is of default on interest payment.

interest rate risk The risk associated with investments relating to the sensitivity of price or value to fluctuation in the current level of interest rates; also, the risk that involves the competitive cost of money. This term is generally associated with bond prices, but it applies to all investments. In bonds, the price carries an interest risk because if bond prices rise, outstanding bonds will not remain competitive unless their yields and prices are adjusted to reflect the current market.

interlocking directorate Two (or more) corporate boards of directors that have individual directors who serve simultaneously on both. The Investment Company Act of 1940 requires that at least 40% of the board remain independent from the operations of the investment company. The law states that no more than 60% of the directors may also hold an affiliated position within the fund (an affiliated position would be a director who is also the fund's investment adviser, custodian, etc.).

internal rate of return (IRR) That rate of discount at which the present value of future cash flows is exactly equal to the initial capital investment.

international arbitrage A purchase or sale of a security on a securities exchange effected for the purpose of profiting from the difference between the price of the security on that exchange and the price of the security on a securities market not within or subject to the jurisdiction of the U.S. government.

in-the-money An option that has intrinsic value (e.g., a call option in which the stock is selling above the exercise price or a put option in which the stock is selling below the exercise price). *See also* at-the-money, intrinsic value, out-of-the-money.

intrastate offering A conditional offering of unregistered securities limited to companies that do business in one state and sell their securities only to residents of that same state (SEC Rule 147).

intrinsic value The mathematical value of an option (e.g., a call option is said to have intrinsic value when the stock is trading above the exercise price).

introducing broker A broker-dealer that does not hold investors' money or securities. Instead, it introduces those accounts to a clearing broker-dealer, which then handles all cash and securities for those accounts.

inventory turnover ratio A ratio that measures the efficiency with which a company can sell and replace its inventory, calculated by dividing net sales by inventory.

inverted market A futures market in which nearby contracts are selling at higher prices than distant contracts. (*Syn.* backwardation)

inverted yield curve A chart that shows long-term debt instruments having lower yields than short-term debt instruments. *See also* normal yield curve.

invested capital *See* capitalization, capital structure.

investment adviser Any person who, for compensation (a flat fee or percent of assets managed), offers investment advice. For investment companies, the adviser has the day-to-day responsibility of investing the cash and securities held in a mutual fund's portfolio. The adviser must adhere to the objectives as stated in the fund's prospectus. This definition includes persons who issue written reports or analyses for compensation.

The term "investment adviser" does not include:
- institutions such as banks, saving institutions or trust companies;
- professionals such as lawyers, accountants or teachers whose performance of these services is solely incidental to the practice of their profession;
- broker-dealers who offer investment portfolio advice as part of their business of being a broker-dealer and receive no special compensation for that service;
- publishers of any financial publication of general, regular and paid circulation. However, a person who sells subscriptions to investment advisory publications (market letters) is considered an investment adviser under the Uniform Securities Act;
- person whose investment advice relates only to U.S. government securities and certain municipal securities; or
- person having no place of business within the state and whose activities are limited to: (a) professional clients (institutions), (b) a very few solicitations or sales to clients other than those above. For instance, some states limit this activity to no more than five clients in any 12 consecutive months.

The term "investment adviser" also excludes any person that the state administrator of the Uniform Securities Act decides not to include.

investment adviser representative Any partner, officer, director or other individual employed by or associated with an investment adviser who: 1) gives investment advice or makes recommendations, 2) manages client accounts or portfolios, 3) determines which investment recommendations or advice should be given, 4) offers or sells investment advisory services, or 5) supervises employees involved in any of these activities.

investment banker A financial professional who raises capital for corporations and municipalities.

investment banking (securities) business The business carried on by a broker, dealer or municipal or government securities dealer of underwriting or distributing new issues of securities as a dealer or of buying and selling securities on the order and for the benefit of others as a broker.

investment company A company engaged primarily in the business of investing and trading in securities, including face-amount certificate companies, unit investment trusts and management companies.

Investment Company Act Amendments of 1970 Amendments to the Investment Company Act of 1940 requires a registered investment company issuing periodic payment plan certificates (contractual plans) to offer all purchasers withdrawal rights and purchasers of front-end load plans surrender rights.

Investment Company Act Amendments of 1975 Amendments to the Investment Company Act of 1940; in particular, that sales charges must relate to the services a fund provides shareholders.

Investment Company Act of 1940 Congressional legislation enacted to regulate investment companies; it requires any investment company in interstate commerce to register with the SEC.

Investment Company/Variable Contract Products Limited Representative *See* Series 6.

investment grade security A security with a rating (S&P, Moody's, etc.) of BBB/Baa or above.

investment in properties The amount of capital contributions actually paid or allocated to the purchase, development, construction or improvement of properties acquired by the program. The amount available for investment equals the gross proceeds raised less front-end fees.

investment objective Any goal a client hopes to achieve through investing.

investment value The market price at which a convertible security (usually a debenture) would sell if it were not converted into common stock. *See also* convertible bond, debenture.

investor The purchaser of a unit or security, including the sponsor to the extent it purchases units.

invitation for bids The "advertising" for bids to be submitted for the underwriting of a bond issue. Invitations are published in *The Bond Buyer*, newspapers, journals and *Munifacts*.

in-whole-call The call of a bond issue in its entirety by the issuer, as opposed to the redemption of issues based on a lottery held by an independent trustee.

IOC *See* immediate or cancel order.

IOI *See* indication of interest.

IPO *See* initial public offering.

IRA *See* individual retirement account.

IRA rollover The reinvestment of assets that an individual receives as a distribution from a qualified tax-deferred retirement plan into another qualified plan. The individual may reinvest either the entire lump sum or a portion of that sum, and typically does so in an account designated as an IRA rollover account. IRA rollovers differ from IRA transfers in that the account owner takes possession of the cash or securities received from the account rather than directing that the cash and securities be transferred directly from the existing plan custodian to the new plan custodian. *See also* individual retirement account.

IRA transfer The direct movement and reinvestment of assets that an individual receives as a distribution from the custodian of one qualified tax-deferred retirement plan to the custodian of another qualified plan. IRA transfers differ from IRA rollovers in that the account owner never takes possession of the cash or securities received from the account, directing that the cash and securities be transferred directly from the existing plan custodian to the new plan custodian. *See also* individual retirement account.

IRR *See* internal rate of return.

issued stock Stock that has been sold to the public.

issuer 1) The corporation or municipality that offers its securities for sale; also, the creator of an option (the issuer of an over-the-counter option is the option writer, and the issuer of a listed option is the Options Clearing Corporation). 2) According to the Uniform Securities Act, any person who issues or proposes to issue any security.

When a corporation or municipality raises additional capital through an offering of securities, that corporation or municipality is the "issuer" of those securities. An issuer transaction is also called a "primary" transaction.

There are two exceptions to the basic definition of issuer. In the case of voting-trust certificates or collateral-trust certificates, "issuer" refers to the person who assumes the duties of depositor or manager. There is considered to be no issuer for certificates of interest or participation in oil, gas, or mining titles or leases where payments are made out of production.

joint account An account in which two or more individuals act as co-tenants or co-owners of the account. The account may be joint tenants in common or joint tenants with right of survivorship. *See also* joint tenants with right of survivorship, joint tenants in common.

joint tenants in common (JTIC) A form of ownership directing that upon the death of one tenant, the decedent's fractional interest in the joint account must be retained by the estate. This form of ownership may be used by any two or more individuals.

joint tenants with right of survivorship (JTWROS) A form of ownership that requires that a deceased tenant's fractional interest in an account be retained by the surviving tenant(s). It is used almost exclusively by husbands and wives. *See also* joint tenants in common.

joint venture The joining of two or more persons in a specific business enterprise, rather than in a continuing relationship, as in a partnership.

JTIC *See* joint tenants in common.

JTWROS *See* joint tenants with right of survivorship.

junior lien debt A bond backed by the same collateral backing a previous issue and having a junior claim to the collateral in the event of default. *See also* open-end pledge. (*Syn.* closed-end pledge)

Keogh plan A qualified tax-deferred retirement plan for persons who are self-employed and unincorporated or who earn extra income through personal services aside from their regular employment. *See also* qualified retirement plan. (*Syn.* HR-10 plan)

L L is a measure of the money supply that includes all of the components of M1, M2 and M3 as well as Treasury bills, savings bonds, commercial paper, bankers' acceptances and Eurodollar holdings of U.S. residents.

last in, first out (LIFO) A method of assessing a company's inventory in which it is assumed that the goods acquired last are the first to be sold. Also used to designate the order in which sales or withdrawals from an investment are made to determine cost basis for tax purposes. *See also* first in, first out.

lease A full or partial interest in the use of an asset; for mineral properties, the interest in the property that authorizes the lessee to drill for, produce and sell oil and gas, other minerals or any combination thereof.

legal investment (legal list) The limited list of securities selected by a state agency (such as a state banking or insurance commission) that can be used in fiduciary accounts (mutual savings banks, pension funds, insurance companies) or in an insurer's general account.

legal opinion of counsel Regardless of the type of municipal bond issued, the bond must be accompanied by a legal opinion of counsel. The opinion of counsel affirms that the issue is a municipal issue and that interest is exempt from federal taxation, among other items.

legislative risk The risk associated with the impact of changes in law on investment.

lending at a premium The act of charging the borrower of securities (the short seller) for the loan of the securities. The charge is stated in terms of dollars per 100 shares per business day.

lending at a rate The act of paying interest on the money received in connection with securities loaned to short sellers.

letter of intent (LOI) A signed purchase agreement under which a fund can sell shares to an investor at a lower overall sales charge, based on the total dollar amount of the intended investment. An LOI is valid only if the investor completes the terms of the purchase agreement within 13 months of the time this agreement is signed. An LOI may be backdated 90 days. (*Syn.* statement of intention)

level debt service Where principal and interest payments remain essentially constant from year to year over the life of the issue.

Level One The basic level of Nasdaq service. It provides registered representatives with the up-to-the-minute inside bid and asked quotations on hundreds of over-the-counter stocks through a desktop quotation machine. *See also* Nasdaq.

Level Two The second level of Nasdaq service. It provides up-to-the-minute inside bid and asked quotations and the bids and askeds of each marker maker for a security through a desktop quotation machine. *See also* Nasdaq.

Level Three The highest level of Nasdaq service. It provides up-to-the-minute inside bid and asked quotations, supplies the bids and askeds of each market maker for a security and allows each market maker to enter changes in those quotes through a desktop quotation machine. *See also* Nasdaq.

leverage The use of borrowed capital to increase earnings. (*Syn.* trading on the equity)

leverage transaction merchant (LTM) An individual or organization registered with the Commodities Futures Trading Commission and permitted to engage in the off-exchange trading of selected futures instruments.

liability A debt owed by an entity; a legal obligation to pay. Current liabilities are debts payable within twelve months. Long-term liabilities are debts payable over a period of more than twelve months.

LIFO *See* last in, first out.

lifting cost An expenditure made and a cost incurred in producing and marketing oil and gas from completed wells. Such costs include, in addition to labor, fuel, repairs, hauling, materials, supplies, utilities and other costs incident to or therefrom, ad valorem and severance taxes, insurance and casualty losses and compensation to well operators or others for services rendered in conducting such operations.

limited partner (LP) A partner who does not participate in the management or control of a partnership and whose liability for partnership debts is limited to the amount invested in the partnership. *See also* participant, passive investor.

limited partnership A form of business organization in which one or more of the partners is liable only to the extent of the amount of dollars they have invested. Limited partners are not involved in management decisions but enjoy direct flow-through of income and expenses. *See also* flow-through.

limited partnership agreement The articles of limited partnership of each limited partnership. The agreement forms the contract between the limited and general partners and states the rights and responsibilities of each.

limited principal A person who has passed a qualifications examination attesting to her knowledge and qualifications to supervise the business of a member in one or more limited areas of expertise. If a limited principal expects to function in one or more of the general fields of expertise reserved for a General Securities Principal, she must also be registered as a General Securities Principal.

limited tax bond A general obligation bond where the security of the bond provided by the issuer's taxing power is limited to a specified maximum rate.

limited trading authorization The authorization for someone other than the customer to have trading privileges in his account. These privileges are limited to purchases and sales; withdrawal of assets is not allowed.

limit order A customer's order with instructions to buy a specified security below a certain price or sell a specified security above a certain price. (*Syn.* or better order)

liquidity The ease with which something can be bought or sold (converted to cash) in the marketplace. A large number of buyers and sellers and a high volume of trading activity are important components of liquidity.

liquidity ratio With a corporation, a measure of the company's ability to meet its current obligations; for investments, the ability to convert the asset into cash without an appreciable loss on the investment. The ratio compares current assets to current liabilities. *See also* current ratio.

listed option An option that can be bought and sold on a national securities exchange in a continuous secondary market. *See also* OTC option. (*Syn.* standardized option)

listed security A security that is traded on a regional or national securities exchange such as the NYSE.

LMV *See* long market value.

loan consent agreement A lending agreement between a brokerage firm and a client that permits the brokerage firm to lend the client's securities. This is part of the margin agreement. (*Syn.* consent to lend agreement)

loaned flat Securities loaned to short sellers without an interest charge.

loans for set amount A type of broker's collateral loan that requires a brokerage firm to deposit new collateral before it can obtain a new loan when additional funds are needed. *See also* broker's loan, call loan.

loan value *See* maximum loan value.

local basis *See* country basis.

local *See* floor trader.

LOI *See* letter of intent.

long The state of owning a security, contract or commodity. A purchase of 5 May wheat contracts would be referred to as *going long May wheat.* The speculator would have a *long* position.

long hedge A long securities or actuals position protected by a long put position. *See also* hedge, short hedge.

long market value (LMV) The current market price of the securities a customer owns, based on the closing prices of the previous day. (*Syn.* current market value)

long straddle Buying a call and a put on the same stock with the same strike price and expiration month.

long-term gain The taxable gain on a capital asset that an investor has owned for more than twelve months. *See also* capital gain, long-term loss.

long-term loss The taxable loss on a capital asset that an investor has owned for more than twelve months. *See also* long-term gain.

loss carryover The capital loss that is carried over to later years for use as a capital loss deduction. *See also* capital loss.

low The lowest price a security or commodity reaches during a given period of time.

LP *See* limited partner.

LTM *See* leverage transaction merchant.

M1 A narrow definition of money supply that includes all coins, currency, demand deposits (checking accounts) and NOW accounts.

M2 A broader definition of money supply that includes all coins, currency, checking deposits, time deposits, savings deposits and noninstitutional money-market funds.

M3 Those currencies included in the M2 definition of money supply plus large time deposits, institutional money-market funds, short-term repurchase agreements and certain other large liquid assets.

maintenance call A brokerage firm's demand that a client deposit money or securities when the client's equity falls below the brokerage firm's minimum maintenance requirement, or the higher maintenance call set by the NYSE. *See also* house maintenance call, NYSE maintenance call.

maintenance excess The difference between the equity in an account and the NYSE minimum margin (25% long and 30% short). *See also* equity, NYSE maintenance requirement.

maintenance requirement *See* NYSE maintenance requirement.

majority vote The vote of limited partners who own more than 50% of the total outstanding units.

Major Market Index (MMI) A 20-stock index designed to track the Dow Jones 30 industrials. The MMI is composed of 15 of the Dow Jones 30 and 5 other large NYSE-listed stocks.

make a market The action of a broker-dealer firm when, on a regular basis, it holds itself out to other firms as ready to buy or sell a particular over-the-counter stock for its own account. Such a firm accepts the risk of holding the position in the security. *See also* market maker.

Maloney Act Section 15 of the Securities Exchange Act of 1934 is known as the Maloney Act, named for its sponsor, the late Sen. Francis Maloney of Connecticut. This legislation provided for the creation of a securities industry association for the specific purpose of supervising the over-the-counter securities market.

managed offering The offering for a sale of securities in which the sponsor uses a dealer-manager to hire soliciting dealers.

management company An investment company that manages a portfolio of various types of securities. *See also* closed-end management company, diversified management company, nondiversified management company, open-end management company.

management fee A fee paid to a sponsor of a program for managing and administering the program.

manager *See* underwriting manager.

manager of the syndicate *See* underwriting manager.

managing partner The sponsor when acting in its capacity as managing partner under the articles of partnership establishing the partnership.

managing underwriter *See* underwriting manager.

mandatory call The redemption of bonds by an issuer based on a predetermined schedule or event. *See also* catastrophe call.

margin The amount of equity as a percentage of current market value in a margin account. *See also* equity, margin call, Regulation T.

margin account An account in which a brokerage firm lends a client part of the purchase price of securities. *See also* Regulation T, special arbitrage account.

margin call A demand for a client to deposit money or securities when a purchase is made in a margin account. *See also* initial margin requirement,

margin. (*Syn.* call, fed call, federal call, federal margin, Reg T call, T call)

margin deficiency The amount by which the required margin exceeds the equity in a margin account. (*Syn.* margin requirement)

margin department The department within a brokerage firm that computes the amount of money a client must deposit in both margin and cash accounts.

margin excess The amount by which the equity in a margin account exceeds the required margin. (*Syn.* excess equity)

margin of profit A ratio used to determine the operating efficiency of a business, calculated by dividing the operating profit by the net sales. (*Syn.* profit margin)

margin requirement *See* margin deficiency.

margin risk The risk that an investor will be required to deposit additional cash if her security positions are subject to adverse price movements.

markdown The difference between the best (highest) current bid price among dealers and the actual price that a dealer pays to a customer.

marketability The ease with which a security can be bought or sold; having a readily available market for trading.

market arbitrage The simultaneous purchase and sale of the same security in different markets to take advantage of a price disparity between the two markets. *See also* arbitrage.

market if touched order (MIT) An order that becomes a market order only if the market touches (or hits) the specified price. A buy MIT order is placed below the current market, and a sell MIT is placed above the current market.

market letter A publication that comments on securities and is distributed to an organization's clients or to the public.

market maker (principal) A dealer willing to accept the risk of holding securities to facilitate trading in a particular security or securities. *See also* make a market.

market NH *See* market not held order.

market not held order A market order for a sizable amount of stock that gives the floor broker discretion about the price or timing of the order's execution. *See also* market NH.

market order An order that is to be executed at the best available price.

market-out clause The standard clause in a firm commitment underwriting agreement that relieves the underwriter of its obligation to underwrite the issue under certain unusual circumstances (e.g., unexpected bad news just before or after the offering date).

market risk That risk due to day-to-day fluctuations in prices at which securities can be bought or sold. *See also* systematic risk.

market value The price at which an investor will buy or sell each share of common stock or each bond at a given time. Market value is determined by the interaction between buyers and sellers in the market. *See also* current market value.

market value on the trade date The gross amount of a long purchase (including commissions) or the net proceeds of a short sale.

market value per share The current price at which a stock is trading in the open market.

mark to the market The act of adjusting the value of an account to the current market value of the security positions in the account; the current valuation of market value and equity.

markup The difference between the best (lowest) current offering price among dealers and the actual price a dealer charges its customer.

markup policy *See* NASD 5% markup policy.

married put When an investor buys a stock and on the same day buys a put on that stock and specifically identifies that position as a hedge. The holding period starts on the day of the purchase and does not end until the stock is sold, through the exercise of the put or otherwise.

matching orders The act of simultaneously entering identical (or nearly identical) orders for the purchase or sale of a security to create the appearance of active trading in the security.

material information Any fact that could affect an investor's decision to buy a certain security.

maturity date The date on which the principal is repaid to the investor. *See also* par value, principal.

maximum loan value The maximum amount a broker-dealer can loan a customer for the purchase of securities, based on the complement of Reg T (e.g., if Reg T were 65%, the maximum loan would be 35%). (*Syn.* loan value)

MBIA *See* Municipal Bond Investors Assurance Corp.

member 1) Of the New York Stock Exchange (NYSE): One of the 1,366 individuals owning a seat on the NYSE. 2) Of the National Association of Securities Dealers (NASD): Any broker or dealer admitted to membership in the NASD.

member firm A firm in which at least one of the principal officers is a member of the New York Stock Exchange, another organized exchange, a self-regulatory organization, or a clearing corporation.

member order An order by a syndicate member for a retail or an institutional client. Each syndicate member receives the commission on orders filled by the syndicate manager. Member orders generally have the lowest priority during the order period. *See also* designated order, presale order.

membership The members of the New York Stock Exchange, another exchange, a self-regulatory organization or a clearing corporation.

mill rate The tax per dollar of assessed value of property ($.001).

minimum death benefit The amount of the guaranteed death benefit, other than any incidental insurance benefit, payable under a variable life insurance policy, regardless of the investment performance of the separate account.

minimum subscription amount The minimum amount to which a person must initially subscribe in a new offering of a direct participation program.

minus tick An execution price below the previous sale. A short sale may not be executed on a minus tick. *See also* plus tick, plus tick rule. (*Syn.* down tick)

MIT *See* market if touched order.

mixed account A margin account having both long and short positions in different securities. *See also* margin account.

MMI *See* Major Market Index.

Modified Accelerated Cost Recovery System (MACRS) An accounting method used to recover the cost of qualifying depreciable property. The MACRS system eliminated the acceleration of deductions for real property. Deductions are based on percentages prescribed in the Internal Revenue Code.

monetary policy The policies and actions of the Federal Reserve Board that determine the rate of growth and size of the money supply, which in turn affect interest rates.

money market The securities market that deals in short-term (less than one year) debt. Money market instruments are forms of debt that mature in less than a year and are very liquid. Treasury bills make up the bulk of trading in the money markets.

money-market fund An open-end investment company investing in money market instruments. Generally sold with no load, the fund offers draft-writing privileges and low opening investments.

money spread *See* price spread.

moral obligation bond A revenue bond issued with nonbinding legislative authority to apportion monies for shortfalls in revenues backing the bond.

mortgage bond A debt obligation secured by a property pledge. Mortgage bonds are liens or mortgages against the issuing corporation's properties and real estate assets.

municipal bond fund A type of mutual fund that invests in municipal bonds, operating either as a unit investment trust (units of interest in an existing portfolio of tax-exempt bonds) or as an open-end fund. *See also* mutual fund, open-end management company, unit investment trust.

Municipal Bond Investors Assurance Corp. (MBIA) A public corporation offering insurance as to timely payment of principal and interest when due on qualified municipal issues. Issues with MBIA insurance are generally rated AAA by Standard & Poor's.

municipal broker's broker A broker acting for another broker in the municipal market. The broker's broker does not take positions in the issue, nor does the broker transact orders for the public. *See also* broker's broker.

Municipal Securities Representative *See* Series 52.

municipal security A debt security issued by a state, a municipality or another subdivision (such as a school, a park, or a sanitary or some other local taxing district) to raise money to finance its capital expenditures. Such expenditures might include the construction of highways, public works or school buildings.

Munifacts A news wire service for the municipal bond industry; a product of *The Bond Buyer*.

mutual exclusion doctrine The doctrine that established the federal tax exemption status of municipal bond interest. This doctrine says that states and municipalities must not tax government-owned properties. The federal government reciprocates by excluding local government properties from federal taxation. (*Syn.* mutual reciprocity, reciprocal immunity)

mutual fund A type of investment company that offers for sale or has outstanding securities that it has issued that are redeemable on demand by the fund at current net asset value. All owners in the fund share in the gains or losses of the fund. (*Syn.* open-end management company)

mutual fund custodian Usually a national bank, a trust company or another qualified institution that physically safeguards securities. It does not manage investments; its function is solely clerical.

mutual reciprocity *See* mutual exclusion doctrine.

naked call (put) writer Any investor who writes a call (put) without owning the underlying stock or other related assets that would enable the writer to deliver the stock (or purchase the stock) should the option be exercised. (*Syn.* uncovered call [put] writer)

NASD *See* National Association of Securities Dealers.

Nasdaq *See* National Association of Securities Dealers Automated Quotation System.

Nasdaq National Market (NNM) Two hundred of the most actively traded over-the-counter stocks within the 4,000 stocks quoted on Nasdaq. Trades are reported as they occur.

Nasdaq 100 An index of the largest 100 nonfinancial stocks on Nasdaq, weighted by capitalization.

NASD Automated Quotation System *See* National Association of Securities Dealers Automated Quotation System.

NASD Bylaws The body of laws that describes how the NASD functions, defines its powers and determines the qualifications and registration requirements for brokers.

NASD District Business Conduct Committee (DBCC) A committee composed of up to twelve NASD members from within a district who serve as administrators for the district. The NASD is divided into 13 local districts to maximize the degree of local administration. The DBCC has original jurisdiction for hearings and judging complaints.

NASD 5% markup policy A guideline for reasonable markups, markdowns and commissions for secondary over-the-counter transactions. (*Syn.* markup policy)

NASD Rules of Fair Practice In general, these rules complement and serve as extensions of the 1934 act rules and also the rules under the 1933 act and the Investment Company Act of 1940.

NASD Small Order Execution System (SOES) An automatic order execution system designed to facilitate the trading of small public market and executable limit orders (500 or fewer shares). Any Nasdaq or NNM security with at least one active SOES market maker is eligible for trading through SOES. All NNM market makers (but not firms that make a market in Nasdaq securities not on the NNM list) are required also to participate in SOES. NNM market makers cannot voluntarily withdraw from SOES participation.

SOES electronically matches and executes orders, locks in a price and sends confirms directly to the broker-dealers on both sides of the trade. Small orders may be aggregated if the total is less than the maximum 500-share limit, but broker-dealers may not split up large orders for the purpose of avoiding the 500-share limitation.

Institutions and broker-dealers may not employ the system to trade for their own accounts. Only public market and executable limit orders are accepted by SOES.

National Association of Securities Dealers (NASD) The self-regulatory organization (SRO) for the over-the-counter (OTC) market. The NASD was recognized as the SRO for the OTC market by the Maloney Act of 1938.

National Association of Securities Dealers Automated Quotation System (Nasdaq) The nationwide electronic quotation system for up-to-the-minute bid and asked quotations on approximately 4,000 over-the-counter stocks.

National Futures Association NFA The self-regulatory organization of the commodities futures industry to which all futures exchange members, commodity-trading advisers (CTAs) and commodity pool operators (CPOs) must belong. The NFA is responsible to the Commodities Futures Trading Commission.

NAV *See* net asset value.

nearby contract Of two or more futures contracts, the contract with the shortest time remaining to expiration. (*Syn.* nearby delivery [month])

nearby delivery (month) *See* nearby contract.

negotiable certificate of deposit (CD) A negotiable certificate that evidences a time deposit of funds with a bank. It is an unsecured promissory note normally issued in $100,000 denominations.

negotiated underwriting An underwriting in which a brokerage firm consults with the issuer and arrives at a consensus about the most suitable price and timing of a forthcoming securities offering. *See also* competitive bidding.

net asset value (NAV) The value of a mutual fund share, calculated by deducting the fund's liabilities from the total assets of the portfolio and dividing this amount by the number of shares outstanding. This is calculated once a day, based on the closing market price for each security in the fund's portfolio. *See also* mutual fund. (*Syn.* bid price)

net capital Liquid capital (cash and assets readily convertible into cash) maintained by a broker-dealer. The uniform net capital rules are the SEC's primary means of regulating broker-dealers and making sure that firms have enough

money (capitalization) to deal responsibly with the investing public. Net capital rules include:
- minimum dollar requirements for net capital;
- definition of and how to compute net capital;
- allowable aggregate indebtedness of broker-dealers;
- maximum aggregate indebtedness to net capital ratios;
- subordinated loan capital contribution rules; and
- maximum debt to equity ratios.

net change The difference between the closing price on the trading day reported and the previous day's closing price. In over-the-counter transactions, the term refers to the difference between the closing bids.

net current asset value per share The calculation of book value per share that excludes all fixed assets. *See also* book value per share.

net income to net sales A ratio that measures the after-tax profitability of a company, calculated by dividing net income by net sales. (*Syn.* net profit margin, net profits to sales, profits after taxes, profit ratio, return on sales)

net investment income The sum of dividends, interest, rents, royalties and short-term gains minus investment expenses. For mutual funds, net investment income represents the source for dividend payments.

net investment return The rate of investment return in a separate account to be applied to the benefit base.

net proceeds The total gross proceeds less expenses incurred, to be paid by the partnership in organizing the partnership and in offering units to the public.

net profit margin *See* net income to net sales.

net profits interest In a net profits interest arrangement, the sponsor shares in revenues after payments for royalties and operating expenses have been made. This payment is made to the sponsor, who has no other interest in the program (such as an overriding royalty) for packaging the deal. Net profits interest is limited to private placement.

net profits to sales *See* net income to net sales.

net revenue pledge A pledge of revenues funding a bond after payment of operating and maintenance expenses. The pledge is contained in the trust indenture. *See also* gross revenue pledge.

net tangible assets per bond A measure of the amount of producing assets behind each corporate bond, calculated by dividing net tangible assets by funded debt. (*Syn.* book value per bond)

net tangible assets per share *See* book value per share.

net worth The amount by which assets exceed liabilities. (*Syn.* shareholders' equity)

New Housing Authority bond (NHA) A municipal bond issued by local public housing authorities to redevelop and improve certain areas. (*Syn.* Public Housing Authority bond)

New Issues Act Another name for the Securities Act of 1933.

New York plan A financing method for the purchase of equipment similar to a conditional sale: a company purchases equipment by issuing bonds, and as the bonds are paid off, the company acquires full title to the equipment. *See also* equipment trust certificate.

New York Stock Exchange (NYSE) A corporation operated by a board of directors responsible for setting policy, supervising Exchange and member activities, listing securities, overseeing the transfer of members' seats on the Exchange and judging whether an applicant is qualified to be a specialist.

New York Stock Exchange maintenance call *See* NYSE maintenance call.

New York Stock Exchange maintenance requirement *See* NYSE maintenance requirement.

New York Stock Exchange Super Designated Order Turnaround system (SuperDot) The NYSE's computerized trading and execution system. Broker-dealers use this order routing system to choose the destination of an order and the route that order will take. An order can be routed directly to the appropriate specialist at his trading post on the floor of the Exchange, or it can be sent to the brokerage firm's house booth for handling by the Exchange member (commission broker) who represents the broker-dealer. Once the order is received by the specialist or commission broker, the order is presented in the auction market. If the order is executed, the specialist or commission broker uses the same automated routing system to send an execution report back to the firm that submitted the order. The broker-dealer then notifies the registered representative, who notifies the customer that the order was executed. Orders executed through the SuperDot routing system are often confirmed back to the broker in less than 60 seconds.

NFA *See* National Futures Association.

NH *See* not held order.

NHA *See* New Housing Authority bond.

nine bond rule The NYSE rule that requires orders for listed bonds in quantities of nine bonds or fewer to be sent to the floor of the NYSE before being traded in the over-the-counter market.

NNM *See* Nasdaq National Market.

no-load fund A mutual fund whose shares are sold without a sales charge added to the net asset value. *See also* mutual fund, net asset value, sales charge.

nominal quote A quotation given for informational purposes only. (*Syn.* subject quote)

nominal yield The interest rate that is stated on the face of a bond representing the amount of interest paid by the issuer on the principal of the issue. (*Syn.* coupon rate, stated yield, yield)

nominee The person in whose name securities are registered if that person is other than the beneficial owner. This is the role of the brokerage firm when customer securities purchased on margin are registered in street name.

nonaccredited investor An investor not meeting the net worth requirements of Regulation D. Nonaccredited investors are counted for purposes of the 35-investor limitation under Rules 505 and 506 of Regulation D.

noncumulative preferred stock A type of preferred stock that does not have to pay any dividends in arrears to the holders. *See also* cumulative preferred stock, preferred stock.

nondiversified management company A management company that is not restricted in its choice of securities or by the concentration of interest it has in those securities. *See also* diversified management company, management company, mutual fund.

nonissuer The term "nonissuer" refers to a person other than the issuer of a security. In a nonissuer securities transaction, for example, the issuer is not one of the parties in the transaction, and the transaction is therefore not, according to the law, directly or indirectly for the benefit of the issuer.

When the Uniform Securities Act refers to a nonissuer transaction, it is referring to a transaction in which the proceeds of the sale go to the selling stockholder. For example, a trade of 100 shares of RCA on the New York Stock Exchange is a typical nonissuer transaction. Most nonissuer transactions are also called secondary transactions.

nonmanaged offering A method of distributing direct participation program interests. Rather than organizing a syndicate to distribute the interest, the program sponsor will contract with individual broker-dealers to offer the interests to the public. A wholesaler (broker-dealer) is often hired by the sponsor to arrange selling agreements with each firm.

nonrecourse financing Financing in which the property is made security for the debt, but there is no personal liability on the part of the borrower.

nonspecified property program A program where, at the time a securities registration is ordered effective, less than 75% of the net proceeds from the sale of program interests are allocated to the purchase, construction or improvement of identified properties or are allocated to a program in which the proceeds from any sale or refinancing of properties may be reinvested. Reserves shall be included in the nonspecified 25%. (*Syn.* blind pool, unspecified property program)

no-par value Stock issued without a stated value. *See also* par value.

normal market A futures market in which nearby contracts are selling at lower prices than distant contracts. (*Syn.* carrying charge market, contango)

normal yield curve A chart that shows long-term debt instruments having higher yields than short-term debt instruments. *See also* inverted yield curve.

not held order (NH) A market order for a sizable amount of stock that gives the floor broker discretion as to the price and timing of execution of the order. (*Syn.* market not held order)

numbered account An account titled with something other than a client's name, such as a number, symbol or special title. The client must sign a form designating ownership of the account.

NYSE *See* New York Stock Exchange.

NYSE maintenance call A demand for a client to deposit money or securities if the client's equity falls below the NYSE minimum maintenance level. *See also* equity.

NYSE maintenance requirement The minimum amount of equity that must be maintained in a margin account at all times according to NYSE rules. The minimum maintenance for corporate securities is 25% of the current market value for a long position.

OB *See* limit order.

OCC *See* Office of the Comptroller of the Currency, Options Clearing Corporation.

OCC Disclosure Document The disclosure document published by the Options Clearing Corporation that must be provided to every investor at the time the investor is approved for standardized options trading.

OCO *See* one cancels other.

odd lot Less than the normal unit of trading, which is less than 100 shares of stock or five bonds.

odd-lot differential The price differential that is often charged when an odd-lot order is executed on an exchange (usually the charge is 12.5 cents [1/8th of a point] per share).

odd-lot order An order for less than the normal unit of trading (normally 100 shares of stock).

odd-lot theory A technical theory based on the assumption that the public is always wrong. According to the theory, if odd-lot sales are up—that is, the public is selling stock—it is probably a good time to buy.

offer 1) An indication by an investor, a trader or a dealer of a willingness to sell a security or commodity. 2) Under the Uniform Securities Act, every attempt to solicit a purchase or sale in a security for value. *See also* bid. (*Syn.* ask, quotation, quote)

offering circular A document that contains information about a corporation's issue of securities. The information included is similar to that made available in the prospectus but abbreviated. Its use is restricted to Regulation A offerings. *See also* Regulation A.

offering price With mutual funds, the price an investor will pay per share. The offering price is the net asset value plus a sales charge (for funds that have a sales charge). *See also* mutual fund, net asset value. (*Syn.* current price)

office of supervisory jurisdiction (OSJ) Any office at which one or more of the following occur:
- order execution and/or market making;
- formation or structuring of public offerings or private placements;
- maintenance of custody of customer funds and/or securities;
- final approval of new accounts on behalf of the member;
- review and endorsement of customer orders;
- final approval of advertising or sales literature for use by persons associated with the member; and
- supervision of activities of persons at one or more of the member's branch offices.

Office of the Comptroller of the Currency (OCC) The bureau of the U.S. Treasury Department that regulates the corporate structure and banking practices of national banks. The Comptroller is appointed by the president, with Senate approval.

Office of Thrift Supervision (OTS) A bureau of the U.S. Treasury Department, authorized by Congress under the Financial Institution Reform, Recovery and Enforcement Act of 1989 to charter, regulate, examine and supervise thrift institutions.

official notice of sale The notification of bidding sent to prospective underwriters specifying such bid procedures as date, time and place of sale, description of the issue, maturities, call provisions and amount of good faith deposit required.

official statement (OS) A statement concerning the municipal issue offered (disclosing the underwriting spread, fees received by brokers for acting as agents of the issuer and initial offering price of each maturity), prepared by the underwriter from information provided by the issuer.

offset To enter an equivalent but opposite closing transaction. To offset an initial purchase, a sale would be made. To offset an initial sale, a purchase would be made.

OID *See* original issue discount.

oil and gas program A direct participation program that has as its primary purpose oil and gas exploration, development or purchase of production.

oil depletion allowance A percentage of revenue from oil production allowed as a deduction from gross revenues generated from the sale of oil and gas. The percentage allowable is 15% (subject to certain limits).

one cancels other (OCO) A dual order submitted with two sets of instructions. At the moment either order is executed, the other order is canceled.

open-end investment company *See* open-end management company.

open-end management company A management company that continually issues new shares. Its shares are redeemable on any business day at the net asset value. Open-end management companies may sell only common stock. (*Syn.* mutual fund, open-end investment company)

open-end pledge A provision in the trust indenture allowing the issuer to use collateral backing a bond for future borrowing. New creditors have the same claim on the collateral as existing creditors.

opening purchase transaction The act of entering the options market by buying calls or puts.

opening range *See* range.

opening sale transaction The act of entering the options market by selling calls or puts.

open market operations The buying and selling of securities (primarily government or agency debt) by the Federal Open Market Committee for increasing or decreasing the level of bank reserves to effect control of the money supply.

open order *See* good till canceled order.

operating expense Any production or leasehold expense of an oil and gas program incurred in the operation of a producing lease, including district expense; direct out-of-pocket expenses for labor, materials and supplies; shares of taxes and transportation charges not borne by overriding royalty interests; and, for other programs, the day-to-day expenses involved in operating the business for a profit.

operating ratio The ratio of operating expenses to net sales, the complement to the profit margin.

operator A person designated to supervise and manage the exploration, drilling, mining, production and leasehold operations of an oil and gas or mining program or a portion of such a program.

option The right to buy (or sell) a specified amount of a security (stocks, bonds, futures contracts, etc.) at a specified price within a specified time. An option represents a right acquired by the purchaser, but it is an obligation only on the part of the option seller.

option agreement The agreement a customer must sign within 15 days of being approved for options trading. In it the client agrees to abide by the rules of the listed options exchanges and not to exceed the exchanges' position or exercise limits.

Options Clearing Corporation (OCC) The organization through which the various options exchanges clear their trades. The OCC supervises the listing of new options and is considered the issuer of standardized options.

option term adjustment An automatic adjustment that is made to the terms of an option on the ex-dividend date when a stock pays a cash dividend (if over the counter) or a stock dividend or if there is a stock split.

order department The department within a brokerage firm responsible for transmitting an order to the proper market for execution. (*Syn.* order room, wire room)

order memorandum The paper form completed by a registered rep that contains the customer's instructions regarding the placement of an order. The order memorandum contains such information as the customer's name and account number, a description of the security, the type of transaction (buy, sell, sell short, etc.) and any special instructions (such as time or price limits). (*Syn.* order memo, order ticket)

order room *See* order department.

order ticket *See* order memorandum.

ordinary income Any income or gain that is not capital gain.

organization and offering expense Any expense that is incurred in preparing a direct participation program for registration and subsequently offering and distributing it to the public, including sales commissions paid to broker-dealers in connection with the distribution of the program.

original issue discount (OID) A bond issued at a discount from face value at maturity. The bond may or may not pay interest, and the discount is taxed as if accrued annually as ordinary income. (*Syn.* stripped bonds)

ORS *See* Chicago Board Options Exchange ORS.

OS *See* official statement.

OSJ *See* office of supervisory jurisdiction.

OTC *See* over the counter.

OTC Bulletin Board An electronic quotation system for non-Nasdaq securities; a computerized *Pink Sheet* for non-Nasdaq stock.

OTC option A put or call option that is not listed on an options exchange. All terms of the contract are negotiated between buyer and seller. *See also* listed option.

OTS *See* Office of Thrift Supervision.

out-of-the-money A term referring to an option that has no intrinsic value (e.g., a put option in which the stock is selling above the exercise price or a call option in which the stock is selling below the exercise price). *See also* at-the-money, in-the-money, intrinsic value.

outstanding stock Issued stock minus treasury stock (stock reacquired by the issuing corporation); stock that is in the hands of the public.

overbought A technical analyst's opinion that more and stronger buying has occurred in a market than the market fundamentals would justify.

overlapping debt A condition resulting when property in a municipality is subject to multiple taxing authorities or tax districts, each having tax collection powers and recourse to the residents of that municipality.

overriding royalty interest An interest in the production of an oil and gas well, carved out of the working interest without liability for any costs of extraction; a form of sharing arrangement in an oil and gas direct participation program paid to someone (generally the sponsor) other than the mineral rights owner.

oversold A technical analyst's opinion that more and stronger selling has occurred in a market than the market fundamentals would justify.

over the counter (OTC) 1) A security that is not listed or traded on a recognized exchange. 2) The non-exchange market for securities.

Both listed and unlisted (OTC) securities as well as municipal and U.S. government securities are traded in the OTC market. OTC trading takes place over computer and telephone networks that link brokers and dealers around the world.

overtrading *See* churning.

owners' equity (*Syn.* shareholders' equity)

PACE *See* Philadelphia Stock Exchange PACE.

Pacific Stock Exchange (PSE) SCOREX The PSE uses the Securities Communication, Order Routing and Execution (SCOREX) system to automatically route and execute orders. SCOREX serves the PSE as an automatic link between the national and regional stock exchanges, and quotes on SCOREX are based on quotes from each exchange trading that particular stock or option.

SCOREX accepts all types of orders, including market, good till canceled and limit orders in both odd and round lots. The specialists at the SCOREX terminals will execute orders up to the 10,099-share SCOREX limit and have the ability to waive that limit for larger orders.

paid-in capital That portion of shareholders' equity that has been generated through issuing stock above its stated value or through assets that have been received as gifts. (*Syn.* paid-in surplus)

paid-in surplus *See* paid-in capital.

parallel shift An up or down movement in a yield curve approximately the same percentage for all maturities.

parity In an auction, *parity* refers to all brokers that have an equal standing in terms of the bidding procedure. The term also refers to the intrinsic value of a convertible security in terms of the common stock into which it can be converted.

partial call The call by an issuer of a portion of a bond issue outstanding prior to the maturity date.

participant Any person who represents stockholders for or against management in a proxy contest; the purchaser or holder of an interest in a direct participation program. *See also* limited partner.

participating preferred stock A type of preferred stock that offers the holder a share of the earnings remaining after all senior securities have been paid. This payment is made in addition to the fixed dividend received. Dividends may be cumulative or noncumulative. *See also* convertible preferred stock, cumulative preferred stock, noncumulative preferred stock, preferred stock.

partnership A form of business organization in which two or more individuals manage the business and are equally and personally liable for its debts.

partnership management fee The fee payable to the general partners for operating the partnership function.

par value An arbitrary dollar value assigned to each share of stock at the time of issuance; the principal amount (face value) of a bond on which interest is calculated. *See also* maturity date. (*Syn.* principal, stated value)

passive income The income from a business in which the individual does not regularly and materially participate, as with a limited partnership income.

passive investor *See* limited partner.

passive loss Any loss from a business in which the individual does not regularly and materially participate, as with limited partnership losses. Passive losses can be used to offset only passive income and not wage or portfolio income.

pass-through certificate A security backed by a pool of conventional (or Department of Veterans Affairs and Farmers Home Administration) mortgages, the principal and interest payment of which are received by the pool and passed through to the certificate holder. Payments may or may not be guaranteed. *See also* Federal National Mortgage Association, Government National Mortgage Association.

pattern A repetitive series of price movements on a chart used by a technical analyst to predict future movements of the market.

payment date The day on which a declared dividend is paid.

PE *See* price-earnings ratio.

pegging The act of effecting transactions in a security for fixing or stabilizing the price of the security above the established offering price. (*Syn.* fixing)

penalty plan *See* contractual plan.

PE ratio *See* price-earnings ratio.

percentage depletion A method of depletion whereby a statutory percentage of gross income from the sale of a mineral resource is a deductible expense. Percentage depletion is available to small producers only and not to purchasers of producing interests.

periodic payment plan A mutual fund sales contract in which the customer commits to buying shares in the fund on a monthly basis over a long term (10 or 20 years).

person An individual, a corporation, a partnership, an association, a fund, a joint stock company, an unincorporated organization, a trust in which the interests of the beneficiaries are evidenced by a security, a government or a political subdivision of a government.

PHA *See* Public Housing Authority bond.

Philadelphia plan A type of financing for railroad equipment trust obligations that involves a vendor delivering equipment to a trustee. The vendor receives equipment trust certificates that are sold to investors. The railroad leases the equipment and pays a periodic rental fee, which covers interest installments and principal when due. When all rental payments are made, the title is transferred to the railroad.

Philadelphia Stock Exchange (PHLX) PACE The PHLX developed the PHLX Automated Communication and Execution (PACE) system in 1975 to automatically route and execute orders. PACE is designed to handle market and limit orders of up to 3,099 shares for over 1,100 actively traded stocks. The PACE system can provide electronic executions within approximately 15 seconds of order receipt and can get confirmations back to the originating broker-dealer in only a few seconds more.

PHLX An acronym for the Philadelphia Stock Exchange.

Pink Sheets The daily quotation sheets that publish the interdealer wholesale quotes for over-the-counter stocks.

placement ratio A ratio compiled by *The Bond Buyer* indicating the number of new municipal issues that have sold within the last week.

plus tick An execution price above the previous sale. *See also* minus tick, plus tick rule. (*Syn.* up tick)

plus tick rule The Securities and Exchange Commission regulation governing the market price at which a short sale may be made. No short sale may be executed at a price below the price of the last sale. *See also* minus tick, zero-plus tick. (*Syn.* up tick rule)

point *See* basis point.

policy processing day The day on which charges authorized in the policy are deducted from the policy's cash value.

POP An acronym for public offering price. *See also* offering price.

portfolio income The income from interest, dividends and other nonbusiness investments.

possession (of securities) *See* control (of securities).

position The amount of a security (shares, contracts, bonds, etc.) either owned (a long position) or owed (a short position) by an individual. A dealer will also take positions in specific securities to maintain an inventory to facilitate trading.

position limit The limitation established by the listed options exchanges that prohibits an investor from having a position of more than a specific number of contracts on the same side of the market.

position trading 1) Occurs when a dealer acquires or sells an inventory in a security. *See also* dealer, principal, make a market. 2) Occurs when a commodities speculator buys or sells positions in the futures markets as a means of speculating on long-term price movements. *See also* scalper, spreader.

precedence In an auction, the ranking of bids and offers according to size (the number of shares in a bid or an offer).

preemptive right The legal right of stockholders to purchase new stock in proportion to their holdings before the new stock is offered to the public.

preferred dividend coverage A financial ratio used to determine the margin of safety with which the fixed dividend requirements are covered for a preferred stockholder, computed by dividing preferred dividends by net income.

preferred stock An equity security that represents ownership in a corporation. Preferred stock has a fixed dividend, with dividend and asset preference over common stock, and it generally carries no voting rights.

preliminary prospectus Any prospectus that is distributed during the cooling-off period and includes the essential facts about the forthcoming offering except for the underwriting spread, final public offering price and date the shares will be delivered. (*Syn.* red herring)

premium The market price of an option; the cash price that the option buyer pays to the option writer; the price paid for a security over and above its face amount. Also, the selling price of an option.

premium bond A bond that sells above par (above 100% of $1,000); that is, the purchase price of the bond is greater than the par value (principal amount). *See also* par value; principal.

prepaid charge plan *See* contractual plan.

prerefunding *See* advance refunding.

presale order An order communicated to the syndicate manager prior to formulation of the bid. If the syndicate wins the bid, the order is already considered sold. A presale order normally has the highest priority in a municipal underwriting.

price-earnings ratio (PE) The ratio of the current market value of the stock divided by the annual earnings per share.

price spread A spread involving the purchase and sale of two options on the same stock with the same expiration date but with different exercise prices. (*Syn.* money spread, vertical spread)

primary distribution *See* primary offering.

primary earnings per share The earnings per share if all rights, stock options and warrants have been converted (if their total conversion will cause at least a 3% increase in the number of shares outstanding). (*Syn.* earnings per share fully diluted)

primary offering An offering in which the proceeds of the underwriting (either equity or debt) go to the issuing corporation or municipality. A corporation increases its capitalization by selling stock (either a new issue or a previously authorized but unissued stock). It may do this at any time and in any amount, provided the total stock outstanding never exceeds the amount authorized in the corporation's bylaws. A municipality raises money by issuing debt. (*Syn.* primary distribution)

prime rate The interest rate that commercial banks charge their prime or most creditworthy customers (generally large corporations).

principal 1) A person who positions trades in the secondary or primary market, including sole proprietors, officers, directors or partners of a company and managers of offices of supervision; also, an investment banker who assumes risk by actually buying securities from the issuer and reselling them. (*Syn.* dealer). 2) An arbitrary dollar value assigned to each share of stock at the time of issuance; the principal amount (face value) of a bond on which interest is calculated. *See also* maturity date. (*Syn.* par value, stated value)

principal transaction A transaction in which a broker-dealer or bank dealer buys stocks or bonds from customers and takes them into its own inventory. It then sells stocks or bonds to customers from its inventory.

priority In an auction, the first person to bid or offer at a given price establishes priority. Only one person can have priority.

prior preferred stock A class of preferred stock that has prior claim over other preferred stock in receipt of dividends, as well as in distribution of assets in the event of liquidation. *See also* preferred stock.

private placement An offering that complies with Regulation D (Rule 505 and Rule 506); generally speaking, the offer of an unregistered security to no more than 35 nonaccredited investors or to an unlimited number of accredited investors. *See also* Regulation D.

productive well Any well that is not a dry hole. As used here, *production* refers to the commercial marketing of oil or gas produced as a result of the recovery of a mineral resource.

profitability The ability of a company to generate a level of income and gain in excess of expense.

profitability ratio A ratio describing profit or income as a percent or multiple of sales.

profit after taxes *See* net income to net sales.

profit margin *See* margin of profit.

profit ratio *See* net income to net sales.

program A limited or general partnership, a joint venture, an unincorporated association or a similar organization other than a corporation formed and operated for the primary purpose of investment in, operation of, or gain from an interest in real property, oil and gas property, or another suitable property.

program interest The limited partnership unit or some other indication of ownership in a direct participation program.

program management fee A fee paid to the sponsor or some other person(s) for managing and administering the program.

progressive tax A tax that takes a larger percentage of the income of high-income people (e.g., the graduated income tax). *See also* regressive tax.

project note A short-term debt instrument issued in anticipation of a later issuance of Public Housing Authority bonds.

property management fee The fee paid to a sponsor or some other person for day-to-day property management services in connection with a real estate program's real property project.

proprietorship A business organization in which a single owner has total control over the business and makes all management decisions.

prospect An area in which a partnership intends to acquire an oil or gas interest or property.

prospectus The legal document that must be given to every investor who purchases registered securities in an offering. It describes the details of the company and the particular offering. (*Syn.* final prospectus)

Prospectus Act Another name for the Securities Act of 1933.

proxy In order to vote on corporate matters, a stockholder must attend the annual meeting. If the stockholder is unable to attend, the stockholder may still vote by proxy. A proxy is given in writing, authorizing another to vote for the stockholder according to the stockholder's instructions.

prudent man rule A legal maxim that restricts discretion in a client's account to investments in only those securities that a reasonably prudent person seeking reasonable income and preservation of capital might buy.

PSE An acronym for the Pacific Stock Exchange.

Public Housing Authority bond (PHA) A bond issued by the Public Housing Authority. (*Syn.* Housing Authority bond)

public offering *See* initial public offering.

public offering price (POP) The price of new shares that is established in the issuing corporation's prospectus; also, the price to investors for mutual fund shares.

purchase and sales department The department within a brokerage firm that computes commissions and taxes and sends confirmations to clients. *See also* trade confirmation.

purchasing power risk The risk that due to inflation a certain amount of money will not purchase as much in the future as it does today. (*Syn.* inflation risk)

put 1) An option contract that gives the owner the right to sell a specified number of shares of stock at a specified price within a specified time. 2) The act of exercising a put option.

put bond A bond requiring the issuer to purchase the bond at the bondholder's discretion, normally at a prescribed time. (*Syn.* tender bond)

put buyer An investor who pays a premium for an option contract and has, for a specified time, the right to sell the underlying security at a specified price.

put spread An investment in which an investor purchases one put on a particular stock and sells another put on the same stock but with a different expiration date, exercise price or both.

put writer An investor who receives a premium and takes on, for a specified time, the obligation to buy the underlying security at a specified price at the put buyer's discretion.

qualified block positioner A dealer that enters into block purchases or sales with customers and that meets all of its minimum net capital requirements.

qualified independent appraiser A person, including a qualified independent petroleum engineer and a qualified independent real estate appraiser, who holds himself out as an appraiser of a particular type of property and who:

    A. is licensed or registered to practice his profession with the appropriate professional or regulatory body, if any, within the state of his business activity, if such is required, and who can demonstrate himself to be qualified to appraise the type of property in respect to which he holds himself out; and

    B. is totally independent in that:

- he is informed of the purpose for which the appraisal is to be used and that it is to be relied upon for the public program;
- he has relied upon sufficient competent evidence of value and has based the appraisal on his own experience and judgment;
- he has no present interest or contemplated future interest, either legal or beneficial, in the property appraised;
- he has no interest in any proposed transaction involving the property or in the parties to such transaction;
- his employment and compensation are not contingent on any value found by him or on anything other than the delivery of his report for a predetermined fee; and
- he is not an affiliate of a sponsor.

qualified legal opinion A conditional opinion of the legality or tax-exempt status of a municipal bond. *See also* legal opinion of counsel.

qualified OTC market maker A dealer that makes a market in an over-the-counter (OTC) margin security and that meets minimum net capital requirements.

qualified retirement plan A retirement plan that qualifies under sections 401 and 501 of the Internal Revenue Code. *See also* individual retirement account, Keogh plan. (*Syn.* approved plan)

qualified third-market maker A dealer that makes a market in an exchange-listed stock and that meets minimum net capital requirements.

quality adjustment The amount a settlement price is adjusted on a futures transaction when the delivered commodity differs from that specified in the original contract.

quality allowance *See* allowance.

quarterly securities count Every broker-dealer must conduct a count of securities in its control, verify securities in transit, compare counts with its securities records and record all unresolved securities differences at least quarterly.

quick ratio A test of a company's liquidity, computed by dividing current assets (cash, cash equivalents and receivables) by current liabilities.

quotation The bid and ask of a particular security.

quote (bond) Like stock quotes, bond prices are quoted in the financial press and most daily newspapers. Corporate bonds are quoted in 1/8ths. Government bonds are quoted in 1/32nds. The quotes for corporate and government bonds are percentages of the bonds' face value ($1,000). Municipal bonds may be quoted on a dollar basis or on a yield to maturity.

quote (stock) Many stocks traded are quoted in the financial press and most daily newspapers. A stock is quoted in points, with each point equal to $1. The price of the stock is further broken down into 1/8ths of a point, where 1/8th equals 12.5 cents.

RAES *See* Chicago Board Options Exchange RAES.

RAN *See* revenue anticipation note.

range A security's low price and high price for a particular trading period (e.g., close of the day's trading, opening of the day's trading, day, month, year). (*Syn.* opening range)

rate covenant A revenue coverage minimum set in a trust indenture for payment of maintenance, debt service and reserve requirements to establish safety margins on the issue.

rating Bonds are rated for safety by various organizations such as Standard & Poor's and Moody's. These firms rate the companies and municipalities issuing bonds according to their ability to repay and make interest payments. Ratings range from AAA or Aaa (the highest) to C or D (representing a company in default).

rating service A company such as Moody's or Standard & Poor's that rates various debt and preferred stock issues for safety of payment of principal, interest or dividends. The issuing company or municipality pays a fee for the rating. *See also* rating.

ratio writing An option position in which the investor writes more than one call option for every 100 shares of underlying stock (or for every call option) that she owns.

R coefficient A statistical measure of how closely the movements of a security's price track with the movements of the market.

real estate investment trust (REIT) An investment trust that operates through the pooled capital of many investors who buy its shares. Investments are in direct ownership of either income property or mortgage loans.

real estate program A direct participation program that has as its primary purpose the investment in or operation of real property for a gain.

realized gain The amount of gain the taxpayer actually has on the sale or other disposition of property.

reallowance *See* concession.

recapitalization The act of converting a short-term liability into a long-term liability.

recapture The treatment as ordinary income of gain that should otherwise be treated as capital gain on the sale or other disposition of a capital asset because of previous deductions from ordinary income that are now treated as being excessive or otherwise not allowed.

reciprocal immunity *See* mutual exclusion doctrine.

reclamation The right of a party to a securities transaction to recover any loss incurred due to bad delivery or another irregularity in the settlement process.

record date The date established by the issuing corporation that determines which stockholders are entitled to receive dividends or rights distributions.

recourse financing Financing in which the taxpayer is personally liable for the debt.

redemption The return of an investor's interest (net asset value) in a mutual fund. By law, redemption must occur within seven days of receiving instruction from the investor to sell shares in the fund.

redemption notice A notice that a company or municipality is redeeming (or calling) a certain issue of bonds.

red herring *See* preliminary prospectus.

refinancing Issuing equity, the proceeds of which are used to retire debt.

refunding A method of retiring an outstanding bond issue using the money from the sale of a new offering. This may occur before maturity (advance refunding) or at maturity (refunding).

regional fund *See* specialized fund.

registered as to principal only A bond on which the name of the owner is printed but that has unregistered coupons payable to the bearer.

registered bond A bond on which the name of the owner appears on the certificate.

registered options principal (ROP) The officer or partner of a brokerage firm who approves in writing certain accounts for certain types of options transactions.

registered principal Anyone associated with a member who manages or supervises the member's investment banking or securities business must be registered as a principal with the NASD. This includes those people involved in training associated persons and in soliciting business. Unless the member firm is a sole proprietorship, there must be at least two registered principals per firm, one of whom must be registered as a General Securities Principal (Series 24).

In addition to having at least one general principal, each member must have at least one Financial and Operations Principal (FinOp—Series 27). If the member does options business with the public, there must be at least one Registered Options Principal (ROP—Series 4).

registered representative (RR) For NASD registration and exam and licensing purposes, the category of *registered representative* includes all associated persons engaged in the investment banking and securities business. This includes:
- assistant officers (who are not principals);
- individuals who supervise, solicit or conduct business in securities; and
- individuals who train people to supervise, solicit or conduct business in securities.

Anyone who is not a principal and not engaged in clerical or brokerage administration is subject to registration and exam licensing as a registered representative—except for foreign associates. (*Syn.* account executive, stockbroker)

registered secondary distribution *See* secondary distribution.

registered trader A member of an exchange who trades primarily for a personal account and at personal risk.

registrar An independent organization or part of a corporation charged with the responsibility of seeing that the corporation does not have more stock outstanding than is accounted for on the corporation's books.

registration by coordination A security is eligible for blue sky registration by coordination in a state if the issuer has filed for registration of that security under the Securities Act of 1933 and files duplicates of the registration documents with the state administrator. The state registration becomes effective at the same time the federal registration statement becomes effective.

registration by notification (filing) A security is eligible for blue sky registration by notification (also known as registration by filing) in a state if the issuer has filed for registration of that security under the Securities Act of 1933, meets minimum net worth and other requirements, and notifies the state of this eligibility by filing certain documents with the state administrator. The state registration becomes effective at the same time the federal registration statement becomes effective.

registration by qualification Any security is eligible for blue sky registration by qualification in a state if the issuer files registration documents for that security with the state administrator, meeting minimum net worth, disclosure and other requirements, and filing appropriate registration fees. The state registration becomes effective when the administrator so orders.

registration statement Before nonexempt securities can be offered to the public, they require registration under the Securities Act of 1933. The registration statement must disclose all pertinent information concerning the issuer and the offering. This statement is submitted to the SEC in accordance with the requirements of the 1933 act.

regressive tax A tax that takes a larger percentage of the income of low-income people (e.g., gasoline and cigarette taxes). *See also* progressive tax.

Reg T call *See* margin call.

regular way A settlement contract that calls for delivery and payment on the fifth business day following the date of trade. This is the usual type of settlement. For government securities, regular way is the next business day.

regulated investment company An investment company granted special status by Subchapter M of the Internal Revenue Code allowing the flow-through of tax consequences on a distribution to shareholders. If 90% of income is passed through to shareholders, the company is not subject to tax on the earnings.

Regulation A The securities regulation that exempts small public offerings from registration (those valued at no more than $5 million worth of securities offered during a twelve-month period).

Regulation D The securities regulation that exempts from registration certain small offerings and sales to specified individuals during a twelve-month period. *See also* private placement.

Regulation G The Federal Reserve Board regulation governing the extension of credit by persons other than banks, brokers or dealers. *See also* Regulation T, Regulation U.

Regulation Q The Federal Reserve Board regulation that establishes how much interest banks may pay on savings accounts. Reg Q was phased out in 1986.

Regulation T The Federal Reserve Board regulation governing the credit that brokerage firms and dealers may extend to clients for the purchase of securities. Regulation T also governs cash accounts.

Regulation T excess *See* excess equity.

Regulation U The Federal Reserve Board regulation governing loans by banks for the purchase of securities. Call loans are exempt from Reg U. *See also* broker's loan, call loan, time loan.

reinstatement privilege A term referring to the fund allowing an investor the privilege of withdrawing the money from the account and redepositing the money without paying a second sales charge.

reinvested earnings *See* retained earnings.

reinvestment For mutual funds, distributions (dividends and gains) are reinvested in the fund to purchase additional shares instead of receiving distributions in cash.

REIT *See* real estate investment trust.

rejection The right of a broker-dealer to refuse to accept securities delivered in completion of a trade because they do not meet the requirements of good delivery (e.g., missing signature, missing the coupons, mutilated, etc.).

reoffering scale The prices or yields at which municipal securities are sold to the public by the underwriters of a municipal offering.

repo *See* repurchase agreement.

repurchase agreement A sale and an attendant agreement to repurchase the securities sold at a higher price on an agreed upon future date. The difference between the sale price and the repurchase price represents the interest earned by the investor. In a repurchase agreement, the seller initiates the deal. Repos are commonly used by government securities dealers as a means of raising capital, typically to finance an inventory of securities. Repos are considered money-market instruments. *See also* reverse repurchase agreement. (*Syn.* repo)

reserves The money that a bank has in its vault or on deposit with the Federal Reserve Bank. A bank is required to maintain a certain percentage of reserves as set by the Fed.

resistance A term used in technical analysis to describe the top of a stock's trading range.

restricted account A margin account in which the equity is less than the Regulation T initial requirement. *See also* equity, initial margin requirements, margin account.

restricted security An unregistered nonexempt security acquired either directly or indirectly from the issuer or an affiliate of the issuer in a transaction that does not involve a public offering. *See also* holding period.

retail transaction A trade in which a client buys an over-the-counter stock from or through a broker-dealer or sells one to or through a broker-dealer. *See also* wholesale transaction.

retained earnings The amount of net income that remains after all dividends have been paid to preferred and common stockholders. (*Syn.* earned surplus, reinvested earnings)

retained earnings ratio The ratio of retained earnings to net income available for common stock. It is the complement of the dividend payout ratio. *See also* dividend payout ratio.

retention The securities that an underwriter sells directly to its own clients. The securities that it underwrites but does not retain are turned back to the manager to be sold by another firm.

retention requirement The proportion of sale proceeds that must be retained to reduce the debit balance if securities are sold from a restricted margin account. The retention requirement is 50%. *See also* restricted account.

retiring bonds The act of calling bonds by a notice in the newspaper, by purchasing bonds in the open market or by repaying bondholders the principal amount at maturity.

return on sales *See* net income to net sales.

revenue anticipation note (RAN) A municipal note issued in anticipation of revenue to be received.

revenue bond A bond whose interest and principal are payable only from specific earnings of an income-producing (revenue-producing) enterprise. *See also* municipal bond.

reverse repurchase agreement A purchase and an attendant agreement to resell the securities sold at a higher price on an agreed-upon future date. The difference between the purchase price and the sale price represents the interest earned by the investor. In a reverse repurchase agreement, the purchaser initiates the deal. *See also* repurchase agreement. (*Syn.* repo)

reversionary interest An interest in a program the benefits of which accrue in the future upon the occurrence of some event.

right A security representing a stockholder's right to purchase new securities in proportion to the number of shares already owned. Rights, also known as stock rights, are stock purchase options issued to existing stockholders only. The right is an option to purchase a company's new issue of stock at a predetermined price (normally for less than the stock's current market price). The right is issued for a short period of time, normally for 30 days, with the option expiring after that time. *See also* preemptive right, subscription right. (*Syn.* subscription right certificate)

right of accumulation The right to apply reduced sales loads (breakpoints) based on the dollar position held by the investor in a mutual fund.

rights offering An offering that gives each stockholder an opportunity to maintain a proportionate ownership in the company before the shares are offered to the public.

riskless and simultaneous transaction *See* riskless transaction.

riskless transaction An over-the-counter transaction in which a brokerage firm buys or sells a security to fill an order previously received from a client for the same security. Although the firm is technically acting as a principal in this trade, the transaction is relatively riskless because the purchase and sale are consummated almost simultaneously. (*Syn.* riskless and simultaneous transaction)

rolling forward (*Syn.* switching)

ROP *See* registered options principal.

royalty interest The right of a mineral rights owner to receive a share in the production of the resource, if and when production begins. The royalty interest retained is free from costs of production.

RR *See* registered representative.

Rule 144 A rule that covers the sale of two kinds of securities: control securities and restricted securities. Under Rule 144, persons who hold control or restricted securities can sell them only in limited quantities. All sales of restricted stock by control persons must be reported to the SEC by the filing of Form 144—Notice of Proposed Sale of Securities. *See also* control security, restricted security.

Rule 145 Rule 145 requires that whenever an offer is made to the stockholders of a publicly owned corporation, soliciting their vote or consent to a plan for reorganizing the company, full disclosure of all material facts must be made in a prospectus, which must be in the hands of the stockholders before the announced voting date.

Rule 147 Rule 147 provides exemption from the registration statement and prospectus requirements of the 1933 act for securities offered and sold exclusively intrastate.

Rule 15c2-1 SEC 15c2-1 governs the safekeeping of securities in customer margin accounts. Broker-dealers are prohibited from using customer securities in excess of customer aggregate indebtedness as collateral to secure loans (rehypothecation) without the express written permission of the customer. Broker-dealers are also prohibited from commingling customer securities without the customers' written permission.

Rule 15c3-1 SEC 15c3-1 governs the net capital requirements of broker-dealers. Net capital requirements differ for different types of broker-dealers and for different amounts of aggregate indebtedness.

Rule 15c3-2 SEC 15c3-2 requires broker-dealers to inform customers of their free credit balances at least quarterly.

Rule 15c3-3 SEC 15c3-3 is known as the *customer protection rule* and regulates the location, segregation and handling of customer funds and securities. Under 15c3-3, broker-dealers must segregate all customer fully paid and excess margin securities in a special reserve bank account for the exclusive benefit of customers.

Rule 405 The NYSE rule stating that each member organization must exercise due diligence to learn the essential facts about every customer; also known as the *know your customer rule*.

Rule 406 The NYSE rule stating that no member organization may carry an account designated by a number or symbol unless the customer has signed a written statement attesting to ownership of the account and the statement is on file with the member organization.

Rule 407 The NYSE rule stating that an employee of the NYSE or any of its members and certain non-member organizations must have written permission from their employers before opening either cash or margin accounts but that employee banks, trust companies and insurance companies need their employers' permission only when opening margin accounts.

Rule 409 The NYSE rule stating that a customer's written instructions and the written approval of a member or an allied member are necessary before a customer's mail can be held.

Rule 504 A private placement offering of less than $1,000,000 during any twelve-month period may qualify for registration under Rule 504. Rule 504 does not restrict the number of accredited or non-accredited purchasers.

Rule 505 A private placement offering of $1,000,000 to $5,000,000 during any twelve-month period may qualify for registration under Rule 505. Rule 505 restricts the number of non-accredited purchasers to 35; there is no restriction on accredited purchasers.

Rule 506 A private placement offering of more than $5,000,000 may qualify for registration under Rule 506. Rule 506 restricts the number of non-accredited purchasers to 35; there is no restriction on accredited purchasers.

Rules of Fair Practice The NASD rules that detail how member firms deal with the public.

sale leaseback A method of raising cash whereby a person sells property to a buyer and leases it back from him.

sales charge With mutual funds, the amount added to the net asset value (NAV) of mutual fund shares. The investor will pay the NAV and the sales charge, which equal the offering price. *See also* mutual fund, net asset value, offering price. (*Syn.* sales load)

sales literature Any written material used to help sell a product and that is distributed by the firm in a controlled manner. *See also* advertising, market letter.

sales load *See* sales charge.

satellite office A member location not identified as either an office of supervisory jurisdiction or a branch office is considered a satellite office (in general, a location not held out to the public as a place of business for the member).

scale Important data concerning each of the scheduled maturities in a new serial bond issue, including the number of bonds, date, maturity, coupon rate and offering price.

scalper A commodities trader who buys and sells many commodities contracts during a single day in the anticipation of profiting from small price fluctuations. Scalpers rarely carry positions from one day to the next, and their buying and selling activity contributes greatly to the liquidity of the commodities markets. *See also* position trading, spreader.

scheduled premium policy Any variable life insurance policy under which both the amount and the timing of premium payments are fixed by the insurer.

Schedule 13D A form that must be filed by an individual (or individuals acting in concert) after acquiring beneficial ownership of 5% or more of any nonexempt equity security. It must be sent within ten business days to the: issuing company, exchange where the stock is trading and the SEC.

Schedule 13e-3 A form that must be filed by a public company whenever it engages in a strategy to take the company private (e.g., when a transaction would decrease the number of stockholders to such a point that the company would no longer be required to file reports with the SEC [under 300 stockholders], a schedule 13e-3 would need to be filed). The transaction could also be a merger, tender offer or reverse stock split. The results of such a transaction must be reported promptly, but no later than ten days after the transaction. The schedule would seek disclosure of all the terms and the fairness of the transaction to unaffiliated stockholders.

Schedule 13e-4 A form also known as an issuer tender offer statement that must be filed by public companies when they make tender offers for their own securities. Schedule 13e-4 reporting must occur no later than ten days after the termination of the tender.

Schedule 13g An abbreviated 13D form that is used principally by broker-dealers, banks and insurance companies only if they acquire a 5% position in the normal course of business and not for the purpose of changing or influencing control of the companies. This schedule must be filed 45 days after the first calendar year end when the broker-dealer or bank becomes subject to the requirement.

SCOREX *See* Pacific Stock Exchange SCOREX.

SEC *See* Securities and Exchange Commission.

secondary distribution A distribution with a prospectus that involves securities owned by major stockholders (typically founders or principal owners of a corporation). In a secondary distribution, sale proceeds go to the sellers of the stock, not to the issuer. (*Syn.* registered secondary distributor)

secondary offering An offering in which one or more major stockholders in a company are selling all or a major portion of their holdings. The underwriting proceeds are paid to the stockholders, rather than to the corporation itself. Typically secondary offerings occur in situations where the founder of a business and perhaps some of the original financial backers determine that there is more to be gained by going public than by staying private. This offering does not increase the number of shares of stock outstanding. Also, a secondary offering is a block trading procedure for very large blocks that is executed off the floor of an exchange after the market closes. *See also* secondary distribution.

secured bond A bond backed by some form of collateral. In the event the company defaults on payment, the bondholders may attach the collateral backing the bond.

Securities Act of 1933 The federal legislation requiring the full and fair disclosure of all material information about the issuance of new securities.

Securities and Exchange Commission (SEC) The commission created by Congress to protect investors. The Commission enforces the Securities Act of 1933, the Securities Exchange Act of 1934, the Trust Indenture Act of 1939, the Investment Company Act of 1940, the Investment Advisers Act of 1940 and others.

Securities Exchange Act of 1934 The federal legislation establishing the Securities and Exchange Commission. Its purpose is to provide regulation of securities exchanges and over-the-counter markets and to protect investors from unfair and inequitable practices.

Securities Industry Association (SIA) The nonprofit organization that represents the collective business interests of its over 600 leading securities firm members headquartered throughout North America. SIA activities include government relations, industry research and educational and informational services for its members.

Securities Investor Protection Corporation (SIPC) A nonprofit membership corporation created by an act of Congress to protect clients of brokerage firms that are forced into bankruptcy. Membership is composed of all brokers and dealers registered under the Securities Exchange Act of 1934, all members of national securities exchanges and most NASD members. SIPC provides customers of these firms up to $500,000 coverage for their cash and securities held by the firms (although coverage of cash is limited to $100,000).

security Under the act of 1934, any note, stock, bond, investment contract, debenture, certificate of interest in profit-sharing or partnership agreement, certificate of deposit, collateral trust certificate, preorganization certificate, option on a security or other instrument of investment commonly known as a security.

Also categorized as "securities" are interests in the following: oil and gas drilling programs, real estate condominiums and cooperatives, farmland or animals, commodity option contracts, whiskey warehouse receipts, multilevel distributorship arrangements, and merchandising marketing programs.

The accurate determination of what is a security is crucial to registered representatives conducting their activities in compliance with state securities laws. In general, a security can be defined as any piece of securitized paper that can be traded for value, except an insurance policy or a fixed annuity. As established by the federal courts, the basic test for determining whether a specific investment comes within the definition of a "security" is whether the person invests his money in a common enterprise and is led to expect profits from the managerial efforts of the promoter or a third party.

security arbitrage The simultaneous purchase and sale of related or convertible securities to take advantage of a price disparity between the two securities. *See also* arbitrage.

security cage *See* cashiering department.

segregation The separation of client-owned securities and those securities owned by the brokerage firm. *See also* commingling.

self-regulatory organization (SRO) Each SRO is accountable to the SEC for the enforcement of federal securities laws, as well as the supervision of securities practices, within an assigned field of jurisdiction. Eight SROs function under the oversight of the Commission. Selected jurisdictions include:

- New York Stock Exchange (NYSE). All matters related to trading in NYSE-listed securities and the conduct of NYSE member firms and associated persons.
- National Association of Securities Dealers (NASD). All matters related to investment banking (securities underwriting) and trading in the over-the-counter market and the conduct of NASD member firms and associated persons.
- Municipal Securities Rulemaking Board (MSRB). All matters related to the underwriting and trading of state and municipal securities.
- Chicago Board Options Exchange (CBOE). All matters related to the writing and trading of standardized options and related contracts listed on that exchange.

sell The term "sale" or "sell" refers to every contract to sell a security or interest in a security. This definition is broad and specifically includes the following:
- Any security given or delivered with or as a bonus for any purchase of securities is considered to have been offered and sold for value.
- A gift of assessable stock is considered to involve an offer and sale.
- Every sale or offer of a warrant or right to purchase or subscribe to another security is considered to include an offer of the other security.

The term "sale" or "sell" does not include a bona fide pledge or loan, or a stock dividend if nothing of value is given by the stockholders for the dividend.

seller *See* writer.

seller's option A settlement contract that calls for delivery and payment according to the number of days specified by the seller. Settlement occurs from six business days to the expiration of the option.

selling a hedge The sale of futures options as a means of protecting against a decrease in commodities prices in the future. *See also* buying a hedge, long hedge, short hedge.

selling concession The portion of an underwriting spread that is paid to a selling group member on the securities it sells to the public during an offering.

selling dividends The illegal practice of inducing clients to buy mutual fund shares by implying that a pending distribution will benefit them; also, the act of combining dividend and gains distributions in the calculation of current yield.

selling group Brokerage firms that sell securities in an offering but that are not members of the underwriting syndicate.

sell-out A procedure that occurs when a buyer fails to accept delivery of securities as stipulated in a contract. The seller can close the contract by selling the securities at the best available price and holding the buyer liable for the price of the securities and the resulting transaction costs.

senior lien debt A bond issue sharing the same collateral backing as other issues but having a prior claim to the collateral in the event of default.

separate account With a variable annuity contract, the account in which the insurance company invests funds paid by contract holders. The funds are kept separate from the company's general investment account. *See also* accumulation unit, annuity.

separately identifiable department or division Under Municipal Securities Rulemaking Board (MSRB) rules, a department or division under the direct supervision of an officer of the bank. If a bank has such a department or division that engages in the business of buying or selling municipal securities, it is classified as a municipal securities dealer and must comply with MSRB regulations.

serial bond A bond issued under a type of maturity schedule in which parts of an outstanding issue of bonds mature at intervals until the issue's final maturity date. Most municipal bonds are serial bonds. *See also* series bond. (*Syn.* serial bond)

series Options of the same class that have the same exercise price and the same expiration date. *See also* class, type.

Series 6 The Series 6 is the Investment Company/Variable Contract Products Limited Representative license. This license entitles the representative to sell mutual funds and variable annuities and is used by many firms selling primarily insurance-related products. It can serve as the prerequisite for the Series 26.

Series 7 A Series 7 General Securities Registered Representative license allows a registered rep to sell all types of securities products, with the exception of commodities futures (which requires a Series 3). This is the most comprehensive of the NASD representative licenses available and serves as a prerequisite for most of the NASD's principals examinations.

Series 11 The Series 11 registration (Assistant Representative—Order Processing) allows a registered sales assistant to take unsolicited orders, enter order tickets, update client information, fill out client new account forms and provide to customers quotes and other pro forma information relating to securities. This registration does not permit the assistant rep to determine suitability, make recommendations of transactions or provide advice to customers.

A broker-dealer may only compensate assistant representatives—order processing on a salary or hourly wage basis. Compensation, including bonuses and commissions, may not be related to the number or size of the transactions effected for customers.

Series 22 The Series 22 Direct Participation Programs Limited Representative license entitles the representative to sell oil and gas, real estate, motion picture and other types of limited partnerships and is used by many firms selling tax-advantaged limited partnership products. It can serve as a prerequisite for the Series 39.

Series 52 The Series 52 Municipal Securities Representative license entitles the representative to sell municipal and government securities and is used by many firms selling primarily municipal debt products. It can serve as a prerequisite for the Series 53.

Series 62 The Series 62 Corporate Securities Limited Representative license entitles the representative to sell all types of corporate securities but not municipal securities, options, direct participation programs or a limited number of other products. It is used by many firms selling general securities products that want to limit their representatives to corporate securities. The Series 62 can serve as a prerequisite for the Series 24.

series bond A bond issued in a scheduled series of public offerings. Series bonds have the same priority claim against corporate assets. *See also* serial bond.

Series EE bond A nonmarketable U.S. government savings bond issued at a discount from par.

Series HH bond A nonmarketable interest-bearing U.S. government savings bond issued at par.

settlement The completion of a securities trade through the delivery of the security (or commodity) for cash or another consideration.

settlement date The date on which a transaction must be settled (exchange of cash for securities).

shareholders' equity This is calculated by subtracting total liabilities from total assets. (*Syn.* net worth; owners' equity)

share identification An accounting method whereby the shares selected for liquidation are identified in any order.

sharing arrangement A method of determining responsibility for expenses and the right to share in revenues between the sponsor and limited partners.

shelf offering An offering that allows an issuer to register a new issue security without selling the entire issue at once. The issuer can sell limited portions of a registered shelf offering over a two-year period without having to reregister the security or incurring penalties. Shelf offerings provide issuers and their investment bankers with flexibility—money can be raised and expenses incurred only as needed.

short The state of having sold a security, contract or commodity. A sale of 10 September silver contracts would be referred to as *going short,* or shorting, September silver. The speculator would have a *short* position.

short against the box The sale of a security that the seller owns but prefers not to deliver; frequently done in an arbitrage account.

short exempt transaction A short sale in an arbitrage transaction that is exempt from the SEC plus tick rule.

short hedge A short securities or actuals position protected by a long call position. *See also* hedge, long hedge.

short interest theory A technical theory that measures the ratio of short sales to volume in a stock. A high ratio of short interest is considered bullish.

short sale The sale of a security that the seller does not own or any sale consummated by the delivery of a security borrowed by or for the account of the seller.

short straddle The position established by writing a call and a put on the same stock with the same strike price and expiration month. *See also* long straddle, spread.

short-term capital gain The taxable gain on a capital asset that is owned for twelve months or less. *See also* capital gain, capital loss, short-term capital loss.

short-term capital loss The taxable loss on a capital asset that is owned for twelve months or less. *See also* short-term capital gain, capital gain, capital loss.

simplified arbitration Disputes not involving customers can be submitted for resolution under simplified industry arbitration proceedings provided the dollar amount of the claim does not exceed $5,000. Under simplified industry arbitration, an arbitration panel consisting of at least one arbitrator (but not more than three) will review evidence and pleadings from both sides of the dispute and render a decision, usually without need for a hearing. All awards under simplified industry arbitration are made within 30 business days from the date the arbitration panel declares the disputed matter closed.

sinking fund A fund established by a corporation or municipality into which money is regularly deposited so that the corporation or municipality has the funds to redeem its bonds, debentures or preferred stock.

sinking fund call The early redemption of bonds from the proceeds of the sinking fund set up for this purpose. *See also* sinking fund.

SIPC *See* Securities Investor Protection Corporation.

SMA *See* special memorandum account.

Small Order Execution System *See* NASD Small Order Execution System.

SOES *See* NASD Small Order Execution System.

sole proprietorship A form of business organization in which a single owner has total control over her own business and makes all managerial decisions.

solvency The measure of a company's ability both to meet its long-term fixed charges and to have adequate money for long-term expansion and growth.

special arbitrage account A type of margin account for arbitrage transactions. *See also* market arbitrage, security arbitrage.

special assessment bond A revenue bond payable only from assessments on property owners who benefit from the services or improvements provided by the proceeds from the bond issue.

special bid *See* special offering.

special cash account *See* cash account.

specialist block purchase (sale) A block trading procedure for smaller blocks in which the specialist purchases (or sells) the block in a private transaction.

specialized fund A type of mutual fund that tries to achieve its investment objectives by concentrating its investments within a single industry or group of related industries.

special memorandum account (SMA) A notation on a customer's general or margin account. Funds are credited to the SMA on a memo basis, and the SMA is used much like a line of credit with a bank. The SMA preserves the customer's right to use excess equity. (*Syn.* special miscellaneous account)

special miscellaneous account *See* special memorandum account.

special offering A block trading procedure in which a block of stock is offered for sale after a prior announcement on the broad tape. (*Syn.* special bid)

special reserve bank account An account maintained by a broker-dealer for the exclusive use of customers and for the required deposits of customer funds.

special situation fund A type of mutual fund that invests in companies in special situations, such as firms undergoing reorganization or firms considered to be takeover candidates.

special tax bond A type of municipal bond that is payable only from the proceeds of a special tax, other than an ad valorem tax. *See also* municipal bond.

speculation The buying and selling of goods or securities solely for the purpose of profiting from those trades and not as a means of hedging or protecting other positions.

split offering An offering combining aspects of both a primary and a secondary offering. A portion of the securities is newly issued, and the proceeds of the sale go to the corporation itself. The remainder of the issue is a secondary offering, the proceeds of which go to the selling stockholders.

sponsor Any person directly or indirectly instrumental in organizing, wholly or in part, a partnership or any person who will manage or participate in the management of a partnership.

spot commodity The actual good as it is being traded, as opposed to futures or options on that good.

spot market A market in which goods are traded for immediate delivery and immediate payment.

spot price The actual price a particular good can be bought or sold for at a specified time and place.

spot secondary distribution A block trading procedure in which a secondary distribution is not registered and is announced suddenly. (*Syn.* unregistered secondary distribution)

spread In a quotation, the difference between the bid and offer; with options, simultaneously having a long and a short option position within the same class but not the same series.

spreader A commodities trader who attempts to profit from the price differences between commodities, markets or delivery months; a commodities arbitrageur. *See also* position trading, scalper.

spread-load option With mutual funds, a system of sales charges for contractual plans. It permits a decreasing scale of sales charges, with no more than 20% of the cost deducted in any one year and no more than an average of 16% of the cost deducted in a consecutive 48-month period. The maximum that may be deducted over the life of the plan is still 9%. Rights of withdrawal exist for 45 days, during which time the client may receive a return of all sales charges deducted plus the current value of the account. After 45 days, the client is entitled to the current net asset value only.

SRO *See* self-regulatory organization.

stabilizing The condition that occurs when a dealer appointed by the managing underwriter buys a security at or below the public offering price to prevent the price from dropping sharply.

stagflation Stagnation in the economy accompanied by a rise in prices.

Standard & Poor's 500 A market indicator composed of 400 industrial stocks, 20 transportation stocks, 40 financial stocks and 40 public utility stocks.

standardized option *See* listed option.

standby underwriter A brokerage firm that agrees to purchase any part of an issue that has not been subscribed to through a rights offering.

stated value *See* par value.

stated yield. *See* nominal yield.

statement of intention *See* letter of intent.

statutory disqualification A person is statutorily disqualified from association with a member organization if that person has been expelled, barred or suspended from association with a member of a self-regulatory organization; has had his registration suspended, denied or revoked by the SEC; has been the cause of someone else's suspension, barment or revocation; has been convicted of certain specified crimes; or has falsified any application or report that he is required to file with or on behalf of a membership organization.

statutory voting rights A voting procedure that permits a stockholder to cast one vote per share owned for each director.

steer averaging The act of investing fixed amounts of capital in cattle over a period of time in staged amounts, with the proceeds from the sale of the cattle automatically reinvested.

step-out well A well or prospect adjacent to a field of proven reserves.

stock ahead A limit order at a specific price that is not filled because other orders at that same price were entered before that order.

stockbroker *See* registered representative.

stock certificate Written evidence of ownership in a corporation.

stock dividend *See* dividend.

stockholders' equity *See* shareholders' equity.

stock power A standard form that duplicates the back of a stock certificate. It is used if the registered owner of a security does not have the certificate available for signature endorsement. *See also* assignment.

stock split A reduction in the par value of stock caused by the issuance of additional stock. A reverse split increases the stock's par value by reducing the number of shares outstanding.

stop limit order A stop order that becomes a limit order once the market price reaches or passes the specific price stated in the stop order. *See also* stop order.

stop order 1) An order by the SEC that suspends the sale of securities to the public. 2) An order that becomes a market order when the market price of the security reaches or exceeds the specific price stated in the stop order.

stopping stock When a specialist guarantees execution at a specific price for a public order submitted by a floor broker.

straddle Either a long or short position in a call and a put on the same security with the same expiration date and exercise price.

straddle—long The act of buying a call and a put on a stock with the same strike price and expiration.

straddle—short The act of writing a call and a put on a stock with the same strike price and expiration.

straight-line depreciation A method of depreciation by which a corporation writes off the cost of an asset in equal amounts each year over the asset's useful life.

strangle A combination of a put and a call where both options are out-of-the-money. A strangle can be profitable only if the market is highly volatile and makes a major move in either direction.

strap The purchase of two calls and one put on the same security with the same terms.

street name Securities held by a brokerage firm in its own name but owned by a client are referred to as being held in street name. *See also* in-street-name account.

strengthening basis A narrowing of the spread between the cash (spot) price and the futures price of a commodity.

strike price The price at which the underlying security will be sold if the option buyer exercises her rights in the contract. (*Syn.* exercise price)

striking price *See* strike price.

strip The purchase of two puts and one call on the same security with the same terms.

strip bond A bond stripped of its coupons, repackaged and sold at a deep discount and maturing at full face value.

stripper bond *See* original issue discount.

stripper well A well producing fewer than ten barrels of oil per day. Stripping a field means pumping the field occasionally and letting it rest between the pumping periods.

subject quote A quote that does not represent actual offers to buy or sell when prices are quoted. It represents an indication of how the market stands. (*Syn.* nominal quote)

subordinated debenture A debt obligation that has unsecured junior claims to interest and principal

subordinated to ordinary debentures and all other liabilities of the issuing corporation. *See also* debenture.

subordinated debt A form of long-term capitalization used by broker-dealers, in which the claims of lenders are subordinated to the claims of other creditors. Subordinated financing is considered part of the broker-dealer's capital structure and is added to net worth (shareholders' equity) to compute total available capital when computing net capital.

subordinated interest An interest that is junior to the rights of participants until such time as the participants have received cumulative distributed cash or net revenues in an amount at least equal to their capital contributions.

subordinated reversionary working interest In this type of sharing arrangement, the sponsor bears no drilling cost and does not share in revenues until investors achieve payout. Payout occurs when an investor receives all monies invested plus a predetermined rate of return (normally 6% compounded annually). At payout, the program sponsor will receive a percentage of the revenues generated and share in additional expenses.

subscription agreement An agreement whereby an investor agrees to purchase securities and in addition agrees to become a limited partner and abide by the limited partnership agreement.

subscription amount The total dollar amount for which a participant in a direct participation program has subscribed for her participation in the program.

subscription right A stockholder's privilege of having the first opportunity to purchase new stock issued by the corporation so that the stockholder may retain his proportionate ownership in the corporation. Generally the price for subscription stock is lower than the current market value. *See also* preemptive right, right.

subscription right certificate *See* right.

sum-of-the-years-digits (SOYD) A method of depreciation in which a corporation writes off more of the value of an asset during its early years of use than during its later years of use.

SuperDot *See* New York Stock Exchange Super Designated Order Turnaround system.

supervision The act of ensuring that the employees and associated persons of a broker-dealer comply with the applicable securities rules and regulations of the SEC, exchanges and SROs.

support A term used in technical analysis to describe the bottom of a stock's trading range.

switching The act of closing or offsetting a position that specifies one delivery (futures) or expiration (options) month and opening a position for the same commodity or security in another, more distant month. (*Syn.* rolling forward)

syndicate A group of broker-dealers formed to handle the distribution and sale of an issuer's security. The typical syndicate has several firms managing the underwriting effort. Each member of the syndicate is then assigned responsibility for the sale and distribution of a portion of the issue. *See also* Eastern account, Western account.

systematic risk The risk inherent in all securities of the same type (commodities, stocks, bonds, etc.) that cannot be eliminated through diversification or similar strategies. *See also* market risk.

takedown The discount at which a syndicate member buys securities from the syndicate. *See also* concession.

TAN *See* tax anticipation note.

Tape *See* Consolidated Tape.

taxability The risk of the erosion of investment income through taxation.

tax and revenue anticipation note (TRAN) A short-term municipal debt security.

tax anticipation note (TAN) A short-term municipal debt security to be paid off from tax revenues.

tax swap *See* bond swap.

T call *See* margin call.

technical analysis A method of securities analysis that analyzes statistics generated by market activity, such as past prices and volume. Technical analysis does not attempt to measure a security's intrinsic value.

tenants in common *See* joint tenants in common (JTIC).

tender bond *See* put bond.

tender offer An offer to buy securities for cash or for cash and securities.

term bond *See* term maturity.

term maturity A type of maturity in which the entire bond issue matures on a single date. *See also* maturity date. (*Syn.* term bond)

testamentary trustee A person authorized to administer a trust, including brokerage accounts, created by a decedent. The authority of the testamentary trustee is created by the last will of the decedent who created the trust.

third market The trading of listed securities in the over-the-counter market. Institutional investors are the primary users of the third market.

time loan A collateral loan of a brokerage firm that matures on a date agreed upon by the lender and the borrower and has a constant interest rate for the duration of the contract. *See also* broker's loan.

time spread A spread that involves different expiration dates but the same exercise price. (*Syn.* calendar spread, horizontal spread)

time value A term that refers to any current market value of an option above and beyond its intrinsic value. *See also* intrinsic value.

tombstone An advertisement that announces a securities offering and identifies the name of the issuer, the type of security, the underwriters and where additional information is available.

total outstanding units All units issued at or before the closing date.

trade comparison The memorandum or ticket exchanged by the two broker-dealers engaged in a trade. It is used to compare and confirm the details of the transaction.

trade confirmation A bill or comparison of a trade that is sent to a customer on or before the first day of business following the trade date.

trade date The date on which a transaction occurs.

trading authorization *See* full trading authorization, limited trading authorization.

TRAN *See* tax and revenue anticipation note.

transfer agent A person or an organization responsible for recording the names of registered stockholders and the number of shares owned, seeing that the certificates are signed by the appropriate corporate officers, affixing the corporate seal and delivering the securities to the transferee.

Treasury bill A marketable, short-term (90 days to one year) U.S. government debt security issued through a competitive bidding process at a discount from par value. There is no fixed interest rate.

Treasury bond A marketable, long-term (10 to 30 years), fixed-interest U.S. government debt security.

Treasury note A marketable, medium-term (one to ten years), fixed-interest U.S. government debt security.

treasury stock Common stock that has been issued and reacquired (purchased) by the corporation from the public at the current market price.

trendline The line that traces a stock's movement by connecting the reaction lows in an upward trend or the rally highs in a downward trend.

triangle A pattern on a chart that shows a narrowing of the price range in which a security is trading. The left side of the triangle typically shows the widest range, and the right side narrows to a point.

trust agreement *See* trust indenture.

trustee of a living trust A person who administers a trust, including brokerage accounts, created by a living person. The authority is created by a trust agreement, not a will.

trust indenture The written agreement between a corporation and its creditors that details the terms of the debt issue. These terms include such things as the rate of interest, the maturity date, the means of payment and the collateral. (*Syn.* deed of trust, trust agreement)

Trust Indenture, Act of 1939 The legislation requiring that all publicly offered, nonexempt debt securities be registered under the Securities Act of 1933 and issued under a trust indenture.

Trust in Securities Act Another name for the Securities Act of 1933.

12b-1 asset-based fees Under Section 12b-1 of the Investment Company Act of 1940, a company may collect a fee for the promotion, sale or other activity connected with the distribution of its shares, determined annually as a flat dollar amount or as a percentage of the company's average total net asset value during the year. There are certain requirements:
- The percentage of net assets charged must be reasonable (typically 1/2 to 1% of net assets managed), and the annual fee cannot exceed 8.5% of the offering price on a per-share basis.
- The fee must reflect the anticipated level of distribution services.
- The payments must represent charges that would have been paid to a third party (an underwriter) had sales charges been negotiated for services involving sales promotion, services and related activities.

two-dollar broker A member of an exchange who freelances by executing orders for various member firms when their own floor brokers are especially busy. The broker charges a commission for her services. The amount of the commission is negotiated.

type A term that refers to whether an option is a put or a call option. *See also* class, series.

UGMA *See* Uniform Gifts to Minors Act.

UIT *See* unit investment trust.

uncovered call (put) writer An investor who writes a call (or put) without owning the underlying security or some equivalent security. (*Syn.* naked call, put, writer)

underlying securities The futures or securities that are bought or sold when an option is exercised or those on which an option is based.

underwriter The entity responsible for marketing stocks, bonds, mutual fund shares and so on.

underwriting The procedure by which investment bankers channel investment capital from investors to corporations and municipalities.

underwriting compensation The sales charge paid to a broker-dealer firm for its involvement in selling and offering securities.

underwriting discount *See* underwriting spread.

underwriting manager The brokerage firm responsible for organizing a syndicate, preparing the issue, negotiating with the issuer and underwriters and allocating stock to the selling group. (*Syn.* manager, manager of the syndicate, managing underwriter)

underwriting spread The difference between the public offering price and the price the underwriter pays to the issuing corporation. (*Syn.* underwriting discount)

underwriting syndicate A group of brokerage firms that agree in writing to cooperate in a joint venture to distribute a particular offering of securities. (*Syn.* syndicate)

undivided account *See* Eastern account.

unearned income The income that is derived from investments and other sources not related to personal services (e.g., interest from a savings account, bond interest and dividends from stock). *See also* earned income. (*Syn.* passive income)

Uniform Gifts to Minors Act (UGMA) The act that permits gifts of money and securities to be given to minors and allows adults to act as custodians for minors.

Uniform Practice Code The NASD code that governs and makes uniform a firm's dealings with other brokerage firms.

Unit A capital contribution to a partnership entitling the holder of the unit to an interest in the net income, net loss and distributions of the partnership, without regard to capital accounts.

unit investment trust (UIT) An investment company that has its own portfolio of securities in which it invests. It sells interests in this portfolio in the form of redeemable securities. UITs can be of two types: fixed (no portfolio changes are made) and nonfixed (portfolio changes are permissible). Unit investment trusts are organized under a trust indenture, not a corporate charter.

unqualified legal opinion A legal opinion of a security given without condition.

unregistered secondary distribution *See* spot secondary distribution.

unsecured bond *See* debenture.

unspecified property program *See* blind pool.

up tick rule *See* plus tick rule.

variable annuity A variable annuity is one form of annuity issued by life insurance companies. Like fixed annuities, variable annuities guarantee payment for life once the contract is annuitized, and the issuing insurance company accepts the mortality risk for the client. However, unlike fixed annuities, the variable annuity contract does not guarantee the amount of the annuity payment or performance of the account. The annuitant accepts the investment risk, not the company. *See also* annuity.

variable death benefit The amount of the death benefit (other than incidental insurance benefits, payable under a variable life insurance policy) dependent on the investment performance of the separate account, which the insurer would have to pay in the absence of the minimum death benefit.

variable life insurance policy Any individual policy that provides for life insurance, the amount or duration of which varies according to the investment experience of any separate account established and maintained by the insurer as to such policy.

variable ratio plan A defensive policy plan in which the investor makes purchases and sales on the theory that the higher the stock prices are, the riskier they are, whereas bond prices tend to be more stable. Therefore, the ratio of stocks to bonds decreases as the market rises and increases as the market falls.

vertical spread *See* price spread.

visible supply 1) The disclosure of all municipal securities known to be coming to market within the next 30 days that is published in *The Bond Buyer*. 2) All supplies of a commodity in licensed warehouses.

volatility The speed with which and extent to which the price of a security or commodity rises and falls within a given period of time.

volume of trading theory A technical theory that tries to confirm a strong or weak market by measuring the volume of trading.

voluntary accumulation plan A plan under which the client opens an account and voluntarily commits to additional periodic investments.

voting trust The transfer of common stock voting power to a trustee.

voting trust certificate A certificate evidencing the transfer of shares into a voting trust. The certificate does not carry the right to vote the shares.

warrant A security giving the holder the right to purchase securities at a stipulated price. This is usually a long-term instrument, affording the investor the option of buying shares at a later date at the subscription price, subject to the warrant's exercise.

wash sale The purchase of the same (or a substantially identical) security within 30 days before or after the sale establishing the loss. The claimed loss will be disallowed.

weakening basis A widening of the spread between the cash (spot) price and the futures price of a commodity.

Western account An arrangement under which syndicate members and dealers are liable only for the sale of securities allocated to them. *See also* Eastern account. (*Syn.* divided account)

when issued contract A settlement contract that calls for delivery on a day set by the NYSE (for securities listed on the NYSE), based on when the issuing corporation will have the physical certificates available for distribution. For unlisted securities, the NASD sets the delivery date.

when issued security (WI) A security offered for sale in advance of the issuance of the security by the issuer.

White's Tax-Exempt Bond Rating Service A rating service that is no longer in existence; it rated tax-exempt (municipal) debt based on the issue's marketability rather than the creditworthiness of the issuer.

wholesale transaction A trade in which a broker-dealer buys an over-the-counter stock from another broker-dealer. *See also* retail transaction.

WI *See* when issued security.

wire house *See* commission house.

withdrawal plan A plan allowing a client to request the systematic withdrawal of her account periodically. Withdrawals may be based on a fixed dollar amount, fixed number of shares, fixed percentage or fixed period of time. The plan is normally a free service offered by a mutual fund.

working capital ratio *See* current ratio.

working interest An operating interest entitling the holder to a share of production under an oil and gas lease and carrying with it the obligation to bear a corresponding share of all costs associated with the production of income.

workout quote A type of subject quotation in which a brokerage firm estimates the price that it thinks it can get if given reasonable time to enter the market and to find the stock to buy or sell.

writer The seller of an option. (*Syn.* guarantor, seller)

Yellow Sheets Pages that the National Quotation Bureau publishes daily and that contain wholesale quotations of dealers for corporate bonds.

yield The rate of return on an investment, generally expressed as a percentage of the current price. *See also* coupon yield, yield to maturity. (*Syn.* current yield, dividend yield)

yield curve The graphic representation of actual or projected yields of fixed-income securities.

yield to call (YTC) The rate of return on an investment that accounts for the cash difference between a bond's acquisition cost and its proceeds, as well as interest income calculated to the earliest date that the bonds may be called in by the issuing corporation.

yield to maturity (YTM) The rate of return on an investment that accounts for the cash difference between a bond's acquisition cost and its maturity proceeds, as well as interest received from owning the bond.

YTC *See* yield to call.

YTM *See* yield to maturity.

zero-coupon bond *See* original issue discount, strip bond.

zero-minus tick A sale made at a price equal to the price of the last sale but lower than the last different price.

zero-plus tick A sale made at a price equal to the price of the last sale but higher than the last different price.

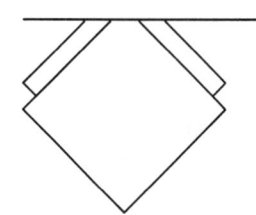

Index

Accounts, customer
　approval and acceptance of, 94
　classification of, 93
　documenting, 94-95
　employees of other brokers, 97
　mutual fund, 191
　new, 93-97
　opening, 94
　ownership, 93
　types of, 98-100
Accumulation plans, 191-96
Accumulation unit, 226, 230
Additional issue market, 76
Adjustable-rate preferred stock, 8
Adjusted gross income, 213
Administrators, 253
ADR, 41
ADS, 41
Adult employee, 218
Advertising, 270-72
　returns, 200
Advisers disclosure, 179
Affiliated person, 174-75, 176
After-contribution income, 217-18
Agency issues, 20, 52-53
　fund, 164
　taxation, 146
Agent, 86-87
Aggressive portfolio, 142
AGI, 213
AIR. See Assumed interest rate
All or none, 78
AMBAC, 56
American depositary receipts (ADRs), 41
Annuity plans
　accounting, 230-32
　payout options, 229-30
　types of contracts, 225-27
　unit, 231
AON, 78
AP. See Associated person
Appeal, 266

Appreciation, 200
Arbitration, 267-69
Artificial transactions, 120
Asset allocation fund, 163
Assets
　claim at dissolution, 8
　coverage, 170-71
　residual claims, 6
Associated person, 115-16, 264
　registration, 260-62
Assumed interest rate (AIR), 231-32, 241-42
Authorized stock, 2

Back-end load, 183
Balanced fund, 163
Balanced portfolio, 143
Balance sheet
　customer, 134
　investment company, 178
Bankers' acceptance, 64
Bank grade bonds, 22
Banking Act, 70-71
Beneficial ownership, 120
Benefits of owning stock, 7
Best efforts, 78
Blue-sky laws, 76
Blue-skying an issue, 75, 76
Board of directors, 173
Bond fund, 163
Bonding of directors, 178
Bonds, 20-30, 170
　characteristics of, 20-23
　corporate, 27-30
　issued by investment companies, 170
　municipal, 20
　purchased at discount, 148-49
　rating and analyzing, 21-23
　U.S. government, 20
　yields, 24-26
Book entry, 48
Book value, 4

Borrowing money
　by investment companies, 170
　from customers, 118
Branch office, 260
Breakpoints, 161, 186-88
Breakpoint sales, 118, 188
Broker, 86-87, 264
　employee accounts, 97
Brokerage support services, 108-11
Brokerage zero-coupon bonds, 50
Broker-dealer, 86-87
　registration, 256, 259
　regulation, 256
Business accounts, 97
Business cycles, 124-25, 130-31
Buyer, 42

Callable preferred stock, 10
Call date, 49
Call risk, 141
Calls, 42
Capital gains, 147-48, 201
　distribution, 199-200
Capital growth, 136
Capital in excess of par, 4
Capital losses, 147-48, 202
Capital market, 61
Capital preservation, 136
Capital risk, 138
Capital surplus, 4
Cash accounts, 95
Cash dividend, 11
Cash trade, 110
Cash value, 239, 242
Cash value life insurance, 214, 238-39
Catch-up provisions, 236
CBOE, 257
Certificate of deposit, 65
Church organizations, 235
Churning, 117
Civil liabilities, 74, 267, 277

337

Claims, 274
Class A, B, C shares, 183
Client account, 91
    new, 93-97
Closed-end investment companies, 157, 158, 169
Code of Arbitration Procedure, 259, 267-69
    amendments to, 268-69
Code of Procedure, 259, 265-67
Collateral trust bond, 27
Combination annuities, 227
Combination fund, 163
Combination preferred stock, 10
Combination privilege, 188
Commercial paper, 64-65
Commissions, 261
Common stock, 2-7, 162, 170
    benefits and risks of, 7
    classifications of, 2-3
    corporate ownership of, 4-6
    value on, 3-4
Competitive bid, 48
Complaint
    resolution process, 265
    sources, 265
Completion of the transactions, 264
Conduit theory, 201
Confidentiality, 119-20
Confirmation, 108
Conflict of interest, 119
Constant dollar plan, 144
Constant dollars, 125
Constant ratio plan, 144
Consumer Price Index (CPI), 126
Continuous public offering securities, 169
Contract, 42, 174
    exchange, 243
Contraction, 124
Contractual accumulation plan, 191-92, 228
Contractual agreement, 225
Control person, 175
Conversion
    parity, 37-38
    price, 37
    ratio (rate), 37
Convertible securities, 10, 35-38
Corporate bond
    taxation, 146
    tracking, 30
    types of, 27-28
Corporate name, 258
Corporate new issue, 75-76
Corporate protection, 6

Corporate retirement plans
    nonqualified, 223-25
    qualified, 220-222
Corporate securities, 23
    underwriting, 75
Corporations, 20, 36, 253
Cost basis, 147, 201, 203
Coverage limits, 253-55
Covered employee, 213
CPI, 126
Credit agreement, 96
Credit regulation, 83
Credit risk, 140
Criminal penalties, 122
Cumulative preferred stock, 9
Cumulative voting, 5
Current yield, 12, 24, 198
Custodial account, 93, 94, 95, 99, 101-3
Custodian, 101-2
    plan, 192-93
Custodian bank, 176
Customer, 180, 264
    account, 93-103, 253-55
    financial profile, 134-35
    investment outlook, 136-37
    legal recourse of, 277
    nonfinancial investment considerations, 135-37
    recommendations, 116, 134-37, 272-73

DBCC. *See* District Business Conduct Committee
Dealer, 86-87, 264
Death
    benefit, 241-42
    UGMA account and, 103
Debentures, 28
Debt securities, 19, 170
Debt-to-equity ratio, 21
Declaration date, 109
Decreasing term insurance, 214, 238
Deed of gift, 101
Default risk, 140
Defensive portfolio, 142
Deferred compensation plan, 224
Defined benefit plan, 220, 221
Defined contribution plan, 220

Definitions
    accumulation stage, 228
    accumulation unit, 226
    additional issue market, 76
    advertising, 270
    affiliated person, 175
    agency, 52

    all or none, 78
    annuity unit, 231
    asset allocation fund, 163
    associated person, 264
    assumed interest rate, 231-32
    authorized stock, 2
    back-end load, 183
    book value, 4
    breakpoint, 186
    broker, 86, 264
    call, 42
    capital market, 61
    cash value, 239
    churning, 117
    closed-end investment companies, 157
    completion of the transaction, 264
    contractual plan, 191, 228
    cooling-off period, 72
    custodian, 101-2
    custodian bank, 176
    customer, 83, 180, 264
    dealer, 86, 264
    debt securities, 19
    defined benefit plan, 220
    defined contribution plan, 220
    discount, 21
    donor, 101
    earned income, 145
    equity option, 42
    excessive trading, 117
    ex-date, 109, 111
    ex-rights date, 111
    ex-warrants date, 111
    face-amount certificate company, 155
    family of funds, 189
    final prospectus, 73
    form letter, 270
    front-running, 121
    generic advertising, 271
    good delivery, 112
    holding period return, 141
    hypothecation agreement, 96
    immediate annuity, 228
    indefeasible title, 101
    ineligible investment, 214
    initial public offering, 76
    inside market, 86
    interested person, 175
    internal rate of return (IRR), 141
    investment company, 153
    management company, 156-59
    member, 264
    mutual fund, 157
    net price, 86

Definitions, cont.
nominal yield, 24
nonqualified plan, 223
open-end investment company, 157
owner employee, 217
passive income, 145
preliminary prospectus, 72
primary market, 84
primary offering, 77
put, 42
record date, 111
red herring, 72
registration statement, 72
regulated investment company, 147, 201
sales literature, 270
secondary market, 84
secondary offering, 77
security, 264
selling away, 115
selling dividend, 117, 199
senior securities, 20
separate account, 226
settlement date, 108, 111
third market, 84
tombstone, 271
trade date, 111
unlisted security, 84

Deflation, 126
Depressions, 124
Disciplinary action/sanctions, 261, 263
Disclaimer clause, 73-74, 170
Disclosure of fund performance, 179
   customer recommendations, 272-73
Discount, bond sold at, 21
Discount rate, 128
Discretionary accounts, 93, 97, 99-100
Disintermediation, 130
Disqualification, 263-65
Distributions, 199-200
District Business Conduct Committee, 258
   decision of, 265-66
Diversification, 136, 142-44
Diversified investment company, 157-59
Dividends, 11-12
   disbursing process, 109-10
   distributions, 198
   exclusions, 203
   preferred stock, 8
   reinvestment, 186, 199-200

   return on investment, 11-12
   selling, 117
   taxation, 147
Dividend department, 109-11
Dividend record date, 109, 110
Doctrine of reciprocal immunity, 54, 146
Dollar cost averaging, 144, 196
Donor, 101
Double-auction market, 85
Dual-purpose fund, 164

Early retirement, 221
Earned income, 145
Economic Recovery Tax Act of 1981, 212
Economics, 124-26
18-month partial refund period, 195
Employee, 235
   elective deferrals, 236
   influencing or rewarding, 117
   Keogh eligibility, 218
Employee Retirement Income Security Act (ERISA), 201-11
Employer contribution plan, 236
Employer contributions, 236
Employment contracts, 117
Equipment trust certificate, 27-28
Equity options, 42
Equity securities, 170-71
   common stock, 2-7
   preferred stock, 8-10
   return on investment, 11-12
   tracking, 13-14
ERISA, 210-11
ERTA, 212
Escrow, 78
Ethics, 113-21
Examinations, 262-63
Excess contribution, 213
Excessive trading, 117, 120
Exchange Act, 82
Exchange hours, 85
Exchange market, 84
Exchanges, family of funds, 189, 203
Ex-dividend date, 109, 110-11, 199
Executive representative, 260
Executors, 253
Exemptions, from registration, 261
Expansion, 124
Expense ratio, 166-67
Ex-rights date, 111
Extension, settlement, 109
Ex-warrant date, 111

Face-amount certificate companies, 155-56
Fair dealing, 116
Fair market value, 203
False information, 121
Family of funds, exchanges, 189, 203
Federal funds, 127-28
Federal funds rate, 65, 128
Federal National Mortgage Association (FNMA), 52-53
Federal Open Market Committee (FOMC), 129
Federal Reserve Board (FRB), 96, 127-29, 165
Fictional names, 275
Fiduciary
   confidentiality, 119-20
   relationship, 120
   responsibility, 102-3
   trading authorization, 93
FIFO, 148, 202
Final prospectus, 73
Financial reports, 178-79
Financial risk, 140
Financial statements, 83
Fines, 267
Fingerprinting, 256
Firm commitment, 77
First in first out, 148, 202
Fiscal policy, 129-31
501(c)3 plan, 234, 235
Fixed annuities, 225, 226
Fixed dollar plan, 197
Fixed income securities, 19
Fixed percentage (fixed-share) plan, 197
Fixed time plan, 197
FNMA, 52-53
Foreign associates, 261
Foreign authority assistance, 122
Foreign securities, 41
Form letter, 270-71
Form 1099B, 161, 200
Form U-4, 260
Form U-5, 260
45-day free look, 194
Forward pricing, 189-90
401K plan, 222
403(B) plan, 234-35
Fourth market, 84
Fraud, 115, 252, 277
FRB. *See* Federal Reserve Board
Free service offers, 274
Freeriding and withholding, 121
Front-end load, 183, 193, 194
Front-running, 121
Frozen account, 109

Full Disclosure Act, 71
Full-time employee, 218
Funded debt, 20

GDP, 125
General account, 240
General obligation bonds, 55
Generic advertising, 271
Generic names, 275-76
Gifts and gratuities, 117
Glass-Steagall Act of 1933, 70-71
GNMA, 53
GO, 55
Going to the discount window, 128
Golden handcuffs clause, 225
Good delivery, 112
Government economic policy, 127-31
Government National Mortgage Association (GNMA), 53
Government securities, 48-50
Gross domestic product (GDP), 125
Growth fund, 162
Guarantee prohibition, 119

Hearing panel, 265
Hearing request, 265
Hidden account, 121
Hiring, 276
Holder, 42
Holding period return, 141
Hot issues, 121
HR-10 plans, 217-19
Hypothecation agreement, 96

IA-1092, 250
Immediate annuity, 228
Income fund, 162-63
Income generation, 136
Income statement
 customer, 134-35
 investment company, 178
Income tax brackets, 145-46
Income taxes, 145
Increasing term insurance, 238
Indefeasible title, 101
Index fund, 164
Indication of interest, 73, 271
Individual retirement accounts (IRAs), 212-16, 219
 contributions, 212-13
 investments, 214
 participation, 212
 rollovers, 214-15
 taxation, 215-16
 tax benefits, 212

 transfers, 215
 withdrawals, 215
Individuals, 253
Ineligibility, 263
Inflation, 125-26
Inflation risk, 138
Initial public offering, 76-77
Inside market, 86
Insider Trading and Securities Fraud Enforcement Act of 1988, 252
INSTINET, 84
Interdealer network, 85
Interest
 bond, 20
 income, 146
 tax-exempt income, 146-47
Interest rate, 65, 130
 risk, 29, 139
Interested person, 175-76
Interlocking directorate, 173
Internal rate of return, 141
Interviews, 276
Investment adviser, 173-74, 250-51
 registration, 250
Investment Advisers Act of 1940, 250-51
Investment banker, 75
Investment banking (securities) business, 264
Investment companies, 153-203
 closed-end, 157, 158
 diversified, 157-59
 management of, 173-79
 nondiversified, 159
 offering, 154-59
 open-end, 157, 158
 operations restrictions, 171-72
 prohibitions, 169, 170, 171
 purpose, 154
 registration, 168-72
 registration exemptions, 169
 securities issued by, 170
 securities registration, 169-71
 types of, 155-59
Investment Company Act of 1940, 154, 193
Investment Company Act of 1970, 193
Investment grade bonds, 22
Investment income, 201
Investment objectives, 161-65
Investment pyramid, 137
Investment recommendations, 116
Investment risks, 138-41
Investor information, 178-79
IPO, 76-77

IRAs, 212-16
IRR, 141
Irrevocable gift, 101
Issuance
 convertible securities, 36
 government securities, 48
 money market, 61
 municipal bonds, 54-55
 rights, 39
 Treasury bill, 48
 Treasury bond, 49
 Treasury note, 48
Issued stock, 3
Issuers, 20

Joint accounts, 98, 253
Joint life with last survivor, 230
Joint tenants in common, 98
Joint tenants with right of survivorship, 98
JTIC, 98
JTWROS, 98

Keogh plans, 217-19
Know Your Customer (NYSE rule 405), 94, 134-37

Legislative risk, 140
Lending money, 118
Letter of acceptance, waiver and consent, 266
Letter of intent (LOI), 77, 187
Level term insurance, 238
Leverage, 21
Life annuity/straight life, 230
Life annuity with period certain, 230
Life contingency, 230
Limited liability, 6
Limited representative licenses, 262-63
Liquidation, 201-2
 priority, 6, 29
Liquidity, 137
 bond's, 23
 money market, 61
 risk, 140
Listed market, 85
Listed security, 84
Loan consent agreement, 96
Loans, 242-43
LOI, 187
Lump-sum account, 192

Mailing instructions, 95
Maloney Act, 71, 83, 255, 257
Management companies, 156-59
 pricing shares, 185

Manipulative devices, 115, 277
Margin
    accounts, 96
    expenses, 149
    mutual fund purchases, 169, 171
Marketability
    bond's, 23
    risk, 140
Marketing, mutual fund, 180
Market maker, 86
Market price influence, 121
Market risk, 29, 139-40
Market value, 4
Maximum sales charge reductions, 186
MBIA, 56
Member, 264
Membership corporation, 257
Mini-max, 78
Minus tick, 85
Misleading information, 121
Misrepresentation, 118
Mixed portfolio, 143
Modern portfolio theory, 143-44
Monetary policy, 127-29
    money-market fund and, 165
Money market, 61-65
Money-market fund, 164-65
Moody's, 21-22
Mortgage bonds, 27
MSRB, 257
Municipalities, 20
Municipal securities, 20, 23, 54-56, 62
    taxation, 146-47
Municipal Securities Rulemaking Board, 257
Mutual fund. *See also* Investment companies
    characteristics of, 160-67
    comparing, 165-67
    distributions, 198-200
    dividend taxation, 147
    marketing, 180
    performance, 179
    pricing, 184-86
    purchasing on margin, 169
    recommendations, 273-74
    share cancellation, 190
    share redemption, 189-90
    taxation, 201-3
    types of accounts, 191
    variable annuities and, 227

Names, use of members', 275-76
NASD. *See* National Association of Securities Dealers
Nasdaq, 84
NASD Manual, 259
National Association of Securities Dealers, 76
    bylaws, 257-64
    corporate name use, 258
    dues, assessments, 258
    manual, 259
    membership, registration, 259-62
    National Arbitration Board, 268
    public communication, 272-77
    regulation review, 276-77
Net asset value (NAV), 157, 181-90
Net capital rule, 83
Net investment income, 198-99
Net price, 86
New account form, 94-95
New issue
    corporate, 75-76
    market, 76
    regulation, 70-74
    types of offerings, 76-77
New Issues Act, 71
New York Stock Exchange, 257
    transactions listing, 13
No-load fund, 180, 184
Nominal yield, 24
Noncompetitive bid, 48
Noncovered employee, 213
Nondiscrimination, 210
Nondiversified investment company, 159
Non-investment grade bonds, 22
Nonmarketable government securities, 51
Nonparticipating employee, 213
Nonpublic information, 119
Nonqualified corporate retirement plans, 223-24
Nonsystematic risk, 143
Notice of right to refund, 195-96
Numbered account, 120
NYSE. *See* New York Stock Exchange

Obligation, 42
OID, 148-49
Open account, 191
Open-end investment companies, 157, 158, 160, 168
Open-market operations, 129
Open repo, 63
Opinions, 274
Options, 42-43
Original issue discount, 148-49

OTC. *See* Over-the-counter market
Outside business activity, 115-16
Outstanding stock, 3
Over-the-counter market, 84-86
    business hours, 85
Owner, 42

Paid-in capital/surplus, 4
Par, 21
Parity, 37-38
Partial withdrawals, 195
Participating employee, 213
Participating preferred stock, 9-10
Partnerships, 253
Par value
    bonds, 21
    stock, 3-4
Passive income, 145
Payable date, 110
Payment, benefits, 221
Payroll deduction plan, 223
Peak, 124
Penalties, 266
Pension Benefit Guaranty Corporation, 210
Pension Reform Act, 210-11
Periodic investment plans, 274
Periodic-payment annuities, 228
Periodic payment plan, 192-93
Permanent life insurance, 238-39
Personal contributions, 236
Pipeline theory, 201
Plan completion insurance, 195
Plan custodian, 192-93
Plan termination, 194-96
Plus tick, 85
Policy value fund, 239
POP, 180
Portfolio, 142
    analysis, 142-44
    diversification, 136-37
    income, 145
    intermediaries, 154
    manager, 173-74
    turnover, 167
Position limits, 42
Position trading, 86
Positive yield curve, 25-26
Power of attorney, 97, 99
Preemptive right, 6, 39, 78
Preferred stock, 8-10, 170-71
    classes of, 9-10
    fund, 163
Preliminary prospectus, 72-73
Premium
    bond sold at, 21
    deductions, 241

Present value, 141
Price
    bond, 22
    conversion, 37
    mutual fund, 184-86
    risk, 29
    Treasury bill, 48
    Treasury bond, 49
    Treasury note, 49
    yield relationship to, 24, 25
Primary market, 71, 84
Primary offering, 77
Prime rate, 65
Principal, 86-87
Prior preferred stock, 9
Private securities transactions, 115-16
Profit-sharing plan, 222
Prohibited practices, 115-21, 171
Property dividend, 11
Prospectus, 72-74, 169-71, 178, 271
    contractual plans, 192
    untruths in, 74
    updating, 169
Prospectus Act, 71
Prosperity, 124
Public educational 403(b) institutions, 234-35
Publicly traded funds, 157
Public offering, 168-69
Public offering price, 180, 183-90
Purchasing power risk, 138
Puts, 42

Qualifications, 262-63
Qualified annuity plans, 234-37
Quantity discounts, 186-88
Quotation, corporate bond, 30

Rating securities, 21
Real estate investment trusts, (REITs), 169
Recessions, 124
Reciprocal immunity, 54, 146
Recommendations, 116, 134-37, 272-75
Record date, 110, 111
Recovery, 124
Recruitment advertising, 276
Redeemable securities, 157
Redemption
    of shares, 189
    variable annuity, 229
Red herring, 72
Refunds, 243-45
Registered representative, 262
Registered security, 48

Registration
    associated person, 260-62
    branch office, 260
    broker-dealer, 256, 259
    by coordination, 76
    by notification, 76
    by qualification, 76
    exchanges and firms, 82-83
    exemptions, 169, 261-62
    investment adviser, 250
    investment company, 168-72
    investment company securities, 169-71
    of new issues, 71
    security, 71-74
    UGMA securities, 102
Registration statement, 72, 170, 271
    changes in, 171-72
    untruths in, 74
Regular way settlement, 108-9
Regulated investment company, 147, 201
Regulation
    broker-dealer, 256
    credit, 83
    new issues, 70-74
    trading, 82-83
Regulation G, 83
Regulation T, 83, 96, 108
Regulation U, 83
Reinvestment privileges, 161, 199-200
Reinvestment risk, 29, 50, 139
REITs, 169
Release IA-1092, 250
Reports prepared by others, 118
Repurchase agreement, 63-64, 190
Reserve requirement, 127
Residual claims, 6
Retirement account agreements, 97
Retirement plans, 209-44
Return on investment (ROI), 11-12
Revenue bonds, 56
Review, 266
Right, 42
Right of withdrawal, 194
Right to refund, 195-96
Rights, 39-40
    ADR holder, 41
    mutual fund holder, 160-61, 171-72
    stockholder, 4-6
Rights of accumulation, 186-88
Rights offering, 39

Risk, 138-41
    management, 143-44
    of owning stock, 7
    of zero-coupon bonds, 29
Rollovers, 214-15, 219
Round lot, 2, 112
Rules of Fair Practice, 259

Sales agreements, variable annuity, 229
Sales charge, 166, 182-84, 243
    quantity discounts and, 186-88
    rate, 185
    reductions, 188
    variable annuities, 228
Sales literature, 270-72
    identification, 272
    withdrawal plan, 197
Savings bonds, 51
Scheduled premium VLI, 240
SEC. *See* Securities and Exchange Commission
Secondary market, 84
Secondary market discount, 149
Secondary offering, 77
Secured bonds, 27-28
Securities Act of 1933, 70-72, 82
    civil liabilities under, 74
Securities and Exchange Commission, 75, 82
    appeal to, 267
    broker-dealer sanctions, 256
    disclaimer, 73, 170
    investigations, 252
    public offering, 168-69
    review, 73
Securities Exchange Act of 1934, 71, 82-83
Securities Investor Protection Corporation (SIPC), 253-55
Securities market, 84-86
    types of offering, 76-77
Security, 264
    receipt and delivery, 108
    safety of, 23
Selection risk, 139
Selling away, 115-16
Selling dividends, 117, 199
Senior debt (lien) securities, 27
Senior securities, 20
Separate account, 226-27, 240-41
Separate customer, 253
Series 6, 262-63
Series EE, HH bonds, 51
Settlement, 108-9, 111
Settlement procedure, 266
75-5-10 test, 158
Share identification, 202

Shared account, 119
Shareholder
    right to vote, 171-72
    sales load reductions, 188
Shares of beneficial interest, 156
Short sales, 171
Signature card, 95
Single accounts, 98
Single-payment annuities, 228
SIPC, 253-55
Specialist, 85
Specialized (sector) fund, 163
Speculation, 137
Speculative bonds, 22
Spousal account, 212
Spread load, 193-94
Standard & Poor's, 21-22, 165
Standby underwriting, 78
Statement of intention, 187
Statutory disqualification, 263
Statutory voting, 5
Stock
    classification, 2-3
    dividend, 11
    ownership, 2
    value of, 3-4
Stockholder
    rights, 4-6
    stock approval, 39
Stock market, 130
STRIPS, 50
Subordinated debentures, 28
Subscription right certificate, 39-40
Subscription rights offering, 78
Suitability, 116, 138
Summary complaint, 266
Systematic risk, 143
Systematic withdrawal plans, 197

Taxation, 145-49
    agency issues, 52
    annuities, 232-33
    capital gains, 167
    current rates, 136
    deferred compensation plan, 225
    dividends, 147
    FNMA issues, 53
    GNMA issues, 53
    investment portfolios and, 146-49
    investment returns, 203
    IRA, 212
    IRA distributions, 215-16
    IRAs, 212
    Keogh plan, 217

    municipal bonds, 54
    mutual fund, 167, 201-3
    nonqualified plans, 223
    of distributions, 221
    qualified annuity plans, 234
    qualified retirement plans, 219
    TDA distributions, 237
    UGMA account, 103
    zero-coupon bond, 29
Tax-deferred annuities (TDAs), 234-37
Tax-equivalent yield, 54
Tax-exempt interest income, 146-47
Tax-free accumulation, 234
Tax-free (tax-exempt) bond fund, 164
Tax-sheltered annuities (TSAs), 234-37
TDA, 234-37
Tender, 48
Tenured employee, 218
Term life insurance, 214, 238
Term life premiums, 238
Terminations, 261
Testimonials, 274
Third market, 84
Thrift plans, 222
Timing risk, 139
Title 1, 2, 3, 4, 210
Tombstone, 271-72
Top heavy plan, 218
Trade confirmations, 108
Trade date, 111
Traded flat, 48
Trade regulation, 82-83
Trade settlement, 108-9
Trading
    hours, 85
    Treasury bills, 48
    Treasury bond, 49
    Treasury note, 48
    unsuitable, 138
Trading authorization, 93, 97, 99-100
Transactions, 108-9
Transfer agent, 177
Transfers, IRA, 215
Treasury bills, 48
Treasury bond, 49-50
Treasury notes, 48-49
Treasury receipts, 50
Treasury stock, 3
Trough, 124
Trust accounts, 253
Trust indenture, 71
Trust Indenture Act of 1939, 71
Truth in Securities Act, 71

TSA, 234-37
12b-1 asset-based fees, 184

UGMA, 101-3
UIT. See Unit investment trust
ULI, 239
Underlying instruments, 42
Underwriter, 76, 177
Underwriting
    group, 157
    process, 75-78
    types of, 77-78
Uniform delivery ticket, 112
Uniform Gifts to Minors Act accounts, 101-3
Uniform Practice Code, 259
Uniform Transfers to Minors Act, 101
U.S. government fund, 164
U.S. government securities, 20, 23, 48-53, 62
    taxation, 146
Unit investment trust (UIT), 156, 192
Unit refund annuity, 230
Unit (share) of beneficial interest, 156
Universal life insurance (ULI), 239
Unlawful representations, 74
Unlisted security, 84
Unsecured bond, 28
UTMA, 101

Valuation, 181-82
Variable annuities, 225-33
Variable annuity payment, 227
Variable life insurance (VLI), 238-42
Variable universal life (VUL), 244
Venue, 265
Vesting, 210
    Keogh, 218
VLI, 239-44
Voluntary accumulation plan, 191
Voting rights, 4-5, 161, 171-72, 244
VUL, 244

Wall Street, 81
Warrant, 40
Wash sales, 148, 202
Whole life insurance, 238-40, 243
Whole life premiums, 239
Withdrawal plans, 197
Withdrawals, IRA, 215-16
Withholding, 215
Withholding tax, 202

WLI, 238-39
Written supervisory procedures, 252

Yield
 agency issues, 52
 bond, 22, 24-26
 current, 12, 24
 curve, 26
 mutual fund, 198-99
 tax-equivalent, 54
Yield to maturity (YTM), 25

Zero-coupon bonds, 28-29, 50

Notes

Notes

Notes

Notes